D1118037

EAT, DRINK, THINK in SPANISH

EAT, DRINK, THINK
in SPANISH

An English-Spanish / Spanish-English
Kitchen Companion

Lourdes Castro

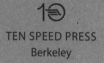

TEN SPEED PRESS
Berkeley

To my late grandmother, Eva Rodriguez Cuetara,
an extraordinary Spanish teacher whose love of the language was contagious.

Copyright © 2009 by Lourdes Castro
Cover illustration copyright © 2009 by Ediciones Malinalco, www.edicionesmalinalco.com

Published in the United States by Ten Speed Press, an imprint of
the Crown Publishing Group, a division of Random House, Inc., New York.
www.crownpublishing.com
www.tenspeed.com

Ten Speed Press and the Ten Speed Press colophon are registered
trademarks of Random House, Inc.

Library of Congress Cataloging-in-Publication Data
is on file with the publisher

ISBN: 978-1-58008-954-8

Printed in Canada

Design by Nancy Austin

10 9 8 7 6 5 4 3 2 1

First Edition

CONTENTS

INTRODUCTION

"Necessity, who is the mother of invention."
—Plato, *The Republic*

A few years ago, I was asked by organizers of an event for the James Beard Foundation to serve as a translator for famed Spanish chef Juan Mari Arzak. I was to sit next to chef Arzak during a dinner cooked by several of Spain's brightest culinary stars. My responsibility was simple—help him navigate the media and offer assistance with dinner guests who did not speak Spanish.

In the process of working out the logistics for a dinner cooked by seven foreign-based chefs, it became evident to the organizers that they needed help communicating with the Spanish chefs. Specific ingredients needed to be sourced and equipment ordered. As a native Spanish speaker, I stepped in as a liaison.

The menus were intricate, and, before I knew it, I was mentally searching for the English word for *cigalas* and *percebes* while at the same time coming up with the Spanish word for fennel and pig's cheeks. I had anticipated issues with regional ingredients but I had taken for granted that these items would have a readily available English translation.

A few months after the Spanish dinner, I was presented with another priceless experience: I was asked to serve as a personal translator for renowned Australian chef Tetsuya Wakuda during his weeklong stay in Madrid for a culinary conference. Talk about a reversal of fortune. This time I was to pair my American English with Chef Wakuda's Australian dialect, and then use my Cuban Spanish to translate the information for Spaniards. If there was ever a need for a Spanish/English dictionary of culinary terms, that was it.

One Language for Many Cultures and Cuisines

While the differences in vernacular among Spanish-speaking countries are well known among native speakers, the divergence is not often recognized by those new to the language. And never is this more apparent than when speaking of food. Not only does each Latin American country have its own cuisine and culinary history, the words used to refer to ingredients, equipment, and technique vary among the countries. Take a banana, for example: the fruit may be referred to as *plátano, cambur, banano,* or *gineo,* depending on what country one is from.

Eat, Drink, Think in Spanish was written as a tool to help English and Spanish speakers communicate more effectively regarding matters of gastronomy. I outline the various Spanish words used to refer to an ingredient, provide phonetic pronunciations, and touch on country specific terms and national dishes.

To bring order to all this information, the book was compiled and organized in a specific manner. The following notes will help you navigate the dictionary and get the most out of its information.

Notes for Using this Book

This book is divided into two parts. The first half of the book lists terms alphabetically in English, followed by the Spanish translation. The second half of the book lists terms alphabetically in Spanish, followed by the English translation. All entries contain the following: term name, translated term, Spanish phonetic pronunciation, term category (see below), and the definition.

TERMS

About two thirds of the terms have both English and Spanish names (i.e. water/ *agua*), which are found in both parts of the book and are easily cross-referenced. You will also see cases where the terms are cognates, with the same word serving in both languages. I've included entries for these terms because it would not be readily apparent otherwise that they are cognates. The remaining terms do not have English translations (i.e. *fajita, chimichurri, tortilla*); such words are found only in the Spanish-English part of the book.

Some terms have more than one Spanish translation. For example, peach can be referred to interchangeably as *durazno* or *melocotón.* In these cases, you will see multiple Spanish words listed with the English term in the English-Spanish part of the book. However, the Spanish-English part includes entries for each of the Spanish synonyms; I encourage you to use those entries to help you select the most appropriate translation.

In some cases, the translation depends on the form of the word—whether it's used as a noun or a verb. You will see definitions for each form in such entries.

Lastly, like most reference books, similar terms are grouped together: for example, the many varieties of beans are listed as "bean, green," "bean, navy," "bean, pinto". Likewise, cuts for specific types of meat follow the main entry for that type of meat; you will find sirloin steak listed under Beef, sirloin.

CATEGORIES

As a way of helping you further understand the meaning of a term, all terms are identified under one of the following categories: Baking & Pastry, Beverage, Condiments, Cooking Method/Technique, Descriptor, Dish, Equipment, Fish & Shellfish, Fruit & Vegetables, Game, General, Grains & Cereals, Herbs & Spices, Meat, and Nuts & Oils.

Categories are especially helpful with terms that have multiple meanings. For example, *whisk* can either refer to a kitchen tool (*agitador*) or a technique (*batir*). In these cases, both definitions will be listed in the entry for *whisk*, with each definition accompanied by its Spanish translation and category.

Whisk Agitador *ah-hee-tah-DOHR*
  EQUIPMENT Definition text.

  Batir *bah-TEER*
  COOKING METHOD/TECHNIQUE Definition text.

SPANISH WORDS WITHOUT AN ENGLISH TRANSLATION

Most Spanish terms that do not have an English translation are country specific, meaning that they are words used to describe a Spanish speaking country's national or typical dish, or its indigenous ingredients. In these cases, the country is listed in parentheses next to the term. For example, *chimichurri* is a raw oil-based sauce made with lots of parsley. It is commonly served alongside meat in Argentina. It is also the name of a similar style sauce served in Nicaragua. This entry appears as follows:

Chimichurri *chee-mee-CHOO-rree*
  CONDIMENT (Argentina) Definition text.
  (Nicaragua) Definition text.

PRONUNCIATION GUIDE

All Spanish terms are directly followed by a phonetic pronunciation. Keep the following in mind when pronouncing Spanish words:

- For the most part Spanish vowels are short.

Vowel	Sounds like	As in...
A	ah	F**a**ther
E	eh	B**e**t
I	ee	B**ee**r
O	oh	C**o**at
U	oo	F**oo**d

- Accented syllables are capitalized. For example, the pronunciation for tequila is written *teh-KEE-lah*.

- Syllables for a single word are connected with hyphens. The phonetic pronunciation of two words are separated by a space. For example, chile jalapeño is written *CHEE-leh hah-lah-PEH-nyo*.

- The pronunciation of the letter V is very similar in sound to B. You will notice I use B instead of V in the phonetic pronunciations, as I feel it results in a more authentic sound.

- The letter H is always silent.

- The letter Ñ is not pronounced like an N but rather like *ny* as in ca**ny**on.

- RR signifies a rolling r sound.

QUICK REFERENCE

In the appendix you will find a quick reference chart listing the cuts of meat (beef, chicken, veal, and so on). This is very helpful as there are various Spanish names for each cut of meat.

ENGLISH-SPANISH

A

Abalone Abalón / Abulón *ah-bah-LOHN / ah-boo-LOHN*
FISH & SHELLFISH A mollusk found along the coastline of California, Mexico, and northern Spain. An abalone is a univalve whose shell is the source of mother-of-pearl. Fresh abalone is a delicacy but it can also be found canned, dried, and salted.

Acid Ácido *AH-see-doh*
GENERAL From the Latin *acidus*, meaning sour, the taste associated with ingredients (vinegar, citrus fruit) possessing a pH below 7. Because acid breaks down cell walls it can change the texture and appearance of foods.

Acidulate Acidular *ah-see-doo-LAHR*
COOKING METHOD / TECHNIQUE To add an acid. Acidulated water is water that has had some vinegar or lemon juice added to it.

Acorn Bellota *beh-YOH-tah*
NUTS & OILS The nut of the oak tree. Acorns are consumed primarily by wildlife.

Additive Aditivo *ah-dee-TEE-voh*
GENERAL Substances added (intentionally or not) to food to preserve its flavor, nutrition, or quality, or to aid in its processing or preparation.

Aerate Gasificar *gah-see-fee-KAHR*
COOKING METHOD / TECHNIQUE To incorporate air.

Agar Agar *ah-GAHR*
HERBS & SPICES A setting agent or thickener derived from seaweed. Often referred to as Japanese gelatin, agar differs from gelatin in that it sets at room temperature and is five times more powerful than gelatin, requiring less to be used. It is tasteless and serves as a vegetarian option to gelatin.

Agave Agave *ah-GAH-veh*
FRUIT & VEGETABLES A succulent (water-retaining) plant that grows in Mexico, Central America, and the southwest United States. Poisonous when raw, agave develops a mildly sweet flavor when cooked. The sap collected from the agave plant is used to make tequila. Agave nectar is also used as a sugar substitute.

Air dry Secar al aire *seh-KAHR ahl AH-ee-reh*
COOKING METHOD / TECHNIQUE To dehydrate through exposure to air.

Albumin Albumina *ahl-boo-MEE-nah*
GENERAL The protein found in egg whites. Albumen, spelled with an "e," is another word for egg white.

Alcohol Alcohol *ahl-KOHL*
BEVERAGE Ethyl/ethanol that is found in alcoholic beverages. It is produced by distilling fermented sugars obtained from fruit or grains. Pure ethyl alcohol boils at 173°F and freezes at -173°F.

Alfalfa sprout **Brote de alfalfa** *BROH-teh deh ahl-FAHL-fah*
FRUIT & VEGETABLES A thin, long stem produced by a sprouted alfalfa seed. They are often used in salads and sandwiches.

Allspice **Pimienta de Jamaica** *pee-mee-EHN-tah deh hah-MAH-ee-kah*
HERBS & SPICES A berry of the evergreen pimiento tree. The name comes from its flavor, which is a combination of nutmeg, cinnamon, black pepper, and cloves. The spice can be purchased in whole or ground form. It is used in both sweet and savory cooking and is also referred to as Jamaica pepper.

Almond **Almendra** *ahl-MEHN-drah*
NUTS & OILS The kernel of the almond tree encased in a hard, inedible shell. Almonds are available in markets blanched (without their thin, brown skin) or with the skin on.

Almond extract **Esencia de almendra / Extracto de almendra** *eh-SEHN-see-ah deh ahl-MEHN-drah / eks-TRAK-toh deh ahl-MENH-drah*
CONDIMENTS A flavoring produced by combining almond oil with ethyl alcohol. Since the flavor of almond extract is intense, use the proper amount of the best-quality extract you can find.

Almond oil **Aceite de almendra** *ah-SAY-teh deh ahl-MENH-drah*
NUTS & OILS A specialty oil that is made by pressing almonds.

Almonds, ground **Almendras molidas** *ahl-MENH-drahs moh-LEE-dahs*
NUTS & OILS Almonds that have been pulverized into a coarse powder. This is achieved with a food processor or mortar and pestle. When almonds are ground, a small amount of sugar is typically added to absorb some of the oil and prevent a paste from forming.

Almonds, sliced **Almendras troceadas** *ahl-MENH-drahs troh-seh-AH-dahs*
NUTS & OILS Almonds that have been sliced thinly lengthwise.

Aluminum foil **Papel de aluminio** *pah-PEHL deh ah-loo-MEE-nee-oh*
EQUIPMENT Thin sheets of aluminum. Aluminum foil can be found in rolls or individual sheets. The foil is opaque and extremely pliable and can withstand freezing temperatures and very high heat.

Amaranth **Amaranto** *ah-mah-RAHN-toh*
GRAINS & CEREALS A plant high in protein. Both the seeds and leaves of amaranth can be eaten. Most commonly the seeds are ground into a flour, which does not contain gluten, and used to make breads. The leaves can be cooked or eaten raw in a salad.

Anchovy **Anchoa / Boquerón** *ahn-CHOH-ah / boh-keh-ROHN*
FISH & SHELLFISH A small, silvery blue fish from the Mediterranean coastline that is filleted, salt-cured, and canned. Some are also smoked. Anchovies are salty and tend to be used sparingly.

ENGLISH-SPANISH A

Anchovy paste Pasta de anchoas *PAHS-tah deh ahn-CHOH-ahs*
CONDIMENTS A paste made from a combination of mashed anchovies, water, vinegar, and spices used as a condiment for its distinctive salty taste. It can be used in recipes or spread on toast as a canapé.

Angelica Angélica *ahn-HEH-lee-kah*
HERBS & SPICES An aromatic herb that is a member of the parsley family and thrives in northern, cold climates. Its stems and leaves are commonly used in baking, often blanched and candied for decorating cakes and pastries. The roots and seeds are also used for making liqueurs.

Anise Anís *ah-NEES*
HERBS & SPICES An herbaceous plant that is a member of the parsley family and has a distinctive sweet licorice flavor. Its leaves and seeds are used in both sweet and savory preparations. This is the flavor found in liqueurs such as anisette (*anís* in Spanish), aguardiente, and pastis.

Annatto paste Pasta de annatto *PAHS-tah deh åh-NAH-toh*
HERBS & SPICES The pulp surrounding the achiote seed in an annatto tree. Found as well in powder form, this derivative is used primarily as a coloring agent for items such as cheese, rice, and butter.

Annatto seed Achiote *ah-chee-OH-teh*
HERBS & SPICES The seed of the annatto tree, sometimes referred to as achiote seed. This spice is used as much for coloring (bright orange red) as flavor (earthy, slightly musky). It can be found in whole or powdered form.

Antioxidant Antioxidante *ahn-tee-ohks-ee-DAHN-teh*
GENERAL A substance that inhibits oxidation. From a culinary point of view, oxidation results in browning and in food becoming rancid. Ascorbic acid (vitamin C), for example, is a natural antioxidant that is often used in food preparation against oxidation.

Appellation Apelación / Denominación *ah-peh-lah-see-OHN / deh-noh-mee-nah-see-OHN*
DESCRIPTOR A geographical designation applied to a grape-growing area controlled by governmental rules. The rules of appellation address issues such as grape varieties and yields per acre and vary by country and even by region. The goal of an appellation is to produce a high-quality product.

Appetizer Aperitivo *ah-peh-ree-TEE-voh*
GENERAL Technically the first course served at the table. An appetizer should be bite-size and is meant to stimulate the appetite. The term is often wrongly interchanged with hors d'oeuvre.

Apple Manzana *mahn-SAH-nah*
FRUIT & VEGETABLES One of the oldest cultivated fruits. The apple has over a thousand varieties that vary in color, texture, and flavor. Apples can be eaten raw or

cooked and are used in both savory and sweet recipes. They are available year-round but are best in the fall.

Apple corer **Despepitador de manzana** *dehs-peh-pee-tah-DOHR deh mahn-SAH-nah*

EQUIPMENT A kitchen tool used to cut and remove the center of an apple. There are a few kinds of apple corers, but the classic one is a long cylinder tube that is serrated on one end and has a handle on the other.

Applesauce **Salsa de manzana** *SAHL-sah deh mahn-SAH-nah*

CONDIMENTS A cooked puree of apples. Sugar and spices can be added for flavor.

Apricot **Albaricoque** *ahl-bah-ree-KOH-keh*

FRUIT & VEGETABLES A relative of the peach that has been grown for over four thousand years. Its thin, furry, orange skin can be cut through without difficulty, exposing a seed that falls out easily.

Aroma **Aroma** *ah-ROH-mah*

DESCRIPTOR A sense of smell that is usually associated with a pleasant odor.

Aromatics **Aromatícos** *ah-roh-MAH-tee-kohs*

DESCRIPTOR Plant products—vegetables, herbs, spices—that contribute vivid aromas and flavors to food preparation.

Arrowroot **Arrurruz** *ah-rroo-RROOS*

GRAINS & CEREALS The starchy tuber of the tropical arrowroot plant. The root is ground into a flour that is used primarily as a thickener. A unique characteristic of the thickener is that it remains clear when heated; it also does not impart a raw, chalky taste if undercooked. The flour should be mixed with a small amount of water before being added to hot liquid in order to maximize it effectiveness.

Artichoke **Alcachofa** *ahl-kah-CHOH-fah*

FRUIT & VEGETABLES The unopened flower bud of the globe artichoke plant. An artichoke needs to be trimmed when mature but can be eaten in its entirety when young. The mature variety is usually boiled or steamed and care must be taken when getting close to the heart as it's surrounded by an inedible fur (the "choke") that must be removed. The stem can be eaten if peeled and has a flavor very similar to that of the heart. Other vegetables have the word "artichoke" in their name, but the true artichoke is the globe artichoke.

Arugula **Rúcula / Roqueta** *ROO-koo-lah / roh-KEH-tah*

FRUIT & VEGETABLES A bitter salad green with a pepper flavor. Arugla can be found in both young and mature stages. The younger the leaf, the more mild tasting it is.

Asafoetida **Asafetida** *AH-sah-feh-TEE-dah*

HERBS & SPICES An herbaceous fennel-like plant that grows mainly in Iran and India. When raw, it has a pungent garlic smell but it mellows when cooked, imparting flavors and aromas reminiscent of sautéed onion and garlic. Asafetida can be found in both powdered and lump form.

Asparagus Espárrago *ehs-PAH-rrah-goh*
FRUIT & VEGETABLES A member of the lily family that has an herbaceous, sweet flavor and gets significantly tougher as it matures. There are four types of asparagus: green (*verde*), the most common type; white (*blanco*), popular in Europe, where it grows underground and as such does not develop chlorophyll; purple (*morado*), which remains purple when fresh or lightly sautéed but turns green with prolonged cooking; and wild (*silvestre*), which is tender and very thin.

Astringent Astringente *ahs-treen-HENH-teh*
DESCRIPTOR Dry, puckering mouthfeel typically caused by tannins.

Au gratin Gratinado *grah-tee-NAH-doh*
COOKING METHOD / TECHNIQUE The technique of creating a golden brown crust by broiling a topping of cheese and/or bread crumbs mixed with butter. Also the name given to a dish made with this technique.

Avocado Aguacate *ah-gwah-KAH-teh*
FRUIT & VEGETABLES A fruit with a buttery texture and nutty flavor and flesh that goes from pale yellow to green. It matures on the tree but ripens off the tree. The Hass variety, which is small and dark, is most commonly used in the United States.

B

Bacon Beicon / Bacon / Tocino *BEH-ee-kohn / BEH-ee-kohn / toh-SEE-noh*
MEAT Traditionally, smoked and cured pork belly. However, other cuts of pork can be used as well.

Bain-marie Baño Maria *bah-NYOH mah-REE-ah*
EQUIPMENT A piece of equipment that cooks food gently by the heat of steam. Traditionally it is made up of a large bowl or pot fitted atop a slightly smaller pot that contains a couple of inches of water and placed over low heat. The steam produced heats the top pot / bowl and its contents. *See also* **Water bath** and **Double boiler**.
COOKING METHOD / TECHNIQUE The technique using a bain-marie to cook delicate foods, that can burn or curdle easily, by the heat of steam as well as keep cooked foods warm.

Baked goods Pastelería *pahs-teh-leh-REE-ah*
BAKING & PASTRY Items produced by the baking process including breads, cakes, pastries, pies, tarts, quiches, and cookies.

Bakery Pastelería *pahs-teh-leh-REE-ah*
BAKING & PASTRY An operation that produces and/or sells baked goods.

Bakeware Equipo de pastelería *eh-KEE-poh deh pahs-teh-leh-REE-ah*
EQUIPMENT Equipment used to make baked goods.

Baking Hornear / Hornada *ohr-neh-AHR / ohr-NAH-dah*
COOKING METHOD / TECHNIQUE Technique of cooking in an oven with dry heat to produce baked goods.

Baking beans Pesas de hornear *PEH-sahs deh ohr-neh-AHR*
EQUIPMENT Small, round, often ceramic balls used when blind baking. Baking paper is placed over pastry and then topped with the balls, which allows for even heat distribution and keeps the pastry from rising too much. Dried beans and rice can be substituted for the ceramic balls.

Baking powder Levadura en polvo *leh-bah-DOO-rah ehn POHL-boh*
BAKING & PASTRY A leavener made up of baking soda, an acid, and a moisture absorber. It is typically used when a recipe does not have an acidic component or does not have enough of one. Baking powder has a limited shelf life.

Baking sheet Bandeja de hornear *bahn-DEH-hah deh ohr-neh-AHR*
EQUIPMENT A flat, firm sheet of metal that typically has an upward curved edge.

Baking soda Bicarbonato de sodio *bee-kahr-boh-NAH-toh deh SOH-dee-oh*
BAKING & PASTRY An alkali that when combined with an acid and moisture functions as a leavener for baked goods. Also known as sodium bicarbonate, it is typically used when a recipe has an acidic component.

Balsamic vinegar Vinagre balsámico *bee-NAH-greh bahl-SAH-mee-koh*
CONDIMENTS A condiment made from the fermented juice of the Italian Trebbiano grape and aged in wooden barrels for a number of years. This aging process produces a dark-colored, sweet-flavored vinegar.

Bamboo mat Tejido de bambú / Alfombrilla de bambú *teh-HEE-doh deh bahm-BOO / ahl-fohm-BREE-yah deh bahm-BOO*
EQUIPMENT A flexible mat made of thin bamboo sticks tied together by string. Bamboo mats are primarily used for rolling sushi.

Bamboo shoot Brote de bambú *BROH-teh deh bahm-BOO*
FRUIT & VEGETABLES The ivory-colored shoot of an edible bamboo species. It is cut as soon as it appears above ground to ensure its tenderness. Bamboo shoots are typically found canned but can be also found fresh.

Bamboo steamer Olla de bambú al vapor / Cesta de bambú *OH-yah deh bahm-BOO ahl bah-POHR / SEHS-tah deh bahm-BOO*
EQUIPMENT A round, stackable steamer made from bamboo wood and used in Asian food preparation. It has bamboo sides and wooden bamboo sticks that make up the grates that form the bottom.

Banana Plátano / Banano / Cambur / Gineo *PLAH-tah-noh / bah-NAH-noh / kahm-boor / gee-NEH-oh*
FRUIT & VEGETABLES A long, curved fruit that changes color from green to yellow to brown as it ripens. Its flesh is a pale beige color and softens as the fruit matures. Bananas grow in clusters and ripen best off the plant.

Banana leaves **Hoja de plátano** *OH-hah deh PLAH-tah-noh*
FRUIT & VEGETABLES The large, flexible leaves of a banana plant. Used in Latin American and Asian cooking to wrap or cover food, they impart a unique smoky flavor. The spines need to be removed in order to make the leaves pliable and able to be cut to the appropriate size for cooking. They are usually found frozen.

Banana pepper **Pimiento italiano** *pee-mee-EHN-toh ee-tah-lee-AH-noh*
FRUIT & VEGETABLES Part of the chile pepper family, a long, yellow pepper that is slightly sweet with mild heat. Its shape resembles that of a banana.

Barbecue adj. **Barbacoa / Asado a la brasa** *bahr-bah-KOH-ah / ah-SAH-do / ah lah BRAH-sah*
COOKING METHOD / TECHNIQUE The method of cooking meat and poultry slowly and indirectly through hot coals or wood. The meat is covered and often basted with a sauce to keep it moist.

n. **Asador / Barbacoa** *ah-sah-DOHR / bahr-bah-KOH-ah*
EQUIPMENT A covered outdoor oven with a grate in its center, which can be heated by electricity, gas, coals, or wood. Some barbecues are fitted with a spit/rotisserie.

Barbecue sauce **Salsa barbacoa** *SAHL-sah bahr-bah-KOH-ah*
CONDIMENTS A sauce used to baste barbecued meat and poultry. It typically contains tomatoes, vinegar, sugar, mustard, and spices.

Barding **Albardillar** *ahl-bahr-dee-YAHR*
COOKING METHOD / TECHNIQUE To add or place fat over lean pieces of meat, especially game, to make it moist and tender.

Barley **Cebada** *seh-BAH-dah*
GRAINS & CEREALS An ancient grain often used for animal fodder. When malted, barley can make beer or whiskey. Pearl barley has the bran removed and is often used in soups.

Barley, pearl **Cebada perlada** *seh-BAH-dah pehr-LAH-dah*
GRAINS & CEREALS Barley that has had its husk and bran layer removed resulting in a softer texture and whiter color. Pearl barley cooks faster than regular barley.

Barramundi **Barramundi** *bah-rrah-MOON-dee*
FISH & SHELLFISH A firm, white, flaky, saltwater fish from the Pacific West region. Popular in Australia, it is now being raised in aquaculture.

Basil **Albahaca** *ahl-BAH-kah*
HERBS & SPICES An herb that is a member of the mint family. Basil is key to Mediterranean cooking, especially Italian cuisine, and it is also often used in Asian cooking. There are a few varieties but the most popular is sweet basil, which has a slight anise and licorice flavor.

Bass **Lubina / Corvina** *loo-BEE-nah / kohr-BEE-nah*
FISH & SHELLFISH A white, flaky fish with a fine texture and mild, sweet flesh. It can grow to be three feet long and twenty pounds in weight.

Baste Regar con grasa *reh-GAHR kohn GRAH-sah*

COOKING METHOD / TECHNIQUE To brush, squeeze, or spoon fat or liquid over meat while it is cooking.

Baster Regador *reh-gah-DOHR*

EQUIPMENT A tool used for basting. Typically, it is a long, hollow cylinder with an opening on one end and a rubber bulb on the other that sucks liquid in when squeezed and pours it out when the pressure is let go.

Batter Pasta para rebozar / Batido / Pasta culinaria *PAHS-tah PAH-rah reh-boh-SAHR / bah-TEE-doh / PAHS-tah koo-lee-NAH-ree-ah*

BAKING & PASTRY An uncooked mixture containing flour and/or eggs. Batter can be thick (semisolid) or thin (liquid) and is typically cooked in an oven.

Bay leaf Hoja de laurel *OH-hah deh lah-oo-REHL*

HERBS & SPICES An herb native to the Mediterranean, also known as a laurel leaf. There are two varieties: the long, thin, and more flavorful California bay leaf and the more oval and subtle Turkish bay leaf. Bay leaves can be purchased dried or fresh, which are more difficult to find.

Bean Judía / Alubia / Frijol / Pororo / Grano / Habichuela / Ejote / Vainita / Chaucha *hoo-DEE-ah / ah-LOO-bee-ah / free-HOHL / poh-ROH-roh / GRAH-noh / ah-bee-choo-EH-lah / eh-HOH-teh / bah-ee-NEE-tah / cha-OO-cha*

FRUIT & VEGETABLES A seed from a pod. Beans can be fresh or dried. If fresh, they can be unripe (the entire pod and bean is eaten) or ripe (the beans must be removed from the pods). *See also* **Snow pea**.

Bean, black Frijole negro / Caraota negra *free-HOH-leh NEH-groh / kah-rah-OH-tah NEH-grah*

FRUIT & VEGETABLES A small, shiny bean with a creamy and meaty flesh that can be purchased dried or canned. Very popular in Latin American cuisines, black beans are served as a soup or side dish.

Bean, broad / Fava Haba *AH-bah*

FRUIT & VEGETABLES A large bean, also known as a fava bean, that comes in a pod and is inedible unless very young. Once removed from the pod, the fresh bean must be blanched to remove its tough skin. Broad beans can be purchased fresh, dried, or canned.

Bean, cannellini Judía cannellini *hoo-DEE-ah kah-neh-LEE-nee*

FRUIT & VEGETABLES A white, kidney-shaped bean prized for its smooth texture. Cannellini beans can be found canned or dried.

Bean, Chinese Judía china *hoo-DEE-ah CHEE-nah*

FRUIT & VEGETABLES Also known as a yard-long bean, a green bean that averages at least one foot in length. Picked before they are mature, Chinese beans are grown abundantly in Southeast Asia. They are treated as regular green beans and often cut into smaller pieces.

ENGLISH-SPANISH B

Bean, dried Legumbre / Frijol seco *leh-GOOM-breh / free-HOHL SEH-koh*
FRUIT & VEGETABLES The seeded pod of a legume that has been dried. Common examples are black beans, chickpeas, and pinto beans.

Bean, fava Haba *AH-bah*
See **Bean, broad**.

Bean, French Judía francesa *hoo-DEE-ah frahn-SEH-sah*
FRUIT & VEGETABLES A tender, young, green bean that can be eaten with its pod.

Bean, green Judía verde / Chaucha *hoo-DEE-ah BEHR-deh / cha-OO-cha*
FRUIT & VEGETABLES An immature or unripe fruit of a bean plant. The small seeds are found inside an edible pod. Some varieties have a fibrous string that needs to be pulled off, but many do not. Also referred to as a common bean, it is available fresh, frozen, and canned.

Bean, lima Judía lima / Pallares *hoo-DEE-ah LEE-mah / pah-YAH-rehs*
FRUIT & VEGETABLES Named after Lima, Peru, where they were discovered more than one hundred years ago, a plump, pale green, kidney-shaped bean that has a mild but meaty flavor. When fresh, lima beans are found in pods that must be removed before cooking. They are also available frozen or canned. Also called butter beans.

Bean, navy Judía navy *hoo-DEE-ah NAH-bee*
FRUIT & VEGETABLES A small, pea-size, dried bean that is white in color. It is mild flavored, dense, and creamy.

Bean, pinto Judía pinta / Frijol colorado *hoo-DEE-ah PEEN-tah / free-HOHL koh-loh-RAH-doh*
FRUIT & VEGETABLES A small, light pink, dried bean coated with black spots. Popular in southwest United States and northern Mexico, it is the bean commonly used for refried beans.

Bean, red kidney Judía roja / Caparrón *hoo-DEE-ah ROH-hah / kah-pah-RROHN*
FRUIT & VEGETABLE A firm, medium-size bean that is shaped like a kidney. It has a dark red skin with a meaty flesh and full-bodied flavor.

Bean, wax Judía amarilla *hoo-DEE-ah ah-mah-REE-ah*
FRUIT & VEGETABLES A light yellow variety of green bean.

Bean thread noodles Fideos de celofán *fee-DEH-ohs deh seh-loh-FAHN*
GRAINS & CEREALS Dried translucent noodles made from the starch of green mung beans. They are also known as cellophane noodles or glass noodles.

Beef Vacuno / Carne de res *bah-KOO-noh / KAHR-neh deh rehs*
MEAT Cattle raised for its meat. The term refers to the animal's muscles, which are portioned into cuts and graded on quality by the USDA (prime, choice, select). *See individual cuts, entries under* **Carne de Res**, *and the Quick Reference*.

Beef, chuck Espadilla *ehs-pah-DEE-yah*

MEAT An inexpensive cut of meat located between the neck and shoulder. It is a tough cut that must be cooked slowly to be tenderized. It is a popular cut for making hamburgers.

Beef, diced Carne troceada *KAHR-neh troh-seh-AH-dah*

MEAT Any cut of beef that has been cut into a dice before or after cooking.

Beef, fillet steak Filete / Corte de solomillo *fee-LEH-teh / KOHR-teh deh soh-loh-MEE-yoh*

MEAT An individual portion of the tenderloin. Also referred to as filet mignon.

Beef, flank steak Falda / Vacio / Tapabarriga *FAHL-dah / bah-SEE-oh / tah-pah-bah-RREE-gah*

MEAT A flat and fibrous cut of beef from the belly muscle of the cow. It is almost always marinated before cooking because, while very flavorful, it is tough and needs tenderizing.

Beef, ground Carne molida *KAHR-neh moh-LEE-dah*

MEAT A cut of beef that has been ground. Depending on the cut used, fat may be incorporated into it.

Beef, porterhouse Bife ancho con costilla / Lomo vetado con costilla / Churrasco redondo *BEE-feh AHN-choh kohn kohs-TEE-yah / LOH-moh beh-TAH-doh kohn kohs-TEE-yah / choo-RRAHS-koh reh-DOHN-doh*

MEAT Taken from the rear and end of the short loin, this is a large cut of beef with the bone still attached. Similar to the T-bone, it consists of both the tenderloin and strip steak. (A porterhouse steak is a large T-bone taken from the rear of the short loin.)

Beef, rib eye Filete de lomo alto / Bife ancho / Lomo vetado *fee-LEH-teh deh LOH-moh AHL-toh / BEE-feh AHN-choh / LOH-moh beh-TAH-doh*

MEAT A cut from the rib section, this very tender steak is available with or without the bone.

Beef, rump steak Bistec de cadera / Colita de cuadril / Punta de picana / Empuje *bees-TEHK deh kah-DEH-rah / koh-LEE-tah deh kwah-DREEL / POON-tah deh pee-KAH-nah / ehm-POO-heh*

MEAT A steak cut from the top round (tail end) section, it is the most tender part of the round. Lean and moderately tough, it is best when braised.

Beef, short plate Tapa de asado / Plateada / Planchuela *TAH-pah deh ah-SAH-doh / plah-teh-AH-dah / plahn-choo-EH-lah*

MEAT A cut from the belly area below the ribs. It is best when slow cooked by moist heat.

Beef, short ribs Asado de tira / Costilla cargada *ah-SAH-doh deh TEE-rah / kohs-TEE-yah kahr-GAH-dah*

MEAT The cut of meat that comes from the short plate of cattle. Specifically, it is found in the bottom portion of the ribs, close to the belly. It is a very flavorful but fatty cut of meat filled with connective tissue. It is the same cut as the St. Louis–style sparerib in pork.

Beef, sirloin Solomillo / Bife angosto / Lomo liso / Bife chico soh-loh-MEE-yoh / BEE-feh ahn-GOHS-toh / LOH-moh LEE-soh / BEE-feh CHEE-koh

MEAT The cut of beef located between the short loin and round. Typically cut into steaks, it is a flavorful cut with a firm texture.

Beef, skirt steak Entraña / Arrachera ehn-TRAH-nya / ah-rrah-CHEH-rah

MEAT A cut taken from the plate or belly of cattle, specifically, the diaphram muscle. Flat and long, it is flavorful but a bit fatty and tough. It is the cut most often used to make fajitas.

Beef, T-bone Chuleta con solomillo / Bife angosto con lomo / Entrecot choo-LEH-tah kohn soh-loh-MEE-yoh / BEE-feh ahn-GOHS-toh kohn LOH-moh / ehn-treh-KOHT

MEAT A cut from the middle section of the short loin, it consists of a T-shaped bone with meat on either side—a strip steak and a tenderloin.

Beef, top round Tapa plana / Tapa de cuadril / Punta de ganso / Cadera TAH-pah PLAH-nah / TAH-pah deh kwah-DREEL / POON-tah deh GAHN-soh / kah-DEH-rah

MEAT The top portion of the round (tail end) section of the cattle.

Beef, whole tenderloin Solomillo entero / Lomo soh-loh-MEE-yoh ehn-TEH-roh / LOH-moh

MEAT Considered the most tender cut of beef. Because it is located in the loin section of the cattle (the middle of its back), this muscle does very little work and remains tender.

Beef jerky Tasajo / Cecina tah-SAH-hoh / seh-SEE-nah

MEAT Beef that has been stripped of fat, cut into strips, marinated, cured, and dried.

Beef patty Carne molida en forma KAHR-neh moh-LEE-dah ehn FOHR-mah

MEAT See **Meat patty**.

Beef stock Caldo oscuro KAHL-doh ohs-KOO-roh

MEAT A strained liquid of simmered browned beef bones and aromatic vegetables.

Beer Cerveza sehr-VEH-sah

BEVERAGE An alcoholic beverage made from a mixture of malted cereals, hops, yeast, and water. It is the most-consumed alcoholic beverage in the world.

Beet Remolacha reh-moh-LAH-chah

FRUIT & VEGETABLES A round root vegetable whose color ranges from white to blood beet red. The root is a storage house for carbohydrates. A beet is prized as much for its edible, nutritious leaves as it is for its sweet flesh.

Belgian endive Endibia bélgica ehn-DEE-bee-ah BEHL-hee-kah

FRUIT & VEGETABLES A type of endive that is made up of a tightly packed head of leaves shaped like a small torpedo. The long, white leaves have pale yellow tips.

The plant is grown in complete darkness to prevent the leaves from turning green. Slightly bitter in flavor, endive can be eaten raw or cooked.

Bell pepper **Ají / Pimiento / Chiltoma** *ah-HEE / pee-mee-EHN-toh / cheel-TOH-mah*

FRUIT & VEGETABLES A fruit and member of the *capsicum* genus. It has a mildly sweet flavor and crisp, juicy texture. Its color ranges from green to orange to red and gets its name from its bell shape.

Bell pepper, green **Pimiento verde / Ají verde** *pee-mee-EHN-toh BEHR-deh / ah-HEE BEHR-deh*

FRUIT & VEGETABLES A mild and slightly sweet-flavored bell pepper with a crisp and juicy texture. When young, all bell peppers are green and according to the variety will turn yellow, red, or orange if allowed to mature on the vine.

Bell pepper, red **Pimiento rojo / Ají rojo** *pee-mee-EHN-toh ROH-hoh / ah-HEE ROH-hoh*

FRUIT & VEGETABLES A bell-shaped pepper with a sweet flavor and crisp, juicy flesh. It is a green pepper that has been allowed to ripen on the vine, resulting in its red color and sweet flavor.

Bergamot **Bergamota** *behr-gah-MOH-tah*

HERBS & SPICES A small, sour citrus fruit whose peel and essence are used to flavor Earl Grey tea.

Berries **Bayas** *BAH-yahs*

FRUIT & VEGETABLES Small, round, edible fruit that tend to be juicy, sweet, and sometimes tart. They have small edible seeds but do not have a pit.

Beta-carotene **Beta-carotina** *BEH-tah kah-roh-TEE-nah*

A powerful antioxidant that is the precursor (will turn into) to vitamin A. Found only in plant products, beta-carotene is not toxic if consumed in excess as the body will eliminate it.

Beverage **Bebida** *beh-BEE-dah*

BEVERAGE A liquid prepared and consumed by humans. Alcohol and/or other substances such as caffeine can form part of a beverage.

Bias cut **Cortado al bies** *kohr-TAH-doh ahl BEE-ehs*

COOKING METHOD / TECHNIQUE A diagonal slice or cut made with a knife.

Bind **Ligar / Unir** *lee-GAHR / oo-NEER*

COOKING METHOD / TECHNIQUE To add an ingredient to a mixture to make it all stick together. Eggs, mayonnaise, bread crumbs, and mustard are common binders.

Biscuit **Galleta / Tortita** *gah-YEH-tah / tohr-TEE-tah*

GRAINS & CEREALS A sweet or savory quick bread leavened with baking powder or baking soda. A biscuit can also refer to a thin, sweet cookie.

Bitter **Amargo** *ah-MAHR-goh*

One of the four basic tastes. It is perceived to be acrid and unpleasant.

Bitters Bitter *BEE-tehr*
CONDIMENTS An alcoholic beverage made with herbs, roots, bark, and other parts of a plant and used to flavor cocktails. Bitters have a high alcohol content and bitter taste. They are also consumed as a digestif.

Bivalve Bivalvo *bee-VAHL-voh*
FISH & SHELLFISH A mollusk, such as a clam, oyster, or mussel, that contains two shells hinged together.

Blackberry Mora *MOH-rah*
FRUIT & VEGETABLES Purple black in color, a berry that is very tart when immature. Blackberries grow on bushes and have small, plump, round clusters that make up their flesh.

Blackened Apimentado *ah-pee-mehn-TAH-doh*
COOKING METHOD / TECHNIQUE Coated with ground black pepper and spices.

Black-eyed pea Alubia de ojo *ah-LOO-bee-ah deh OH-hoh*
FRUIT & VEGETABLES A small, beige bean with a black spot said to have come to America through the slave trade. Black-eyed peas are very popular in the southern United States.

Black olive paste Pasta de aceitunas *PAHS-tah deh ah-seh-ee-TOO-nahs*
CONDIMENTS Crushed black olives that may be seasoned with lemon, anchovies, and olive oil. Black olive paste is used as a condiment or spread over toast as a canapé.

Black peppercorn Pimienta negra *pee-mee-EHN-tah NEH-grah*
HERBS & SPICES Picked and dried unripe berries from the pepper plant. Black is the strongest-flavored peppercorn.

Black sapote Sapote negro *sah-POH-teh NEH-groh*
FRUIT & VEGETABLES A round fruit that looks like a rotting green tomato. The flesh of the black sapote turns a soft dark brown when ripe with an appearance similar to that of chocolate pudding. Its flavor is somewhat bland.

Black Tea Té negro *teh NEH-groh*
BEVERAGE Tea leaves that are fermented and oxidized before they are dried. This results in tea that has a very strong flavor and dark amber color.

Blanch Escaldar *ehs-kahl-DAHR*
COOKING METHOD / TECHNIQUE To quickly cook and cool food by plunging it in boiling water and then cooling it in an ice-water bath. Blanching is typically performed on fruit and vegetables to loosen the skin, brighten the color, and enhance the flavor. It is another word for scald.

Blend Mezclar *mehs-KLAHR*
COOKING METHOD / TECHNIQUE To mix two or more substances together until well combined.

Blender Liquadora / Batidora *lee-kwah-DOH-rah / bah-tee-DOH-rah*
EQUIPMENT A small electric appliance used to blend, crush, and puree, ingredients. It typically consists of a tall pitcher with sharp rotary blades at its base connected to an electric stand.

Blind bake Hornear a ciegas *ohr-neh-AHR ah see-EH-gahs*
COOKING METHOD / TECHNIQUE To bake an empty pie crust before adding the filling. Often the crust is pierced with a fork and/or lined with parchment paper and topped with baking beans to prevent the pastry from rising and help it bake evenly.

Blood orange Naranja sanguina *nah-RAHN-hah sahn-GWEE-nah*
FRUIT & VEGETABLES A sweet yet tart orange with bright red flesh.

Blood sausage Morcilla *mohr-SEE-yah*
MEAT Pork sausage made with the blood of the pig. Blood sausage can contain other ingredients such as bread crumbs, rice, nuts, and spices. It is generally consumed fried.

Blueberry Arandano negro *ah-RAHN-dah-noh NEH-groh*
FRUIT & VEGETABLES A small, round blackish blue fruit that grows on a bush. Its translucent flesh is sweet while its dark skin can be tart.

Blue cheese Queso azul *KEH-soh ah-SOOL*
DAIRY A type of cheese that has been injected with a special mold that causes the cheese to develop blue and green veins. The mold also contributes to the cheese's characteristic flavor.

Blue crab Cangrejo azul *kahn-GREH-hoh ah-SOOL*
FISH & SHELLFISH A crustacean that is found along the Atlantic Coast and the Gulf of Mexico. It has blue claws and a blue green shell and can be both hard- or soft-shelled.

Boil Hervìr *ehr-BEER*
COOKING METHOD / TECHNIQUE To cook by raising the temperature of water to 212°F.

Bok choy Bok choy *bohk choy*
FRUIT & VEGETABLES A vegetable that has a white crunchy stalk and dark green leaves and grows in bunches. Its flavor is very mild and it is often used in Asian cooking.

Bone v. Deshuesar *dehs-weh-SAHR*
COOKING METHOD / TECHNIQUE To remove the bone from a piece of meat, poultry, or fish.

n. Hueso *WEH-soh*
MEAT Porous connective tissue that forms the skeleton of animals.

Boned and rolled meat Carne deshuesado y listo *KAHR-neh dehs-weh-SAH-doh ee LEES-toh*
MEAT A piece of meat with all bones removed, tightly rolled, and tied with twine (cooking string).

Bonito Bonito *boh-NEE-toh*
FISH & SHELLFISH A variety of tuna (skip jack) that is a member of the mackerel family. It is often preserved for canning or drying (dried into bonito flakes).

Borage Borraja *boh-RRAH-hah*
HERBS & SPICES An herb with blue five-point flowers and green leaves. Popular in Europe, it is eaten both raw and cooked. If raw, it must be finely chopped in order to make sure its hairy texture isn't overwhelming.

Bordeaux wine Vino de Burdeo *BEE-noh deh boor-DEH-oh*
BEVERAGE Wine made from grapes grown in southwest France. In Britain, this wine is referred to as claret.

Bouillon cube Pastilla de caldo / Cubito de caldo *pahs-TEE-yah deh KAHL-doh / koo-BEE-toh deh KAHL-doh*
CONDIMENTS Dehydrated beef, chicken, or vegetable stock that has been compressed and shaped into a small cube. It is also known as stock cube.

Bouquet garni Bouquet garni *boo-KEH gahr-NEE*
HERBS & SPICES A bunch of herbs that have been tied together with string or bundled in a pouch made of cheesecloth. The traditional combination is parsley, thyme, and bay leaf but any herb combination can be made.

Bowl Plato hondo / Bol *PLAH-toh OHN-doh / bohl*
EQUIPMENT A deep, open-top vessel used to serve food. It can be small for individual use or large to serve a group.

Boysenberry Boysenberry *boy-sehn-BEH-rree*
FRUIT & VEGETABLES A berry that looks like a large, purple raspberry and has a slight sweet, tart flavor. It was made by crossing a raspberry, blackberry, and loganberry in the early 1920s.

Brain Sesos *SEH-sohs*
MEAT Organ located within the skull of an animal. Contents from beef, lamb, and pork are eaten and referred to as a type of offal.

Braise Estofar *ehs-toh-FAHR*
COOKING METHOD / TECHNIQUE To cook slowly to develop flavors and tenderize tough cuts of meat. The meat is first browned in fat, then a liquid is added and the mixture is covered tightly with a lid. The meat is left to cook in the oven or on the range at a low temperature for a long period of time. Braising is also used for vegetables.

Bran Salvado *sahl-VAH-doh*
GRAINS & CEREALS The outer layer of cereal grains (wheat, oats, rice) that is typically removed during the milling process. High in fiber and vitamins and minerals, bran is used in breakfast cereals and as an ingredient in baked goods.

Brandy snaps Cañitas al brandy *kah-NYEE-tahs ahl BRAHN-dee*
BAKING & PASTRY Thin, crisp cookies baked in the oven until golden brown. They remain pliable when hot and are shaped into tubes or baskets stuffed or filled with cream and/or fruit. Brandy snaps may or may not contain brandy but are made with a good amount of butter, sugar, and corn syrup, which allows them to be shaped when hot.

Bran flakes Copos de salvado *KOH-pohs deh sahl-BAH-doh*
GRAINS & CEREALS A dry, ready-to-eat whole grain cereal irregularly shaped into small, thin sheets.

Brazil nut Nuez de Brasil *noo-EHS deh brah-SEEL*
NUTS & OILS The large seed of a giant tree of the same name found in the Amazon. The seed is often mistakenly referred to as a nut.

Bread v. Empanizar *ehm-pah-nee-SAHR*
COOKING METHOD / TECHNIQUE To coat an ingredient with bread crumbs, flour, or another ground grain. Often the food is dipped in egg or a liquid to help the bread crumbs adhere before being fried or baked. This creates a crispy exterior while maintaining a moist interior.

n. Pan *pahn*
GRAINS & CEREALS A baked good made with flour, salt, water, and sometimes a leavener. It can be baked, steamed, or fried.

Bread, sandwich Pan de molde *pahn de MOHL-deh*
GRAINS & CEREALS A pullman loaf of bread that is made with white flour and baked in a long, narrow pan. Its slices are square and have four flat crusts.

Bread crumbs Pan rallado *pahn rah-YAH-doh*
CONDIMENTS Fresh or dried bread that has been ground to crumbs. Dried bread can be stale bread or bread that has been toasted.

Breadfruit Fruta del pan *FROO-tah dehl pahn*
FRUIT & VEGETABLES A large, green-skinned fruit native to the Caribbean. The cream-colored flesh is eaten when the fruit is unripe or before it becomes too sweet. Breadfruit can be made sweet or savory by frying, grilling, baking, or stewing.

Break Cortado / Cortar *kohr-TAH-doh / kohr-TAHR*
COOKING METHOD / TECHNIQUE A situation where at least two substances from an emulsion separate.

Breakfast Desayuno *deh-sah-YOO-noh*
GENERAL The first meal of the day typically eaten in the morning.

Bream Brema común *BREH-mah koh-MOON*
FISH & SHELLFISH A general term for a species of fish found all over the world in both fresh and salt waters. They have a firm, white flesh that is low in fat. Popular

varieties include sea bream (Japan), dorada (Spain), daurade (France), and porgy (United States).

Brine Salmuera / Agua salada *sahl-moo-EH-rah / AH-gwah sah-LAH-dah*
COOKING METHOD / TECHNIQUE A highly concentrated solution of salt and water. Sugar is sometimes added to the solution. Brine is used to preserve, flavor, and increase the juiciness of meats.

Broccoli Brecol *breh-KOHL*
FRUIT & VEGETABLES A relative of the cabbage and cauliflower family, a vegetable that is made up of clusters of dark green buds held by edible stems. It resembles cauliflower.

Broil Asar a fuego directo *ah-SAHR ah foo-EH-goh dee-REHK-toh*
COOKING METHOD / TECHNIQUE To cook food directly under a heat source.

Broth Caldo *KAHL-doh*
CONDIMENTS A liquid obtained from simmering vegetables with meat, poultry, or fish in water.

Brown Dorar *doh-RAHR*
COOKING METHOD / TECHNIQUE To develop a brown color on meat or vegetables by cooking quickly over high heat. This also develops the flavors.

Brush Brocha *BROH-cha*
EQUIPMENT A handheld instrument containing bristles that is used to spread liquid, paste, or powder.

Brussels sprouts Coles de Bruselas *KOH-lehs deh broo-SEH-lahs*
FRUIT & VEGETABLES A member of the cabbage family that looks like miniature cabbage heads. Brussels sprouts are grown on stalks with many small heads lined up in rows.

Buckwheat Alforfón *ahl-fohr-FOHN*
GRAINS & CEREALS Though technically an herb, buckwheat is categorized here under its common usage as a cereal grain. A relative of sorrel and rhubarb, its seeds are used to make a flour, the key ingredient to Russian blini and soba noodles.

Buffalo Búfalo *BOO-fah-loh*
GAME An animal also known as a bison. Its meat is lower in fat than beef yet very tender and the flavor is very mild. Its milk is used to make cheese.

Buffet Bufé *boo-FEH*
GENERAL A meal where food is set out on tables and guests help themselves or are served a helping before sitting down to eat.

Bulgur Bulgur *BOOL-guhr*
GRAINS & CEREALS Wheat kernels that have had the bran removed and then are boiled and dried. Often confused with cracked wheat, bulgur is often used in the Middle East.

Bunch Manojo *mah-NOH-hoh*
MEASUREMENTS An inexact measurement generally adding up to a handful.

Bundt pan Molde Bundt *MOHL-deh boont*
EQUIPMENT A tube pan with a rounded bottom with ridges. A typical pan holds twelve cups of batter.

Burgundy wine Vino de Borgona *BEE-noh deh bohr-GOH-nah*
BEVERAGE Wine made from grapes grown in eastern France. The most common grapes from the region are the Pinot Noir and Chardonnay.

Burn Quemar *keh-MAHR*
COOKING METHOD / TECHNIQUE To overcook to the point that the food is dehydrated and has begun to be converted to ash.

Butter Mantequilla *mahn-teh-KEE-yah*
DAIRY Cream that is beaten (or churned) until it solidifies. Butter can be salted or unsalted. U.S. law states that butter must be 80 percent fat; the remaining ingredients are water and milk solids.

Butter, brown Mantequilla marron *mahn-teh-KEE-yah mah-RROHN*
DAIRY Butter that has been heated until the milk solids caramelize and become brown. This must be done slowly to prevent the butter from burning. It results in a butter with a deep nutty flavor. Brown butter is used as a sauce and a condiment and in pastry making.

Butter, clarified Mantequilla clarificada *mahn-teh-KEE-yah klah-ree-fee-KAH-dah*
DAIRY Butter that has been melted and its milk solids removed. It has a higher smoke point than regular butter and a milder flavor. Also known as drawn butter, in east India it is referred to as ghee.

Buttercream Crema de mantequilla *KREH-mah deh mahn-teh-KEE-yah*
DAIRY A sweet and creamy icing. In its simplest form, buttercream is made by whipping butter with powdered sugar.

Butterfly Cortar en forma libro *kohr-TAHR ehn FOHR-mah LEE-broh*
COOKING METHOD / TECHNIQUE To cut a food item so as to split its thickness in half. Once the item is split, it is opened like a book. This technique is used most often on thick pieces of meat or fish.

Buttermilk Leche mazada *LEH-cheh mah-SAH-dah*
DAIRY Nonfat or low-fat milk that has bacteria added to it. It has a thick consistency and tangy flavor. Acidic in nature, buttermilk has a low pH.

C

Cabbage Col *kohl*

FRUIT & VEGETABLES A leafy green vegetable that is a relative of cauliflower, broccoli, and Brussels sprouts. Its color can range from white to green to red, and its leaves can be flat or curly. Cabbage can grow as a compact head or a loose group of leaves. *See also* **Kale**.

Cabbage, Chinese Col china *kohl CHEE-nah*

FRUIT & VEGETABLES Thin, green, wavy leaves connected to wide, white stalks, both of which are eaten. Chinese cabbage, also known as napa cabbage, is thinner and crisper than other cabbage varieties.

Cabbage, green Col verde *kohl BEHR-deh*

FRUIT & VEGETABLES The most common variety of cabbage, with a tight head and thick hearty green leaves. It is used to make coleslaw.

Cabbage, red Col lombarda *kohl lohm-BAHR-dah*

FRUIT & VEGETABLES A tight head of cabbage with dusty blue red–colored leaves. The cabbage will turn blue if exposed to an alkaline solution, but will become a bright red when an acid like vinegar is added. It can be eaten raw or cooked.

Cabbage, savoy Col savoy *kohl sah-BOY*

FRUIT & VEGETABLES A tight head of cabbage with crinkled leaves that have a netted texture. Its mild flavor and crisp leaves make it one of the best varieties for eating. Its outer leaves are green with veins that turn progressively white as they get closer to the center of the head.

Cabbage, white Repollo *reh-POH-yoh*

FRUIT & VEGETABLES The white-colored variety of this tight-headed, leafy green vegetable.

Cabrales cheese Queso cabrales *KEH-soh kah-BRAH-lehs*

DAIRY An assertive Spanish blue cheese from the region of Asturias in northern Spain. It is typically made from cow's milk but can also be blended with sheep's or goat's milk. It was traditionally wrapped in sycamore maple leaves but is now covered in a dark aluminum wrapper with a protected stamp signaling its authenticity.

Cachaça Cachaça *kah-CHA-sah*

BEVERAGE A Brazilian distilled alcoholic beverage made from fresh sugarcane juice. The caipirinha is the most popular cachaça-based cocktail.

Cactus Nopales *noh-PAH-lehs*

FRUIT & VEGETABLES The oval, dark green leaves of the nopal cactus. Tart in flavor, the leaves' thorns are cut off before they are sliced and cooked. Nopales are available fresh and canned.

Caffeine **Cafeína** *kah-feh-EE-nah*
GENERAL A stimulant found naturally in some foods. It affects the nervous system, heart, and kidneys, and also dilates blood vessels.

Cake **Torta / Pastel** *TOHR-tah / pahs-TEHL*
BAKING & PASTRY A baked good made with flour, sugar, and eggs as well as some sort of leavener. It is typically baked in a pan or mold in the oven.

Cake flour **Harina de repostería** *ah-REE-nah deh reh-pohs-teh-REE-ah*
GRAINS & CEREALS A soft wheat flour that is low in protein and high in starch content. Cake flour produces tender cakes with a fine crumb.

Cake pan **Molde para pastel** *MOHL-deh PAH-rah pahs-TEHL*
EQUIPMENT A mold used for baking cakes. Traditional shapes are round, square, and rectangle and there are specialty forms such as heart-shaped and tube pans. Cake pan materials vary and can be metal based or silicone.

Cake slicer **Rebanador de torta** *reh-bah-nah-DOHR deh TOHR-tah*
EQUIPMENT A long, thin, bull-nosed serrated knife used to slice cakes.

Calorie **Caloria** *kah-loh-REE-ah*
MEASUREMENTS Unit of measure for food energy value. The four sources of calories are carbohydrates, proteins, fats, and alcohol.

Can n. **Lata** *LAH-tah*
EQUIPMENT An airtight metal container used to store beverages and food.

v. **Enlatar / Envasar / Conservar** *ehn-lah-TAHR / ehn-bah-SAHR / kohn-sehr-VAHR*
COOKING METHOD / TECHNIQUE To preserve food by processing and sealing in an airtight container.

Candied fruit **Fruta cristalizada / Fruta confitada / Fruta escarchada / Fruta glaseada** *FROO-tah krees-tah-lee-SAH-dah / FROO-tah kohn-fee-TAH-dah / FROO-tah ehs-kahr-CHAH-dah / FROO-tah glah-seh-AH-dah*
BAKING & PASTRY Pieces of fruit that have been dipped in sugar syrup and then dried. Granulated sugar can also be dusted over them before they dry for added texture.

Candied ginger **Jenjibre en conserva** *hehn-HEE-breh ehn kohn-SEHR-bah*
BAKING & PASTRY Peeled pieces of ginger that have been boiled in sugar syrup, dusted with granulated sugar, and then dried.

Candied peel **Piel de fruta escarchada** *pee-EHL deh FROO-tah ehs-kahr-CHAH-dah*
BAKING & PASTRY The skin of fresh fruit, typically citrus fruit, cut into strips, boiled in sugar syrup, dusted with granulated sugar, and then dried. It can be eaten as is or used as a garnish.

Candy **Caramelo / Dulces** *kah-rah-MEH-loh / DOOL-sehs*
BAKING & PASTRY A generic term for a sweet confection. Candy can be hard or soft and made with or without chocolate.

Canola oil Aceite de colza *ah-SAY-teh deh KOHL-zah*
NUTS & OILS A neutral-tasting oil made from pressed rapeseeds. It has the lowest amount of saturated fat of any oil and almost as much monounsaturated fat as olive oil.

Can opener Abrelata *ah-breh-LAH-tah*
EQUIPMENT An instrument used to open a can. A can opener can be manual or electric.

Cantaloupe Cantaloup *kahn-tah-LOOP*
FRUIT & VEGETABLES A fruit whose skin is netted with a greenish gray color and has orange flesh. The cantaloupes found in the United States are really muskmelons; true cantaloupes are found in Europe.

Caper Alcaparra *ahl-kah-PAH-rrah*
HERBS & SPICES The sun-dried flower bud of a bush native to the Mediterranean. The dried bud is pickled then packed in a brined solution or salted. Capers have a sharp, salty, vinegary flavor.

Carambola Carambola / Fruta estrella *kah-rahm-BOH-lah / FROO-tah ehs-TREH-yah*
FRUIT & VEGETABLES A tropical fruit with a waxy skin that has five prominent protrusions. When sliced crosswise it takes the shape of a star, which is why it is also referred to as star fruit. A carambola has a fresh, slightly tart flavor.

Caramel Caramelo *kah-rah-MEH-loh*
BAKING & PASTRY Melted sugar that has been heated until it turns into an amber-colored syrup. A small amount of water can be added to thin it. When the liquid cools it becomes hard and brittle. Butter or cream can be added to make a soft caramel.

Caramelize Caramelizar *kah-rah-meh-lee-ZAHR*
COOKING METHOD / TECHNIQUE To heat sugar until it melts and turns a dark golden brown color.

Caramelized Caramelizado *kah-rah-meh-lee-ZAH-doh*
The browning that occurs when heating food that contains carbohydrates.

Caraway Alcaravea *ahl-kah-rah-VEH-ah*
HERBS & SPICES A seed whose flavor is very similar to that of anise. It comes from a plant that is a member of the parsley family.

Carbohydrate Carbohidrato *kahr-boh-ee-DRAH-toh*
GENERAL A nutrient needed to sustain life and the most common source of energy. Sugar, starch, and fiber are all carbohydrates.

Cardamom Cardamomo *kahr-dah-MOH-moh*
HERBS & SPICES A member of the ginger family, a spice with a light green pod filled with small, black seeds. If the whole pod is used, it should be lightly crushed in order

to help extract the flavor of the seeds. The aroma and flavor are warm, sweet, and strong. A little goes a long way except the ground variety, which is much weaker.

Carob Algarroba *ahl-gah-RROH-bah*
FRUIT & VEGETABLES The pulp, pods, and seeds of the carob tree. When they are dried, roasted, and ground into a powder, carob is used as a flavoring in baked goods. Its flavor is sweet and possessing and similar to that of chocolate. Because of its low fat content, it is often used as a chocolate substitute.

Carp Carpa *KAHR-pah*
FISH & SHELLFISH A freshwater fish native to Asia. The most popular use of it in the United States is as the main ingredient in gefilte fish.

Carrageenan Carageena *kah-rah-GEE-nah*
GENERAL A thickener and stabilizer that gels like gelatin and is able to do so at room temperature. Derived from a seaweed, it is a vegetarian alternative to gelatin.

Carrot Zanahoria *sah-nah-OH-ree-ah*
FRUIT & VEGETABLES A root vegetable, long, thin, and typically orange, with curly green tops that grow above ground. The root is sweet and the tops are not eaten. The skin is thin and is usually peeled. There are also white, purple, yellow, and red heirloom carrots.

Carve Trinchar *treen-CHAHR*
COOKING METHOD / TECHNIQUE To cut portions of cooked meat using a carving knife.

Casein Caseína *kah-seh-EE-nah*
DAIRY The principal protein found in milk. Casein coagulates or thickens when mixed with rennin, forming cheese.

Cashew Anacardo *ah-nah-KAHR-doh*
NUTS & OILS A kidney-shaped nut that grows on the cashew tree. The shell is very toxic and must be carefully removed. The nut is made up of almost 50 percent fat.

Casing Piel *pee-EHL*
MEAT The thin, tubular membrane from animal (sheep, hogs, cattle) intestines that has been cleaned and dried and is used to encase sausage stuffing.

Cask Barril *bah-RREEL*
EQUIPMENT A large wooden barrel typically made of oak used to store or age wine or spirits.

Cassava Yuca / Mandioca / Cazabe *YOO-kah / mahn-dee-OH-kah / kah-SAH-beh*
FRUIT & VEGETABLES Also known as yucca or manioc, a root vegetable with a very tough and inedible brown skin and milky white flesh. It is high in starch and has a neutral flavor. It is used to make tapioca.

Casserole Cazuela cacerola *kah-soo-EH-lah kah-seh-ROH-lah*
EQUIPMENT A deep, ovenproof dish that goes from oven to table. It can be round, square, or rectangular and may have handles and a lid.

Cast-iron skillet **Sartén de hierro** *sahr-TEHN deh ee-EH-rroh*
EQUIPMENT A long-handled frying pan made from ironware, typically round with sloping sides. Ironware is prized for its heat-absorbing and -retaining qualities. A cast-iron skillet has a nonstick finish when seasoned.

Catfish **Siluro** *see-LOO-roh*
FISH & SHELLFISH A freshwater fish that has prominent barbels extending from its mouth area resembling whiskers. Its skin is thick and slippery with no scales and should be removed before cooking.

Cauliflower **Coliflor** *koh-LEE-flohr*
FRUIT & VEGETABLES A cruciferous vegetable made up of a bunch of florets attached to a stalk. Typically white in color, it can also be green or purple, which turns light green when cooked.

Cayenne pepper **Cayena** *kah-YEH-nah*
FRUIT & VEGETABLES A bright red, hot chile pepper available in both fresh and dried form. When dried and crushed, it is referred to as crushed red pepper. When dried and ground, it is referred to as cayenne pepper.

Celeriac **Apio-nabo** *AH-pee-oh NAH-boh*
FRUIT & VEGETABLES Also known as celery root, the root of a special type of celery plant. It has a brown and knobby exterior and a beige-colored interior that browns easily and must be soaked in acidulated water. It has a mild celery flavor.

Celery **Apio** *AH-pee-oh*
FRUIT & VEGETABLES A green, fibrous, ribbed stalk that grows in bunches. The stalks get more tender and lighter in color toward the center of the bunch.

Celery seed **Semilla de apio** *seh-MEE-yah deh AH-pee-oh*
HERBS & SPICES The seed of a celery plant. It is available whole or ground and has a strong celery flavor.

Cereal **Cereal** *SEH-reh-ahl*
GRAINS & CEREALS A plant from the grass family that produces an edible seed. Rice, corn, wheat, and oats are popular examples.

Chamomile **Manzanilla** *mahn-sah-NEE-yah*
HERBS & SPICES A dried flower used for making tea. The tea is both herbal and noncaffeinated.

Champagne **Champaña / Champán** *cham-PAH-nya / cham-PAHN*
BEVERAGE A sparkling wine from the northeast region of France called Champagne. Its color can range from light yellow to blush rose. Its sweetness varies from bone dry to very sweet.

Charbroil **Asar en parrilla** *ah-SAHR ehn pah-REE-yah*
COOKING METHOD / TECHNIQUE To cook food directly over dry heat. The food is typically placed on a metal grate that leaves grill marks on it.

Chayote Chayote *cha-YOH-teh*
FRUIT & VEGETABLES A pear-shaped fruit with a pale green, slightly wrinkled, edible skin. Its white flesh is bland tasting but some say it resembles a cucumber. It has a soft seed in its center that is not eaten. Chayote can be eaten cooked or raw and can be treated similarly to a summer squash.

Cheese Queso *KEH-soh*
DAIRY A dairy product made from the milk of cows, goats, sheep, and buffalo. The milk protein casein is coagulated through the addition of rennet, an enzyme. The resulting solids are separated from the liquid, pressed, and then aged.

Cheesecake Tarta de queso *TAHR-tah deh KEH-soh*
BAKING & PASTRY A cheese-based tart made with a fresh cheese—typically cream cheese (New York style) or ricotta (Italian style). It can have a crust or be crustless and its texture can range from dense to light and airy.

Cheesecloth Estopilla / Paño de muselina *ehs-toh-PEE-yah / PAH-nyoh deh moo-seh-LEE-nah*
EQUIPMENT A lightweight cotton cloth used in cooking that will stay intact when wet and will not impart a flavor. It is used for straining liquids, lining molds, and creating packets of herbs.

Cherimoya Annon / Chirimoya *ah-NOHN / chee-ree-MOH-yah*
FRUIT & VEGETABLES A round, green-skinned fruit with a scalelike pattern. The flesh is milky and creamy with embedded black seeds. Its flavor is a blend of banana and papaya.

Cherry Cereza *seh-REH-sah*
FRUIT & VEGETABLES A small, round fruit surrounding a seed, ranging in color from bright red to purplish black to golden. Cherries can be either sweet or sour. The sour variety is too tart to be eaten raw and is used for baking or confections.

Chervil Perifollo *peh-ree-FOH-yoh*
HERBS & SPICES A member of the parsley family, an herb with tender green leaves that impart a mild anise flavor. It is one of the classic ingredients in fines herbes.

Chestnut Castaña *kahs-TAH-nyah*
NUTS & OILS A nut encased in a hard, dark shell that must be removed along with its bitter inner skin before being eaten. The nut can be eaten raw, but that isn't common in the United States. Typically the nut is roasted, boiled, pureed, or candied, resulting in a nut with a soft texture and sweet flavor.

Chew Masticar *mahs-tee-KAHR*
GENERAL To crush food with the teeth.

Chicken Pollo *POH-yoh*
  MEAT A domesticated fowl. Its meat is a type of poultry and its flavor is mild and
  somewhat neutral. A chicken can weigh between two and ten pounds. Almost the
  entire bird and its eggs are eaten. *See also individual cuts.*

Chicken, breast fillet Filete de pechuga de pollo *fee-LEH-teh deh
peh-CHOO-gah deh POH-yoh*
  MEAT A white meat portion found in front of the ribs, this is the most popular chicken
  part.

Chicken, diced Pollo troceado *POH-yoh troh-seh-AH-doh*
  MEAT Chicken meat that has been cubed.

Chicken, double breast Pecho entero de pollo *PEH-choh ehn-TEH-roh deh
POH-yoh*
  MEAT The entire breast portion of one chicken, it is made up of two individual breast
  fillets that are still attached to each other.

Chicken, drumstick Muslito de pollo *moos-LEE-toh deh POH-yoh*
  MEAT The bottom portion of the chicken leg, below the knee joint. It contains all
  dark meat.

Chicken, half Medio pollo *MEH-dee-oh POH-yoh*
  MEAT Half of a whole chicken: one breast, wing, thigh, and drumstick.

Chicken, leg Muslo de pollo *MOOS-loh deh POH-yoh*
  MEAT An all dark meat chicken made up of two parts: the thigh and drumstick.

Chicken, liver Hígado de pollo *EE-gah-doh deh POH-yoh*
  MEAT Organ meat. It is mild tasting, as far as liver goes. Chicken livers are sold whole
  due to their small size.

Chicken, quarters Cuartos de pollo *KWAHR-tohs deh POH-yoh*
  MEAT A quarter of a whole chicken, made up of the leg or breast meat. Leg quarters
  contain one thigh and one drumstick, and the breast quarter contains one breast
  and one wing.

Chicken, strips Tiras de pollo *TEE-rahs deh POH-yoh*
  MEAT Chicken meat that has been cut into thin strips. Strips can be cut from both
  white and dark meat, but they are usually made from breast meat.

Chicken, thigh Medio muslo de pollo *MEH-dee-oh MOOS-loh deh POH-yoh*
  MEAT The portion of the chicken's leg above the knee joint. It contains all dark meat.

Chicken, wing Ala de pollo *AH-lah deh POH-yoh*
  MEAT Considered white meat, chicken wings are sold individually or kept attached
  to the breast and sold together.

Chicken carcass Carcasa de pollo *kahr-KAH-sah deh POH-yoh*
  MEAT The entire body of the chicken after it has been slaughtered.

Chicken stock Caldo de pollo / Caldo blanco *KAHL-doh deh POH-yoh / KAHL-doh BLAHN-koh*

MEAT The strained liquid resulting from simmering chicken bones, vegetables, and water. It is used as a base for soups, stews, and sauces.

Chickpea Garbanzo *gahr-BAHN-soh*

FRUIT & VEGETABLES A round, beige-colored legume that has a firm texture and nutty flavor. It can be found dried or canned.

Chickpea flour Harina de garbanzos *ah-REE-nah deh gahr-BAHN-sohs*

GRAINS & CEREALS Dried chickpeas ground into a flour.

Chicory Achicoria *ah-chee-koh-REE-ah*

FRUIT & VEGETABLES A relative of the endive, with leaves that are green and curly with white stalks. Its flavor is slightly bitter and it can be eaten raw or cooked.

Chicory coffee Café de achicoria *kah-FEH deh ah-chee-koh-REE-ah*

BEVERAGE A blend of ground coffee beans and ground chicory root. The root comes from a special variety of chicory that has been dried and roasted.

Chihuahua cheese Queso Chihuahua *KEH-soh chee-WAH-wah*

DAIRY A Mexican cheese made from cow's milk that melts well, becoming soft and stringy. Found in braids or balls, the white cheese is similar in flavor to Monterey Jack cheese. It is named after the Mexican state in which it is made.

Chile Chile / Guindilla *CHEE-leh / geen-DEE-yah*

HERBS & SPICES The pod of a plant of the *Capsicum* genus. There are more than two hundred varieties, ranging greatly in length and width. The guindilla originated in the Americas and has long been associated with Mexican cuisine. It is widely known for the heat it imparts, which varies from mild to blistering hot. *See also* **Banana pepper**; **Cayenne pepper**.

Chile, Anaheim Chile Anaheim / Guindilla Anaheim *CHEE-leh ah-nah-eh-EEM / geen-DEE-yah ah-nah-eh-EEM*

HERBS & SPICES A long and narrowly shaped, slightly sweet and mild chile that comes in green and red varieties. One of the most commonly used varieties in the United States, it and can be purchased fresh or dried and is frequently stuffed.

Chile, ancho Chile ancho / Guindilla ancho *CHEE-leh AHN-choh / geen-DEE-yah AHN-choh*

HERBS & SPICES A dried poblano chile. The sweetest of the dried chiles, an ancho chile's heat is mild and its color is a deep, reddish brown. It gets its name from its broad width (*ancho* means wide in Spanish).

Chile, chilaca Chile chilaca / Guindilla chilaca *CHEE-leh chee-LAH-kah / geen-DEE-yah chee-LAH-kah*

HERBS & SPICES A very long and thin, fresh pepper measuring up to nine inches in length. Richly flavored with medium heat, it is dark green in color and turns dark brown when ripe. When dried, it is a pasilla chile or chile negro.

Chile, chipotle Chile chipotle / Guindilla chipotle *CHEE-leh chee-POHT-leh /*
geen-DEE-yah chee-POHT-leh

HERBS & SPICES A dried and smoked jalapeño. Dark brown with wrinkled skin, chipotles are hot with a smoky, slightly sweet flavor. They are available dried or canned in
adobo.

Chile, habanero Chile habanero / Guindilla habanero *CHEE-leh ah-bah-NEH-*
roh / geen-DEE-yah ah-bah-NEH-roh

HERBS & SPICES A very hot chile that has a slight fruity flavor. Small and round, it is
typically green in color but turns orange when ripe.

Chile, jalapeño Chile jalapeño / Guindilla jalapeño *CHEE-leh hah-lah-*
peh-NYOH / geen-DEE-yah hah-lah-peh-NYOH

HERBS & SPICES A small, hot chile pepper that averages about two inches in length.
Its smooth skin is green when unripe and turns red if the chile is left to mature on the
vine. Its seeds and veins, which hold most of the heat, can be easily removed. Jalapeños are available fresh or canned. Dried, smoked jalapeños are called chipotles.

Chile, mulatto Chile mulato / Guindilla mulato *CHEE-leh moo-LAH-toh /*
geen-DEE-yah moo-LAH-toh

HERBS & SPICES A type of dried poblano chile that is dark brown, wrinkled, and measures about four inches long. Darker and sweeter than other varieties, it has a mild
spice and a chocolate, licorice flavor.

Chile, pasilla Chile pasilla / Guindilla pasilla *CHEE-leh pah-SEE-yah /*
geen-DEE-yah pah-SEE-yah

HERBS & SPICES A long, thin, dried chile measuring about seven inches in length.
Black and wrinkled, it is sometimes referred to as chile negro (black chile). Richly
flavored but mildly hot, it is the dried version of the chilaca chile.

Chile, pasilla Oaxaca Chile pasilla Oaxaca / Guindilla pasilla Oaxaca
CHEE-leh pah-SEE-yah wah-HAH-kah / geen-DEE-yah pah-SEE-yah wah-HAH-kah

HERBS & SPICES The smoked pasilla chile. It is hotter than the chipotle chile.

Chile, poblano Chile poblano / Guindilla poblano *CHEE-leh pohb-LAH-noh /*
gèen-DEE-yah pohb-LAH-noh

HERBS & SPICES A dark green, mild chile whose flavor is more intense the darker
its skin is. It measures about two by four inches and is very commonly roasted and
stuffed. It gets its name from Puebla, Mexico, where it originates. When dried, it is
called ancho or mulato chile.

Chile, serrano Chile serrano / Guindilla serrano *CHEE-leh seh-RRAH-noh /*
geen-DEE-yah seh-RRAH-noh

HERBS & SPICES A small, thin, hot and spicy chile pepper averaging about three
inches in length. Its smooth skin turns red or orange when ripe. Because of its meaty
flesh, it does not dry well and is available only fresh, canned, or pickled.

Chile, Thai Chile tailandés / Guindilla tailandés *CHEE-leh tah-ee-lahn-DEHS / geen-DEE-yah tah-ee-lahn-DEHS*

HERBS & SPICES A small, thin-skinned but very spicy chile commonly found in Thailand and other Southeast Asian countries. Green when unripe, it turns a bright red color when it matures.

Chill (Poner a) Enfriar *(poh-NEHR ah) en-free-AHR*

COOKING METHOD / TECHNIQUE To cool down. This can be done in the refrigerator or on ice.

Chinese black beans, dried Frijoles negros chinos *free-HOHL-ehs NEH-grohs CHEE-nohs*

FRUIT & VEGETABLES Small, fermented soybeans that turn black and soft as a result of the drying process. They are preserved in salt and take on a complex pungent and salty flavor. Mostly used as a condiment, Chinese black beans are typically finely chopped before added to a dish. They are also known as fermented black beans.

Chinese broccoli Brecol chino *breh-KOHL CHEE-noh*

FRUIT & VEGETABLES Also known as Chinese kale , a vegetable with wide green leaves connected to a steam, often with small white flower heads attached. The entire vegetable is eaten; it has a slight bitter taste and is often used in stir-fry dishes.

Chive Cebollino *seh-boh-YEE-noh*

HERBS & SPICES A green herb with a long, thin stem that has a mild onion flavor. A member of the onion family, it produces small flowers that can be eaten but are mostly used for garnish. It is one of the herbs in fines herbes.

Chocolate Chocolate *choh-koh-LAH-teh*

BAKING & PASTRY Food made from seeds of the cacao tree. The seeds are removed from the pods, fermented, dried, and roasted. They are then cracked and the chocolate liquor is separated from the cocoa butter in the nibs. The chocolate liquor is used to make various chocolate products.

Chocolate, baking Chocolate de repostería *choh-koh-LAH-teh deh rehs-pohs-teh-REE-ah*

BAKING & PASTRY Pure, unadulterated chocolate (chocolate liquor) mixed with some cocoa butter in order to make a solid. It is also known as bittersweet chocolate.

Chocolate, couverture Chocolate de cobertura *choh-koh-LAH-teh deh koh-behr-TOO-rah*

BAKING & PASTRY Extremely glossy and high-quality coating chocolate. It must contain a minimum of 32 percent cocoa butter as the more it contains the higher the sheen, the firmer the snap, and creamier the flavor of the chocolate. It is typically found only in specialty shops.

Chocolate, dark Chocolate negro / Chocolate oscuro *choh-koh-LAH-teh NEH-groh / choh-koh-LAH-teh ohs-KOO-roh*
BAKING & PASTRY Chocolate made by adding fat and sugar to chocolate liquor (ground from the nibs of the cacao bean). The amount of fat and sugar varies, resulting in a range of intensity in chocolate flavor in dark chocolate. Milk is never added.

Chocolate, Mexican Chocolate mexicano *choh-koh-LAH-teh meh-hee-KAH-noh*
BAKING & PASTRY Grainy-textured, dark chocolate that has cinnamon and sugar added. Ground almonds can also be included. It is used for making hot chocolate or as an ingredient in mole poblano.

Chocolate, milk Chocolate con leche *choh-koh-LAH-teh kohn LEH-che*
BAKING & PASTRY Chocolate that has dry milk powder and sugar added to it. It must contain 12 percent milk solids and 10 percent chocolate liquor.

Chocolate, semisweet Chocolate semidulce *choh-koh-LAH-teh seh-mee-DOOL-seh*
BAKING & PASTRY Unsweetened dark chocolate that has had sugar, lecithin, and vanilla added to it. It must contain at least 50 percent chocolate liquor, but the amount of sugar added is not regulated, resulting in a high disparity in flavor among brands.

Chocolate, white Chocolate blanco *choh-koh-LAH-teh BLAHN-koh*
BAKING & PASTRY A confection of sugar, cocoa butter, and milk solids. White chocolate cannot be classified as real chocolate because it contains no chocolate liquor.

Chocolate chips Pepitas de chocolate *peh-PEE-tahs deh choh-koh-LAH-teh*
CONDIMENTS Small round chunks of chocolate.

Chop v. Cortar / Trocear / Picar *kohr-TAHR / troh-seh-AHR / pee-KAHR*
COOKING METHOD / TECHNIQUE To cut food into irregularly shaped bite-size pieces.

n. Chuleta *choo-LEH-tah*
MEAT An individual portion of meat taken from the rib section with an attached rib bone. *See also individual types of meat.*

Chopsticks Palillos chinos *pah-LEE-yohs CHEE-nohs*
EQUIPMENT Long, thin eating or cooking utensils used throughout Asia. Made up of two even-length sticks typically made from wood, bamboo, or plastic, they range in length from five to twelve inches.

Chorizo Chorizo *choh-REE-soh*
MEAT Highly seasoned pork sausage popular in Mexico and Spain. Fresh pork is used in the Mexican variety, while smoked pork is used for the Spanish. The spices and flavorings used vary according to the region in which they are made. Both types are used to flavor recipes; Spanish chorizo can be eaten raw.

Chutney Chutney *CHOOT-nee*
CONDIMENTS A condiment made from cooked fruit. Chutney can be chunky or smooth, mild or hot. Vinegar and spices are added to it for flavor.

Cider **Sidra** *SEE-drah*
BEVERAGE A fermented fruit juice typically made from apples. The alcohol content ranges from 3 to 9 percent. Most ciders are sparkling but some can be found still, and there are nonalcoholic varieties.

Cider vinegar **Vinagre de sidra** *bee-NAH-greh deh SEE-drah*
CONDIMENTS Vinegar made from cider.

Cilantro **Cilantro / Perejil chino** *see-LAHN-troh / peh-reh-HEEL CHEE-noh*
HERBS & SPICES The green leaves and stems of the coriander plant used as an herb. Both the leaves and stronger-flavored stems can be eaten. Sold in bunches, cilantro, also known as Chinese parsley, has a bright pungent flavor.

Cinnamon **Canela** *kah-NEH-lah*
HERBS & SPICES The dried inner bark of the evergreen tree. This brick red–colored spice can be purchased as sticks or ground powder. It has a pungent bittersweet flavor that is used in both sweet and savory dishes.

Citron **Cidra** *SEE-drah*
FRUIT & VEGETABLES A large, round, yellow citrus fruit. The pulp is very tart. The peel is used for its lemony flavoring and aroma.

Citrus **Cítrico** *SEE-tree-koh*
FRUIT & VEGETABLES A family of fruit that thrives in tropical to temperate climates. Juice laden, it has a tart flavor due to the high amounts of citric acid found in the pulp. Oranges, limes, lemons, and grapefruit are the most common types.

Clam **Almeja** *ahl-MEH-hah*
FISH & SHELLFISH A bivalve that burrows in sediment. It comes in three different sizes: littleneck (small), cherrystone (medium), and chowder (large).

Clarify **Clarificar** *klah-ree-FEE-kahr*
COOKING METHOD / TECHNIQUE To clear a cloudy liquid.

Clean (to) **Limpiar** *leem-pee-AHR*
COOKING METHOD / TECHNIQUE To remove dirt or marks.

Cleaver **Cuchillo de carnicero** *koo-CHEE-yoh deh kahr-nee-SEH-roh*
EQUIPMENT A cutting tool with a large, rectangular blade. It is used by butchers for its ability to cut through bones. The flat side of the blade can be used for pounding.

Clementine **Clementina** *kleh-mehn-TEE-nah*
FRUIT & VEGETABLES A small mandarin orange with a thin skin that easily peels off. Usually seedless, it has a very sweet flavor.

Clover honey **Miel de trébol** *mee-EHL deh TREH-bohl*
CONDIMENTS Honey made from the nectar of the clover flower.

Cloves **Clavos** *KLAH-vohs*
HERBS & SPICES The dried, unopened flower buds of the evergreen clove tree. Nail-shaped and dark brown in color, cloves are sold whole or ground. The spice has a warm flavor that is used to flavor sweet and savory dishes.

Coat **Cubrir / Bañar** *koo-BREER / bah-NYAHR*
COOKING METHOD / TECHNIQUE To cover food with another ingredient usually by rolling, dipping, or pressing.

Cockle **Berberecho** *behr-beh-REH-choh*
FISH & SHELLFISH A small bivalve with a tricolor ribbed shell. It can be eaten raw or cooked.

Cocktail **Cóctel** *KOHK-tehl*
BEVERAGE An alcoholic beverage made by combining a spirit with a mixer (juice or soda).

Cocoa butter **Crema de cacao** *KREH-mah deh kah-KAH-oh*
CONDIMENTS The vegetable fat extracted from cocoa beans. It is used to add smoothness and flavor to foods.

Cocoa powder **Cacao en polvo** *kah-KAH-oh ehn POHL-voh*
CONDIMENTS Dried ground cocoa beans that have had their cocoa butter removed. Dutch cocoa is cocoa powder that has been treated with an alkali to neutralize its acidity.

Coconut **Coco** *KOH-koh*
NUTS & OILS The dried nut of the coconut palm tree. The very hard and inedible outer husk is green when immature and brown and hairy when ripe. The hollow nut holds a thin coconut juice in its center, which is consumed as a refreshing beverage. The white coconut meat, which is attached to the husk is cut or grated loose. It can be found fresh or dried.

Coconut cream **Crema de coco** *KREH-mah deh KOH-koh*
CONDIMENTS A liquid made by simmering four parts shredded coconut with one part water or milk and then straining it. It is different from cream of coconut, which is sweetened.

Coconut flakes **Copos de coco** *KOH-pohs deh KOH-koh*
CONDIMENTS Dried, shredded coconut that can be sweetened or unsweetened. It is available canned or in bags.

Coconut milk **Leche de coco** *LEH-cheh deh KOH-koh*
CONDIMENTS A liquid made by simmering equal amounts of shredded coconut with water and then straining it.

Coconut oil **Aceite de coco** *ah-SAY-teh deh KOH-koh*
NUTS & OILS A highly saturated fat that is extracted from the dried meat of the coconut. It is used for frying and in packaged foods.

Cod **Bacalao** *bah-kah-LAH-oh*
FISH & SHELLFISH A white and firm saltwater fish from the north Atlantic. It is lean and has a mild flavor. In Spain and Latin America it is typically found as salt cod. Cod fillets are preserved through drying and salting.

Coddle Cocer a media *koh-SEHR ah MEH-dee-ah*
COOKING METHOD / TECHNIQUE To slowly cook food in individual, covered containers placed in simmering water. Coddling is often used with eggs.

Coffee Café *kah-FEH*
BEVERAGE A caffeinated beverage made by extracting the flavor of ground coffee beans.

Coffee, decaffeinated Café descaffeinado *kah-FEH dehs-kah-feh-ee-NAH-doh*
BEVERAGE Coffee that has had the caffeine removed. This can be achieved through steaming and removing the caffeine-containing outer layer of the coffee bean or by chemically removing it with the addition of a solvent.

Coffee, instant Café instantáneo *kah-FEH eens-tahn-TAH-neh-oh*
BEVERAGE Powdered coffee made by heat drying freshly brewed coffee.

Coffee maker Cafetera *kah-feh-TEH-rah*
EQUIPMENT An appliance that makes coffee.

Colander Colador / Coladera *koh-LAH-dohr / koh-lah-DEH-rah*
EQUIPMENT A perforated bowl used to drain liquids.

Cold Frío *FREE-oh*
DESCRIPTOR Having a low temperature.

Combine Combinar *kohm-bee-NAHR*
COOKING METHOD / TECHNIQUE To mix or incorporate two substances.

Compote Compota *kohm-POH-tah*
BAKING & PASTRY A dessert of slowly cooked whole or chopped fruit in simple syrup and spices. A compote can be served chilled or warm.

Conch Caracola *kah-rah-KOH-lah*
FISH & SHELLFISH A mollusk found in a single spiral shell in southern warm waters. The muscle can be eaten raw but must be tenderized by being pounded or finely chopped if cooked.

Condensed milk Leche condensada *LEH-cheh kohn-dehn-SAH-dah*
DAIRY A combination of whole milk and sugar that is heated until 60 percent of the water content is evaporated and the mixture is reduced to a sweet, thick consistency.

Condiment Condimento *kohn-dee-MEHN-toh*
CONDIMENTS A savory accompaniment to food. A condiment can be a sauce or spice mixture.

Connective tissue Tejido conjuntivo *teh-HEE-doh kohn-hoon-TEE-boh*
MEAT The tough, fibrous tissue that surrounds muscle fibers. Collagen and elastin are forms of this tissue that must either be removed (elastin) or slowly cooked in moist heat to allow it to break down and gelatinize (collagen).

Cookbook Recetario / Libro de cocina *reh-seh-TAH-ree-oh / LEE-broh deh koh-SEE-nah*
GENERAL A book of recipes.

Cookie Galleta / Bizcocho *gah-YEH-tah / bees-KOH-choh*
BAKING & PASTRY A small, sweet cake made with flour, sugar, eggs, and a high ratio of fat. Its texture can be crispy, crunchy, soft, or cakey.

Cookie-crumb crust Base de migas *BAH-seh deh MEE-gahs*
BAKING & PASTRY A pasty dough or crust made up of crushed cookies bound by a fat such as melted butter.

Cookie cutter Cortador de pastel *kohr-tah-DOHR deh pahs-TEHL*
EQUIPMENT A plastic or metal tool used to cut shapes from rolled-out cookie dough. Cookie cutters come in various shapes and sizes.

Cooking Cocinando / Cocinar *koh-see-NAHN-doh / koh-SEE-nahr*
COOKING METHOD / TECHNIQUE The process of preparing food by selecting, measuring, and cooking ingredients.

Cooking wine Vino para cocinar *BEE-noh PAH-rah koh-see-NAHR*
CONDIMENTS An inferior wine that has been fortified with salt. Solely used for cooking, it cannot be drunk straight.

Cool Refrescar *reh-frehs-KAHR*
COOKING METHOD / TECHNIQUE To lower the temperature.

Cooling rack Rejilla *reh-HEE-yah*
EQUIPMENT A flat, metal grate used to cool baked goods. It has short legs that raises the grate above a tabletop allowing for air circulation.

Core Quitar el corazón / Descorazonar *kee-TAHR ehl koh-rah-SOHN / dehs-koh-rah-soh-NAHR*
COOKING METHOD / TECHNIQUE To remove the center portion of a fruit or vegetable.

Coriander Coriandro *koh-ree-AHN-droh*
HERBS & SPICES A plant related to the parsley family that is used for its seeds, leaves, and stems. The seeds are small and tan, have a lemony flavor, and can be found whole or ground. The leaves and stems, known as cilantro, have a pungent flavor that is not at all similar to the flavor of the seeds.

Corkscrew Sacacorcho *sah-kah-KOHR-choh*
EQUIPMENT A tool used to remove the cork from a bottle.

Corn Maíz *mah-EES*
FRUIT & VEGETABLES A cereal grain that grows on stalks. Yellow, white, or sometimes blue kernels are attached to a cob and surrounded by silk and layers of papery husks. The sweet-tasting kernels can be cooked and eaten directly off the cob, or cut off before cooking.

Corn, baby **Maíz baby** *mah-EES BAY-bee*
FRUIT & VEGETABLES Immature ears of corn that are picked right after the silk of the corn is formed. They can be purchased raw or canned and are mostly imported from Asia.

Cornflakes **Copos de maíz** *KOH-pohs deh mah-EES*
GRAINS & CEREALS A breakfast cereal made from milled corn. Small, irregularly shaped, thin cornflakes are light yellow in color.

Corn husk **Hoja de maíz / Hoja de tamal** *OH-hah deh mah-EES / OH-hah deh tah-MAHL*
FRUIT & VEGETABLES The inedible, papery outer layer surrounding corn kernels. Corn husks are primarily used to wrap tamales. Fresh husks are green, while dried ones are beige in color and must be soaked in hot water for about twenty minutes to soften before being used.

Cornmeal **Harina de maíz** *ah-REE-nah deh mah-EES*
GRAINS & CEREALS Dried corn kernels that are ground to a specific texture—fine, medium, or coarse. Its color can be yellow, white, or blue and depends on the type of corn used.

Corn oil **Aceite de maíz** *ah-SAY-teh deh mah-EES*
NUTS & OILS A tasteless and colorless oil made from pressing corn kernels. It is a highly unsaturated fat with a high smoke point (410ºF).

Cornstarch **Maizena** *mah-ee-SEH-nah*
GRAINS & CEREALS The flour made from the interior of the dried corn kernel (endosperm). Used as a thickening agent, it must be combined with a small amount of cool water before being added to a hot liquid in order to prevent it from clumping.

Corn syrup **Jarabe de maíz** *hah-RAH-beh deh mah-EES*
CONDIMENTS A sweet, dense, sticky syrup made by processing cornstarch with acids. There are two varieties: light and dark. The light has been clarified to remove color and the dark has caramel flavoring and coloring added.

Cottage cheese **Requesón** *reh-keh-SOHN*
DAIRY A mild-flavored, fresh cheese made from pasteurized cow's milk that has been curdled by the addition of an acid and sometimes an enzyme. Cottage cheese stays moist as not all of the whey gets drained. Its texture is lumpy with curds ranging in size from small to large.

Couscous **Cuscus** *COOS-coos*
GRAINS & CEREALS Very small, round-shaped pasta made from semolina flour. Most packaged varieties are precooked and require only a small amount of boiling liquid poured over the grains to steam them for about five minutes. It is a staple starch of North African countries.

Crab Cangrejo / Buey / Jaiba / Centollo *kahn-GREH-hoh / boo-WAY / HAY-ee-bah / sehn-TOH-yoh*
> FISH & SHELLFISH A crustacean found in fresh or salt water. Of the more than four-thousand varieties of crabs, all have two claws in addition to their legs. Crabmeat is sweet and can be served cold or hot after it's been cooked and removed from its shell. It is available fresh, canned, or frozen.

Cracker Galleta *gah-YEH-tah*
> GRAINS & CEREALS A salted or savory thin biscuit or wafer.

Cracklings Chicharrones *chee-cha-RROH-nehs*
> MEAT Crisp, browned pork skin that has been fried or roasted. It can have meat still attached to it.

Cranberry Arandano rojo *ah-RAHN-dah-noh ROH-hoh*
> FRUIT & VEGETABLES A round, bright red berry with a tart flavor. Cranberries are available fresh (in bags), frozen, and dried. There are many processed products derived from the cranberries such as juice, jelly, and canned sauce.

Cream v. Batir *bah-TEER*
> COOKING METHOD / TECHNIQUE To beat two or more ingredients until they are smooth and well incorporated with no sign of individual particles. This process also helps to incorporate air into the mixture.

n. Crema / Nata *KREH-mah / NAH-tah*
> DAIRY A pasteurized dairy product consisting primarily of the fat found in milk. The fat content can vary from 18 percent (light) to 36 percent (heavy).

Cream, clotted Crema extra espesa / Nata extra espesa *KREH-mah EKS-tra ehs-PEH-sah / NAH-tah EKS-trah ehs-PEH-sah*
> DAIRY Cream that is made from unpasteurized milk heated until a layer of cream forms on the surface. The cream is removed and cooled. Typically used as a spread, it is a specialty of Devonshire, England.

Cream, double Crema doble / Nata doble crema *KREH-mah DOH-bleh / NAH-tah DOH-bleh KREH-mah*
> DAIRY Cream with a milk fat content of approximately 48 percent. It is most often found in Europe and Britain.

Cream, heavy Crema espesa / Nata espesa *KREH-mah ehs-PEH-sah / NAH-tah ehs-PEH-sah*
> DAIRY Cream with a milk fat content between 36 and 40 percent.

Cream, light Crema semidesnatada / Nata semidesnatada
KREH-mah seh-mee-dehs-nah-TAH-dah / NAH-tah seh-mee-dehs-nah-TAH-dah
> DAIRY Cream that contains between 18 and 30 percent milk fat. It is the lightest form of cream. It is often used to lighten coffee.

Cream, whipped Crema batida / Nata batida *KREH-mah bah-TEE-dah / NAH-tah bah-TEE-dah*
> DAIRY Cream that has been beaten by hand or machine until light and airy.

Cream, whipping Crema montada / Nata montada *KREH-mah mohn-TAH-dah / NAH-tah mohn-TAH-dah*
> DAIRY Cream that contains 30 to 36 percent milk fat.

Cream cheese Queso crema *KEH-soh KREH-mah*
> DAIRY A soft, white, unripe, spreadable cheese made from cow's milk. Found in tubs and bars, it has a slight tangy flavor.

Cream of coconut Crema de coco endulsada *KREH-mah deh KOH-koh ehn-dool-SAH-dah*
> CONDIMENTS A thick sweet mixture of coconut paste and sugar. It is a main ingredient in piña coladas.

Cream of tartar Cremor tártaro *kreh-MOHR TAHR-tah-roh*
> CONDIMENTS A crystallized acid found in the interior of wine barrels. This white powder is used when an acidic ingredient is needed in a recipe. It is used in baking to help the leavening process and improves the stability and volume of whipped egg whites.

Cream sauce Salsa de crema *SAHL-sah deh KREH-mah*
> CONDIMENTS Also known as béchamel, a sauce made by adding milk or cream to a flour and butter paste (a roux). The thickness of the sauce is dependent on the ratio of flour to liquid.

Crème anglaise Crema inglesa *KREH-mah een-GLEH-sah*
> BAKING & PASTRY A very thin custard used as a dessert sauce. It is made with sugar, egg yolks, milk, and vanilla.

Crème fraîche Crema fresca / Nata fresca *KREH-mah FREHS-kah / NAH-tah FREHS-kah*
> DAIRY Developed by the French, a high-fat soured cream made from unpasteurized cream that thickens with the bacterial cultures naturally present at room temperature. The variety found in the United States is slightly different and is made with pasteurized cream that has bacteria added to it. Its high fat content prevents it from breaking at a high temperature.

Crepe Crepe / Crepa *krehp / KREH-pah*
> BAKING & PASTRY Paper-thin pancakes that are rolled or folded and topped with a sauce. They can be sweet or savory and are often stuffed with a filling.

Crispy Crujiente *kroo-hee-EHN-teh*
> DESCRIPTOR The brittle texture typically obtained from a thin product that is firm but easily broken.

ENGLISH-SPANISH C

Croquettes Croquetas *kroh-KEH-tahs*
DISH Ground meat, fish, or cheese mixed with a thick cream sauce (béchamel), then shaped into small logs, breaded, and fried.

Crunchy Crocante *kroh-KAHN-teh*
DESCRIPTOR The noisy, crackling sound made when chewing. Also the term used to describe a food item that produces a crackling sensation.

Crush Aplastar *ah-plahs-TAHR*
COOKING METHOD / TECHNIQUE To break, pound, or grind into small fragments or powder. Tools used to obtain this result include a mortar and pestle, rolling pin, meat pounder, and the bottom of a heavy pan.

Crust Corteza *kohr-TEH-sah*
BAKING & PASTRY The hardened outer layer of a baked good. A hard, crisp covering added to an ingredient such as a meat, vegetable, or fruit.

Crustacean Crustaceo *kroos-TAH-seh-oh*
FISH & SHELLFISH One of two types of shellfish. A crustacean is made up of a jointed external skeleton that is also referred to as a shell. Crab, shrimp, and lobster are examples.

Crusted Rebozado / Capeado *reh-boh-SAH-doh / kah-peh-AH-doh*
COOKING METHOD / TECHNIQUE Having a hardened covering. Common covering ingredients are bread crumbs, cheese, peppercorns, and herbs and spices.

Cuban coffee Café cubano *kah-FEH koo-BAH-noh*
BEVERAGE Strong espresso coffee that has a sweet sugar-foam floating on top of the coffee. The foam is made by creaming sugar with a few drops of espresso coffee, then pouring the coffee over the creamed sugar. It is served in small, one-ounce quantities

Cucumber Pepino *peh-PEE-noh*
FRUIT & VEGETABLES A long, green cylindrical fruit with a thin, edible skin. At times the skin is waxed and is then peeled and not eaten. The flesh is white and mildly flavored with a juicy and crisp texture. A cucumber has small, edible seeds found along the center that are sometimes removed. It is typically eaten raw.

Culantro Recao *reh-KAH-oh*
HERBS & SPICES Long, narrow, green leaves with an intense and pungent cilantro flavor.

Cumin Comino *koh-MEE-noh*
HERBS & SPICES A flat, dark brown seed that resembles caraway. It must be ground before being used and delivers a strong, nutty, and lemony flavor. It is often used in Cuban and Mexican cooking.

Cup Taza *TAH-sah*

MEASUREMENTS A unit of measure for either wet or dry ingredients. A cup measures 8 fluid ounces for wet ingredients but varies in weight when measuring dry ingredients.

Curdle Cortar *kohr-TAHR*

COOKING METHOD / TECHNIQUE To separate, as a dairy product separates into curds and whey. The curds form as a result of proteins that coagulate from exposure to heat or an acid.

Cured Curado *koo-RAH-doh*

COOKING METHOD / TECHNIQUE Preserved with smoke, salt, or an acid (pickling).

Curly endive Escarola *ehs-kah-ROH-lah*

FRUIT & VEGETABLES A member of the endive family that has a loose head of green, slightly furry leaves that curl at the tips. The leaves have a slight bitter taste. Endive is often confused with chicory.

Currant Grosella *groh-SEH-yah*

FRUIT & VEGETABLES A small berry related to the gooseberry. There are three different varieties, which come in three different colors: black, red, and white. The black currant must be cooked and is used to make cassis liqueur. The red and white currants can be eaten raw.

Curry leaf Hoja de curry *OH-hah deh KOO-ree*

HERBS & SPICES The leaf of the curry tree. Fresh, dark green curry leaves are small (about three inches) and have a short shelf life. They freeze well but will lose flavor. They are available in dried form, but the flavor is inferior.

Curry powder Curry en polvo *KOO-ree ehn POHL-voh*

HERBS & SPICES A blend of about twenty spices. Popular in India and the Caribbean, the combination of spices varies regionally, but most blends contain coriander, tumeric, cumin, and nutmeg. The spices can be ground and mixed or purchased commercially. The flavor of curry can be sweet and/or hot. Hot curry is known as Madras curry.

Custard Natilla / Flan *nah-TEE-yah / flahn*

BAKING & PASTRY A pudding-style dessert made in the oven or on the stovetop. Typically flavored with vanilla, it is served on its own or as part of a tart or pie.

Cut Cortar *kohr-TAHR*

COOKING METHOD / TECHNIQUE To separate into parts with a knife.

Cutting board Tabla de picar *TAH-blah deh pee-KAHR*

EQUIPMENT A flat surface made of wood, plastic, or glass to cut on. It can be rectangular or round.

Cuttlefish Sepia *SEH-pee-ah*
FISH & SHELLFISH A relative of the squid and octopus that has eight arms and two tentacles. It resembles a squid and also has ink sacs. It is often tenderized before cooking due to its tough and chewy meat.

D

Daikon Rábano daikon *RAH-bah-noh dah-EE-kohn*
FRUIT & VEGETABLES A large radish with a sweet flavor. Its skin is beige and its flesh is white, crisp, and juicy.

Daiquiri Daiquirí *dah-ee-kee-REE*
BEVERAGE A rum-based cocktail made with lime juice, fruit, and sugar. A frozen daiquiri is made by pureeing the mixture with ice cubes in a blender.

Danish Danesa *dah-NEH-sah*
BAKING & PASTRY An open-faced, flaky breakfast pastry that is filled with fruit, cream cheese, and/or nuts. The pastry is made from a slightly sweetened yeast dough flavored with vanilla.

Date Datil *DAH-teel*
FRUIT & VEGETABLES The brown, oval-shaped fruit of the date palm. Found abundantly in the Middle East, it has a sweet flesh that surrounds a single narrow seed. The fruit must be picked unripe and allowed to mature off the tree. Dates can be found in fresh or dried form. They can be eaten as is, or pitted and stuffed.

Deep-fat fryer Freidora *freh-ee-DOH-rah*
EQUIPMENT A small appliance used for deep-frying foods. It is a deep container with an adjustable electric thermometer that controls the temperature of the oil it contains.

Deep-fry Freir *freh-EER*
COOKING METHOD / TECHNIQUE To cook by completely submerging a food in hot fat.

Degas / Deflate Desinflar *dehs-een-FLAHR*
COOKING METHOD / TECHNIQUE To reduce an object's volume through the removal of air.

Deglaze Deglasar *deh-glah-SAHR*
COOKING METHOD / TECHNIQUE To loosen brown bits of food that have stuck to the bottom of a sauté pan by pouring in a liquid and scraping the bottom of the pan. The result is a very flavorful base that is used for a sauce or within a recipe.

Degrease Desgrasar *dehs-grah-SAHR*
COOKING METHOD / TECHNIQUE To remove fat from a liquid. This can be done by skimming the fat off with a spoon, patting the fat that floats to the top with a paper towel, or chilling the liquid until the fat floats to the top, solidifies, and then is removed.

Dehydrate Deshidratar *dehs-ee-drah-TAHR*
COOKING METHOD / TECHNIQUE To remove the moisture content from food by slowly heating it. The drying can be done by sun, air, or in the oven.

Dessert Postre *POHS-treh*
BAKING & PASTRY Typically the last course of a meal made up of predominantly sweet food such as cakes, cookies, fruit, and chocolate.

Devein Desvenar *dehs-veh-NAHR*
COOKING METHOD / TECHNIQUE To remove the intestinal tract from a shrimp, which is located along its back.

Dextrose Dextrosa *deks-TROH-sah*
CONDIMENTS The commercial name for glucose when it is derived from cornstarch. Glucose is the most basic form of sugar and is found in almost all carbohydrates. Dextrose is also known as corn sugar.

Diagonal cut Corte rombiodales *KOHR-teh rohm-bee-oh-DAH-lehs*
COOKING METHOD / TECHNIQUE A slanted, square pattern of cuts.

Dice Cortar en dados / Trocear *kohr-TAHR ehn DAH-dohs / troh-seh-AHR*
COOKING METHOD / TECHNIQUE To cut food into cubes. They can be small, medium, or large, measuring 1/8 to 1/4 inch.

Digestion Digestión *dee-hehs-tee-OHN*
GENERAL The breakdown of food inside the body into small components that can be absorbed into the bloodstream.

Digestive Digestivo *dee-hehs-TEE-voh*
BEVERAGE An alcoholic beverage taken after a meal to aid in digestion.

Dill Eneldo *eh-NEHL-doh*
HERBS & SPICES An herb with a slender stem and feathery green leaves that resemble fennel tops. It has a very delicate flavor reminiscent of anise that is lost when heated. It is available in fresh and dried form.

Dill pickle Pepino en vinagre al eneldo *peh-PEE-noh ehn bee-NAH-greh ahl eh-NEHL-doh*
CONDIMENTS A cucumber that has been pickled in brine flavored with dill seed.

Dill seed Semilla de eneldo *seh-MEE-yah deh eh-NEHL-doh*
HERBS & SPICES The seed of the dill plant with a flavor and appearance similar to that of the caraway seed. Brown, flat, and oval-shaped, it has a stronger flavor than that of the leaves of the dill plant, which are used as an herb.

Dilute Diluir / Diluido *dee-loo-EER / dee-loo-EE-doh*
COOKING METHOD / TECHNIQUE To decrease a flavor's intensity through the addition of water or another liquid.

Dining room Comedor *koh-meh-DOHR*
GENERAL The room in a house or restaurant where tables are set and guests sit to eat.

Dinner Cena *SEH-nah*
GENERAL The evening meal. In the United States it is the main meal of the day; in other countries it may be a light supper eaten after 9:00 p.m.

Dishwasher Lavaplatos *lah-bah-PLAH-tohs*
EQUIPMENT (1) An electric machine that washes dishes and utensils. (2) A person who washes dishes in a restaurant or other commercial setting.

Dissolve Disolver *dee-sohl-BEHR*
COOKING METHOD / TECHNIQUE To cause a solid to disappear into a liquid.

Distillation Destilacíon *dehs-tee-lah-see-OHN*
COOKING METHOD / TECHNIQUE The process of purifying a liquid by boiling it, collecting its vapors, and cooling the vapors until they turn into liquid form.

Distilled water Agua destilada *AH-gwah dehs-tee-LAH-dah*
BEVERAGE Water that has been purified through distillation.

Double boiler Baño Maria *bah-NYOH mah-REE-ah*
EQUIPMENT A pot that is made to fit securely on top of another. The bottom pot contains a small amount of water that simmers and heats the top pot with its steam. A double boiler is used to heat delicate foods that can burn or curdle easily.

Dough Masa *MAH-sah*
BAKING & PASTRY A stiff mixture made primarily of flour and water. It has a pliable texture that can be worked, scooped, and/or kneaded by hand. It is the precursor to breads, cookies, pie crust, and pasta.

Doughnut Buñuelo *boo-ny-WEH-loh*
BAKING & PASTRY Fried dough that has been leavened with yeast or baking powder. Traditionally, a doughnut is ring-shaped and topped with dusted sugar, chocolate, or sugar glaze. It can also be round and filled with jelly, custard, or pastry cream.

Dragon Fruit Pitahaya *pee-tah-AH-ya*
FRUIT & VEG See **Pitahaya**.

Drain Desaguar / Escurrir / Desague *deh-sah-GWAHR / ehs-koo-REER / deh-SAH-gweh*
COOKING METHOD / TECHNIQUE To remove excess liquid or fat from an item by using a colander or placing the item on top of a paper towel to absorb the excess moisture or fat.

Dredge Rebozar / Cubrir *reh-boh-SAHR / koo-BREER*
COOKING METHOD / TECHNIQUE To lightly coat a food with a dry ingredient, most commonly flour or bread crumbs.

Dress Aderezar / Aliñar *ah-deh-reh-ZAHR / ah-lee-NYAR*
COOKING METHOD / TECHNIQUE To add a sauce or dressing to a salad, vegetable, fish, or meat.

Dressing Aderezo / Aliño *ah-deh-REH-zoh / ah-LEE-nyoh*
CONDIMENTS A sauce used to coat and flavor salads, vegetables, fish, or meat.

Dried bonito flakes Copos de bonito *KOH-pohs deh boh-NEE-toh*
FISH & SHELLFISH Dried fermented and smoked skipjack tuna, which is also known as bonito. The dried fish is pink in color and shaved as needed. The shavings can be purchased in bags and are the main ingredient in dashi.

Dried currant Pasa de corinto *PAH-sah deh koh-REEN-toh*
FRUIT & VEGETABLES A small, dried, seedless Zante grape. Similar to a raisin, it has an intense flavor and is used mostly in baking. It is not in the same family as the fresh black, red, and white currant, which are related to the gooseberry.

Dried fruit Fruta seca *FROO-tah SEH-kah*
FRUIT & VEGETABLES Fruit that has been severely dehydrated resulting in a concentrated and intense sweet flavor. The fruit is dried by the sun or by a special oven.

Drizzle Escurrir *ehs-koo-REER*
COOKING METHOD / TECHNIQUE To pour a liquid over food in a thin stream.

Drop Dejar caer / Gota *deh-HAHR kah-ehr / GOH-tah*
COOKING METHOD / TECHNIQUE To let fall.

Dry Seco / Secar *SEH-koh / seh-KAHR*
DESCRIPTOR (1) Without moisture. (2) Said of a wine that is not sweet.

Dry ice Hielo seco *ee-EH-loh SEH-koh*
GENERAL Solid carbon dioxide that is used for long-term chilling. It turns into a gas, not a liquid, and as such will not produce water. Dry ice will produce burns if it comes in contact with skin.

Dry yeast Levadura seca *leh-bah-DOO-rah SEH-kah*
BAKING & PASTRY Small, dehydrated granules of yeast. The lack of moisture causes the living microorganism (yeast) to be in a dormant state. It is revived when the yeast granules are rehydrated.

Duck Pato *PAH-toh*
MEAT A bird whose characteristic dark red–colored flesh is much darker than that of chicken. It has a thick layer of fat surrounding its breast that is prized as a cooking fat when rendered. Both domesticated and wild varieties of duck are eaten.

Duck, breast Pechuga de pato *peh-CHOO-gah deh PAH-toh*
MEAT The cut of meat found directly in front of the rib cage. It is dark red in color and has a layer of fat under its skin.

Duck, liver Hígado de pato *EE-gah-doh deh PAH-toh*
MEAT An organ meat that is very fatty and rich tasting. It is used in making the delicacy foie gras.

Duck, thigh Medio muslo de pato *MEH-dee-oh MOOS-loh deh PAH-toh*
MEAT The dark meat found in the upper leg portion. It is used for making duck confit.

Duck egg Huevo de pato *WEH-voh deh PAH-toh*
DAIRY The egg from a duck. It is similar in taste to a chicken egg but slightly larger in size.

Dumplings Bolas de masa *BOH-lahs deh MAH-sah*
GRAINS & CEREALS Balls of dough that are steamed, fried, or baked. They can be sweet or savory and are often stuffed with a filling.

Durian Durian *doo-ree-AHN*
FRUIT & VEGETABLES The fruit of the durian tree that is known as much for its succulent texture and sweet flavor as it is for its offensive odor. It is the size and shape of a football; its skin is brown and covered with spikes. Outlawed by commercial airliners, it can be found in the United States canned or frozen.

Dust Polvorear / Espolvorear *pohl-boh-reh-AHR / ehs-pohl-boh-reh-AHR*
COOKING METHOD / TECHNIQUE To lightly coat food with a powdered substance.

E

Eel Anguila *ahn-GEE-lah*
FISH & SHELLFISH A long, dark gray, snakelike-looking fish that is found in both fresh and salt water. Its thick skin is tough and rubbery and must be removed before cooking its flesh, which is meaty and often smoked.

Egg Huevo *WEH-voh*
DAIRY A reproductive body with an oval-shaped, thin shell protecting a yellow yolk surrounded by a clear, protein-rich membrane. The most common egg used for eating comes from a hen but can also come from a female duck, goose, or quail. The shell can be either brown or white, which is due to the hen's breed and has no impact on the egg's taste or nutritional content. Although the shell is not commonly eaten, every part of the egg is edible.

Eggplant Berenjena *beh-rehn-HEH-nah*
FRUIT & VEGETABLES A member of the nightshade family, a pear-shaped fruit with a smooth skin that is typically dark purple but can also be white. Its beige-colored flesh has a spongy texture and is filled with very small, edible, brown seeds. It can vary substantially in thickness and length. Although it is technically a fruit, eggplant is typically prepared as a savory ingredient. The flesh takes on a meaty and creamy texture when cooked.

Egg wash Bañar con huevo / Baño de huevo / Glaseado de huevo *bah-NYAR kohn WEH-voh / BAH-nyoh deh WEH-voh / glah-seh-AH-doh deh WEH-voh*
COOKING METHOD / TECHNIQUE A mixture of egg or egg yolk with a small amount of water or milk. It is brushed on a baked good before baking to give it a golden brown color and shine.

Egg white Clara de huevo *KLAH-rah deh WEH-voh*
DAIRY The inside of an egg that is primarily made of albumin protein and makes up two-thirds of the egg's weight. It is transparent in its raw state and turns opaque white when cooked.

Egg yolk **Yema de huevo** *YEH-mah deh WEH-voh*

DAIRY The yellow middle of an egg that makes up one-third of the egg's weight. It is spherical in shape and is found within the egg white. It contains protein, fat, and phospholipids, most notably lecithin, whose main function is in acting as an emulsifier bringing two immiscible liquids together. The depth of its yellow color is determined by the animal's diet.

Elderberry **Sauco** *sah-OO-koh*

FRUIT & VEGETABLES The dark, purplish black berry of the elder tree. It is very tart, and while it can be eaten raw, it is best when cooked. Elderberries are most often used for making preserves or wine.

Emulsifier **Emulsionante / Emulsivo** *eh-mool-see-oh-NAHN-teh / eh-mool-SEE-voh*

COOKING METHOD / TECHNIQUE A substance that binds together two ingredients that normally do not blend with each other.

Emulsion **Emulsión** *eh-mool-see-OHN*

COOKING METHOD / TECHNIQUE A mixture made up of an emulsifier and two ingredients that normally would not blend with each other. The mixture can be thick or thin and can stay blended permanently or temporarily.

Endive **Endibia** *ehn-DEE-bee-ah*

FRUIT & VEGETABLES An herb that is a relative of chicory. There are three main varieties used in cooking: Belgian endive, curly endive, and escarole. It can be eaten raw or cooked.

Enrich **Enriquecer** *ehn-ree-keh-SEHR*

COOKING METHOD / TECHNIQUE (1) To increase the flavor intensity or nutrient content of a dish through the addition of an ingredient. (2) To increase the viscosity or thickness of a liquid through the addition of cream or a fat.

Entrée **Plato principal / Plato fuerte** *PLAH-toh preen-see-PAHL / PLAH-toh foo-EHR-teh*

GENERAL The main course of a meal.

Espresso **Espresso / Café solo** *ehs-PREH-soh / kah-FEH SOH-loh*

BEVERAGE A strong, dark coffee made by forcing hot water through packed, finely ground coffee beans. It is served in small quantities in a special cup called a demitasse.

Ethylene **Etileno** *eh-tee-LEH-noh*

GENERAL An odorless, colorless, and tasteless gas that is naturally present in many fruit and vegetables. It is a plant hormone that increases as a fruit matures and accelerates the aging process. Avocados, apples, bananas, peaches, and melons produce a large amount of the gas and can help speed the ripening process of other fruit.

Evaporated milk Leche evaporada *LEH-cheh eh-bah-poh-RAH-dah*
DAIRY Milk that has been heated to between 110°F and 140°F until it has lost half of its water. Its tan color and slight caramel flavor are a result of the caramelization that occurs to the milk sugar during the heating process. It has a creamy texture and mouthfeel. Available in cans, it has a long shelf life if kept unopened.

Eviscerate Eviscerar *eh-bee-seh-RAHR*
COOKING METHOD / TECHNIQUE To remove an animal's internal organs.

Expiration date Fecha de caducidad / Fecha de vencimiento *FEH-chah deh kow-see-DAHD / FEH-chah deh behn-see-mee-EHN-toh*
GENERAL A date stamped on a food package informing the consumer when the product will most likely not be usable.

Extract v. Extraear *eks-trah-EHR*
COOKING METHOD / TECHNIQUE To remove. To draw out. To pull out.

n. Esencia / Extracto *eh-SEHN-see-ah / eks-TRAK-toh*
CONDIMENT A concentrated flavor derived from food by distillation. They are most commonly found in liquid form but are also available in powder or gel. *See also individual extracts.*

F

Farmer cheese Queso blanco *KEH-soh BLAHN-koh*
DAIRY A fresh cheese made by pressing out most of the moisture from cottage cheese. It is formed into a solid rectangular or round shape which can be sliced or crumbled. Made from cow, sheep, or goat's milk, it has a slightly sour flavor.

Fat Grasa *GRAH-sah*
GENERAL A macronutrient necessary for human survival that contains nine calories per gram. From a culinary standpoint it refers to triglycerides that are both in the solid and liquid state, but technically fats are solid and oils are liquid. Its functions are varied and include adding flavor, richness, color, and tenderness to foods.

Fennel Hinojo *ee-NOH-hoh*
FRUIT & VEGETABLES An aromatic plant with a licorice and aniselike flavor. Its base is a white bulb that is used as a vegetable and can be eaten raw or cooked. It has a number of green stems protruding from the bulb that have thin, feathery, green leaves similar in taste and texture to those of dill. The leaves have a very delicate flavor and should not be cooked.

Fennel seed Semilla de hinojo *seh-MEE-yah deh ee-NOH-hoh*
HERBS & SPICES An oval, brownish green seed from the fennel plant. Fennel seeds are similar in flavor and appearance to anise seeds except they are larger. Available whole or ground, they can be used in sweet or savory recipes.

Fenugreek Fenogreco *feh-noh-GREH-koh*
HERBS & SPICES An aromatic plant whose leaves and seeds are popular in Indian cooking. Its round, yellow seeds of the same name are more commonly used and are available in whole or ground form Often an ingredient in curries and for pickling, it is also a main one in artificial maple syrup flavoring.

Fermentation Fermentación *fehr-mehn-tah-see-OHN*
COOKING METHOD / TECHNIQUE A chemical change that occurs in food and beverages wherein enzymes from yeast or bacteria cause alcohol and carbon dioxide to form. It results in a change in appearance, texture, and flavor.

Fiber Fibra *FEE-brah*
GENERAL (1) The indigestible portion of plant-based foods. (2) The striations found in an animal's muscles.

Fig Higo *EE-goh*
FRUIT & VEGETABLES The fruit from the fig tree. On average it has a two-inch diameter and color range of golden yellow to dark purplish–black. The interior of a fresh fig is red with lots of small, edible seeds. Both the skin and flesh can be eaten and are very sweet. Figs are available fresh or dried and are eaten raw or cooked.

Fill Llenar *yeh-NAHR*
COOKING METHOD / TECHNIQUE (1) To add. (2) To make full.

Fillet v. Filetiar / Cortar en filete *fee-leh-tee-AHR / kohr-TAHR ehn fee-LEH-teh*
COOKING METHOD / TECHNIQUE To cut off a boneless piece of fish or meat.
n. Filete *fee-LEH-teh*
MEAT A boneless piece of fish or meat.

Filter Filtrar *feel-TRAHR*
COOKING METHOD / TECHNIQUE To pass a solid or liquid through a strainer, cheesecloth, or paper so as to remove impurities or unwanted ingredients.

Fines herbes Finas hierbas *FEE-nahs ee-EHR-bahs*
HERBS & SPICES A classic combination of fresh chervil, chives, parsley, and tarragon that are finely chopped. Fines herbes are often used in French cooking.

First course Entrada / Primer plato *ehn-TRAH-dah / pree-MEHR PLAH-toh*
GENERAL The first course of a meal. It can also be called the appetizer.

Fish Pescado *pehs-KAH-doh*
FISH & SHELLFISH An aquatic animal that has fins, a backbone, and gills. Fish range in shapes and sizes and can come from both fresh and salt water. Saltwater fish have larger bones which are easier to remove than those of freshwater fish.

Fish bone Espina *ehs-PEE-nah*
FISH & SHELLFISH A small, thin bone of a fish.

Fish fillet Filete de pescado *fee-LEH-teh deh pehs-KAH-doh*
FISH & SHELLFISH A single boneless piece of fish that is cut from the top or side of a fish.

Fish fin Aleta *ah-LEH-tah*
FISH & SHELLFISH A flat and wing-shaped piece of anatomy on a fish. It helps a fish steer and provides stability.

Fish gills Agallas *ah-GAH-yahs*
FISH & SHELLFISH The respiratory organ found in aquatic animals. Its main function is to take in oxygen from the water and release carbon dioxide.

Fish poacher Besuguera *beh-soo-GEH-rah*
EQUIPMENT A long, thin cooking vessel used to poach fish. It has a tight-fitting lid and an internal rack. A flavored liquid is added and the fish is placed onto the rack before the covered poacher is placed in the oven or over heat.

Fish sauce Salsa de pescado *SAHL-sah deh pehs-KAH-doh*
CONDIMENTS A dark brown sauce made from fermented fish. A staple in Southeast Asian cooking, it has a pungent aroma and salty flavor. Fish sauce is used in cooking and as a condiment and in dipping sauces.

Fish steak Rueda de pescado / Rodaja de pescado *roo-EH-dah deh pehs-KAH-doh / roh-DAH-hah deh pehs-KAH-doh*
FISH & SHELLFISH On average, a one-inch-thick, crosswise cut from a large fish that has been eviscerated.

Fish stew Caldereta *kahl-deh-REH-tah*
FISH & SHELLFISH A dish prepared by slowly simmering fish and vegetables in a liquid until the liquid thickens up. The slow, moist cooking method allows for the fish to tenderize and the flavors to blend.

Five-spice powder Mezcla de cinco especias en polvo *MEHS-klah deh SEEN-koh eh-SPEH-see-ahs ehn POHL-voh*
HERBS & SPICES A mixture of five ground spices used in Chinese cooking: cinnamon, cloves, fennel seed, star anise, and Szechuan peppercorns.

Flaky Escamoso *ehs-kah-MOH-soh*
DESCRIPTOR The term used to describe pastry whose texture is made up of dry, flat, thin layers of sheets stacked upon each other.

Flambé Flamear *flah-meh-AHR*
COOKING METHOD / TECHNIQUE The technique of lighting food on fire after sprinkling it with a liquor just before serving. It is the French word for "flamed."

Flan pan Molde de flan *MOHL-deh deh flahn*
EQUIPMENT Any type of pan used to cook flan. Typically round, it can be large or small and made of various materials.

Flat fish Pescado plano *pehs-KAH-doh PLAH-noh*
FISH & SHELLFISH A flat and oval-shaped fish whose eyes both lie on the same side of its head. Flat fish are firm, white-fleshed fish that are easy to fillet. Flounder, halibut, sole, and turbot are examples.

Flavor Sabor *sah-BOHR*
DESCRIPTOR A sensory experience gotten from the combination of taste, aroma, and touch.

Flip Voltear *bohl-teh-AHR*
COOKING METHOD / TECHNIQUE To turn over. To throw as to reverse the position.

Floating island Isla flotante *EES-lah floh-TAHN-teh*
BAKING & PASTRY A dessert comprising islands of meringue floating in a sea of crème anglaise. Lightly beaten egg whites are poached in sweetened hot milk and set aside while the milk is used to make the crème anglaise.

Flounder Fleso *FLEH-soh*
FISH & SHELLFISH A flat, saltwater, white-flesh fish with a brownish tan skin that allows it to camouflage itself in the ocean. It has a delicate flavor.

Flour Harina *ah-REE-nah*
GRAINS & CEREALS The finely ground kernel of a cereal grain. Flour can contain the entire kernel or just parts of it.

Flour, all-purpose Harina sin mezcla *ah-REE-nah seen MEHS-klah*
GRAINS & CEREALS A flour blend of low-gluten soft wheat and high-gluten hard wheat. Because of this combination, this flour can be used for many purposes in the kitchen. All-purpose flour is milled solely from the inner part of the wheat (the endosperm); it does not contain germ or bran. It is also referred to as AP flour.

Flour, bread Harina de fuerza *ah-REE-nah deh foo-EHR-sah*
GRAINS & CEREALS An unbleached wheat flour that is high in gluten protein and used for bread making. Bread flour is made from 99 percent hard wheat flour.

Flour, durum Harina de trigo duro *ah-REE-nah deh TREE-goh DOO-roh*
GRAINS & CEREALS Durum is one of the three major types of wheat that is high in protein but is inelastic and does not rise well. For this reason it is not used for bread making but is the flour of choice for pasta making since it can be boiled for a long period of time without falling apart.

Flour, oat Harina de avena *ah-REE-nah deh ah-BEH-nah*
GRAINS & CEREALS Toasted and hulled whole oats that have been ground into a powder. Oat flour does not contain gluten.

Flour, rice Harina de arroz *ah-REE-nah deh ah-RROHS*
GRAINS & CEREALS Dried, uncooked, white rice that has been ground to a fine powder. It does not contain gluten. Rice powder is used for making baked goods.

Flour, self-rising Harina leudada *ah-REE-nah leh-oo-DAH-dah*
GRAINS & CEREALS All-purpose flour that has had baking powder and salt added to it.

Flour, white Harina blanca *ah-REE-nah BLAHN-kah*
GRAINS & CEREALS Flour made only from the endosperm (starchy part) of the wheat kernel.

ENGLISH-SPANISH **F**

Flour, whole wheat Harina de trigo integral *ah-REE-nah deh TREE-goh een-teh-GRAHL*
> GRAINS & CEREALS Flour made from the milling of the wheat's whole grain.

Flowers, edible Flores comestibles *FLOH-rehs koh-mehs-TEE-blehs*
> FRUIT & VEGETABLES Flowers that are not sprayed with pesticides and have a desirable flavor and appearance. They are used for garnish, steeping in oil, and making teas or other beverages.

Fold Doblar *doh-BLAHR*
> COOKING METHOD / TECHNIQUE To combine two ingredients of different weights, the lighter of which has typically been aerated. The lighter ingredient is slowly incorporated into the heavier one by gently scooping up the heavy ingredient and turning it onto the lighter one until the mixture is well blended. This technique maintains the volume and light texture of the mixture.

Food coloring Colorantes alimenticios *koh-loh-RAHN-tehs ah-lee-mehn-TEE-see-ohs*
> CONDIMENTS Edible dyes used to color food. Available in liquid, paste, or powder form, food coloring is used most often in baking to tint frosting and icings.

Food mill Molinillo / Pasapuré *moh-lee-NEE-yoh / pah-sah-poo-REH*
> EQUIPMENT
> A mechanical kitchen tool that breaks down food into a puree and separates skins and seeds from the flesh. Typically it is used only with fruit and vegetables that are very soft or have been cooked.

Food processor Trituradora *tree-too-rah-DOH-rah*
> EQUIPMENT A small, electric kitchen appliance that chops, grinds, slices, and purees food. It consists of a work bowl fitted with an S-shaped blade and a lid that must be securely fastened in place before it can be turned on. Food can be added directly to the bowl or put through the feed tube found on the lid. Food processors come in various sizes.

Fork Tenedor *teh-neh-DOHR*
> EQUIPMENT A handheld utensil used for eating or serving food. It is made of a handle that has two to five tines protruding from it. Used mostly in the West for eating, a fork stabs or lifts food that then gets lifted to the mouth or taken to the plate.

Form Formar *fohr-MAHR*
> COOKING METHOD / TECHNIQUE (1) To put together. (2) To shape.

Freeze Congelar *kohn-HEH-lahr*
> COOKING METHOD / TECHNIQUE (1) To turn into ice. (2) To convert from a liquid to a solid by decreasing the temperature of an item below freezing.

Freezer Congelador *kohn-heh-lah-DOHR*
> EQUIPMENT An electric appliance with a temperature-controlled compartment that maintains the temperature below the freezing point of water. All items placed in the

compartment become frozen. Freezers come in various sizes, and some form part of a unit with a refrigerator.

Freezer burn **Quemadura de congelador** *keh-mah-DOO-rah deh kohn-heh-lah-DOHR*

DESCRIPTOR The loss of moisture from food that has been frozen. It results from improperly wrapped food that has been stored in the freezer. Freezer burn irreversibly changes the texture, appearance, and flavor of food.

French bread **Pan francés** *pahn frahn-SEHS*

GRAINS & CEREALS A crusty and light-textured bread made from a fat-free yeast dough. The texture of the crust is achieved by spraying the dough with water during the baking process. Its typical shape is the baguette, which is long and thin and has slits running along its topside. During baking these slits allow steam to escape and a light crust to form.

French fries **Papas fritas** *PAH-pahs FREE-tahs*

DISH Potatoes that are cut into thick or thin strips and then deep-fried. The term refers to the technique of cutting a potato into long, lengthwise strips, which is called frenching.

French style **A la francesa** *ah lah frahn-SEH-sah*

COOKING METHOD / TECHNIQUE v. To cut a vegetable into lengthwise strips.
DESCRIPTOR n. A preparation for a cut of raw meat that is still attached to a rib bone. The protruding bone is thoroughly cleaned and stripped of all meat and fat.

French toast **Torreja** *toh-RREH-hah*

BAKING & PASTRY A dish made from slices of bread that have been dipped in an egg-and-milk mixture and panfried on both sides until golden brown. It is typically topped with maple syrup, fresh fruit, and/or whipped cream.

Fritter **Buñuelo** *boo-ny-WEH-loh*

BAKING & PASTRY A fried ball of dough. The batter for a fritter can be plain or mixed with a ground meat, shredded vegetable, or flavorful condiment.

Frog's legs **Ancas de rana** *AHN-kahs deh RAH-nah*

GAME The hind legs of a frog that are its only edible part. Their flavor and texture is often compared to that of a tender chicken breast.

Frost **Escarchar** *ehs-kahr-CHAR*

COOKING METHOD / TECHNIQUE To cover a baked good with icing or frosting.

Fructose **Fructosa** *frook-TOH-sah*

CONDIMENTS A simple carbohydrate that is sweeter than sucrose (table sugar) but loses its sweetness when heated. It can safely be consumed by diabetics and comes in powdered or liquid form. It cannot be evenly substituted with granulated table sugar.

Fruit cocktail Cóctel de frutas *KOHK-tehl deh FROO-tahs*
FRUIT & VEGETABLES A mixture of various fruit that have been chopped up into bite-size pieces. The fruit can be mixed with a sweet syrup or left plain with a small amount of lemon juice tossed in to prevent them from browning.

Fry Freír / Frito *freh-EER / FREE-toh*
COOKING METHOD / TECHNIQUE To cook food in hot fat. The food can be completely submerged (deep-fried), partially submerged (panfried), or quickly cooked in a small amount of fat (sautéed).

Frying pan / Skillet Sartén *sahr-TEHN*
EQUIPMENT A shallow, round cooking vessel with sloped sides used to cook food with a hot fat. It ranges from eight to twelve inches in width. Its shallowness is important as it allows the vapors from the pan to evaporate quickly and prevents the food from steaming.

G

Galangal Galangal *gah-LAHN-gahl*
HERBS & SPICES A root tuber that has a hot peppery, citrus flavor used for seasoning. It is similar in appearance to, and used as a substitute for, fresh ginger with a thin skin that needs to be peeled. Its flesh is creamy white in color. Galangal is available fresh or dried.

Gallon Galón *gah-LOHN*
MEASUREMENTS A liquid measurement equivalent to 16 cups or 8 pints or 4 quarts.

Game Caza *KAH-sah*
GAME Hunted wild animals suitable for human consumption. Popular examples are duck, boar, rabbit, and venison.

Game birds Aves caseras *AH-behs kah-SEH-rahs*
GAME Hunted wild birds suitable for human consumption. The sizes of the birds range from small (partridge, dove) to medium (pheasant) to large (goose, turkey).

Garam masala Garam masala *GAH-rahm mah-SAH-lah*
HERBS & SPICES / CONDIMENTS A mixture of dry-roasted and ground spices that is traditional in northern India. The combination varies according to personal preference but typically contains about twelve different spices. The spice blends can be made at home or purchased commercially. Garam masala gives an earthy and warm flavor to dishes.

Garlic Ajo *AH-hoh*
FRUIT & VEGETABLES A member of the lily family, a bulb that grows underground and is made up of sections that are individually wrapped in a paperlike skin called cloves. The entire bulb is called a head. Garlic has a pungent, spicy flavor that is strong when raw, but mellows as it cooks, even becoming sweet if cooked slowly for a long period

of time. Related to onions, leeks, and chives, it is used as an aromatic seasoning in many dishes. It is available fresh, dried, or in powdered form.

Garlic powder **Ajo en polvo** *AH-hoh ehn POHL-boh*
HERBS & SPICES Dehydrated garlic that has been ground to a fine powder.

Garnish **Guarnición** *gwar-nee-see-OHN*
COOKING METHOD / TECHNIQUE A final decorative and edible component of a dish. It should be visually appealing and reflect the flavor and/or composition of the dish.

Garrotxa **Garrotxa** *gah-RROCH-ah*
DAIRY A goat's milk cheese named after the town where it is made in the northeast section of Spain. It is a semisoft cheese with a nutty flavor and a soft and slightly moldy blue gray rind.

Gastronomy **Gastronomía** *gahs-troh-noh-MEE-ah*
The art and science of preparing good food.

Gelatin **Gelatina** *geh-lah-TEE-nah*
CONDIMENTS A thickener or setting agent derived from the collagen found inside an animal's bones. It melts when it is heated and solidifies into a jellylike texture when it is cooled. It is odorless, tasteless, and colorless and is available in sheets or powdered form.

Germ **Germen** *HEHR-mehn*
GRAINS & CEREALS The embryo or seed of a cereal grain. Located in the kernel, the germ contains many nutrients including vitamins, fiber, and fatty acids. It is a component of a whole grain but can be removed and sold independently.

Gherkin **Pepinillo** *peh-pee-NEE-yoh*
CONDIMENTS A very small cucumber, one to three inches in length, that is pickled and sold in jars or cans. The French call it a cornichon.

Gilthead sea bream **Dorada** *doh-RAH-dah*
FISH & SHELLFISH A fish of the bream species. Prized in Europe for its great taste and versatility, it is considered to be the best tasting of the breams.

Gin **Ginebra** *hee-NEH-brah*
BEVERAGE A grain alcohol that is redistilled and flavored with juniper berries and other botanicals. It is a very dry spirit with a sharp and distinct flavor.

Ginger **Jengibre** *hehn-HEE-breh*
HERBS & SPICES A tuber root of the ginger plant. Its light brown and very bumpy skin must be peeled off. Its flesh is pale yellow in color and very fibrous, which is why it tends to be grated and its juice extracted for use. Ginger has a strong peppery and soapy flavor that is very aromatic. A staple in Asian cooking, it is used in both sweet and savory recipes. It can be found in powdered form, but it is inferior in taste to the fresh.

Gizzards Mollejas *moh-YEH-hahs*
> MEAT (1) Organs found in the digestive tract of birds that grind up food. Often sold with whole birds, they are packaged in small bags and placed in the bird's cavity, but they can also be purchased separately. They must be cooked with by a slow moist heat method in order to tenderize the tough meat. (2) Classified as offal, lamb, beef, or pork thymus glands and/or pancreas.

Glassware Cristalería *krees-tah-leh-REE-ah*
> EQUIPMENT Tableware made with glass. Glassware most often refers specifically to drinking vessels.

Glaze v. Glasear / Barnizar / Glasedo *glah-seh-AHR / bahr-nee-SAHR / glah-seh-AH-doh*
> COOKING METHOD / TECHNIQUE To brush on or coat a food with a sweet or savory sauce that will set on the food and produce a shine.

n. Glaseado *glah-seh-AH-doh*
> A thick or thin sauce that is used to coat food and adds color, shine, and flavor. It can be sweet or savory.

Glucose Glucosa *gloo-KOH-sah*
> GENERAL Generally referred to as dextrose, a simple sugar that is not as sweet as table sugar. It does not crystallize and is often used in commercial food preparation.

Gluten Gluten *GLOO-tehn*
> GENERAL A combination of the proteins glutenin and gliadin, which are found in cereal grains, most commonly wheat. The two proteins must be hydrated in order to activate gluten which is responsible for creating a strong network structure in baked goods.

Glycerin Glicerina *glee-seh-REE-nah*
> GENERAL A component of a triglyceride obtained from fats. A common name for glycerol, glycerin is a thick, colorless liquid used to add sweetness and retain moisture in foods.

Goat Chivo (male) / Cabra (female) *CHEE-boh / KAH-brah*
> MEAT A four-legged, cloven-hoofed animal that is a bovine related to sheep. The meat of mature animals has a strong flavor and is tough, while that of young animals, called kids, is tender.

Goat, young Cabrito *kah-BREE-toh*
> MEAT Meat from a young goat.

Goat's milk Leche de cabra *LEH-cheh deh KAH-brah*
> DAIRY The milk extracted from a goat. Available fresh or canned, it can be drunk or made into cheese.

Goose Oca *OH-kah*

MEAT A web-footed animal much larger than a duck. It can be wild or domesticated and while its meat is eaten, it is most popular for its creamy, rich liver that results from force feeding.

Gooseberries Uvas espinas *OO-bahs ehs-PEE-nahs*

FRUIT & VEGETABLES Large berries with a tart-flavored flesh that grow on bushes. Their soft furry skin comes in a variety of colors of green, white, yellow, and red.

Grain Grano *GRAH-noh*

GRAINS & CEREALS The dried, edible portion of the cereal plant. Examples of plants from which grains are removed include corn, wheat, rice, oats, and barley. The word "grain" is often used interchangeably with cereal.

Gram Gramo *GRAH-moh*

MEASUREMENTS The most popular dry unit of measure in the metric system. It is equivalent to $1/1,000$ kilogram or 0.0022 pound.

Grand reserve Gran reserva *grahn reh-SEHR-bah*

BEVERAGES A term given to wine that has been aged for at least five years. It is also intended to be given to wines made in exceptional years, but that is up to the discretion of the winemaker.

Grapefruit Toronja *toh-ROHN-hah*

FRUIT & VEGETABLES A large citrus fruit that is more tart than sweet and somewhat bitter. Its fragrant yellow skin must be peeled and its white pith removed. The interior flesh is made up of juicy segments that can range in color from yellow to a deep reddish pink. Its juice is a popular morning beverage.

Grape leaves Hojas de parra *OH-hahs deh PAH-rrah*

FRUIT & VEGETABLES The large, edible green leaves of a grapevine that are often used in Greek and Middle Eastern cooking for wrapping foods. Sold in jars, they are typically rolled up and kept in a brine solution to keep them preserved.

Grapes Uvas *OOH-bahs*

FRUIT & VEGETABLES The edible berries that grow in clusters on vines or shrubs. They can have small seeds in their center or be seedless, and the color of their thin, edible skin ranges from light green to dark purplish black. There are more than a thousand varieties, and depending on their flavor profile, they can be used for wine making, eating, drying, or making into preserves.

Grapeseed oil Aceite de pepita de uva *ah-SAY-teh deh peh-PEE-tah deh OO-bah*

NUT & OILS Oil extracted from the seeds of grapes. Its neutral flavor and high smoke point make it good for sautéing or pan frying.

Grater Rallador *rah-yah-DOHR*

EQUIPMENT A kitchen tool used to grate or shred food into thin strips or crumbs. It consists of a metal plate that is perforated with holes on which a food is slid back and forth. The size of the holes determines the size of the grate. The typical configuration of a handheld grater is a tall four- to six-sided box where each side can grate food to a different thickness and size. Most graters are manual but electric versions also exist.

Gratin dish Cacerola de gratinado *kah-seh-ROH-lah deh grah-tee-NAH-doh*
EQUIPMENT A special ovenproof dish used to hold food that is to be gratinéed (set under the broiler or in the oven) and immediately brought to the table.

Grease v. Engrasar *ehn-grah-SAHR*
COOKING METHOD / TECHNIQUE To coat or slather a baking dish or pan with a fat so as to make it a nonstick surface.

n. Grasa *GRAH-sah*
MEAT Rendered animal fat.

Green peppercorns Pimientas verdes *pee-mee-EHN-tahs BEHR-dehs*
HERBS & SPICES The soft unripe berries of the pepper plant that are preserved in brine or salt.

Grenadine Granadina *grah-nah-DEE-nah*
CONDIMENTS Originally made from real pomegranates, a dark red, artificially sweetened, pomegranate- flavored syrup used to color and flavor drinks.

Griddle Plancha *PLAHN-chah*
EQUIPMENT A flat, often rimless cooking pan. It can be a freestanding pan placed over a burner or be built into a stove-top.

Grilled A la parrilla / Asado a la parrilla *ah lah pah-RREE-yah / ah-SAH-doh ah lah pah-RREE-yah*
COOKING METHOD / TECHNIQUE Cooked on a metal grate that is placed over hot coals or a heat source.

Grind Moler *MOH-lehr*
COOKING METHOD / TECHNIQUE To breakdown food to very small particles. This can be accomplished with an electric grinder, meat grinder, mortar and pestle, or food processor.

Grinder Molinillo / Trituradora *moh-lee-NEE-yoh / tree-too-rah-DOH-rah*
EQUIPMENT A manual or electric kitchen tool used to grind food.

Grouper Cherna *CHEHR-nah*
FISH & SHELLFISH A firm white fish, a member of the sea bass family, from the warm Atlantic or Gulf waters. Its skin has a very strong flavor and should be removed before cooking.

Grouse Foja *FOH-hah*
GAME A small game bird similar to a chicken in size.

Guava Guayaba *gwah-YAH-bah*
FRUIT & VEGETABLES A small, oval-shaped, tropical fruit with a bumpy skin that ranges in color from yellow green when unripe to dark purple when mature. The

red flesh can be eaten only when the fruit is ripe and is often used to make juice or preserves. Guava is available fresh and canned and is very popular in Mexico and the Caribbean.

Guava paste **Pasta de guayaba / Bocadillo** *PAHS-tah deh gwah-YAH-bah / boh-kah-DEE-yoh*

FRUIT & VEGETABLES Guava fruit pulp that has been cooked with pectin and sugar and flavored with citric acid. It is set and shaped into a firm block that can be sliced and served as a snack or dessert. It is used as a pastry filling or served with cheese.

Guinea fowl **Pintada** *peen-TAH-dah*

GAME A small bird with a dark, strongly flavored meat. It ranges from one to four pounds in weight. Care must be given when cooking the bird as it can dry out easily.

H

Haddock **Abadejo / Eglefino** *ah-bah-DEH-hoh / ehg-leh-FEE-noh*

FISH & SHELLFISH A saltwater fish that has a firm texture and very mild flavor. A cousin of cod, it is a popular fish that is used in a variety of ways. Its skin is white and has a black line running along its side. Haddock is available fresh, smoked, canned, or frozen.

Hake **Merluza** *mehr-LOO-sah*

FISH & SHELLFISH A saltwater fish that is a relative of the cod and found in northern Pacific and Atlantic waters. It is a delicate-flavored, white fish that has a firm texture. It is very popular in Spain.

Halibut **Fletán** *fleh-TAHN*

FISH & SHELLFISH A very large, white, and firm-fleshed fish that comes from the waters of the north Pacific and Atlantic oceans. Low-fat and mild-flavored, halibut is available in steaks and fillets.

Ham **Jamón** *hah-MOHN*

MEAT The cooked or fresh meat from the hog's hind leg. The meat is taken from the hip down to the middle shank and is cured to some degree. Often it is also smoked after it is cured. Ham is available boneless or with the bone in.

Hamburger **Hamburguesa** *ahm-boor-GEH-sah*

MEAT Ground beef patties that are cooked to a desired doneness and sandwiched between two round buns.

Handful **Manojo** *mah-NOH-hoh*

MEASUREMENTS A measure of how much a hand can grasp.

Hand mixer (electric) **Batidor de varilla** *bah-tee-DOHR deh bah-REE-yah*

EQUIPMENT A small handheld electric appliance used to whip, beat, and mix ingredients. Two beaters are connected to a handled base that contains the motor. The beaters are submerged into the ingredients before the motor is started.

Hard-boiled egg Huevo cocido *WEH-voh koh-SEE-doh*
COOKING METHOD / TECHNIQUE An egg in its shell that has been submerged into boiling water long enough for the yolk and white to firm up. It takes about eight minutes for the egg to become solidified. Hard-boiled eggs can be kept in their shells in the refrigerator for up to a week.

Hare Kiebre *kee-EH-breh*
GAME A relative of a rabbit that is very fast moving. Its flesh is stronger in flavor and darker in color than that of a rabbit. It is available domesticated or wild and needs to be tenderized or cooked by a moist heat method to prevent the meat from becoming tough.

Haute cuisine Alta cocina *AHL-tah koh-SEE-nah*
GENERAL Food prepared and served in an elegant and highly technical manner. It is the French term for "high cooking."

Hazelnut Avellana *ah-beh-YAH-nah*
NUTS & OILS The small, round nut that grows on the hazel tree. Its hard brown shell must be cracked open, and inside the nut has a thin, brown skin that is slightly bitter and should be removed. Used in both savory and sweet recipes, hazelnuts can be ground, chopped, or left whole.

Hazelnut oil Aceite de avellana *ah-SAY-teh deh ah-beh-YAH-nah*
NUTS & OILS The oil extracted from pressed hazelnuts. Due to its pronounced and intense flavor, it is often blended with a light and neutral oil.

Heart Corazón *koh-rah-SOHN*
MEAT Organ meat that is made up almost entirely of muscle. Its very low-fat content means it can become tough if cooked improperly or for too long. It can come from cattle, calves, chickens, or lambs.

Hearts of palm Palmitas *pahl-MEE-tahs*
FRUIT & VEGETABLES Pale white tube ranging in width from one-half to two inches. Since hearts of palm are found in the inner core of the bark of a special palm tree, the tree must be killed for them to be harvested. The flavor is reminiscent of that of an artichoke. Popular in Brazil, they are typically tossed in salads. They are available canned or fresh.

Herbs Hierbas *ee-EHR-bahs*
HERBS & SPICES Fresh or dried leaves of plants used in small amounts to add flavor to food. Herbs offer very little nutritional value.

Herbes de Provence Hierbas de Provenza *ee-EHR-bahs deh proh-BEHN-sah*
HERBS & SPICES A mixture of dried herbs commonly used in the South of France. Lavender is a key ingredient and others include basil, rosemary, sage, fennel seed, thyme, and bay leaf. It is used on meats and vegetables.

Herring Arenque *ah-REHN-keh*
FISH & SHELLFISH Small fish that swim in large pools and are found in cold salt water. Oily and silver-colored, they grow no larger than a pound in weight. Young herrings are often used as a substitute for sardines. Fresh herring can be baked, grilled, or sautéed and is often also cured or pickled.

Hijiki Alga hijiki *AHL-gah hee-GEE-kee*
FRUIT & VEGETABLES A long, thin, Japanese seaweed that is boiled and dried after it has been harvested from the ocean. It must be reconstituted before using. Often prepared as a salad or used in recipes, it has a salty, licoricelike flavor.

Hock Codillo ahumado *koh-DEE-yoh ah-oo-MAH-doh*
MEAT The portion of an animal's leg located between the foot and the thigh. It does not have much meat but it does have a large amount of bone and connective tissue, which is good for flavoring and thickening food.

Honey Miel *mee-EHL*
CONDIMENTS A thick, sweet syrup made from flower nectar by bees. The type of flower determines its color and flavor. Honey offers the same amount of sweetness as table sugar but with added flavor and texture/mouthfeel. It is used for cooking, baking, as a spread, and as a beverage sweetener. At times it is sold with its honeycomb and is available pasteurized so that it will not crystallize.

Honey, orange blossom Miel de azahar *mee-EHL deh ah-sah-AHR*
CONDIMENTS Honey derived from the nectar of the orange blossom.

Honeycomb Panal de miel *pah-NAHL deh mee-EHL*
CONDIMENTS A wax structure, made up of a number of six-sided individual compartments, made by honeybees to store their honey. The bees produce their own wax to construct it.

Honeydew Melón de miel *meh-LOHN deh MEE-ehl*
FRUIT & VEGETABLES A round fruit with a smooth and pale green skin that is inedible. The flesh is slightly darker than the peel and can be very juicy and sweet. A member of the muskmelon family, it is similar to a cantaloupe in that it contains a number of small seeds in its center that must be removed before eating.

Honing steel Chaira *CHAH-ee-rah*
EQUIPMENT A metal rod that is coated with a special fine abrasive. A knife is passed over it at a specific angle to align the material on the blade's edge, but does not reshape or sharpen it.

Hors d'oeuvre Entremeses *ehn-treh-MEH-sehs*
GENERAL Small, bite-size appetizers served before a meal and often accompanied by cocktails. They can be hot or cold and are almost always savory. They can be served before or after taking a seat at the dinner table.

ENGLISH-SPANISH H

Horseradish Rábano picante *RAH-bah-noh pee-KAHN-teh*
HERBS & SPICES A plant grown mainly for its large white root. Pungent and spicy in flavor, horseradish is used as a seasoning or condiment—never on its own. When used fresh, it is typically grated. It is also available bottled, preserved in brine.

Hot Caliente *kah-lee-EHN-teh*
DESCRIPTOR A descriptive measure of a high temperature.

Hot dog Perro caliente *PEH-rroh kah-lee-EHN-teh*
MEAT An American-style frankfurter, a cured sausage made from pork or beef and served in a special oblong, soft bun. Typical accompaniments include ketchup, mustard, and pickle relish.

Hothouse cucumber Pepino hothouse *peh-PEE-noh hoht house*
FRUIT & VEGETABLES A practically seedless cucumber with a thin, bumpy skin. It is longer than a traditional cucumber (at least one foot long) and is packaged in plastic for protection since its skin is not covered in wax. It is also known as an English cucumber.

Hybrid Híbrido *EE-bree-doh*
DESCRIPTOR A result of crossbreeding.

I

Iberian Ibérico *ee-BEH-ree-koh*
DESCRIPTOR Relating or belonging to the Iberian peninsula, which is comprised of Spain and Portugal.

Ice v. Poner en hielo *poh-NEHR ehn ee-EH-loh*
COOKING METHOD / TECHNIQUE To decrease the temperature of a food by placing it over ice or in an ice bath.

n. Hielo *ee-EH-loh*
BEVERAGE The frozen state of water.

Ice cream Helado / Nieve *eh-LAH-doh / nee-EH-beh*
BAKING & PASTRY A frozen dessert made with cream, milk (fresh or powdered), and a sweetener (sugar, honey, or an artificial sweetener). A flavoring such as chocolate, caramel, or nuts can be added. Commercial ice creams usually contain stabilizers and thickeners to help improve and maintain their texture.

Ice cream cone Barquillo *bahr-KEE-yoh*
BAKING & PASTRY A thin wafer cookie that is molded into a cone shape and used as an edible container that holds ice cream.

Ice cream maker Máquina de hacer helado *MAH-kee-nah deh ah-SEHR eh-LAH-doh*
EQUIPMENT A manual or electric kitchen tool used for making ice cream. When ice cream is made manually, a cream mixture is put in a canister and constantly stirred

while being frozen to prevent ice crystals from forming. The electric version stirs the container for you. Ice cream makers come in various sizes and price points but all work on same principal.

Ice cream scoop Paleta de helado *pah-LEH-tah deh eh-LAH-doh*
EQUIPMENT A kitchen tool and utensil used to serve ice cream. Depending on the type of scoop used, the ice cream can be formed into a spherical ball or a long egg shape. Scoops come in various sizes.

Idiazabal Idiazabal *ee-dee-ah-SAH-bahl*
DAIRY An unpasteurized sheep's milk cheese from the Basque region of Spain. It is a pressed cheese that may be lightly smoked during the aging process, giving it a nutty and slightly smoky flavor. Idiazabal is formed in rounds and shares manchego's characteristic zigzag pattern on its rind.

Incorporate Incorporar *een-kohr-poh-RAHR*
COOKING METHOD / TECHNIQUE To mix two or more ingredients until well blended.

Infuse Infundir *een-foon-DEER*
COOKING METHOD / TECHNIQUE To extract the flavor of a food by soaking it in a hot liquid.

Infusion Infusión *een-foo-see-OHN*
COOKING METHOD / TECHNIQUE The flavor that has been extracted from a food by having soaked it in a hot liquid.

Irradiate Irradiar / Irradiado *ee-rrah-dee-AHR / ee-rah-dee-AH-do*
GENERAL To extend the shelf life of food by exposing it to low doses of X-rays or gamma rays in order to eliminate the presence of microorganisms. The process is approved by the FDA and all foods that have undergone this process must bear an international symbol.

Israeli couscous Cuscus israelí *COOS-coos ees-rah-eh-LEE*
GRAINS & CEREALS Closer to orzo than couscous, a small, round wheat pasta that is much larger than regular couscous. It is often used as a substitute for rice.

J

Jackfruit Fruta de jack *FROO-tah deh yahk*
FRUIT & VEGETABLES A very large, oval-shaped tropical fruit with green, spiky skin that can grow up to one hundred pounds in weight. Its faintly sweet flesh is cream colored with seeds dispersed throughout it. Jackfruit is used in savory dishes when unripe and sweet recipes when mature.

Jam Mermelada *mehr-meh-LAH-dah*
CONDIMENTS A spreadable product made from fruit puree that has been simmered with water and sugar until the plant's natural pectins thicken the mixture. It is used as a spread or in desserts.

Jelly Jalea *hah-LEH-ah*
CONDIMENTS A spreadable product made from fruit juice, sugar, and pectin. The pectin, which is responsible for thickening the product, can be naturally occurring in the fruit or can be added in powdered form.

Jerusalem artichoke Aguaturma / Tupinambo *ah-gwah-TOOR-mah / too-pee-NAHM-boh*
FRUIT & VEGETABLES A tuber from the sunflower plant similar in appearance to fresh ginger. The thin skin is light brown and bumpy, and the white flesh is crunchy and sweet with a faint nutty flavor. It can be eaten raw, or cooked with or without its skin. It is also known as sunchoke.

Jewfish Mero *MEH-roh*
FISH & SHELLFISH A member of the sea bass family, the largest member of the grouper species, averaging 75 to 150 pounds in weight. It can be found in the warm waters of the Atlantic and Gulf of Mexico and parts of the Pacific. It is a firm, white fish with a mild flavor. Jewfish is also known as black bass but its name was officially changed to goliath grouper in 2001.

Jicama Jícama / Nabo dulce *HEE-kah-mah / NAH-boh DOOL-seh*
FRUIT & VEGETABLES A large root vegetable that averages one and a half pounds in weight. Its white flesh is crunchy with a texture and flavor similar to those of a water chestnut; its very thin, brown skin is inedible. Jícama can be eaten raw or cooked.

John Dory Pez de San Pedro *pehs deh sahn PEH-droh*
FISH & SHELLFISH A deep-sea fish with long spines protruding from its head. Its skin is light yellow to green in color with a dark circular spot on its side. Its mild-tasting flesh is versatile and can be cooked in a number of ways.

Juice v. Extraer el jugo *eks-trah-EHR ehl HOO-goh*
COOKING METHOD / TECHNIQUE To extract the liquid (juice) found in a fruit or vegetable.

n. Jugo *HOO-goh*
BEVERAGE The liquid extracted from a fruit or vegetable.

Juicer Exprimidor / Exprimidor de cítricos *eks-pree-mee-DOHR / eks-pree-mee-DOHR deh SEE-tree-kohs*
EQUIPMENT A manual or electric kitchen tool used to extract liquid from a fruit or vegetable. Juicers vary in size, with some being small handheld devices and others counter-mounted small electric appliances.

Julienne v. Cortar a la juliana *kohr-TAHR ah lah hoo-lee-AH-nah*
COOKING METHOD / TECHNIQUE To cut food into thin strips.

n. Juliana *hoo-lee-AH-nah*
DESCRIPTOR Food that has been cut into thin strips. The length of the food is not important.

Juniper berry **Baya de enebro** *BAH-yah deh eh-NEH-broh*
HERBS & SPICES A dark purple–colored berry that resembles a blueberry. Juniper berries have a strong herbaceous flavor with lots of tannins and are used often with game meats in European cooking. Typically they are used dried because they are very bitter when raw.

Junk food **Comida basura** *koh-MEE-dah bah-SOO-rah*
GENERAL Food that has little or no nutritional value.

K

Kaffir lime **Lima kaffir** *LEE-mah kah-FEER*
FRUIT & VEGETABLES The small, bumpy, green-skinned citrus fruit that grows on the kaffir tree. The fruit's rind and the tree's leaves have the most flavor and aroma and are used most to add flavor to food. Most often found dried, the leaves can be purchased fresh and have a more intense flavor.

Kale **Col rizada** *kohl ree-ZAH-dah*
FRUIT & VEGETABLES A member of the cabbage family that has dark green leaves with very curly edges that are attached at its base but do not form a tight head. The hearty cabbage-flavored leaves have a thick center stem that should be removed before they are cooked or eaten. The leaves can be treated like spinach.

Ketchup **Ketchup** *KEH-choop*
CONDIMENTS A tangy tomato-based condiment made with sugar, vinegar, and other spices. Often used as an ingredient in recipes, it is typically used as a topping on hamburgers and french fries.

Kidney **Riñón** *ree-NYOHN*
MEAT A glandular organ taken from cattle, swine, or lambs. Beef kidney is most recognizable as it is multilobed. Kidney is best from younger animals as it is more tender and mild flavored.

Kitchen shears **Tijeras de cocina** *tee-HEH-rahs deh koh-SEE-nah*
EQUIPMENT Scissors used for cutting food and other kitchen tasks.

Kiwi **Kiwi** *KEE-wee*
FRUIT & VEGETABLES A small, egg-shaped fruit with brown, furry skin that is not eaten. The flesh is bright green with a small white center dotted with edible, tiny, black seeds. It has a juicy texture and a sweet tart flavor that is slightly astringent.

Knead **Amasar** *ah-mah-SAHR*
COOKING METHOD / TECHNIQUE A technique used on bread dough to blend its ingredients and work the gluten strands in order to add strength to the dough. It can be done manually or by a machine. The process consists of stretching and folding the dough onto itself until a smooth and elastic dough forms.

Knife Cuchillo *koo-CHEE-yoh*
EQUIPMENT A sharp-edged, handheld tool used to cut food. It consists of a handle attached to a blade. Knives come in a variety of sizes and materials.

Knife, chef's Cuchillo de chef *koo-CHEE-yoh deh chehf*
EQUIPMENT Also known as a French knife, an all-purpose knife with a blade six to twelve inches long. The tip is curved allowing for a rocking motion to occur when chopping or handling the knife.

Knife, paring Cuchillo de vegetal *koo-CHEE-yoh deh beh-heh-TAHL*
EQUIPMENT A small knife with a blade three inches long. It is used for specific detailed tasks such as hulling strawberries, deveining shrimp, and creating intricate garnishes.

Knife, serrated Cuchillo serrado / Cuchillo de sierra *koo-CHEE-yoh seh-RRAH-doh / koo-CHEE-yoh deh see-EH-rrah*
EQUIPMENT A knife with a sawlike blade used to slice through very delicate foods such as terrines or cakes or foods with a tough crust or skin such as breads or sausages. It can cut through food without squeezing it or applying undo pressure.

Knife sharpener Afilador de cuchillo *ah-fee-lah-DOHR deh koo-CHEE-yoh*
EQUIPMENT An instrument used to fine-tune the sharp cutting edge of a knife by grinding the edge against a rough, hard surface at a specific angle (twenty degrees). Knife sharpeners come in manual or electric versions.

Kohlrabi Colinabo *koh-lee-NAH-boh*
FRUIT & VEGETABLES A member of the turnip family that has a white or purple bulb with thin stems and dark green leaves. The bulb is used more than the leaves, although both are edible. The bulb has a mild sweet flavor reminiscent of a turnip. Its texture is similar to that of a potato.

Kombu Alga kombu *AHL-gah KOHM-boo*
FRUIT & VEGETABLES Long, wide pieces of seaweed that are dried and sold as long strips or sheets. Kombu is cultivated off the coasts of China, Japan, and Korea. Popular in Japanese cuisine, its one of the main ingredients in dashi.

Kosher Kosher / Conforme a la ley judaica *KOH-shehr / kohn-FOHR-meh ah lah LEH-ee hoo-dee-AH-kah*
DESCRIPTOR Conforming to Jewish dietary law, which states what foods can be eaten and in what combination they can be eaten. It also applies to the kitchen / facility in which the food is prepared.

Kumquat Naranja china / Naranja enana / Kumquat *nah-RAHN-hah CHEE-nah / nah-RAHN-hah eh-NAH-nah / KOOM-kwaht*
FRUIT & VEGETABLES A very small, oval-shaped citrus fruit. Both the tart orange rind and sweet flesh are edible. Kumquats are available fresh and canned.

L

Lactic acid Ácido láctico *AH-see-doh LAHK-tee-koh*
GENERAL A tart and bitter-tasting acid that forms when a particular bacteria combines with the milk-sugar lactose. It is responsible for the distinctive taste of soured milk and the tartness found in yogurt.

Ladle Cucharrón *koo-cha-RROHN*
EQUIPMENT A large, deep-bowled spoon with a long handle used to serve soup or other liquids.

Ladyfinger banana Plátano enano *PLAH-tah-noh eh-NAH-noh*
FRUIT & VEGETABLES A small, stubby banana that has a thin skin and sweet flavor.

Lamb Cordero *kohr-DEH-roh*
MEAT The meat from domesticated sheep that are less than one year old. The flesh is tender with a pronounced meaty flavor.

Lamb, chop Chuleta de cordero *choo-LEH-tah deh kohr-DEH-roh*
MEAT An individual cut of lamb that still has the rib bone attached.

Lamb, crown Corona de cordero *koh-ROH-nah deh kohr-DEH-roh*
MEAT Two racks of lamb ribs that are cooked, placed upright, and curved to form a circular shape. Paper truffles are traditionally placed over the top of each rib bone.

Lamb, French trimmed Costilla de cordero a la francesa *kohs-TEE-yah deh kohr-DEH-roh ah lah frahn-SEH-sah*
MEAT Lamb chops that have had all the meat and fat trimmed off the rib bone.

Lamb, leg of Pierna de cordero *pee-EHR-nah deh kohr-DEH-roh*
MEAT An entire hind leg from the lamb.

Lamb, rack of Costillar de cordero *kohs-tee-YAHR deh kohr-DEH-roh*
MEAT The cut taken from the rib section. About eight rib bones and their meat are attached to each other. It is typically served in one piece.

Lamb, shoulder of Paletilla de cordero *pah-leh-TEE-yah deh kohr-DEH-roh*
MEAT The cut located right below the neck. It is an economical cut that is flavorful but can get tough and chewy if not cooked properly. The entire shoulder is typically sold boneless and can be cooked as a roast.

Lamb, shoulder steak Corte de paletilla de cordero *KOHR-teh deh pah-leh-TEE-yah deh kohr-DEH-roh*
MEAT An individual sliced portion of the lamb shoulder.

Langoustine Cigala *see-GAH-lah*
FISH & SHELLFISH A deep-sea crustacean that looks like a small lobster and can grow up to eight inches long. The colder the waters it comes from, the more flavor it has. It is also known as Norway lobster.

Lard Manteca *mahn-TEH-kah*
MEAT Rendered pork fat that is used for both cooking and baking. It is prized for its high smoke point and distinct flavor. Fat taken from the area surrounding the pig's kidneys is considered the best.

Lavender Lavanda *lah-BAHN-dah*
HERBS & SPICES A member of the mint family, a plant that produces a purple flower that is used in both savory and sweet recipes for its floral aroma and flavor. When dried, the flower serves as a key ingredient in herbes de Provence. It also produces a nectar that bees use to make honey. The flowers are often candied and used as a garnish in baked goods.

Leavening Levadura / Fermento *leh-bah-DOO-rah / fehr-MEHN-toh*
BAKING & PASTRY A substance used in batters and doughs that reacts with moisture, heat, and acidity to trigger a reaction causing the creation of a gas. This gas lightens the batter or dough allowing it to rise and gain volume.

Lecithin Lecitina *leh-see-TEE-nah*
GENERAL A member of the lipid family, a diglyceride that falls under the category of phospholipid. It acts as an emulsifier, which is an agent that binds two ingredients that do not normally mix creating a smooth and homogenized mixture. Lecithin is found abundantly in egg yolks.

Leek Puerro *poo-EH-rroh*
FRUIT & VEGETABLES A member of the onion and garlic family, but much milder in flavor, that resembles a giant scallion. The white flesh, closest to the roots, has a more pronounced onion flavor than the thick, dark green leaves that shoot up from it. The entire leek is edible but the tops of the greens need trimming as they are tough and offer little flavor. Leeks are used in the same way onions are used.

Leg Pierna *pee-EHR-nah*
MEAT A limb that supports an animal's body and is used for locomotion. Animals can have 2 to 4 legs.

Lemon Limón *lee-MOHN*
FRUIT & VEGETABLES The small, egg-shaped citrus fruit that grows on a lemon tree. The flesh and skin are both yellow in color and edible. The juicy flesh has a bright flavor that is tart and acidic. The skin is full of natural oils and can be grated and used for flavoring. It is best to remove the white pith that separates the skin from the flesh as it is bitter.

Lemonade Limonada *lee-moh-NAH-dah*
BEVERAGE A beverage made by mixing lemon juice, water, and sugar.

Lemon curd Crema de limón *KREH-mah deh lee-MOHN*
CONDIMENTS A thick and creamy mixture made predominately from lemon juice and egg yolks that have been sweetened with sugar. It is simmered until it thickens and can be used in desserts or as a spread.

Lemongrass Hierba de limón *ee-EHR-bah deh lee-MOHN*

HERBS & SPICES A tall grass used as an herb. The section closest to the root contains the most citrus lemon flavor and is cylindrical in shape with layers resembling a scallion. It must be crushed or chopped in order to allow its flavor to be infused into the dish. Lemongrass is available fresh or dried.

Lemon sole Pelaya *peh-LAH-yah*

FISH & SHELLFISH A small, white-fleshed fish that is mild in flavor and low in fat. A species of flounder, it is also known as English sole.

Lemon squeezer Exprimidor de cítricos *eks-pree-mee-DOHR deh SEE-tree-kohs*

EQUIPMENT A handheld kitchen tool used to extract the juice from a lemon or lime. A lemon squeezer comes in different shapes and sizes but must be made with an acid-resistant material.

Lemon verbena Maria Luisa *mah-REE-ah loo-EE-sah*

HERBS & SPICES An herb with long, thin, soft green leaves that have a very pronounced lemon flavor. It is used to flavor dishes as well as make tea and lemon oil.

Lentil Lenteja *lehn-TEH-hah*

FRUIT & VEGETABLES The seed of the lentil plant that grows in a pod. The seeds are dried as soon as they are ripe. Lentils come in a variety of colors—brown, green, yellow, and red—that are determined by the presence or absence of a husk. They do not need to be soaked before cooking. They are legumes containing a high amount of protein and are often used as a meat substitute.

Lettuce Lechuga *leh-CHOO-gah*

FRUIT & VEGETABLES A plant that produces edible leafy greens. Grown throughout the world, lettuce falls under one of four main families—crisphead, romaine, looseleaf, and butterhead. Typically eaten raw, lettuce is the base of most salads. Its flavor is described as grassy, and its texture is crisp. *See also* **Mâche**; **Mesclun**.

Lettuce, butterhead Lechuga trocadero *leh-CHOO-gah troh-kah-DEH-roh*

FRUIT & VEGETABLES Small loose heads of a light green lettuce in the same family as Bibb and Boston lettuce. Its leaves are tender and have a buttery texture.

Lettuce, iceberg Lechuga iceberg *leh-CHOO-gah EES-behrg*

FRUIT & VEGETABLES Thin, light green leaves that are wrapped into a tight head of lettuce. Its neutral flavor and crisp texture are due to its high water content. It is also known as crisphead lettuce.

Lettuce, lollo rosso Lechuga lollo rojo *leh-CHOO-gah LOH-yoh ROH-hoh*

FRUIT & VEGETABLES A looseleaf lettuce with very curly red leaves. The core is pale green in color. The leaves are tender but crisp.

Lettuce, oak leaf (red or green) Hoja de roble (roja o verde) *OH-hah deh ROHB-leh (ROH-hah oh BEHR-deh)*
> FRUIT & VEGETABLES A looseleaf lettuce whose leaves are attached at the base of its head. Its flavorful, soft, wavy leaves are predominantly green with splashes of red.

Licorice Regaliz *reh-gah-LEES*
> HERBS & SPICES The dark brown root of the licorice plant from which an anise or tarragon-like flavor can be extracted. It is used to flavor candies, soft drinks, and medicines.

Light Ligero *lee-GEH-roh*
> DESCRIPTOR (1) Of little weight or density. (2) Having few calories.

Claro *KLAH-roh*
> DESCRIPTOR Pale in color.

Lime Lima / Limón verde *LEE-mah / lee-MOHN BEHR-deh*
> FRUIT & VEGETABLES The small, round fruit of the lime tree that grows in tropical regions. About three inches in diameter, the fruit has a thin, green skin that turns yellow as it ripens. Its seedless flesh is pale green and juicy with a tart citrus flavor.

Lipid Lípido *LEE-pee-doh*
> GENERAL A fatty substance that falls under one of three categories: triglyceride, phospholipid, and cholesterol. Lipids cannot dissolve in water. Fats and oils are both members of this family.

Liqueur Licor *lee-KOHR*
> BEVERAGE A spirit that has been sweetened and flavored with items such as seeds, spices, flowers, or roots; a drinkable, distilled beverage containing ethanol.

Liter Litro *LEE-troh*
> MEASUREMENTS A metric unit of measure of volume. It is slightly more than 1 quart, approximately equivalent to 4 fluid cups.

Liver Hígado *EE-gah-doh*
> MEAT A large organ that is prized for its rich taste and creamy texture. It is best consumed from young animals as the liver from older ones can be tough and stronger flavored. Most liver consumed comes from calves, cattle, geese, and poultry. Depending on the animal source, it is available fresh or frozen, whole or sliced.

Loaf pan Molde de pan *MOHL-deh deh pahn*
> EQUIPMENT A deep, rectangular pan used for making meat loaf and pound cake. It comes in a range of sizes, but the most common is nine inches long by five inches wide by three inches deep.

Lobster Langosta / Bogavante *lahn-GOHS-tah / boh-gah-BAHN-teh*
> FISH & SHELLFISH A crustacean found all over the world in both cold and warm waters, ranging in weight from one to six pounds. There are two main types: Maine lobster, which is found in cold waters and has claws and a sweet, tender flesh, and spiny or

rock lobster, which is found in warm waters and has no claws and firmer meat that is found only in the tail. Lobsters are available live and fresh or dead and frozen.

Lobster claws **Pinzas** *PEEN-sahs*
FISH & SHELLFISH Pincers; the sharp and curved extremities of a lobster.

Locust bean **Algarroba** *ahl-gah-RROH-bah*
FRUIT & VEGETABLES The seeds found inside the carob pod. They are the source of locust bean gum, which is used as a thickener in processed foods. *See* **Carob**.

Loganberry **Mora logan** *MOH-rah LOH-gahn*
FRUIT & VEGETABLES A berry that looks like a hybrid between a raspberry and blackberry. It has the form of a blackberry with the color of a raspberry and the flavor of both. Loganberries can be eaten raw or used as an ingredient in desserts or jams.

Loin **Lomo** *LOH-moh*
MEAT A tender section of meat located on either side of the backbone or spine. It is typically cut into steaks or chops.

Loquat **Níspero** *NEES-peh-roh*
FRUIT & VEGETABLES A yellow, pear-shaped fruit. Its flesh is crisp and juicy and its texture is similar to that of an apple. It has a tart flavor and can be eaten raw or used as an ingredient in desserts. High in pectin, loquats are good for making jam.

Lotus root **Loto** *LOH-toh*
FRUIT & VEGETABLES The edible root of the aquatic lotus plant. Cylindrical in shape, it measures about three inches in diameter. A cross-section of the root shows the white-colored flesh filled with spongelike holes. The root has a crisp-textured flesh surrounded by a thin, reddish-colored skin that must be removed before eating. Its flavor is similar to that of a water chestnut. Lotus root is available fresh, canned, and dried.

Lovage **Levístico** *leh-BEES-tee-koh*
HERBS & SPICES A plant whose dark green leaves and seeds are used as an herb and spice. Its flavor and aroma are similar to those of celery and is often used as a substitute for celery seed. It is very popular in southern Europe, especially the Liguria region of Italy.

Low fat **Bajo en grasa** *BAH-hoh ehn GRAH-sah*
DESCRIPTOR Not deriving a large amount of calories from fat. According to U.S. labeling guidelines, low fat refers to food that has three grams of fat or less per serving.

Lukewarm **Tibio** *TEE-bee-oh*
DESCRIPTOR Tepid. Moderately warm. Neither hot nor cold.

Lunch **Almuerzo / Comida** *ahl-MWEHR-soh / koh-MEE-dah*
GENERAL The midday meal. For many countries, this is the main meal of the day.

Lychee **Lichi** *LEE-chee*
FRUIT & VEGETABLES The small, round tropical fruit that grows on the lychee tree. About the size of a cherry, it has a rough and hard, red outer skin that is inedible but

easy to remove. The juicy flesh is creamy white and surrounds a single large seed. Mildly sweet in flavor, it is available fresh, canned, or frozen.

M

Macadamia nut **Nuez macadamia** *noo-EHS mah-kah-DAH-mee-ah*
NUTS & OILS The nut of the macadamia tree which is native to Australia. Buttery sweet in flavor, it is round and beige colored. It is almost always sold shelled since its shell is very hard and difficult to crack.

Mace **Macis** *MAH-sees*
HERBS & SPICES A spice taken from the nutmeg tree. It is the dried, red covering of the nutmeg seed and as such its flavor is very similar to that of nutmeg. Its color is a bit more red and vivid than nutmeg's and is used when imparting color is important in a dish. Mace is sold in powdered form.

Macerate **Macerar** *mah-seh-RAHR*
COOKING METHOD / TECHNIQUE To steep or soak a food in a liquid in order to infuse the food with the flavor of the liquid.

Mâche **Mache** *mahsh*
FRUIT & VEGETABLES Narrow, dark green leaves that are used in salads for their slight nutlike flavor. They are very delicate and tender. Mâche is also known as corn salad or lamb's lettuce.

Mackerel **Caballa** *kah-BAH-yah*
FISH & SHELLFISH A firm and fatty saltwater fish with a pleasantly strong flavor. Mackerels are sold whole when small or in fillets or steaks. They spoil quickly as a result of their high fat content and are often smoked to help preserve them. The most popular types are king mackerel and Spanish mackerel.

Mahimahi **Mahimahi** *MAH-hee MAH-hee*
FISH & SHELLFISH A medium-size fish that averages about twenty pounds found in warm salt water. Being firm and flavorful with a moderate amount of fat makes it a good grilling fish. It is also known as dolfinfish, but its Hawaiian name—mahimahi—is more commonly used to avoid confusion with the dolphin mammal.

Mahon **Mahón** *mah-OHN*
DAIRY Named after the town where it originated on the island of Minorca, Spain, a firm, cow's milk cheese with a nutty flavor that sharpens as it ages. It has an orange-colored rind that is achieved from its being rubbed with butter, oil, and paprika.

Maillard reaction **Reacción de Maillard** *re-ahk-see-OHN deh MAH-ee-yahrd*
COOKING METHOD / TECHNIQUE A browning reaction that takes place between an amino acid and a sugar. In addition to producing a brown color, it also results in the development of complex meaty flavors and aromas.

Majorero Majorero *mah-hoh-REH-roh*

DAIRY From the island of Fuerteventura in the Canary Islands, a cheese made from the island's goats' milk, which is unusually high in fat. It is firm and pale white in color, and its flavor is buttery and nutty yet mildly tart.

Mallard Pato real *PAH-toh reh-AHL*

GAME One of the ancestors of the domesticated duck. Its green head and yellow bill is very recognizable.

Malt Malta *MAHL-tah*

GRAINS & CEREALS The name given to the process of sprouting a grain underwater then removing and drying it once it is germinated. The dried grain is then ground into a powder and used to flavor foods and beverages. The grain's resulting flavor is deeper and sweeter than it was originally.

Manchego Manchego *mahn-CHEH-goh*

DAIRY A Spanish, semifirm, sheep's milk cheese produced in La Mancha, a region in central Spain just south of Madrid. Considered Spain's most popular cheese, it is protectèd by Denominación de Origen. It has a creamy and slight sharp flavor. Aged for three months to a year in natural caves, manchego comes in ten-inch-round wheels with a recognizable zigzag pattern embossed on its rind.

Mandarin Mandarina *mahn-dah-REE-nah*

FRUIT & VEGETABLES A citrus fruit that resembles an orange but is much smaller. Its skin is loosely attached to its flesh and easily peels off. There are several varieties, each with its own trait, and all have a sweet flavor.

Mandoline Mandolina *mahn-doh-LEE-nah*

EQUIPMENT A kitchen tool used to precisely slice and cut food into juliennes or matchsticks. It consists of a thin, rectangular-shaped box with a sharp blade in its center that adjusts to alter the thickness of the cuts.

Mango Mango *MAHN-goh*

FRUIT & VEGETABLES A tropical fruit that is oblong and green-skinned when unripe, but turns yellow and red and fragrant as it matures. Its flesh is golden yellow with a dense texture that is juicy and sweet. A very large oval seed is found in its center with the flesh attached. The flesh must be cut apart from the seed, and the skin is inedible. More than one hundred different varieties exist; some varieties are more fibrous than others.

Mangosteen Mangostán *mahn-goh-STAHN*

FRUIT & VEGETABLES No relation of the mango, a fruit that grows in Southeast Asia. It looks like a small, round eggplant. Its interior flesh is soft and cream-colored, and divided into segments. Its flavor is refreshingly tart and sweet.

Maple syrup Jarabe de arce *hah-RAH-beh deh AHR-seh*

CONDIMENTS The sap from the maple tree that has been boiled and reduced until a thick liquid forms.

Margarine Margarina *mahr-gah-REE-nah*
CONDIMENTS A butter substitute developed in 1869 by a French chemist as an affordable alternative to butter. Modern margarine is made with vegetable oil that has been hydrogenated until it becomes spreadable. Food coloring, emulsifiers, and preservatives are often used to make it look and taste like butter.

Margarita Margarita *mahr-gah-REE-tah*
BEVERAGE A popular cocktail in Mexico made with tequila, triple sec, and lime juice. It is served straight up or on the rocks or frozen. The rim of a margarita glass is typically dipped in lime juice and coated with salt.

Marinade Adobo *ah-DOH-boh*
CONDIMENTS A liquid mixture containing an acid and other condiments and seasonings used to flavor meats, fish, and vegetables. The acid, usually in the form of citrus juice, vinegar, or wine, is helpful in tenderizing tough cuts of meat.

Marinate Adobar *ah-doh-BAHR*
COOKING METHOD / TECHNIQUE To soak food in a marinade to absorb its flavors or tenderize tough cuts of meat.

Marjoram Mejorana *meh-hoh-RAH-nah*
HERBS & SPICES A member of the mint family that looks and tastes like oregano with a mild sweet flavor. Available fresh and dried, it is often used in Europe.

Marmalade Mermelada *mehr-meh-LAH-dah*
CONDIMENTS A spread made from fruit cooked with sugar and pectin where chunks of fruit are still in tact and pieces of rind are mixed in. Citrus fruit are most commonly used.

Marrowbone Hueso de medular / Hueso de caña *WEH-soh deh meh-doo-LAHR / WEH-soh deh KAH-nya*
MEAT A beef bone, typically from the thigh, that contains marrow.

Marshmallow Nubes *NOO-behs*
CONDIMENTS A confection made from corn syrup, water, gelatin, gums, and flavorings. Cylindrical in shape, it can be large or small and is often white in color. Its spongy texture changes to molten and gooey when heated.

Marzipan Mazapán *mah-sah-PAHN*
CONDIMENTS Almond paste that has added sugar. Its pliable nature makes it ideal for shaping and molding into forms. Food coloring is often added when making decorative shapes.

Mash Machacar / Hacer puré *mah-chah-KAHR / ah-SEHR poo-REH*
COOKING METHOD / TECHNIQUE To compress or squish food and reduce it to a pulp.

Mature Añejo *ahn-NYE-hoh*
DESCRIPTOR Ripe. Fully developed. Aged.

Mayonnaise Mayonesa *mah-yoh-NEH-sah*
CONDIMENTS An emulsion of vegetable oil, egg yolk, and lemon juice or vinegar. It is a thick and creamy condiment used as a spread or in recipes.

Meal Comida *koh-MEE-dah*
GENERAL Food eaten at a set time.

Mealy Harinoso *ah-ree-NOH-soh*
DESCRIPTOR Description of a texture that is slightly dry and crumbly.

Measure v. Medir *meh-DEER*
MEASUREMENTS To assign a value to an attribute such as length, volume, or weight.
n. Medida *meh-DEE-dah*
MEASUREMENTS A unit of measure such as inch, ounce, cup, or gram.

Measuring cups Tazas de medir / Jarras de medir *TAH-sahs deh meh-DEER / HAH-rrahs deh meh-DEER*
EQUIPMENT A kitchen tool used to measure food in liquid or dry form. For dry measurements, cups come in sets that consist of 1/4-, 1/3-, 1/2-, and 1-cup sizes. Liquid measurements are taken with a cup that has markings every 1/4- and 1/3-cup intervals.

Measuring spoons Cucharas de medir *koo-CHA-rahs deh meh-DEER*
EQUIPMENT A kitchen tool used to measure small quantities of dry or liquid ingredients. Measuring spoons are sold in sets that range in size from 1/8 teaspoon to 1 tablespoon.

Meat Carne *KAHR-neh*
MEAT An animal's flesh consumed as food. It can be its muscle or an organ.

Meat patty Carne molida en forma *KAHR-neh moh-LEE-dah ehn FOHR-mah*
MEAT Ground meat that has been shaped into a round, flat disk.

Meatballs Albóndigas *ahl-BOHN-dee-gahs*
MEAT Ground meat that is seasoned, shaped into a ball, and cooked. Bread crumbs and egg are often added to bind and keep the meat from falling apart.

Medium Medio hecho *MEH-dee-oh EH-choh*
COOKING METHOD / TECHNIQUE The doneness of meat described by its internal temperature, color, and juiciness. The meat should be pink and firm in the center and its temperature should reach 140°F-150°F.

Medium rare Poco hecho *POH-koh EH-choh*
COOKING METHOD / TECHNIQUE The doneness of meat described by its internal temperature, color, and juiciness. The meat should be warm and red in the center and its temperature should reach 130°F-140°F.

Melon Melón *meh-LOHN*
FRUIT & VEGETABLES A fruit that grows on a vine. Melon refers to two categories of this fruit. The muskmelon is round with netted or smooth skin. Its seeds are contained in the center of the fruit and its flesh is dense but juicy and sweet as it ripens.

The watermelon, the next category, is oblong with a smooth, green skin and a red, juicy flesh that is dotted with black seeds.

Melon baller **Cortador de melón / Vaciador de melón** *kohr-tah-DOHR deh meh-LOHN / bah-see-ah-DOHR deh meh-LOHN*

EQUIPMENT A handheld kitchen tool with a small, round, hollow half-inch circle connected to a handle. It is used to scoop out balls of melon flesh.

Melt **Derretir** *deh-rreh-TEER*

COOKING METHOD / TECHNIQUE To change the physical property of food from a solid state to a liquid state by heating.

Melted **Derretido** *deh-rreh-TEE-doh*

COOKING METHOD / TECHNIQUE The physical property of food having been changed from a solid to a liquid by applying heat.

Menu **Carta** *KAHR-tah*

GENERAL A list of dishes to be served. A list of options to choose from in order to create a meal.

Meringue **Merengue** *meh-REHN-geh*

BAKING & PASTRY A mixture of egg whites and sugar whipped until peaks are formed. The texture of the peaks ranges from soft to stiff. Meringue can be eaten uncooked and used as a dessert topping or baked in a low oven until completely dry.

Mesclun **Mesclun** *MEHS-kloon*

FRUIT & VEGETABLES A mix of small tender salad greens whose combination and type vary.

Metal skewer **Brocheta de metal** *broh-CHE-tah deh meh-TAHL*

EQUIPMENT A rod or stick made of stainless steel used to pierce through food and hold it while the food is cooked. It is typically used for grilling food.

Mexican wedding cakes **Polvorones** *pohl-boh-ROH-nehs*

BAKING & PASTRY Shortbreadlike cookies that are made with flour, ground nuts, and butter. They are shaped into a ball and rolled in powdered sugar. They are often served at weddings, christenings, and special occasions.

Mezzaluna **Mezzaluna** *meh-sah-LOO-nah*

EQUIPMENT A half-moon-shaped, curved blade with a handle on either side of the blade. It chops by rocking the blade's edge over the food to be cut.

Microwave oven **Microonda** *mee-kroh-OHN-dah*

EQUIPMENT A kitchen appliance that cooks food by using microwave radiation to heat water molecules within the food. It cooks food quickly but does not cause browning or caramelization.

Milk **Leche** *LEH-cheh*

DAIRY The creamy white liquid produced by the mammary glands of mammals. The most common source is a cow, but milk from goats, sheep, and water buffalo is also consumed.

Milk, powdered Leche en polvo *LEH-cheh ehn POHL-voh*
DAIRY Milk that has had all its liquid evaporated. This has a longer shelf life than regular milk and does not need to be refrigerated. It comes in nonfat and whole milk varieties.

Milk shake Batido *bah-TEE-doh*
BEVERAGE A beverage made from milk, ice cream, and a flavoring—fruit, chocolate, or syrup—that is pureed in a blender.

Millet Mijo *MEE-hoh*
GRAINS & CEREALS A cereal grain rich in protein that is more popular for its use in animal feed than for human consumption, although it gets distributed to needy regions of the world. It is prepared in the same manner as rice, has a bland flavor, and serves as a good canvas for other foods.

Milliliter Mililitro *mee-lee-LEE-troh*
MEASUREMENTS A metric unit of measure that calculates length. It is $1/1,000$ meter.

Mince Picar / Desminuzar *pee-KAHR / dehs-mee-noo-SAHR*
COOKING METHOD / TECHNIQUE To cut food into very small irregular-shaped pieces.

Mineral Mineral *mee-neh-RAHL*
GENERAL A nonliving substance that is naturally occurring and has a specific chemical composition. Minerals are required by the body in very small amounts.

Mint Menta *MEHN-tah*
HERBS & SPICES An herb with sturdy, green leaves that delivers a fresh flavor with a cool aftertaste. Its essential oil is extracted and used as a flavoring. It is used in both sweet and savory recipes as well as a number of cocktails. There are more than twenty-five species of mint. Two main varieties are peppermint and spearmint. Yerba buena is a hybrid of the mint family that is used throughout Latin America.

Mixer Batidora *bah-tee-DOH-rah*
EQUIPMENT An electric kitchen tool used to whip or beat ingredients that can be handheld or stationary. The handheld version, used for smaller tasks, has a small motor with two whisks connected to it. The larger stationary machine stands on its own and has a dedicated work bowl with various attachments used to mix ingredients.

Mixing bowl Cuenco / Bol *koo-EHN-koh / bohl*
EQUIPMENT A work bowl used to mix or toss ingredients. It comes in sizes ranging from three-quarters of a quart to more than eight quarts and in materials such as ceramic, glass, and stainless steel.

Molasses Melaza *meh-LAH-sah*
CONDIMENTS Thick, dark brown syrup that is a by-product of sugar refining. It is a result of the boiled-down juice extracted from sugarcane or sugar beets. It has a deep caramel flavor that can be bitter.

Mold **Moho** *MOH-oh*
GENERAL A variety of fungus that grows on food. It causes food spoilage and appears as fuzzy, blue green spots. Some fungus can be desirable such as the one used in cheese making.

Molde *MOHL-deh*
EQUIPMENT A container used to shape food into a specific form. Ingredients are put inside a mold and then cooked or cooled in it in order to take on the mold's shape. Molds come in various shapes and sizes.

Mollusk **Molusco** *moh-LOOS-koh*
FISH & SHELLFISH Invertebrate whose soft body lives inside a shell that is either made up of two pieces and hinged (bivalve) or forms one solid piece (univalve). Mollusk is one of two main categories of shellfish; the other is crustacean.

Monkfish **Rape** *RAH-peh*
FISH & SHELLFISH A flat fish found in northern Atlantic waters that has dark brown skin and is very ugly looking. It buries itself in the ocean floor and lures prey with a thin filament that is connected to its head. Its edible flesh is found in its tail and is sweet, firm, and dense (not flaky) resembling lobster meat.

Mortar and pestle **Molcajete y tejolete / Mortero** *mohl-kah-HEH-teh ee teh-loh-HEH-teh / mohr-TEH-roh*
EQUIPMENT A two-piece kitchen tool made up of a bowl and thick blunt stick used to crush and mash ingredients. The bowl (*molcajete*) is the mortar and the stick (*tejolete*) is the pestle. Each piece is made from the same material, usually wood, marble, ceramic, or rock.

Mount **Montar** *mohn-TAHR*
COOKING METHOD / TECHNIQUE To add small, cold pieces of butter to a sauce and stir constantly until the butter is completely melted and incorporated into the sauce. This is done right before serving to add body and shine to the sauce.

MSG (Monosodium glutamate) **GMS (Glutamato monosódico)** *GLOO-tah-mah-toh moh-noh-SOH-dee-koh*
CONDIMENTS A sodium salt of glutamic acid, one of the twenty-two amino acids. Naturally found in kombu seaweed, it is also commercially synthesized and sold in the form of a white powder. Although flavorless, it has the ability to enhance the flavor of savory foods and provide the unique taste sensation umami.

Muddle **Enturbiar / Machacar** *ehn-too-bee-AHR / mah-cha-KAHR*
COOKING METHOD / TECHNIQUE To crush or mash ingredients with the blunt end of a stick (known as a muddler). This technique is often used when making mixed drinks that are flavored with fresh herbs.

Mullet roe **Mujol** *moo-HOHL*
FISH & SHELLFISH The female fish eggs from mullet fish. It is available fresh or salt-cured. Botargo is the Italian version and karasumi the Japanese.

Mung bean sprout **Brote de judía mungo** *BROH-teh deh hoo-DEE-ah MOON-goh*

FRUIT & VEGETABLES The germinated sprout of the mung bean, which has a long, thin, off-white stem with yellow tips. It has a crunchy texture and an herbaceous, nutty flavor. It is used as a vegetable and served raw or cooked.

Mushroom **Seta / Champiñón / Hongo** *SEH-tah / cham-pee-ny-OHN / OHN-goh*

FRUIT & VEGETABLES An edible fungus. Cultivated or forged in the wild, thousands of varieties exist with different sizes, colors, and shapes. Their flavors range from mild to nutty and earthy, their colors from white to black. Mushrooms are available fresh or dried. *See also* **Porcini**.

Mushroom, chanterelle **Seta cantarela** *kahn-tah-REH-lah*

FRUIT & VEGETABLES A funnel-shaped wild mushroom that is yellow orange in color with gills that run beneath its cap. It has a nutty flavor and chewy, meaty texture. Chanterelles can be found fresh, dried, or canned.

Mushroom, horn of plenty **Trompeta de la muerte** *trohm-PEH-tah deh lah moo-EHR-teh*

FRUIT & VEGETABLES A trumpet-shaped wild mushroom with a wrinkled-edge cap. Dark grayish black in color with a deep earthy and nutty flavor, it is available fresh and dried.

Mushroom, morel **Colmenilla** *kohl-meh-NEE-yah*

FRUIT & VEGETABLES An edible wild mushroom, although some are cultivated. Its cap is cone-shaped and filled with spongelike holes and ranges in size from one to four inches long. Its flavor is earthy and nutty and is more intense in the darker mushrooms. Morels are available fresh, dried, or canned.

Mushroom, oyster **Seta orellanes** *SEH-tah oh-reh-YAH-nehs*

FRUIT & VEGETABLES An edible, creamy white wild mushroom that is now also cultivated. Its name comes from its fanlike shape that resembles an oyster. Its flavor mellows when it is cooked.

Mushroom, portobello **Seta portobello** *SEH-tah pohr-toh-BEH-loh*

FRUIT & VEGETABLES A large, brown cultivated mushroom that is recognizable by its wide flat cap and fully exposed gills. It is a fully mature cremini, which is a variety of the common white mushroom. Its deep flavor and meaty texture are due to its age and reduced moisture content.

Mushroom, shiitake **Seta shiitake** *SEH-tah shee-TAH-kee*

FRUIT & VEGETABLES A cultivated Asian mushroom with a wide dark brown cap and inedible stem. Meaty and a bit chewy in texture, it has a rich flavor. Shiitake mushrooms are available fresh and dried.

Mushroom, wild **Seta salvaje / Champiñón salvaje** *SEH-tah sahl-BAH-heh / cham-pee-ny-OHN sahl-BAH-heh*

FRUIT & VEGETABLES A mushroom that has been harvested from the wild (not cultivated). Wild mushrooms are available fresh or dried.

Mussel Mejillón *meh-hee-YOHN*
> FISH & SHELLFISH A bivalve mollusk found in both salt and fresh water. Its oblong shell is blue black in color with streaks of yellow. Its flesh is dark tan, firm, and meaty. Mussels are available fresh (live) or canned (plain or smoked).

Mustard Mostaza *mohs-TAH-sah*
> CONDIMENTS A paste made from powdered mustard seed mixed with wine, beer, or vinegar, water, and spices. The piquant condiment is used as a spread or in recipes.

Mustard, American Mostaza americana *mohs-TAH-sah ah-meh-ree-KAH-nah*
> CONDIMENTS A paste made from powdered white mustard seeds, water, vinegar, and spices. Often referred to as yellow mustard, turmeric is the spice that gives it its characteristic bright yellow color.

Mustard, Dijon Mostaza de Dijon *mohs-TAH-sah deh dee-HOHN*
> CONDIMENTS A pale yellow mustard that is sharp in flavor. Made from mustard seeds, white wine, and unfermented grape juice (verjuice) instead of vinegar, this recipe was first created in Dijon, France, in 1856

Mustard, French Mostaza francesa *mohs-TAH-sah frahn-SEH-sah*
> CONDIMENTS A prepared mustard made from ground mustard seeds, water, and vinegar. Brown mustard seeds, which are zestier than the white variety, are used.

Mustard, hot English Mostaza inglesa picante *mohs-TAH-sah een-GLEH-sah pee-KAHN-teh*
> CONDIMENTS Prepared mustard made from white and brown mustard seeds mixed with vinegar, water, and other spices. It is bright yellow in color and very spicy hot.

Mustard, whole grain Mostaza a la antigua *mohs-TAH-sah ah lah ahn-TEE-gwah*
> CONDIMENTS Prepared mustard made with mustard seeds that are not ground but left whole and mixed with the other ingredients.

Mustard seed Semillas de mostaza *seh-MEE-yahs deh mohs-TAH-sah*
> HERBS & SPICES The small, round seed of the mustard plant. The seed's color is determined by the type of plant it comes from. The most common mustard seeds are yellow or brown but they can also be black or white.

Mutton Carnero *kahr-NEH-roh*
> MEAT Meat from a domesticated sheep that is more than two years old. It has a stronger flavor and tougher flesh than that of the younger lamb.

N

Nacho Nacho *NAH-choh*
> DISH A dish often associated with Tex-Mex cuisine, made of layers of tortilla chips and melted cheese and topped with a dollop of sour cream, sliced jalapeño, chopped tomato, and sliced black olives.

Nectarine Nectarina *nehk-tah-REE-nah*

FRUIT & VEGETABLES Of the same species as the peach, a fruit that has smooth, red skin with yellow streaks. Its flesh is white or yellow and is sweet and juicy with a single seed in its center that can be loose or clinging to the flesh.

Nonstick frying pan Sartén antiadherente *sahr-TEHN ahn-tee-ahd-eh-REHN-teh*

EQUIPMENT A frying pan coated with Teflon or another material that does not allow food to adhere to it.

Noodles Fideos *fee-DEH-ohs*

GRAINS & CEREALS Pasta made with flour, water, and eggs or egg yolk. The flour can be made from wheat, rice, buckwheat, or another grain. Always flat, noodles can be thin or thick, long or short, or shaped into a square. They are available fresh or dried. *See also* **Ramen; Rice vermicelli**.

Noodles, Asian Fideos asiáticos *fee-DEH-ohs ah-see-AH-tee-kohs*

GRAINS & CEREALS Long, flat noodles made from a dough of wheat, rice, or soy flour, water, and sometimes egg.

Noodles, egg Pasta al huevo / Fideos al huevo *PAHS-tah ahl WEH-voh / fee-DEH-ohs ahl WEH-voh*

GRAINS & CEREALS Pasta made from wheat flour, water, and eggs or egg yolks. Egg noodles are flat and can be thick or thin, long or square-shaped. They are sometimes found wound up in nests and are available fresh or dried.

Noodles, rice Fideos de arroz *fee-DEH-ohs deh ah-RROHS*

GRAINS & CEREALS Long, thin noodles made from rice flour and water. Pale white when dried, they become translucent when cooked.

Noodles, soba Fideos de alforfón *fee-DEH-ohs deh ahl-fohr-FOHN*

GRAINS & CEREALS Thin, dark tan, Japanese noodles made with buckwheat flour.

Noodles, wheat Fideos de trigo *fee-DEH-ohs deh TREE-goh*

GRAINS & CEREALS Noodles made from wheat flour.

Nori Alga nori *AHL-gah NOH-ree*

FRUIT & VEGETABLES The Japanese name for very thin sheets of dried seaweed. It tastes of seawater and marine life and its color ranges from green to black. Usually eaten in dried form, it is used as a wrapper for sushi. Typically nori comes in square shapes but can be cut into any desired form.

Nut Fruto seco *FROO-toh SEH-koh*

NUTS & OILS A large, dried, oily, and edible seed of a plant that is enclosed in a shell.

Nutmeg Nuez moscada *noo-EHS mohs-KAH-dah*

HERBS & SPICES The seed found inside the fruit of the nutmeg tree. The seed is covered with a meshlike membrane that when dried and ground becomes the spice mace. The remaining one-inch- long seed is dried and when grated has a warm, sweet flavor. The brown-colored spice can be purchased whole or ground.

ENGLISH-SPANISH N

O

Oat bran **Salvado de avena** *sahl-VAH-doh deh ah-BEH-nah*
GRAINS & CEREALS The outer edible layer of the oat kernel. It contains a high amount of soluble fiber.

Oatmeal **Avena molida** *ah-BEH-nah moh-LEE-dah*
GRAINS & CEREALS Toasted and hulled whole oats that have been cut, crushed, or steamed and flattened with rollers. Oatmeal is used as a thickener, flavoring, or simply cooked as a breakfast cereal.

Oats **Avena** *ah-BEH-nah*
GRAINS & CEREALS A cereal grass that bears a kernel, which must be removed from its husk in order to be edible for human consumption. Oats can be cooked and served in a manner similar to rice.

Oaxaca cheese **Queso Asadero** *KEH-soh ah-sah-DEH-roh*
DAIRY White, cow's milk Mexican cheese, named after the Mexican state of Oaxaca where the cheese was originally made. Its flavor is similar to that of Monterey Jack. Alike in texture and melting properties to mozzarella, it is often used for quesadillas or for broiling since it melts so well. It is available in braids, balls, and wheels.

Octopus **Pulpo** *POOL-poh*
FISH & SHELLFISH A member of the mollusk family that has eight flexible legs or tentacles and no internal skeleton. It grows to an average extended length of two feet and a weight of three pounds. If not cooked properly, the meat becomes tough and rubbery. The younger the octopus, the more tender the meat.

Offal **Asadura / Despojo** *ah-sah-DOO-rah / dehs-POH-hoh*
MEAT The British word for variety meats. Offal includes internal organs and flesh that is not muscle and is used in cooking or for making sausage.

Oil **Aceite** *ah-SAY-teh*
NUTS & OILS Fat extracted from a plant source that is liquid at room temperature. Oil is a very efficient medium for cooking as it boils at a much higher temperature than water.

Okra **Okra / Quingombó** *OH-krah / keen-gohm-BOH*
FRUIT & VEGETABLES The thin, long, green pods from the okra plant that are harvested when still unripe, and used as a vegetable although technically it is a fruit. Okra has an herbaceous green flavor. When cooked, it lets go of a sticky substance that serves as a thickener. It is most popularly used in gumbo.

Olive **Aceituna / Olivo** *ah-say-TOO-nah / oh-LEE-boh*
FRUIT & VEGETABLES The small, round fruit of the olive tree that contains a high amount of fat and has a seed or pit in its center. An olive's flavor is dependent on its ripeness when it was picked. All unripe olives are green and can stay green or turn a darker color when ripened. After being picked, they can be processed into oil or cured or brined for eating. Some are stuffed with pimientos, anchovies, or almonds.

Olive, black Aceituna negra / Oliva negra *ah-say-TOO-nah NEH-grah / oh-LEE-bah NEH-grah*

FRUIT & VEGETABLES A ripe green olive that is either ripened on the tree or ripened artificially. The ripening process causes it to change to a black color.

Olive, green Aceituna verde / Oliva verde *ah-say-TOO-nah BEHR-deh / oh-LEE-bah BEHR-deh*

FRUIT & VEGETABLES An olive that is harvested when still unripe and then cured. Green olives are often marinated with herbs or pitted and stuffed with pimientos, almonds, or anchovies.

Olive, kalamata Aceituna kalamata *ah-say-TOO-nah kah-lah-MAH-tah*

FRUIT & VEGETABLES A dark purple black–colored Greek olive named after a city in Greece. It has a smooth skin and meaty flavor.

Olive oil Aceite de oliva *ah-SAY-teh deh oh-LEE-bah*

NUTS & OILS The oil extracted from the pressing of olives. Prized for its fruity and sometimes spicy flavor, it ranges in color from light yellow to dark green. It is a monounsaturated fat that is used for cooking.

Olive oil, extra-virgin Aceite de oliva extra-virgen *ah-SAY-teh deh oh-LEE-bah ehks-TRAH BEER-hehn*

NUTS & OILS Olive oil obtained from the first cold pressing of olives and cannot contain more than 1 percent acidity by volume. It is considered the finest olive oil in the world. Its color ranges from olive green to golden yellow and its flavor ranges from fruity to spicy.

Olive oil, light Aceite de oliva ligero *ah-SAY-teh deh oh-LEE-bah lee-HEH-roh*

NUTS & OILS Olive oil that has gone through a filtration process, resulting in a milder flavor, fragrance, and color but with the same amount of fat and calories. The filtration process produces an oil with a higher smoke point. Due to its more neutral flavor, it is used in baking.

Omelet Tortilla *tohr-TEE-yah*

DISH A dish made with beaten eggs cooked in a buttered sauté pan until the eggs set and is then folded in half onto itself. Various fillings such as sautéed vegetables or cheese can be placed inside the folded egg.

Onion Cebolla *seh-BOH-yah*

FRUIT & VEGETABLES The bulb of an onion plant that has an inedible, papery outer skin and a juicy interior flesh made up of concentric layers. Prized for its aroma and flavor it can be eaten raw but is used sparingly due to its pungent and sharp flavor. Cooking mellows its flavor and brings out its sweetness. There are many varieties of onions ranging in color, size, and flavor. *See also* **Scallion**; **Shallot**.

Onion, cocktail Cebollitas en vinagre *seh-boh-YEE-tahs ehn bee-NAH-greh*

CONDIMENTS A pickled, sweet pearl onion that maintains a crunchy texture. It is used as a garnish in cocktails.

Onion, green Cebolla verde *seh-BOH-yah BEHR-deh*
FRUIT & VEGETABLES An immature onion. It has a white base that is beginning to turn into a bulb, which has a stronger flavor, and a straight green top, both of which are edible. It is referred to as a scallion although it is not exactly the same.

Onion, red Cebolla roja *seh-BOH-yah ROH-hah*
FRUIT & VEGETABLES A medium-size onion with a reddish purple–colored skin. It has an intense sweet flavor that decreases when it is cooked. It is also known as an Italian onion or purple onion.

Onion, Spanish Cebolla española *seh-BOH-yah ehs-pah-NYOH-lah*
FRUIT & VEGETABLES A large, round onion that comes in three colors: yellow, red, and white. The yellow variety is sweet and the red is used raw when thinly sliced.

Orange Naranja *nah-RAHN-hah*
FRUIT & VEGETABLES The citrus fruit of the orange tree. Its orange-colored flesh is divided into segments by a white pith, which is surrounded by an orange skin that is fragrant and full of natural oils. Its juicy flesh is sweet tasting and slightly tart.

Orange, Seville Naranja agria *nah-RAHN-hah AH-gree-ah*
FRUIT & VEGETABLES A bitter orange. Its thick skin is pale yellow orange in color. It is not an eating orange as it has a very sour flesh and a high acid content. The juice is used often in marinades, and the skin is used in making bitters.

Oregano Orégano *oh-REH-gah-noh*
HERBS & SPICES A member of the mint family, an herb with small, green leaves, purple flowers, and a pungent flavor that is used in many dishes in the Mediterranean and Latin America. There is a Mexican variety and Mediterranean variety of oregano, the former of which is stronger. Oregano is available fresh or dried.

Organic food Comida orgánica *koh-MEE-dah ohr-GAH-nee-kah*
GENERAL Food grown without the use of synthetic pesticides, fertilizers, antibiotics, or chemicals.

Ostrich Avestruz *ah-behs-TROOS*
GAME A large bird whose meat is often compared to very lean beef. An ostrich egg is equivalent in size to sixteen chicken eggs and is cooked in similar ways.

Ounce Onza *OHN-sah*
MEASUREMENTS A unit of measure of weight equal to 1/16 pound or 28.35 grams.

Oven Horno *OHR-noh*
EQUIPMENT A kitchen appliance powered by gas or electricity. It consists of an enclosed chamber that roasts or bakes food in it through the circulation of hot air.

Oxtail Rabo de buey *RAH-boh deh boo-WEH*
MEAT Meat from the tail of cattle, although it used to come from oxen. Oxtail is bony and filled with lots of connective tissue that must be cooked by a slow and moist method (stewing or braising) in order for it to become tender, but it is very flavorful.

Oyster Ostra *OHS-trah*

FISH & SHELLFISH A bivalve that lives in salt water with a rough, gray, and rocklike shell. Its interior flesh is soft and succulent with a salty, briny flavor and is pale beige in color. The size and flavor vary according to variety of oyster. It can be eaten raw or cooked.

Oyster sauce Salsa de ostras *SAHL-sah deh OHS-trahs*

CONDIMENTS A thick, dark brown condiment made from oysters, soy sauce, brine, and sugar. A savory sauce, it is used in many Asian recipes or as a straight dipping sauce.

P

Palm oil Aceite de palma *ah-SAY-teh deh PAHL-mah*

NUTS & OILS Oil pressed from the fruit of the African palm. Often confused with palm kernel oil, which is oil taken from the seed inside the palm fruit, it has a distinctive flavor and red color that becomes clear when the oil is heated. Very high in saturated fat, it is thick and viscous at room temperature.

Pan Cacerola / Cazuela / Sartén *kah-seh-ROH-lah / kah-soo-EH-lah / sahr-TEHN*

EQUIPMENT A wide, shallow cooking vessel typically made of a metal.

Pancake Panqueque *pahn-KEH-keh*

BAKING & PASTRY A very thin quick bread or cake made from a batter that is poured onto a hot skillet or onto a hot griddle. It can be sweet or savory.

Panfry Freir a la sartén *freh-EER ah lah sahr-TEHN*

COOKING METHOD / TECHNIQUE To cook a food in a small amount of fat in a skillet, making sure the fat does not submerge the food.

Pan roasted Asado al sartén *ah-SAH-doh ahl sahr-TEHN*

COOKING METHOD / TECHNIQUE A two-part cooking technique that begins by searing food in an ovenproof skillet over high heat and then transferring the skillet to the oven to finish the cooking. This allows food to achieve a golden brown sear and maintain its moisture while it cooks internally.

Papaya Papaya *pah-PAH-yah*

FRUIT & VEGETABLES A large, oval-shaped fruit with a smooth, yellow skin that grows to about nine inches in length and two pounds in weight. When ripe, the flesh is densely succulent and sweet with a slight tart flavor. In a papaya's center are numerous edible, black seeds that are often discarded.

Paprika Pimentón *pee-mehn-TOHN*

HERBS & SPICES A spice made from ground, dried sweet red peppers. The type of pepper used determines the color and flavor of the spice which can range from sweet to pungent to hot. The variety also determines the intensity of its red color.

Parboil Sancochar *sahn-koh-CHAHR*
COOKING METHOD / TECHNIQUE To partially cook an ingredient by boiling it briefly. The ingredient will finish being cooked at a later time, most likely with a different technique. Parboiling is a time-saving technique to ensure ingredients with different cooking times will be ready at the same time.

Parrot fish Pez loro *pehs LOH-roh*
FISH & SHELLFISH A saltwater fish found near reefs in warm waters. It is often a bycatch of snapper. Recognizable for its brilliant blue, yellow, pink, and green–colored skin, it gets its name from the shape of its mouth and teeth which resemble the beak of a parrot.

Parsley Perejil *peh-reh-HEEL*
HERBS & SPICES A bright green leaf plant used as an herb. It has a fresh, slightly pungent flavor. Two varieties are used in cooking—curly leaf and flat leaf—which are distinguishable by the shape and texture of their leaves. Available fresh or dried, it is used in recipes, as palate cleansers, and as garnishes. It is one of the classic herbs in fines herbes.

Parsnip Chirivía *chee-ree-BEE-ah*
FRUIT & VEGETABLES A beige-colored root vegetable that looks like a carrot but is sweeter and stronger flavored. Its very thin skin should be peeled off and the parsnip used in the same way you would a carrot, eaten raw or cooked.

Partridge Perdiz *pehr-DEES*
GAME A member of the pheasant family, a medium-size game bird averaging about one to one-and-a-half pounds.

Passion fruit Fruta de la pasión / Granadilla *FROO-tah deh lah pah-see-OHN / grah-nah-DEE-yah*
FRUIT & VEGETABLES A small, egg-shaped, tropical fruit whose skin is typically dark brown but can also be yellow. Similar in structure to a pomegranate, inside it has a white pith that surrounds seeds covered in yellow flesh that are sweet with some sour and tart notes. The seeds can be eaten whole, or pressed through a strainer to extract the juice.

Pasta Pasta *PAHS-tah*
GRAINS & CEREALS Noodles made from a dough of flour, water, and sometimes egg that is cooked by boiling. Pasta comes in hundreds of shapes and sizes and can be dried or fresh. Italian law stipulates that dry pasta can be made only from durum wheat flour. This flour has a slight yellow tinge that gives pasta its characteristic yellow color.

Pasta, dry Pasta seca *PAHS-tah SEH-kah*
GRAINS & CEREALS A pasta, made primarily from durum semolina flour and water or egg, that is shaped and dehydrated by mechanical dryers. It comes in varying shapes from long to short, fat to thin, flat to round.

Pasta, filled Pasta rellena *PAHS-tah reh-YEH-nah*
GRAINS & CEREALS Pasta that has been stuffed with ingredients (a filling).

Pasta, fresh Pasta fresca *PAHS-tah FREHS-kah*
GRAINS & CEREALS Pasta made with semolina flour and egg instead of water. It is highly perishable and must be kept refrigerated prior to cooking. It cooks in only a few minutes—a fraction of the time it takes to cook dry pasta.

Pasta, long Pasta alargada *PAHS-tah ah-lahr-GAH-dah*
GRAINS & CEREALS A type of pasta that is categorized by its length. Longer than it is wide, it averages about ten inches in length. Long pasta can be dried or fresh.

Pasta, short Pasta corta *PAHS-tah KOHR-tah*
GRAINS & CEREALS Pasta that is compact, thicker, and denser than the long variety.

Pasta machine Máquina de hacer pasta *MAH-kee-nah deh ah-SEHR PAHS-tah*
EQUIPMENT A kitchen tool, both manual and electric, used to roll out and cut sheets of pasta dough. The most common type passes the dough between two rollers, flattening it out to the desired thickness.

Pasta sheets Pasta en láminas *PAHS-tah ehn LAH-mee-nahs*
GRAINS & CEREALS Pasta dough that has been flattened into thin layers.

Pasteurize Pasteurizar *pahs-teh-oo-ree-SAHR*
COOKING METHOD / TECHNIQUE To heat food for a short period of time to kill disease-causing pathogens. Pasteurizing is not intended to kill all microorganisms, just most of the ones that are likely to cause disease. Primarily performed on milk, it is also used on juices, wine, and beer.

Pastry Pastel / Masa *pahs-TEHL / MAH-sah*
BAKING & PASTRY Unleavened dough made from flour, water, and a fat to make pies and tarts. It is also a term used to describe baked goods (cakes, pies, tarts).

Pastry arts Pastelería *pahs-teh-leh-REE-ah*
BAKING & PASTRY The art of pastry and dessert making.

Pastry bag Bolsa pastelera *BOHL-sah pahs-teh-LEH-rah*
EQUIPMENT A cone-shaped bag with an opening on either end. A semisoft ingredient is added through the large end and squeezed out of the small opening, which can be fitted with special tips that produce decorative piping. Pastry bags come in various materials including cloth and disposable plastic.

Pastry brush Cepillo para repostería *seh-PEE-yoh PAH-rah reh-pohs-teh-REE-ah*
EQUIPMENT A thin-bristled brush used for a variety of pastry tasks such as wiping off excess flour or brushing egg wash onto pastry.

Pastry cream Crema pastelera *KREH-mah pahs-teh-LEH-rah*
BAKING & PASTRY A thick, sweet custard made from milk, eggs, flour, and sugar. It is used to fill cakes, tarts, éclairs, pies, and other pastries.

Pastry cutter **Mesclador de masa** *mehs-klah-DOHR deh MAH-sah*
EQUIPMENT A handheld kitchen tool used to cut or blend butter into flour. It is made up of a number of curved thin rods attached to a rounded handle.

Pastry wheel **Cortador de pastel** *kohr-tah-DOHR deh pahs-TEHL*
EQUIPMENT A small handheld kitchen tool made up of a slightly sharp, round disk attached to a handle. The edge of the disk can be plain or fluted to give a decorative appearance. Resembling a small pizza cutter, it is used to cut sheets of pastry or cookie dough.

Pea **Guisante** *gee-SAHN-teh*
FRUIT & VEGETABLES A member of the legume family that has edible seeds found inside pods. Some pods are edible and others are not, requiring the seeds (peas) to be removed. Peas are available fresh, canned, frozen, or dried.

Pea, green **Guisante verde** *gee-SAHN-teh BEHR-deh*
FRUIT & VEGETABLES Also known as an English pea or garden pea, an immature bean inside a pod. A pea must be removed from its pod and eaten fresh before its natural sugars turn into starch, dramatically altering its flavor.

Pea, split green **Guisante verde partido / Chicharro** *gee-SAHN-teh BEHR-deh pahr-TEE-doh / CHEE-chah-rroh*
FRUIT & VEGETABLES A dried green sweet pea that has been mechanically split to cook faster.

Pea, split yellow **Guisante amarillo partido** *gee-SAHN-teh ah-mah-REE-yoh pahr-TEE-doh*
FRUIT & VEGETABLES A dried yellow sweet pea that has been mechanically split to cook faster.

Pea, sugar snap **Guisante dulce** *gee-SAHN-teh DOOL-seh*
FRUIT & VEGETABLES A pea with an edible pod. Slightly rounded, it resembles a cross between an English pea and a snow pea.

Peach **Melocotón / Durazno** *meh-loh-koh-TOHN / doo-RAHS-noh*
FRUIT & VEGETABLES The fruit from the peach tree that has a characteristic fuzzy skin ranging in color from white to blush red. Its flesh, either orange yellow or blush white in color, is dense, juicy, and sweet and surrounds one seed / pit.

Peanut **Cacahuete / Maní** *kah-kah-WEH-teh / mah-NEE*
NUTS & OILS Technically a legume, a dried seed enclosed in an inedible shell/pod. Two nuts are enclosed in a beige-colored soft shell that has a netted texture. The nuts have a very thin, dark red, papery skin that is edible. There are several varieties of peanuts, the two most popular being the Spanish peanut and the Virginia peanut. Peanuts can be purchased shelled or in their shells.

Peanut butter Mantequilla de maní / Mantequilla de cacahueta *mahn-teh-KEE-yah deh mah-NEE / mahn-teh-KEE-yah deh kah-kah-WEH-teh*

CONDIMENTS A paste made from grinding roasted peanuts and often mixing them with salt. Some commercial varieties contain sugar and other additives to prevent the naturally present oils from separating.

Peanut butter chips Pepitas de mantequilla de maní / Pepitas de mantequilla de cacahuete *peh-PEE-tahs deh mahn-teh-KEE-yah deh mah-NEE / peh-PEE-tahs deh mahn-teh-KEE-yah deh kah-kah-WEH-teh*

CONDIMENTS Sweetened commercial peanut butter that has been formed into small drops or disks.

Peanut oil Aceite de maní / Aceite de cacahuete *ah-SAY-teh deh mah-NEE / ah-SAY-teh deh kah-kah-WEH-teh*

NUTS & OILS The oil pressed from peanuts that is then filtered and refined. It is mild in flavor and has a high smoke point (450°F), making it a great oil for deep frying. It is high in monounsaturated fat.

Pear Pera *PEH-rah*

FRUIT & VEGETABLES The round or bell-shaped fruit that grows on a pear tree. Its thin edible skin ranges in color from green to yellow to red. Its flesh is cream colored and can be firm or succulent with a slightly sweet flavor. Pears ripen best after they've been picked. There are more than five thousand varieties.

Pecan Pacana *pah-KAH-nah*

NUTS & OILS The nut that grows on the pecan tree. About one inch in length, the smooth, brown shell holds the lighter-colored nut that is recognizable by its ribbed texture. The kernel has a characteristic buttery flavor which is used in both sweet and savory recipes.

Pectin Pectina *pehk-TEE-nah*

GENERAL A substance naturally found in the cell wall of plants that is used as a gelling agent and thickener. Most commonly used to make jelly, jam, and preserves, it is added to fruit mixtures that do not contain enough natural pectin. It is available in liquid and powdered form.

Peel Pelar *peh-LAHR*

COOKING METHOD / TECHNIQUE To remove the outer skin of a fruit or vegetable.

Peppercorn Pimienta *pee-mee-EHN-tah*

HERBS & SPICES The very small berry that grows on the pepper plant (a vine) and is used as a spice for its spicy and hot flavor.

Peppermill Molinillo *moh-lee-NEE-yoh*

EQUIPMENT A handheld kitchen tool used to grind peppercorns.

Peppermint Menta / Hierbabuena / Yerba buena *MEHN-tah / ee-ehr-bah-boo-EH-nah / YEHR-bah boo-EH-nah*

HERBS & SPICES A species of mint that is pungent and peppery-flavored with a high menthol content. Its small leaves are dark green and hearty. It is available dried or fresh.

Pepperoni Chistorra *chees-TOH-rrah*

MEAT The Italian American name for a spicy, cured, dried sausage made from pork and beef.

Perch Perca *PEHR-kah*

FISH & SHELLFISH A small freshwater fish that ranges in size from one-half to three pounds. Mild-flavored and firm-fleshed, it has a yellow green–colored skin with dark vertical stripes. It is also known as yellow perch or river perch.

Persimmon Kaki / Palo santo *KAH-kee / PAH-loh SAHN-toh*

FRUIT & VEGETABLES Resembling an orange tomato, the fruit that grows on the persimmon tree. It comes in two varieties; the more common hachiya is astringent unless fully ripened and has a soft and creamy texture. Like the tomato, both the skin and flesh are eaten either raw or cooked. The other variety, fuyu, is not tart but is also not commonly available.

Pestle Telojete *teh-loh-HEH-teh*

EQUIPMENT One piece of a two-part kitchen tool called a mortar and pestle. It is a thick, blunt stick used to crush and mash ingredients. *See also* **Mortar and pestle**.

Pesto Pesto *PEHS-toh*

CONDIMENTS An uncooked sauce, Italian in origin, made with basil, garlic, pine nuts, Parmesan cheese, and olive oil. Traditionally the ingredients are crushed or pounded in a mortar with a pestle until a sauce forms.

Pheasant Faisán *fah-ee-SAHN*

GAME A medium-size game bird averaging three and a half pounds. It needs care when cooking to prevent the flesh from drying out and is often covered in fat to retain moisture.

Phyllo dough Masa filo *MAH-sah FEE-loh*

BAKING & PASTRY Tissue-thin sheets of unleavened dough. It is used to make sweet and savory recipes and is popular in Greek cuisine. It is available frozen or fresh.

Pickle v. Encutir *ehn-koo-TEER*

COOKING METHOD / TECHNIQUE To preserve or marinate in a vinegar or brine mixture.

n. Pepino *peh-PEE-noh*

FRUIT & VEGETABLES A cucumber that has been marinated in a brine or vinegar mixture.

Pickled egg Huevo en vinagre *WEH-voh ehn bee-NAH-greh*

DAIRY A hard-boiled egg that has been marinated and preserved in a vinegar solution.

Pickled ginger Jengibre encurtido *hehn-HEE-breh ehn-koor-TEE-doh*
CONDIMENTS Thickly sliced ginger that has been marinated in a vinegar solution. Often artificially colored pink, it is served and eaten after sushi.

Pickling spice Condimento para encurtido *kohn-dee-MEHN-toh PAH-rah ehn-koor-TEE-doh*
HERBS & SPICES A spice blend used in a pickling marinade liquid. Blends differ but spices are usually left whole and include peppercorns, bay leaves, cloves, mustard seeds, and coriander seeds among others.

Picos blue Picos / Picón *PEE-kohs / pee-KOHN*
DAIRY A creamy, assertive, and full-flavored cow's milk blue cheese from northern Spain that is wrapped in maple leaves. It is also called Picon.

Pie Pye / Pastel / Empanada *pah-ee / pahs-TEHL / ehm-pah-NAH-dah*
BAKING & PASTRY A dish made with a crust and filling. It can be sweet or savory and can have a single or double crust. Crusts can be made from pie dough, puff pastry, phyllo, and cookie crumbs among other things.

Pie pan Molde de pastel *MOHL-deh deh pahs-TEHL*
EQUIPMENT An ovenproof container used for baking a pie. Pie pans come in a variety of shapes, sizes, and materials, but all have sloping sides.

Pig cheeks Caretas de cerdo *kah-REH-tahs deh SEHR-doh*
MEAT The cheeks of a hog. Also known as hog jowls, they are typically smoked and cured and used for flavoring dishes.

Pig ear Oreja de cerdo *oh-REH-hah deh SEHR-doh*
MEAT The ear of a hog. Due to the high amount of collagen contained in the ear, it becomes incredibly gelatinous when cooked for a long time over low heat. Very popular in Spain, it is served as part of a stew called a *cocido* or simply roasted and served as a tapa.

Pigeon Paloma / Pichón *pah-LOH-mah / pee-CHON*
GAME Also known as wood pigeon, a small game bird popular in Europe.

Pig's feet Pies de cerdo *pee-EHS deh SEHR-doh*
MEAT The feet and ankles of a pig. They contain high amounts of collagen and will turn soft and gelatinous when cooked for a long time over low heat. Also known as trotters, they are available pickled, smoked, and fresh.

Pike Lucio *loo-see-OH*
FISH & SHELLFISH A freshwater fish with a long and thin body of lean and firm flesh with lots of bones. It is often used for fish mousse or stuffing.

Pinch Pisca *PEES-kah*
MEASUREMENTS An imprecise unit of dry measure. An amount of substance held between the thumb and index finger.

ENGLISH-SPANISH P

Pineapple Piña *PEE-nya*
FRUIT & VEGETABLES The tropical fruit that grows on the pineapple plant and is long and cylindrical in shape with thin, pointed leaves sprouting from its top. Its bumpy, inedible skin must be cut off to expose the yellow-colored flesh, which is juicy and sweet but can be acidic and tart depending on ripeness or variety. A pineapple must be picked when mature as it will not ripen off the vine, but its acidity can decrease if it is left at room temperature for a couple of days.

Pine nut Piñón *pee-NYOHN*
NUTS & OILS The small, edible seeds of pine trees found in the pinecone, which require a labor-intensive process to remove. The ivory-colored, high-fat nut is found inside a thin, dark shell that must be removed before eating.

Pistachio nut Pistacho *pees-TAH-choh*
NUTS & OILS The nut that grows on a pistachio tree. Its hard, tan shell splits naturally when ripe and contains a green-colored nut. Pistachio shells are sometimes artificially dyed a red color for aesthetic purposes. Pistachios can be purchased shelled or unshelled.

Pit v. Quitar las espinas *kee-TAHR lahs ehs-PEE-nahs*
COOKING METHOD / TECHNIQUE To remove the seed or stone of a fruit by cutting it out or pushing it out.

n. Carozo / Hueso *kah-ROH-soh / WEH-soh*
FRUIT & VEGETABLES The seed or stone of a fruit located in the center of its flesh.

Pitahaya / Pitaya Pitahaya *pee-tah-AH-yah*
FRUIT & VEGETABLES A member of the cactus family, an oval-shaped fruit that has a prickly, inedible, bright pink skin. Its juicy flesh is white and filled with small, edible seeds that add a crunchy texture. It has a very mild flavor, which is used mostly as a palate cleanser. It is also known as dragon fruit.

Pith (citrus) Albedo *ahl-BEH-doh*
FRUIT & VEGETABLES The soft, white, bitter-tasting membrane that lies between the peel and the flesh of the citrus fruit.

Pitter Despepitador *dehs-peh-pee-tah-DOHR*
EQUIPMENT A handheld kitchen tool used to remove the seed or pit from olives or cherries. A prong pushes the seed out of the center of the fruit.

Plantain Plátano *PLAH-tah-noh*
FRUIT & VEGETABLES A very large variety of banana with a firmer texture and higher starch content. As a plantain matures the skin changes color from green to black and the texture from firm to soft. It can be prepared when ripe or unripe but must it be cooked before being eaten.

Plastic wrap **Envuelve plástico** *ehn-BWEHL-veh PLAHS-tee-koh*
EQUIPMENT Thin plastic film used to wrap food and containers. It has the ability to cling to itself or other surfaces without adhesive, making it a very useful wrapper. It can create an airtight environment if sealed correctly.

Plate **Plato** *PLAH-toh*
EQUIPMENT A flat vessel on which food is served. It can be slightly concave with a rim. Plates come in various shapes and sizes but are traditionally round.

Pluck **Desplumar** *dehs-ploo-MAHR*
COOKING METHOD / TECHNIQUE (1) To remove feathers. (2) To pull off or out quickly.

Plum **Ciruela** *see-roo-EH-lah*
FRUIT & VEGETABLES The small, round fruit, about three inches in diameter, that grows on the plum tree. The edible, thin skin is typically purple red in color but can also be yellow. The yellow flesh is juicy with a sweet tart flavor. A single seed is found in the center. Dried plums are called prunes.

Plum sauce **Salsa de ciruela** *SAHL-sah deh see-roo-EH-lah*
CONDIMENTS A thick, translucent, golden yellow condiment with a sweet and sour flavor. Also known as duck sauce, it is made from plums and apricots that are mixed with sugar, vinegar, and other seasonings.

Poach **Escalfar** *ehs-kahl-FAHR*
COOKING METHOD / TECHNIQUE To cook food gently in simmering liquid. The liquid can be water or a seasoned mixture that imparts flavor to the ingredient.

Polenta **Polenta** *poh-LEHN-tah*
GRAINS & CEREALS A dish made from boiled cornmeal.

Pollack **Abadejo** *ah-bah-DEH-hoh*
FISH & SHELLFISH A member of the cod family found in deep north Atlantic waters. Silver-skinned with a moderate amount of fat, it has a white flesh that is firm with a sweet flavor. It is used in making fish sticks and surimi (imitation crab meat).

Pomegranate **Granada** *grah-NAH-dah*
FRUIT & VEGETABLES A round, red fruit the size of an orange with a small projection jutting from its stem end. The thick skin encloses a large amount of red fleshy seeds that are contained within a beige-colored spongy membrane. The seeds are the only edible part of the pomegranate and have a tart and tannic flavor and underlying sweetness.

Popcorn **Maíz para palomitas** *mah-EES PAH-rah pah-loh-MEE-tahs*
GRAINS & CEREALS A special type of dried corn kernel that pops open when heated. The moisture found inside the kernel turns to steam when heated and cannot escape the hard impermeable husk until enough pressure builds up and explodes the kernel open.

Poppy seed Semillas de adormidera *seh-MEE-yahs deh ah-dohr-mee-DEH-rah*
HERBS & SPICES The very small, dark blue gray seed that comes from the poppy flower. Crunchy and nutty in flavor, poppy seeds are used in sweet and savory recipes and are popular toppings on breads. They are available in whole or ground form.

Porcini, dried Boleto seco *boh-LEH-toh SEH-koh*
FRUIT & VEGETABLES Wild mushroom of the *boletus edulis* species. Light brown in color, porcini have smooth and meaty caps can range in diameter from one to ten inches. They have an intense earthy flavor and are difficult to find fresh, but are available dried year-round.

Pork Cerdo / Puerco / Chancho *SEHR-doh / PWEHR-koh / CHAHN-choh*
MEAT Meat from domesticated pigs that are less than a year old. The meat can be fresh or cured. *See individual cuts, entries under* **Carne de cerdo**.

Pork, boneless leg Pierna deshuesada de cerdo *pee-EHR-nah dehs-weh-SAH-dah deh SEHR-doh*
MEAT Meat of the pork leg that has had the bone removed.

Pork, chop Chuleta de cerdo *choo-LEH-tah deh SEHR-doh*
MEAT The cut of meat from the loin section that is cut perpendicular to the spine and typically has a rib bone attached.

Pork, cutlet Filete de cerdo *fee-LEH-teh deh SEHR-doh*
MEAT A thin, boneless slice of pork.

Pork, diced Carne de cerdo troceada *KAHR-neh deh SEHR-doh troh-seh-AH-dah*
MEAT Any cut of pork that has been cut into small pieces before or after cooking.

Pork, escalope Escalopa de cerdo *ehs-kah-LOH-pah deh SEHR-doh*
MEAT A very thin slice of boneless pork that has been pounded.

Pork, ground Carne de cerdo molido *KAHR-neh deh SEHR-doh moh-LEE-doh*
MEAT A cut of pork that has been ground.

Pork, leg Pierna de cerdo *pee-EHR-nah deh SEHR-doh*
MEAT A cut that is taken from the back legs of the pig. Ham comes from this cut.

Pork, shoulder Paletilla de cerdo / Pernil *pah-leh-TEE-yah deh SEHR-doh / pehr-NEEL*
MEAT The meat from the upper portion of the front leg of the pig. Very flavorful and a bit fatty, it is also known as pork butt.

Pork, tenderloin Solomillo de cerdo *soh-loh-MEE-yoh deh SERH-doh*
MEAT The meat taken from the loin section of the pig. The most tender cut of pork, this thin, elongated muscle is usually sold in pairs.

Pork belly Panceta de cerdo *pahn-SEH-tah deh SEHR-doh*
MEAT The cut of meat taken from the belly of the pig. It is made up of layers meat and flesh. When the cut is cured it becomes bacon.

Pork loin Lomo de cerdo *LOH-moh deh SEHR-doh*

MEAT The cut of meat located on the top (back) of the pig between the leg and the shoulder. Found on either side of the spine / rib cage, it is a very tender and lean cut that will dry out if overcooked.

Pork spareribs Costillas de cerdo *kohs-TEE-yahs deh SEHR-doh*

MEAT The meat that comes from the lower portion of the ribs, the part closest to the underbelly of the pig. Very flavorful, and popular for barbecuing, they have less meat and more fat than baby back ribs that come from the loin section. St. Louis–style ribs are trimmed spare-ribs.

Port Oporto / Vino porto *oh-POHR-toh / BEE-noh POHR-toh*

BEVERAGE A sweet, fortified wine typically made from red grapes, although a white variety exists. Similar types of wines are produced in other areas of the world, but only those made in the Duoro region of Portugal can be called port.

Pot Olla / Cacerola *OH-yah / kah-seh-ROH-lah*

EQUIPMENT A deep cooking vessel with one or two handles and a lid used on the stove-top. This is the common name for most cooking vessels.

Potassium nitrate Salitre *sah-LEE-treh*

GENERAL A chemical compound used as a food preservative. Also known as saltpeter, it is most commonly used in making sausages and other cured meats.

Potato Patata / Papa *pah-TAH-tah / PAH-pah*

FRUIT & VEGETABLES A starchy tuber crop vegetable. Its flesh is creamy white and can be waxy (high moisture/low starch—good for boiling) or starchy (low moisture/high starch—good for baking and mashing). There are hundreds of varieties. All have thin, edible skin and can range in color from white to yellow to red and even blue.

Potato, purple Patata morada / Papa morada *pah-TAH-tah moh-RAH-dah / PAH-pah moh-RAH-da*

FRUIT & VEGETABLES A small, oval potato with a dark grayish black skin. The flesh is purple colored and very dense and holds its shape well. A Peruvian heirloom potato from the Andes, it is believed to be one of the first harvested potatoes.

Potato, russet Patata russet *pah-TAH-tah ROO-seht*

FRUIT & VEGETABLES A large, oblong potato with a rough, brown skin. Its white flesh is high in starch making it suitable for baking, mashing, and frying.

Potato chips Papitas fritas *pah-PEE-tahs FREE-tahs*

FRUIT & VEGETABLES Thinly sliced, deep-fried potatoes.

Potato flour Harina de papa *ah-REE-nah deh PAH-pah*

GRAINS & CEREALS The flour made from boiled then dried potatoes that are ground into a powder. Used as a thickener, it is gluten free. It is also known as potato starch.

Potato masher Aplasta papas *ah-PLAHS-tah PAH-pahs*
EQUIPMENT A handheld kitchen tool used to crush cooked potatoes or other soft ingredient into a mash. A long handle is attached to a metal wire formed into a zig-zag shape or to a flat, blunt sheet of metal.

Potato ricer Pasapuré *pah-sah-poo-REH*
EQUIPMENT A handheld kitchen tool resembling a large garlic press, used to press soft ingredients through the small holes of a metal plate. It breaks food down to the size of grains of rice.

Poultry Aves *AH-behs*
MEAT Domesticated fowl— chickens, turkeys, geese, and ducks—raised for food The flesh and/or eggs are eaten.

Pound v. Espalmar *ehs-pahl-MAHR*
COOKING METHOD / TECHNIQUE To flatten food or an ingredient by striking it with a heavy object.

n. Libra *LEE-brah*
MEASUREMENTS A unit of measure of weight equivalent to 16 ounces.

Pound cake Panetela *pah-neh-TEH-lah*
BAKING & PASTRY A sweet loaf cake traditionally made with a pound each of flour, butter, sugar, and eggs.

Powdered milk Leche en polvo *LEH-cheh ehn POHL-voh*
DAIRY Dehydrated milk. Also known as dry milk, it can come from whole milk, non-fat milk, or buttermilk.

Prawn Gamba *GAHM-bah*
FISH & SHELLFISH A crustacean. A prawn can refer to either a species of the lobster family that looks like a small Maine lobster or a large shrimp that has sweet tasting meat. Although the terms are used interchangeably, prawns and shrimp, though of the same order, are different species.

Prepare Preparar *preh-pah-RAHR*
COOKING METHOD / TECHNIQUE To cook. To put together.

Preserve v. Preservar *preh-sehr-BAHR*
COOKING METHOD / TECHNIQUE To conserve food so that it can be kept for an extended period of time. Techniques include canning, smoking, salting, pickling, and dehydrating.

n. Marmelada / Confitura *mehr-meh-LAH-dah / kohn-fee-TOO-rah*
CONDIMENTS A thick, chunky spread of cooked fruit wherein lumps of fruit are left in tact. Sugar and pectin may be added to it.

Preserved lemons Limones en conserva *lee-MOH-nehs ehn kohn-SEHR-bah*
CONDIMENTS Lemons that are conserved in a salt and acid solution. Spices are often added to infuse flavor. Preserved lemons are common in Middle Eastern cuisine.

Pressure cooker Olla de presión *OH-yah deh preh-see-OHN*
EQUIPMENT A special pot with a sealed air-tight lid that regulates the internal pressure of the pot and does not allow steam or heat to escape. The build-up of steam and pressure inside the pot results in food cooked at a significantly higher temperature. This results in a substantial reduction of cooking time.

Prick Pinchar *peen-CHAHR*
COOKING METHOD / TECHNIQUE To create small holes in food. To slightly pierce.

Prickly pear Higo chumbo / Tuna *EE-goh CHOOM-boh / TOO-nah*
FRUIT & VEGETABLES The small, oval-shaped fruit of the cactus plant that grows off the cactus pad (nopal). Its prickly-textured skin is inedible and ranges in color from green to bright pink. Its flesh is slightly tart, sweet, and juicy. Prickly pear can be eaten raw or cooked.

Processed meat Fiambre *fee-AHM-breh*
MEAT Precooked or cured meats that are thinly sliced and served cold or at room temperature. Also known as cold cuts, they Include ham, turkey, roast beef, bologna, and salami.

Protein Proteína *proh-teh-EE-nah*
GENERAL A large molecule made up of amino acids that is essential to living cells. Protein provides energy to the body and is responsible for repairing cells. It is found predominantly in animal products but is also provided by plant sources.

Prune Ciruela pasa *see-roo-EH-lah PAH-sah*
FRUIT & VEGETABLES A dried plum. It has a very dark purple, wrinkled skin with a chewy texture. Its flesh has an intense sweetness.

Pudding Pudín / Budín *poo-DEEN / boo-DEEN*
BAKING & PASTRY A sweet or savory egg and milk–based custard. Pudding can be baked, steamed, or boiled.

Puff pastry Hojaldre *oh-HAHL-dreh*
BAKING & PASTRY Light, flaky pastry made from chilled layers of butter sandwiched between sheets of dough. The unleavened pastry rises by the steam let go by the butter and separates into many thin layers.

Pulp Pulpa *POOL-pah*
FRUIT & VEGETABLES The soft flesh of a fruit contained within a thin membrane. It contains the juice of the fruit.

Pulverize Pulverizar *pool-beh-ree-SAHR*
COOKING METHOD / TECHNIQUE To make into a powder by crushing, grinding, or pounding.

Pumpernickel Pan de centeno entero / Pan negro *pahn deh sehn-TEH-noh ehn-TEH-roh / pahn NEH-groh*
GRAINS & CEREALS A dark bread made with rye flour and a sourdough starter, which produces a slightly sour taste. Traditionally it was baked very slowly to achieve the

dark color and deep flavor, but now molasses is sometimes added to achieve the same results more quickly.

Pumpkin Calabaza *kah-lah-BAH-zah*
FRUIT & VEGETABLES A large, round, orange fruit that is a winter squash and member of the gourd family. Hard, inedible skin surrounds a sweet dense flesh that must be cooked before being eaten. A cluster of seeds is found within a membrane web in the center of the pumpkin and can be eaten when husked and roasted. Canned pumpkin puree is available year-round.

Pumpkin seeds Pepitas *peh-PEE-tahs*
HERBS & SPICES The small, green seeds of a pumpkin that have had their white husks removed. They have a nutty flavor and a crunchy texture. They are available with or without their husks as well as raw or roasted.

Punch Ponche *POHN-cheh*
BEVERAGE A fruit juice–based beverage made from a mixture of ingredients. It can be alcoholic or soft and is usually made in large quantities and served in a punch bowl. Chunks or slices of fresh fruit are often added as garnish.

Puree v. Hacer puré *ah-SEHR poo-REH*
COOKING METHOD / TECHNIQUE To grind food with a blender, food processor, or food mill until it achieves a smooth consistency.

n. Puré *poo-REH*
DESCRIPTOR Solid food that has been ground to a smooth consistency.

Q

Quail Codorniz *koh-dohr-NEES*
GAME A very small game bird averaging less than half a pound in weight. Its pale flesh has a marked flavor that is not as intense as that of a wild game bird, but is not as bland as that of a domesticated chicken.

Quail egg Huevo de codorniz *WEH-voh deh koh-dohr-NEES*
DAIRY A very small egg about one inch in diameter. Its shell is beige with brown spots. Its flavor is very similar to a chicken egg and it can be cooked and prepared in the same way.

Quart Quarto / Cuarto de galón *KWAHR-toh / KWAHR-toh deh gah-LOHN*
MEASUREMENTS A unit of measure for volume equivalent to 4 cups, 2 pints, or 32 fluid ounces.

Quince Membrillo *mehm-BREE-yoh*
FRUIT & VEGETABLES The yellow, pear-shaped fruit that grows on the quince tree. Its flavor is very tart and astringent and is therefore best when cooked so it mellows out. Due to its naturally high amount of pectin, quince is often used to make jam and preserves. It is often paired with Manchego cheese.

Quinoa Quinoa / Quinua *KEE-noh-ah / KEE-noo-ah*
GRAINS & CEREALS The seed of a leafy green vegetable although it is treated like a grain. Very high in protein, it is considered a complete protein since it contains all eight essential amino acids. Light brown in color when dried, it becomes translucent when cooked with a fluffy texture and nutty flavor. Quinoa was a staple in the ancient Incan diet.

R

Rabbit Conejo *koh-NEH-hoh*
GAME An animal whose flavor and flesh is similar to that of chicken and can be cooked and prepared in a similar manner.

Rack Estante *ehs-TAHN-teh*
EQUIPMENT A framework for holding an object or food item.

Radicchio Radicchio *rah-DEE-kee-oh*
FRUIT & VEGETABLES Red leaf chicory with white veins throughout its leaves. Used often in salads, it has a bitter flavor that mellows when cooked.

Radish Rábano *RAH-bah-noh*
FRUIT & VEGETABLES A root vegetable ranging in shape from round to elongated and in size from small (one-inch in diameter) to large (one and one-half feet in length). Its color can be white, red, purple, or black. Its flavor is peppery and its texture is crisp. It is most commonly served raw.

Rainbow trout Trucha arco iris *TROO-chah AHR-koh EE-rees*
FISH & SHELLFISH The most popular fish of the trout variety. Both farmed and wild, it is easily identified by a broad rainbow-looking band that runs along its side. Its flesh has a mild flavor. It makes spawning trips between fresh and salt water.

Raisin Pasa *PAH-sah*
FRUIT & VEGETABLES A dried grape that is dehydrated mechanically or by the sun. It is intensely sweet with a deep tart flavor and can be eaten raw or used in both sweet and sour recipes. It is available in a variety of sizes and colors—black, green, purple, and yellow.

Rambutan Rambután / Achotillo *rahm-boo-TAHN / ah-choh-TEE-yoh*
FRUIT & VEGETABLES A small, egg-shaped fruit with recognizable long and thin bristles protruding from its skin. Green when unripe, its skin turns a bright red when the fruit matures. The flesh is a translucent cream color that surrounds a single seed. Its flavor is slightly sweet and tart.

Ramekin Posuelo *poh-soo-EH-loh*
EQUIPMENT A small, ovenproof baking dish measuring about four inches in diameter and made of glazed ceramic. It is used for serving individual portions.

Ramen Ramen *RAH-mehn*
GRAINS & CEREALS A Japanese noodle dish served in a broth with pieces of meat and vegetables. Also an instant Asian-style noodle dish sold in plastic packages.

Rare Muy poco hecho *MOO-ee POH-koh EH-choh*
COOKING METHOD / TECHNIQUE The doneness of meat described by its internal temperature, color, and juiciness. The meat should be cold and red in the center and its temperature should reach 125°F-130°F.

Raspberry Frambuesa *frahm-boo-EH-sah*
FRUIT & VEGETABLES A member of the berry family. Very small in size (less than one inch in length) with a bumpy exterior texture, it is cone shaped with a hollow center and an opening on one end. It is traditionally a deep pink red but there are other color varieties—golden and black. Its flavor is sweet and tart.

Raspberry, golden Frambuesa dorada *frahm-boo-EH-sah doh-RAH-dah*
FRUIT & VEGETABLES One of the three main varieties of raspberry (the others are red and black). It is a delicate fruit with a sweet and slightly tart flavor.

Raspberry vinegar Vinagre de frambuesa *bee-NAH-greh deh frahm-boo-EH-sah*
CONDIMENTS Vinegar that has been infused with the flavor of raspberries or has been made with fermented raspberry juice.

Raw Crudo *KROO-doh*
DESCRIPTOR (1) Having not been exposed or treated with heat. (2) A food's natural state.

Red mullet Salmonete *sahl-moh-NEH-teh*
FISH & SHELLFISH A very small saltwater fish primarily found in the Mediterranean Sea. It has reddish-colored skin and a firm, lean flesh that is great for grilling or frying. Despite its name, it is a member of the goatfish family, not the mullet family.

Red pepper flakes Copos de pimiento rojo *KOH-pohs deh pee-mee-EHN-toh ROH-hoh*
HERBS & SPICES A combination of various red chile peppers that are dried and crushed. Because the seeds are included in the mix the flakes are hot and spicy.

Red snapper Pargo / Huachinango *PAHR-goh / wah-chee-NAHN-goh*
FISH & SHELLFISH A saltwater fish found in warm waters. The most popular fish in the snapper family, it gets its name from the red color in its skin and eyes, which comes from the high amounts of carotenoids in its diet. It has firm, white flesh that flakes when cooked.

Reduce Reducir *reh-doo-SEER*
COOKING METHOD / TECHNIQUE To concentrate the flavor and increase the viscosity of a liquid by boiling or simmering it until the water content is decreased through evaporation.

Reduction Reducción *reh-dook-see-OHN*

COOKING METHOD / TECHNIQUE The concentrated solution that results after a liquid is reduced.

Red wine vinegar Vinagre de vino tinto *bee-NAH-greh deh BEE-noh TEEN-toh*

CONDIMENTS A vinegar made from red wine. It is slightly less acidic than distilled white vinegar. Some producers age the vinegar in small wooden casks to deepen and develop its flavor.

Refresh Refrescar *reh-frehs-KAHR*

COOKING METHOD / TECHNIQUE (1) To restore coolness or freshness. (2) To place a food item under cold water to cool down or to stop the cooking process.

Refried beans Frijoles refritos *free-HOH-les reh-FREE-tohs*

DISH Cooked beans that have been mashed and fried in lard or other fat. A traditional dish in Mexican and Tex-Mex cuisine, it is typically made with pinto beans, but black or red beans can be used as well.

Refrigerator Nevera / Refrigerador / Heladera / Frigorífico / Camara frigorífica *neh-BEH-rah / reh-free-geh-rah-DOHR / eh-lah-DEH-rah / free-goh-REE-fee-koh / KAH-mah-rah free-goh-REE-fee-kah*

EQUIPMENT A large electric cooling appliance that keeps its contents at a constant temperature that is below room temperature. Typically shaped like a box, the thermally insulated appliance comes in different sizes and is often connected to a freezer.

Rehydrate Re-hidratar *reh-ee-drah-TAHR*

COOKING METHOD / TECHNIQUE (1) To restore water loss. (2) To add moisture to a dried item.

Relish Salsa condimentada *SAHL-sah kohn-dee-mehn-TAH-dah*

CONDIMENTS A sweet or savory condiment made from chopped fruit or vegetables that have been slowly cooked with added seasonings until it thickens.

Render Derretir *deh-rreh-TEER*

COOKING METHOD / TECHNIQUE To melt animal fat.

Renin Quimosina *kee-moh-SEE-nah*

GENERAL An enzyme used to curdle milk and make cheese. Obtained from the stomach of a young calf, it can be purchased in powdered or tablet form.

Reserve v. Reservar *reh-sehr-BAHR*

COOKING METHOD / TECHNIQUE To keep and save for future use.

n. Reserva *reh-SEHR-bah*

BEVERAGE A term given to a wine of a higher quality, or wine that has been held back and aged before being sold, or both. In some countries, this is regulated but in others it's not.

Rest Reposar *reh-poh-SAHR*

COOKING METHOD / TECHNIQUE To relax. To set aside and not move.

Restaurant Restaurante *rehs-tah-oo-RAHN-teh*
GENERAL A public establishment that prepares and serves food.

Rhubarb Ruibarbo *roo-ee-BAHR-boh*
FRUIT & VEGETABLES Plant with a reddish pink–colored stem and dark green leaves. Although technically a vegetable, it is treated like a fruit. The celerylike stems are the only edible part of the plant. Very tart in flavor, it is always cooked before being eaten and is always mixed with a considerable amount of sugar.

Rib Costilla *kohs-TEE-yah*
MEAT A cut of meat to which muscle and/or flesh is attached. A bone that protrudes from the vertebrae.

Ribbon Cinta *Seen-tah*
EQUIPMENT A strip of material used for tying or trimming.

Rice Arroz *ah-RROHS*
GRAINS & CEREALS The seeds of the rice plant that are processed and used as an edible cereal grain. The small kernels come in different sizes (long, medium, and short) and categories (white and brown) based on the rice variety and how much processing they have undergone. A staple in many cuisines, rice is high in starch, and must be cooked by boiling or steaming before eating. *See also* **Wild rice**.

Rice, Arborio Arroz arborio *ah-RROHS ahr-BOH-ree-oh*
GRAINS & CEREALS A short grain rice with a very high starch content. Named after the Italian town of Arborio, it is used to make risotto as its high starch content is helpful in creating a creamy risotto.

Rice, basmati Arroz basmati *ah-RROHS bahs-MAH-tee*
GRAINS & CEREALS A long grain rice that is grown on the foothills of the Himalayas. It is light textured, very fragrant, and is often used in Indian and Middle Eastern cuisine.

Rice, brown Arroz integral *ah-RROHS een-teh-GRAHL*
GRAINS & CEREALS Rice that contains the entire rice grain with the exception of the inedible husk. It is light brown in color and has a nutty flavor and chewy texture.

Rice, fried Arroz frito *ah-RROHS FREE-toh*
DISH A Chinese dish made with day-old rice stir-fried in a wok with other ingredients and seasonings such as eggs, vegetables, scallions, and soy sauce. Diced chicken, pork, or shrimp is often also added.

Rice, jasmine Arroz jazmín *ah-RROHS hahs-MEEN*
GRAINS & CEREALS Also known as fragrant Thai rice. A long grain rice with a nutty flavor and very fragrant aroma. Its texture is similar to that of Basmati rice.

Rice, long grain Arroz de grano largo *ah-RROHS deh GRAH-noh LAHR-goh*
GRAINS & CEREALS Rice that is four to five times as long as it is wide. It can be of the white or brown variety. Long grains separate easily after being cooked.

Rice, short grain Arroz de grano corto *ah-RROHS deh GRAH-noh KOHR-toh*
GRAINS & CEREALS Rice that is short, stubby, and almost round. It can be of the white or brown variety. It contains a high amount of starch.

Rice, sushi Arroz para sushi *ah-RROHS PAH-rah SOO-shee*
GRAINS & CEREALS A white, short grained, sticky rice with a high starch content. It is boiled or steamed and mixed with a mixture or rice vinegar, sugar, and salt before being used to form sushi. It is washed before it is cooked to remove excess starch.

Rice, white Arroz blanco *ah-RROHS BLAHN-koh*
GRAINS & CEREALS Rice that has had its husk, bran, and germ removed.

Rice bran Salvado de arroz *sahl-VAH-doh deh ah-RROHS*
GRAINS & CEREALS The outer layer of the rice grain. Rice bran is high in soluble fiber.

Rice cracker Galleta de arroz *gah-YEH-tah deh ah-RROHS*
GRAINS & CEREALS A thin cracker made from rice flour. It does not contain gluten.

Rice paper Papel de arroz *pah-PEHL deh ah-RROHS*
GRAINS & CEREALS Very thin, edible sheets made from white rice flour, tapioca, and water. The dried translucent sheets must be rehydrated in hot water to become pliable and workable. Used as a wrapper for meat and vegetables, they can be fried after they have been rehydrated.

Rice vermicelli Fideos muy finos de arroz *fee-DEH-ohs moo-EE FEE-nohs deh ah-RROS*
GRAINS & CEREALS Very thin and long noodle strands made from rice flour. They are also known as rice sticks.

Rice vinegar Vinagre de arroz *bee-NAH-greh deh ah-RROHS*
CONDIMENTS A vinegar made from fermented rice or rice wine. It is popular in Japanese, Chinese, and Korean cuisine.

Ring mold Molde circular *MOHL-deh seer-koo-LAHR*
EQUIPMENT A circular metal form about three inches tall and three to six inches wide. It does not have a top or bottom and is used to shape ingredients into a circle.

Rise Subir *soo-BEER*
COOKING METHOD / TECHNIQUE (1) To lift. (2) To reach a higher position.

Roasted red peppers Pimientos morrones *pee-mee-EHN-tohs moh-RROH-nes*
FRUIT & VEGETABLES Roasted red peppers that are skinned and seeded. They can be made fresh and are also available in jars or cans.

Roasting Asar / Asado *ah-SAHR / ah-SAH-doh*
COOKING METHOD / TECHNIQUE A dry cooking method that subjects food to heat in an oven or another heat source. It causes a browning reaction on the surface of the food resulting in the intensification of flavor.

Roasting pan Cazerola para asar *kah-seh-ROH-lah PAH-rah ah-SAHR*
EQUIPMENT A wide, shallow pan used to roast meats and/or vegetables. It may or may not have handles and is often fitted with a rack to lift the food off the bottom of the pan ensuring even air circulation.

Roasting rack Rejilla *reh-HEE-yah*
EQUIPMENT Fitted inside a roasting pan, a framework of bars that keeps ingredients off the surface of the pan.

Rock salt Sal mineral *sahl mee-neh-RAHL*
CONDIMENTS Unrefined salt sold in large chunks. The impurities left in the salt can cause it to take on pale hues of gray, blue, or pink.

Roe Huevas *WEH-vahs*
FISH & SHELLFISH Female fish eggs.

Roll v. Enrollar / Rollo *ehn-roh-YAHR / ROH-yoh*
COOKING METHOD / TECHNIQUE To cause something to take on a cylindrical shape.
n. Panecillo / Bolillo *pah-neh-SEE-yoh / boh-LEE-yoh*
GRAINS & CEREALS A small, round piece of bread. It is used as a side dish or for making sandwiches.

Rolled oats Copos de avena *KOH-pohs deh ah-BEH-nah*
GRAINS & CEREALS Whole oats that have been steamed and flattened under heavy rollers. They cook more quickly than whole oats and are used in baked goods and for breakfast cereal.

Rolling pin Rodillo *roh-DEE-yoh*
EQUIPMENT A handheld cylindrical-shaped kitchen tool that looks like a thick rod. Its main function is to flatten and stretch out dough, but it is also used to crush, pound, and shape ingredients. Traditionally made of wood, it also comes in silicone, marble, and plastic among other materials.

Roll out Extender *eks-tehn-DEHR*
COOKING METHOD / TECHNIQUE To flatten. To extend or straighten by applying force with a roller or rolling pin.

Roncal Roncal *rohn-KAHL*
DAIRY Spanish sheep's milk cheese. It is a firm cheese with a nutty and piquant flavor made in one of the seven villages in the Valle de Roncal in northern Spain.

Room temperature Temperatura ambiente *tehm-peh-rah-TOO-rah ahm-bee-EHN-teh*
GENERAL Ambient temperature. A comfortable dwelling temperature. For scientific purposes, it is calculated at 70°F.

Rosemary Romero *roh-MEH-roh*
HERBS & SPICES A woody herb with pine needle–shaped leaves that are very fragrant. Its strong flavor and aroma are described as lemony and woodsy.

Rosewater Agua de rosas *AH-gwah deh ROH-sahs*
CONDIMENTS A distillation of rose petals. It has a distinctive flavor and highly floral aroma that is used in recipes especially for baked goods.

Round fish Pescado redondo *pehs-KAH-doh reh-DOHN-doh*
FISH & SHELLFISH A round-bodied fish with eyes on both sides of the head. It has a backbone that runs along its upper body and fillets located on either side. Examples are cod, bass, trout, snapper, and salmon.

Royal icing Glaseado *glah-seh-AH-doh*
BAKING & PASTRY Icing or frosting made of powdered sugar, egg whites, and a drop of lemon juice. It hardens quickly into an opaque white frosting and is used often in cake and cookie decorations.

Rub v. Rozar *roh-SAHR*
COOKING METHOD / TECHNIQUE To massage or work a paste, marinade, or condiment onto an item.

n. Adobo seco *ah-DOH-boh SEH-koh*
CONDIMENTS A mixture of spices that is applied to and worked or massaged into a piece of meat, fish, or vegetable.

Rubber spatula Espátula de goma *ehs-PAH-too-lah deh GOH-mah*
EQUIPMENT A handheld kitchen tool. A spatula with a rubber head whose flexible nature makes it ideal for folding ingredients and mixing and scraping mixtures out of mixing bowls.

Rum Ron *rohn*
BEVERAGE A distilled beverage made from the fermentation of sugarcane by-products and then aged. There are four basic styles: light/white, gold/amber, añejo, and dark.

Rump Cadera *kah-DEH-rah*
MEAT The meat from the back or hind leg of an animal. It is also called round cut.

Rutabaga Rutabaga / Nabo sueco *roo-tah-BAH-gah / NAH-boh soo-EH-koh*
FRUIT & VEGETABLES A root vegetable that is a cross between the cabbage and turnip. Shaped like a wide and stubby turnip, it has a thin, beige skin and creamed-colored flesh. Similar to a carrot, it can be eaten raw or cooked. It is also known as Swede.

Rye Centeno *sehn-TEH-noh*
GRAINS & CEREALS A cereal grass whose grain is harvested and milled into flour. Low in gluten, it is a key ingredient in pumpernickel bread. Rye is also used for making whiskey.

ENGLISH-SPANISH R

S

Saccharin Sacarina *sah-kah-REE-nah*

CONDIMENTS An artificial sweetener that is noncaloric and three hundred times as sweet as sugar. It has a bitter aftertaste and is unstable when heated.

Saddle Silla *SEE-yah*

MEAT The connected two loins found on either side of the backbone. Resembling a saddle placed on top of an animal, it is often a cut of lamb, veal, or venison.

Safflower oil Aceite de cártamo *ah-SAY-teh deh KAR-tah-moh*

NUTS & OILS The oil that is pressed from the seeds of the safflower. Flavorless and colorless, it is the oil with the highest amount of polyunsaturated fat and does not solidify when chilled and as a result is a popular choice for salad dressings. It has a high smoke point, making it a good frying oil.

Saffron Azafrán *ah-sah-FRANH*

HERBS & SPICES A spice made from the dried yellow-orange stigmas of the purple crocus. Because each flower has only three stigmas and because they must be picked by hand, this spice is the world's most expensive spice by weight. It is used for its sweet, grassy flavor and yellow coloring.

Sage Salvia *SAHL-vee-ah*

HERBS & SPICES Light bluish green leaves with a fuzzy texture that are used as an herb. Its flavor is described as earthy, minty, and peppery, and sage is often paired with roasted meats.

Salad Ensalada *ehn-sah-LAH-dah*

FRUIT & VEGETABLES A mixture of raw or cooked food—meat, seafood, fruit, or vegetables—tossed with a moist dressing. A salad typically includes salad greens but does not have to.

Salad spinner Centrifugadora de ensalada / Escurridora de ensalada
sehn-tree-foo-gah-DOH-rah deh ehn-sah-LAH-dah / ehs-koo-ree-DOH-rah deh ehn-sah-LAH-dah

EQUIPMENT A kitchen tool that use centrifugal force to dry its contents, primarily salad greens. A plastic basket containing the food is placed inside a bowl. When the top is sealed, the basket spins and shoots out excess water, which collects in the bowl.

Salmon Salmón *sahl-MOHN*

FISH & SHELLFISH An anadromous fish (meaning it lives in salt water, but returns to spawn in the fresh water where it was born) that has a black, silvery skin and an orange pink–colored flesh. It can be purchased fresh, canned, and smoked.

Salmonella Salmonella *sahl-moh-NEH-lah*

GENERAL A bacterial infection that can be transmitted to the human body through foods such as eggs, poultry, or meat. Other foods can pass along the bacteria via cross contamination.

Salmon roe **Huevas de salmón** *WEH-vahs deh sahl-MOHN*
FISH & SHELLFISH The eggs from a female salmon. Large, round, and a glistening orange in color with a light texture, they explode in your mouth.

Salsify **Salsify** *SAHL-see-fee*
FRUIT & VEGETABLES The root vegetable of the salsify plant. Very long and slender, it has a rough, thin skin that is peeled before cooking. The skin's color is dependent on the variety of salsify and can be pale yellow, gray, or black. Salsify has a faint briny flavor and is sometimes referred to as oyster plant.

Salt **Sal** *sahl*
HERBS & SPICES A dietary mineral made up of sodium chloride. Extracted from salt mines or the sea, it is a solid crystal that can take on a tinge of color (pink, white, gray) as a result of its impurities. It is used both as a seasoning to enhance the flavor of food and as an important preservative.

Salt, sea **Sal marina** *sahl mah-REE-nah*
CONDIMENTS The salt obtained by the evaporation of sea water. In addition to sodium chloride, it has a variety of minerals that give it a unique taste.

Salt cod **Bacalao salado** *bah-kah-LAH-oh sah-LAH-doh*
FISH & SHELLFISH Cod that has been dried and salted. It is sold whole or in portions.

Salty **Salado** *sah-LAH-doh*
DESCRIPTOR Tasting of salt. One of the four basic tastes.

Sandwich **Sándwich / Bocadillo** *SAHN-weech / boh-kah-DEE-yoh*
GENERAL A dish made up of a filling held between two pieces of bread.

Sapodilla **Chicozapote** *chee-koh-sah-POH-teh*
FRUIT & VEGETABLES The small, egg-shaped fruit (two to four inches in diameter) that grows on the sapodilla tree whose bark produces a white gum called chicle, the base for chewing gum. Its skin is brown and scruffy and its flesh is pale beige. Sweet and juicy with a couple of seeds in its center, the fruit does not ripen until picked from the tree.

Sapote **Sapote** *sah-POH-teh*
FRUIT & VEGETABLES The general term for a very soft and ripe fruit. There are three unrelated fruit with sapote as part of their names: mamey sapote, black sapote, and white sapote.

Sardines **Sardinas** *sahr-DEE-nahs*
FISH & SHELLFISH A term that broadly describes small, soft-boned, saltwater fish such as herring and pilchard. Iridescent and silver-skinned, they swim in large schools. These fatty fish and are best grilled or broiled and they are often found canned.

Sashimi **Sashimi** *sah-SHEE-mee*
FISH & SHELLFISH Sliced, fresh raw fish. Sashimi is served accompanied by pickled radish and ginger and a soy dipping sauce.

Saturated fat Grasa saturada *GRAH-sah sah-too-RAH-dah*
GENERAL A triglyceride primarily containing saturated fatty acids, which are hydrocarbon chains that have no double bonds and are filled to capacity with carbon atoms, making them very stable. Found primarily in animal fats, they are solid at room temperature.

Sauce Salsa *SAHL-sah*
CONDIMENTS Flavored liquid used to accompany a food. A sauce can be very thin or very thick, sweet or savory, smooth or chunky.

Saucepan Olla *OH-yah*
EQUIPMENT A round cooking vessel with one long or two short handles and a tight-fitting lid. Saucepans come in sizes ranging from one-half quart to four quarts and can be deep or shallow. They are made out of stainless steel, aluminum, and copper among other materials.

Sauerkraut Col fermentada *kohl fehr-mehn-TAH-dah*
CONDIMENTS A dish made from shredded cabbage fermented in brine.

Sausage Salchicha *sahl-CHEE-chah*
MEAT Ground meat mixed with fat, spices, and seasoning and typically stuffed inside a casing. It can be left fresh, or cured, smoked, or dried to develop its flavor and extend its shelf life.

Sauté Saltear / Salteado *sahl-teh-AHR / sahl-teh-AH-doh*
COOKING METHOD / TECHNIQUE To cook food quickly with little fat in a sauté or frying pan. The food is constantly moved around.

Sauté pan Sartén *sahr-TEHN*
EQUIPMENT A wide, shallow pan with straight or sometimes slightly sloping sides. It has a long handle and comes in a variety of sizes and materials.

Savory Ajedrea *ah-heh-DREH-ah*
HERBS & SPICES A strong-flavored herb that tastes like a blend of thyme, mint, and rosemary. It is similar in appearance to rosemary but its leaves are a bit more delicate.

Scad Jurel *hoo-REHL*
FISH & SHELLFISH A saltwater fish that grows to be about one foot in length. Belonging to the same family as pompanos and jack mackerels, it has very large eyes and silver-colored skin.

Scald Escaldar *ehs-kahl-DAHR*
COOKING METHOD / TECHNIQUE To heat milk just below boiling (about 180°F). Before pasteurization, scalding was done to destroy damaging bacteria and enzymes found in the milk. Currently it is done to raise the temperature of milk and/or infuse a flavor such as vanilla bean or cinnamon stick. It is another word for blanch.

Scales Pesos *PEH-sohs*
EQUIPMENT Devices used to measure the weight of an object.

Escamas *ehs-KAH-mahs*
FISH & SHELLFISH   Small, hard plates that grow on the skin of fish and provide protection.

Scallion Cebolleta *seh-boh-YEH-tah*
FRUIT & VEGETABLES   A member of the onion family that lacks a fully developed bulb and has a mild onion flavor. It has a stronger-flavored white base close to the roots and milder-tasting green tops. Long and straight, the entire vegetable can be eaten raw or cooked. It is also known as spring onion or green onion.

Scallop Vieira *bee-EH-rah*
FISH & SHELLFISH   A marine bivalve mollusk. Most scallops are free living and swim by opening and closing their very ornate fan-shaped shells. The abductor muscle responsible for the shell's movement is what is eaten. Two varieties exist: the smaller and sweeter bay scallop and the larger sea scallop. The shells are often used as serving dishes.

Score Marcar *mahr-KAHR*
COOKING METHOD / TECHNIQUE   To make small shallow gashes in a food or ingredient.

Scotch Scotch *skohch*
BEVERAGE   Barley-based whiskey made in Scotland and that conforms to strict Scottish standards.

Scramble Revolver *reh-bohl-BEHR*
COOKING METHOD / TECHNIQUE   To beat, mix, or stir vigorously.

Scraper Rasqueta *rahs-KEH-tah*
EQUIPMENT   A piece of curved plastic or rubber. It is used to cleanly scrape off batter or dough from a bowl or work area.

Scrubbing brush Cepillo de fregar *seh-PEE-yoh deh freh-GAHR*
EQUIPMENT   A brush made with short, stiff bristles that are rubbed against dirty surfaces for cleaning.

Sea bream Sargo *SAHR-goh*
FISH & SHELLFISH   A small, saltwater fish that lives near the coast and has an average weight of four pounds. It has a round-shaped body and silver-colored skin. It feeds off crustaceans and mollusks which results in its having very flavorful meat.

Sea cucumber Cohombro de mar *koh-OHM-broh deh mahr*
FISH & SHELLFISH   A long-bodied marine animal that lives on the ocean floor. Highly gelatinous, it is often used in soups. Typically found dried, it must be soaked for a day until it doubles in size.

Seafood Mariscos *mah-REES-kohs*
FISH & SHELLFISH   Any fish, shellfish, or marine life eaten as food.

Seal Sellar *seh-YAHR*
COOKING METHOD / TECHNIQUE To make tight. To prevent something from entering or escaping by securely closing its opening.

Sear Sellar / Quemar *seh-YAHR / keh-MAHR*
COOKING METHOD / TECHNIQUE A process that browns meat quickly over high heat and with a small amount of fat. This provides the meat with a golden brown color and crust, and a deep flavor.

Season Sazonar / Condimentar *sah-soh-NAHR / kohn-dee-mehn-TAHR*
COOKING METHOD / TECHNIQUE To enhance the flavor of food by adding a salt or spice.

Seasoning Sazón *sah-SOHN*
CONDIMENTS The salt or spice added to a food to enhance its flavor.

Sea urchin Erizo *eh-REE-soh*
FISH & SHELLFISH A marine animal found in a small, round shell with hard protruding prickly spines. Its orange-colored roe is considered a delicacy and is typically eaten right out of the shell.

Seaweed Algas marinas *AHL-gahs mah-REE-nahs*
FRUIT & VEGETABLES Marine algae. This is used as food primarily in Asian cuisine and is typically found in dried form.

Seedless Sin pepitas / Sin semillas *seen peh-PEE-tahs / seen seh-MEE-yahs*
DESCRIPTOR Without seeds.

Seeds Semillas *seh-MEE-yahs*
HERBS & SPICES Small embryonic plants enclosed in a hard covering. They are also referred to as kernels.

Segment v. Segmentar *sehg-mehn-TAHR*
COOKING METHOD / TECHNIQUE To divide or cut into pieces (segments).

n. Segmento *sehg-MEHN-toh*
The membrane-enclosed sections found inside a citrus fruit.

Semolina Sémola *SEH-moh-lah*
GRAINS & CEREALS Semolina can specifically refer to a coarsely ground hard durum wheat used to make pasta, or a coarsely ground soft wheat used to make breakfast cereal.

Sesame oil Aceite de sésamo / Aceite de ajonjolí *ah-SAY-teh deh SEH-sah-moh / ah-SAY-teh deh ah-hohn-ho-LEE*
NUTS & OILS The oil pressed from sesame seeds. There are two varieties: the cold-pressed oil, which is almost colorless and has a mild nutty flavor, and the toasted oil, which is made from toasted sesame seeds and has a dark, golden brown color and much stronger flavor.

Sesame seed Semilla de sésamo / Ajonjolí *seh-MEE-yah deh SEH-sah-moh / ah-hohn-ho-LEE*

HERBS & SPICES The oil-rich seed of the sesame plant. The small, black- or cream-colored seeds are used whole in dishes and impart a nutty flavor. They are often baked onto breads, bagels, and rolls. Sesame seeds can be ground into a paste called tahini.

Set Cuajar *kwah-HAHR*

COOKING METHOD / TECHNIQUE To become firm. A term often used with custards, eggs, and cheese.

Shallot Escalonia / Chalota *ehs-kah-LOH-nee-ah / chah-LOH-tah*

FRUIT & VEGETABLES A relative of the onion that looks more like a garlic. Its small bulb is made up of individual segments covered entirely by a thin, papery skin. Its flesh is white with a tinge of pink or gray, and it has a sweet mild onion-like flavor.

Shank Morcillo *mohr-SEE-yoh*

MEAT The meat from the lower part of the leg. Typically from beef, veal, lamb, or pork, it is very flavorful but also very tough due to the high amount of connective tissue it contains. It must be cooked over low heat for a long time to be tenderized.

Shape Formar *fohr-MAHR*

COOKING METHOD / TECHNIQUE (1) To give form to. (2) To make something fit a certain way.

Shark Tiburón *tee-boo-ROHN*

FISH & SHELLFISH A very large, saltwater fish with dense, low-fat meat. Sold in steaks or chunks, shark must be soaked in acidulated water before being cooked to remove its natural ammonia odor.

Shaving Viruta *bee-ROO-tah*

COOKING METHOD / TECHNIQUE A very thin, flat slice.

Sheet Lámina *LAH-mee-nah*

GENERAL A thin, expansive, and unbroken surface area of a material.

Shell Caparazón / Concha *kah-pah-rah-SOHN / KOHN-cha*

FISH & SHELLFISH The hard outer covering of many animals. For certain animals it is their skeletal system.

Shellfish Marisco / Crustaceo / Molusco *mah-REES-koh / kroos-tah-SEH-oh / moh-LOOS-koh*

FISH & SHELLFISH An aquatic animal that has a shell. The two main types of shellfish are crustaceans and mollusks.

Sherry Vino de jerez *BEE-noh deh geh-REHS*

BEVERAGE A wine made from white grapes that has been fortified with brandy after fermentation. It is produced in a variety of styles, most notably dry and light, colored and sweet, and dark. Protected by a designation of origin, all sherries must be produced in an area known as the sherry triangle located in the south of Spain.

Sherry vinegar Vinagre de jerez *bee-NAH-greh deh geh-REHS*
CONDIMENTS The wine vinegar made from sherry and aged in oak barrels. It is amber colored with a deep complex flavor.

Shock Asustar *ah-soos-TAHR*
COOKING METHOD / TECHNIQUE To stop the cooking of a food by plunging it in an ice bath.

Shortening Grasa / Aceite solidificado *GRAH-sah / ah-seh-EE-teh soh-lee-dee-fee-KAH-doh*
GENERAL Broadly means any cooking fat that is solid at room temperature.

Shot Chupito / Dedal *choo-PEE-toh / deh-DAHL*
BEVERAGE A small drink of liquor. A shot typically contains one fluid ounce but there is no standard size.

Shoulder Paleta *pah-LEH-tah*
MEAT The cut of meat taken from the front leg, and depending on the animal, it can run from the neck down to the leg. It is very flavorful but very tough due to the high amount of connective tissue present.

Shred v. Triturar / Hacer tiras *tree-too-RAHR / ah-SEHR TEE-rahs*
COOKING METHOD / TECHNIQUE To tear into thin, narrow strips.

n. Tira *TEE-rah*
DESCRIPTOR A thin narrow strip.

Shrimp Camarón *kah-mah-ROHN*
FISH & SHELLFISH Crustaceans found in both fresh and salt water. They come in a variety of colors (pink, light brown, and gray) and sizes. They live on the water's floor and feed by filtering food matter. Their cooked flesh is meaty, sweet, and succulent. There are two main classifications: larger warm-water shrimp and smaller cold-water shrimp. Though the terms prawns and shrimp are used interchangeably, and the crustaceans are of the same order, they are different species.

Shrimp paste Pasta de camarones *PAHS-tah deh kah-mah-ROH-nehs*
CONDIMENTS Pink-colored paste made from ground-up fermented shrimp. Pungent in flavor and odor, it is a condiment used in many Asian recipes.

Shuck Descascarar / Descortezar *dehs-kahs-kah-RAHR / dehs-kohr-teh-SAHR*
COOKING METHOD / TECHNIQUE (1) To remove shellfish from their shell. (2) To peel off the husks from corn.

Sieve Criba / Cedazo / Tamiz *KREE-bah / seh-DAH-soh / tah-MEES*
EQUIPMENT A kitchen tool made with a mesh or net used to strain particles or liquid. Sieves come in various shapes, sizes, and mesh densities.

Sift Tamizar / Cerner *tah-mee-SAHR / sehr-NEHR*
COOKING METHOD / TECHNIQUE To separate dry ingredients by passing food through a strainer or mesh. Sifting is done to incorporate air and help lighten ingredients.

Sifter Cernedor *sehr-neh-DOHR*
EQUIPMENT A handheld kitchen tool used for sifting.

Simmer Cocer a fuego lento *koh-SEHR ah foo-EH-goh LEHN-toh*
COOKING METHOD / TECHNIQUE To cook food gently in a liquid that is heated to just below the boiling point (about 185°F). In a simmer, small bubbles will just begin to rise and break the surface.

Simple syrup Almíbar *ahl-MEE-bahr*
BAKING & PASTRY A solution of sugar and water that is heated until the sugar melts. In an irreversible process that removes the graininess of the sugar crystals, simple syrup can be made in various densities to meet different needs (thin, medium, and heavy). The more sugar that is used, the more viscous the syrup. It is also known as sugar syrup.

Sink Fregadero *freh-gah-DEH-roh*
EQUIPMENT A basin with running water used for washing hands and objects.

Skate Raya *RAH-yah*
FISH & SHELLFISH A kite-shaped flat fish with winglike fins. Mild and sweet tasting, the thin fins are the edible portion of a skate. They are often soaked in acidulated water before being cooked to get rid of a naturally occurring ammonia odor. A skate is also known as a ray.

Skewer Brocheta / Palillo / Pincho *broh-CHE-tah / pah-LEE-yoh / PEEN-cho*
EQUIPMENT A long, thin wooden or metal stick with a pointed end used to pierce food. Food can be cooked on a skewer or it can be used as a serving tool.

Skillet Sartén *sahr-TEHN*
EQUIPMENT Another name for a frying pan. *See* **Frying pan**.

Skim v. Espumar / Quitar espuma *ehs-poo-MAHR / kee-TAHR ehs-POO-mah*
COOKING METHOD / TECHNIQUE To remove foam from the surface.

v. Desnatar / Quitar nata *dehs-nah-TAHR / kee-TAHR NAH-tah*
COOKING METHOD / TECHNIQUE To remove cream from milk.

Skim milk Leche desnatada *LEH-cheh dehs-nah-TAH-dah*
DAIRY Non-fat milk. It is milk that has had its cream (fat) removed.

Skimming spoon Espumadera *ehs-poo-mah-DEH-rah*
EQUIPMENT A kitchen utensil used to remove an item from the surface of a liquid. It is constructed of a spoon whose bowl has mesh netting.

Skin v. Despellejar / Pelar *dehs-peh-yeh-HAHR / peh-LAHR*
COOKING METHOD / TECHNIQUE To peel or strip the skin or outer layer of an ingredient.

n. Piel *pee-EHL*
GENERAL An outer layer or surface. Skin is a naturally occurring protective covering. In plants, it is known as the peel. In animals, it is a source of fat and flavor.

Slice Rebanada / Rodaja / Trozo / Porción *reh-bah-NAH-dah / roh-DAH-hah / TROH-soh / pohr-see-OHN*
  COOKING METHOD / TECHNIQUE (1) A flat cut. A slice can be thick or thin. (2) A slit.

Slimy Baboso *bah-BOH-soh*
  DESCRIPTOR Description of something having a thick, viscous substance (slime) on it.

Slotted spoon Cuchara calada / Cuchara con ranuras *koo-CHA-rah kah-LAH-dah / koo-CHA-rah kohn rah-NOO-rahs*
  EQUIPMENT A spoon with holes or slits in its bowl. It lifts ingredients while allowing liquid to pass or drip through.

Slow cook Cocinar a fuego lento *koh-see-NAHR ah foo-EH-goh LEHN-toh*
  COOKING METHOD / TECHNIQUE To cook food with low and steady moist heat.

Slow Food Comida Lenta *koh-MEE-dah LEHN-tah*
  GENERAL A movement started by Italian journalist Carlo Petrini that promotes the preservation of culture and local cuisine. It began as a response to the opening of the fast-food chain, McDonalds, in Rome.

Slurry Lodo *LOH-doh*
  COOKING METHOD / TECHNIQUE A paste made by mixing a dry starch (flour, corn-starch) with a room-temperature liquid in order to dissolve the starch before adding it to a hot liquid. This is done to prevent the starch from clumping. The mixture is used as a thickener and must be cooked for a few minutes after it has been added.

Smelt Eperlano *eh-pehr-LAH-noh*
  FISH & SHELLFISH A very small (average length seven-inch) fish that lives in salt water but travels to fresh water to spawn (breed). It has a shimmering silver skin with a rich and oily flesh. It is sold and eaten whole.

Smoke Humo *OO-moh*
  GENERAL A vapor emitted when a material combusts.

Ahumar / Ahumado *ah-oo-MAH-doh / ah-oo-MAHR*
  COOKING METHOD / TECHNIQUE The process of flavoring, cooking, or curing a food by exposing it to smoke generated by the burning of a specific wood and/or herbs.

Smoked fish Pescado ahumado *pehs-KAH-doh ah-oo-MAH-doh*
  FISH & SHELLFISH Fresh fish that has been cured and flavored by smoke. Salmon, trout, and white fish are popular for smoking.

Smoked paprika Pimentón ahumado *pee-mehn-TOHN ah-oo-MAH-doh*
  HERBS & SPICES A spice made by slowly drying red peppers over an oak-burning fire for several weeks, resulting in a sweet and smoky flavor. It comes in three varieties: sweet (*dulce*), bittersweet (*agridulce*), and hot (*picante*). Very popular in Spanish cuisine. It is also referred to as pimentón de la Vera, which makes reference to the area in Spain where it is made.

Smoked salmon **Salmón ahumado** *sahl-MOHN ah-oo-MAH-doh*
FISH & SHELLFISH Fresh salmon that has been cured and flavored by smoke.

Smoked trout **Trucha ahumada** *TROO-chah ah-oo-MAH-dah*
FISH & SHELLFISH Fresh trout that has been cured and flavored by smoke.

Smoke point **Punto de inflamación** *POON-toh deh een-flah-mah-see-OHN*
GENERAL The temperature at which a heated fat begins to deteriorate. Once the temperature is reached, the fat will begin to emit smoke. This results in the fat's eventually imparting an unpleasant taste and odor. The higher a fat's smoke point, the better suited it is for frying.

Snack **Tentempié / Botana / Merienda** *tehn-tehm-pee-EH / boh-TAH-nah / meh-ree-EHN-dah*
(1) A canapé or hors d'oeuvre. A small bite offered before a meal. (2) An informal meal or a small amount of food eaten in between meals.

Snail **Caracol** *kah-rah-KOHL*
MEAT A land or water mollusk that has a spiral shell. It has been eaten for thousands of years and is considered a delicacy.

Snapper **Pargo** *PAHR-goh*
FISH & SHELLFISH The common name for the *lutjanidae* family of saltwater fish of which there are about 250 species. Found in tropical and subtropical regions of the ocean, snappers are known for their teeth and snapping mouth that is compared to that of an alligator in quickness.

Snifter **Copita** *koh-PEE-tah*
EQUIPMENT A short-stemmed, wide-bottomed glass used to drink brandy. Its narrow top traps the brandy's aroma in the glass.

Snow pea **Tirabeque** *tee-rah-BEH-keh*
FRUIT & VEGETABLES A flat, green-colored, fresh bean with an edible pod. The thin bean is picked when immature and contains very small peas.

Soak **Empapar / Remojar / Poner en remojo** *ehm-pah-PAHR / reh-moh-HAHR / poh-NEHR ehn reh-MOH-hoh*
COOKING METHOD / TECHNIQUE (1) To immerse in a liquid. (2) To cause something to be wet.

Soda water **Agua de soda** *AH-gwah deh SOH-dah*
BEVERAGE Carbonated water that is effervescent and fizzy. Depending on bottler, it may contain minerals producing a distinct flavor. It is also known as club soda or seltzer water.

Soft-ball stage **(Almibar) a punto de perla** *(ahl-MEE-bahr) ah POON-toh deh PEHR-lah*
BAKING & PASTRY The temperature at which a small amount of sugar syrup forms soft pliable balls when immersed in cold water (234°F–240°F/112°C–116°C).

Soft-crack stage (Almibar) a punto de escarchado *(ahl-MEE-bahr) a POON-toh deh ehs-kahr-CHAH-doh*
BAKING & PASTRY The temperature at which a small amount of sugar syrup separates into hard but flexible threads when immersed in cold water (270°F–290°F/ 132°C–143°C).

Soft drink Refresco *reh-FREHS-koh*
BEVERAGE A broad term for a nonalcoholic beverage.

Soften Ablandar *ah-blahn-DAHR*
COOKING METHOD / TECHNIQUE To make less hard.

Sole Lenguado *lehn-GWAH-doh*
FISH & SHELLFISH A flat fish that dwells in the bottom of the ocean and averages about one foot in length. Its skin is brown gray in color. It has a mild buttery flavor and firm texture. It is known as common or Dover sole and is very popular in Europe.

Sorbet Sorbete *sohr-BEH-teh*
BAKING & PASTRY A frozen dessert made with a water-based mixture flavored with a sweetened fruit puree, chocolate, or wine. It does not contain dairy products.

Sorrel Acedera *ah-seh-DEH-rah*
HERBS & SPICES A green leaf that is used as both a vegetable and an herb. The leaves resemble spinach. When young, the tart leaves are added to salads or cooked like a leafy green. Mature sorrel is more acidic and has a stronger flavor and tends to be used as an herb.

Soufflé dish Cacerola de suflé *kah-seh-ROH-lah deh soo-FLEH*
EQUIPMENT A special round, ovenproof ramekin that has a flat bottom and tall straight sides. Traditionally the exterior is fluted. Soufflé dishes come in various sizes.

Soup Sopa *SOH-pah*
GENERAL A liquid food made by cooking meat and/or vegetables in a water-based solution. Soup can be smooth or chunky, thick or thin.

Sour Agrio / Cortado *AH-gree-oh / kohr-TAH-doh*
DESCRIPTOR One of the four basic tastes. It is described as a sharp, tart taste.

Sour cream Crema agria / Nata agria *KREH-mah AH-gree-ah / NAH-tah AH-gree-ah*
DAIRY A dairy product made by adding a lactic acid–producing bacteria and a small amount of rennet to cream. The added bacteria thickens the cream and gives it a tart and sour taste.

Sourdough Masa agria *MAH-sah AH-gree-ah*
BAKING & PASTRY A yeast starter made with flour, water, sugar, yeast, and a special bacteria called lactobacilli. This bacterial culture produces lactic and acetic acid giv-

ing the starter a distinctive sour and tart flavor. Sourdough bread is leavened with this yeast starter.

Sous vide *Al vacío* *ahl bah-SEE-oh*

COOKING METHOD / TECHNIQUE A cooking technique that seals food in a vacuum-packed bag and cooks it for an extended period of time at a controlled temperature.

Soybean *Soja / Soya* *SOH-hah / SOH-yah*

FRUIT & VEGETABLES A legume whose pod is inedible. A soybean contains all essential amino acids making it a great source of protein. Eaten fresh, it has a nutty and buttery taste and meaty texture. Immature soybeans are steamed and served as edamame. Soybeans are a source for many foods including soy sauce, soy milk, tofu, and soybean oil.

Soybean oil *Aceite de soya / Aceite de soja* *ah-SAY-teh deh SOH-yah / ah-SAY-teh deh SOH-hah*

NUTS & OILS The oil pressed from soybeans. Light yellow in color, it is often labeled "vegetable oil." It is used abundantly in commercially made food products from salad dressings to mayonnaise. It is often hydrogenated and turned into margarine or shortening. It has a high smoke point, making it a great choice for frying.

Soy milk *Leche de soya* *LEH-cheh deh SOH-yah*

BEVERAGE A nondairy beverage made from cooked, ground soybeans that is milky in texture. It is naturally high in protein and low in fat.

Soy sauce *Salsa de soya* *SAHL-sah deh SOH-yah*

CONDIMENTS A dark brown condiment made from fermented soybeans, water, salt, and wheat or barley. It is salty and pungent in flavor.

Spaghetti *Espaguetis* *ehs-pah-GEH-tees*

GRAINS & CEREALS Long, thin, round pasta made from wheat that is Italian in origin.

Spatula *Espátula* *ehs-PAH-too-lah*

EQUIPMENT A handheld kitchen utensil that serves as a multipurpose tool. The material it is made with (rubber, metal, wood, plastic) determines its function, which includes scraping bowls, turning fish, folding ingredients, and stirring mixtures.

Spice *Especia* *ehs-PEH-see-ah*

HERBS & SPICES The dried bark, bud, fruit, root, stem, or seed used for flavoring. Spices are available whole or ground.

Spicy *Picante* *pee-KAHN-teh*

DESCRIPTOR Hot, producing a burning sensation in the mouth.

Spider *Espumadera oriental* *ehs-poo-mah-DEH-rah oh-ree-ehn-TAHL*

EQUIPMENT A type of strainer or skimmer used in Asian kitchens. A long handle is attached to the wide bowl of a spoon that is shallow and has a hollow netted texture that resembles a spiderweb.

Spinach Espinaca *ehs-pee-NAH-kah*
FRUIT & VEGETABLES   A delicate leafy green that can be eaten raw or cooked. Oxalic acid present in the leaves produces a slight bitter taste and leaves the mouth with a powdery, coated sensation. Depending on the variety the dark green leaves can be curled at the edges and take on a range of shapes.

Sponge Esponja *ehs-POHN-hah*
EQUIPMENT   A soft, porous spongy material that absorbs liquid and is used for washing and cleaning.

Spoon Cuchara *koo-CHA-rah*
EQUIPMENT   A utensil. A small, round bowl with a handle attached, used for eating and serving.

Springform cake pan Molde desmontable *MOHL-deh dehs-mohn-TAH-bleh*
EQUIPMENT   A round baking pan whose sides and bottom can be detached. A spring or latch mechanism secures or unmolds the straight edges of the pan from the flat bottom. It is used with tarts and cakes that would be difficult to remove from a traditional pan. Springform pans are available in various sizes.

Sprout Brote *BROH-teh*
FRUIT & VEGETABLES   A baby shoot, a new plant growth. It has a tender texture and mild flavor.

Squab Paloma torcaz *pah-LOH-mah tohr-KAHS*
GAME   A young, usually about four weeks old, domesticated pigeon that has never flown. Its dark red–colored flesh is very tender. Most squabs weigh less than one pound.

Squash Calabaza *kah-lah-BAH-zah*
FRUIT & VEGETABLES   A fruit from the gourd family. There are two main varieties: summer and winter squash. A summer squash has thin, edible skin and seeds with a flesh that is sweet with a high water content. A winter squash has a hard, thick, inedible skin and seeds with a dense but sweet flesh that must be cooked before eating. *See also* **Pumpkin**.

Squash, acorn Calabaza bellota *kah-lah-BAH-zah beh-YOH-tah*
FRUIT & VEGETABLES   A round winter squash with a dark green skin and orange flesh. All winter squashes have hard, thick, inedible skin and seeds that can be removed before or after being cooked.

Squash, butternut Calabaza almizclera *kah-lah-BAH-zah ahl-mees-KLEH-rah*
FRUIT & VEGETABLES   A peanut-shaped winter squash that has pale beige skin and bright orange flesh. It has an average weight of two and a half pounds.

Squash, pattypan Calabaza bonetera *kah-lah-BAH-zah boh-neh-TEH-rah*
FRUIT & VEGETABLES   A small, flat, round summer squash. Its thin and edible skin can be yellow, green, or white. It is cooked and treated the same way as other summer squash.

Squash, spaghetti Calabaza de espaguetti *kah-lah-BAH-zah deh eh-spah-GEH-tee*

FRUIT & VEGETABLES An oblong winter squash measuring about one foot in length with a hard skin that is yellow, orange, or white with green stripes. Its yellow flesh must be cooked to be eaten and separates easily into thin strands that resemble spaghetti pasta.

Squash, yellow Calabacín amarillo *kah-lah-bah-SEEN ah-mah-REE-yoh*

FRUIT & VEGETABLES A variety of summer squash. It can be identified by its crook neck and soft, edible, yellow skin. Its white flesh contains small edible seeds and turns translucent when cooked.

Squash blossoms Flores de calabaza *FLOH-rehs deh kah-lah-BAH-sah*

FRUIT & VEGETABLES The flowers from a summer or winter squash. Yellow or orange in color, they taste vaguely like squash. Often stuffed and fried, they can also be sautéed or left raw and used in a salad or as a garnish.

Squid Calamar / Chipirón *kah-lah-MAHR / chee-pee-ROHN*

FISH & SHELLFISH A marine animal with ten legs. After the insides have been eviscerated, the body can be stuffed or sliced into rings and then cooked. The white-colored flesh is sweet but becomes tough and chewy if not cooked properly. The ink sac inside is used as a coloring and flavoring in a number of recipes.

Squid ink Tinta de calamar *TEEN-tah deh kah-lah-MAHR*

FISH & SHELLFISH The dark purple black ink found inside a sac in the squid. It is used for coloring and flavoring.

Stabilizer Estabilizante *ehs-tah-bee-lee-SAHN-teh*

GENERAL An additive used to keep solutions emulsified and in solution. It prevents ingredients from separating.

Stainless steel Acero inoxidable *ah-SEH-roh een-ohks-ee-DAH-bleh*

EQUIPMENT A steel metal that does not stain or rust as easily as regular steel.

Star anise Anis estrellado *an-NEES ehs-treh-YAH-doh*

HERBS & SPICES A dried star-shaped spice that comes from an evergreen tree grown in China and Japan. It has a licorice / aniselike flavor that is used to flavor sweet and savory dishes as well as to infuse tea. Star anise is available in whole or ground form.

Starch Almidón *ahl-mee-DOHN*

GRAINS & CEREALS A complex carbohydrate (polysaccharide) found in plant products.

Star fruit Carambola / Fruta estrella *kah-rahm-BOH-lah / FROO-tah ehs-TREH-yah*

FRUIT & VEGETABLES A tropical fruit with a waxy skin that has five prominent protrusions. When sliced crosswise it takes the shape of a star, which is why it is referred to as star fruit. When ripe, it has a yellow orange skin and flesh that contains a small dark seed. It is juicy with a refreshingly tart flavor. *See also* **Carambola**.

Steam v. Cocinar al vapor *koh-see-NAHR ahl bah-POHR*
COOKING METHOD / TECHNIQUE To cook with the heat produced by converting water to steam.

n. Vapor *bah-POHR*
GENERAL Water vapor.

Steamer Olla para cocinar al vapor / Vaporera *OH-yah PAH-rah koh-see-NAHR ahl bah-POHR / bah-poh-REH-rah*
EQUIPMENT A device or cooking vessel used to create steam and cook food in it.

Stem Rama *RAH-mah*
HERBS & SPICES The part of the plant that connects the roots and the leaves.

Stew v. Guisar *gee-SAHR*
COOKING METHOD / TECHNIQUE To simmer a food in a thick, flavored liquid for a long time. This tenderizes tough cuts of meat and allows flavors to blend.

n. Guiso *GEE-soh*
GENERAL A dish made by slowly cooking a meat and/or vegetable in a liquid for a long period of time.

Stir Revolver / Remover *reh-bohl-BEHR / reh-moh-BEHR*
COOKING METHOD / TECHNIQUE To move around.

Stir-fry Saltear (a fuego vivo) *sahl-teh-AHR (ah foo-EH-goh BEE-boh)*
COOKING METHOD / TECHNIQUE To quickly fry food in a small amount of fat in a large pan (typically a wok) while constantly stirring. This method is often used in Asian cuisine.

Stock Caldo líquido *KAHL-doh LEE-kee-doh*
CONDIMENTS The flavored liquid resulting from the simmering of vegetables, herbs, and animal bones for a long period of time. The liquid is reduced until the flavors are concentrated and the liquid thickens. Stock is used as a base for sauces, soups, and stews.

Stock cube Cubito de caldo *koo-BEE-toh deh KAHL-doh*
CONDIMENTS Dehydrated beef, chicken, or vegetable stock compressed and shaped into a square. It is also known as a bouillon cube.

Stockpot Caldera / Olla para caldo *kahl-DEH-rah / oh-YAH PAH-rah KAHL-doh*
EQUIPMENT A large pot with sides as tall as the pot is wide that allows the liquid in it to simmer without much reduction. Stockpots come in various sizes ranging from six to thirty-six quarts.

Store Guardar *gwar-DAHR*
COOKING METHOD / TECHNIQUE To set aside for future use.

Stove Estufa *ehs-TOO-fah*
EQUIPMENT A kitchen appliance that cooks food and includes the range (burners) and the oven.

Strain Colar *koh-LAHR*

COOKING METHOD / TECHNIQUE (1) To filter. (2) To remove impurities. (3) To sift and separate ingredients.

Strainer Colador *koh-lah-DOHR*

EQUIPMENT A kitchen tool with a netted, meshed, or perforated bottom used to strain or filter food items or sift dry ingredients. A strainer comes in a variety of sizes and net / mesh densities.

Strawberry Fresa *FREH-sah*

FRUIT & VEGETABLES A red, pointed-end fruit with small, edible yellow seeds surrounding its skin. It is juicy, sweet, and fragrant when ripe. Strawberries are available fresh or frozen.

Stuff Rellenar *reh-yeh-NAHR*

COOKING METHOD / TECHNIQUE To cram into or fill a cavity or opening.

Suckling pig Cochinillo *koh-chee-NEE-yoh*

MEAT A young pig, about two to six weeks old, that is roasted whole. Its weight ranges between ten and twenty-five pounds.

Suet Salsa de riñonada *SAHL-sah deh ree-nyoh-NAH-dah*

CONDIMENTS The fat found surrounding the kidneys in cattle, lambs, swine, and other animals. It must be rendered before being used and must be refrigerated. Suet has a very low melting and smoke point.

Sugar Azúcar *ah-SOO-kahr*

CONDIMENTS A simple carbohydrate derived from sugarcane and sugar beets. The term refers to crystallized sucrose (table sugar). Sugar provides a sweet taste, tenderizes baked goods, and is responsible for the browning reaction of caramelization.

Sugar, brown Azúcar moreno *ah-SOO-kahr moh-REH-noh*

CONDIMENTS White sugar that is mixed with molasses.

Sugar, confectioners' Azúcar glas *ah-SOO-kahr glahs*

CONDIMENTS Granulated sugar ground to a fine powder with a small amount of cornstarch added to prevent it from clumping. It is ground to different degrees of fineness from XXX to 10X—the more X's the finer the grain. Also known as powdered sugar and icing sugar, it is used in recipes for its quick-dissolving property and is dusted over desserts for garnish.

Sugar, dark brown Azúcar moreno oscuro *ah-SOO-kahr moh-REH-noh ohs-KOO-roh*

CONDIMENTS White sugar combined with molasses (6.5 percent of the mixture is molasses). The sugar has a high moisture content due to the water-loving nature of molasses. It is dark brown in color and deep caramel in flavor.

Sugar, Demerara Azúcar Demerara *ah-SOO-kahr deh-meh-RAH-rah*
   CONDIMENTS A form of raw sugar made from sugarcane juice that has been dehydrated. The large brown-colored sugar crystals get their name from the Demerara area of Guyana where the technique is said to have originated.

Sugar, light brown Azúcar moreno claro *ah-SOO-kahr moh-REH-noh KLAH-roh*
   CONDIMENTS Granulated white sugar mixed with molasses. About 3.5 percent of product weight is molasses, which results in a light brown color and distinctive caramel flavor. Its moist texture is due to the water-attracting qualities of molasses.

Sugar, powdered Azúcar en polvo *ah-SOO-kahr ehn POHL-voh*
   CONDIMENTS See **Sugar, confectioners'**.

Sugar, raw Azúcar sin refinar / Azucar en bruto *ah-SOO-kahr seen reh-fee-NAHR / ah-SOO-kahr ehn BROO-toh*
   CONDIMENTS Crystallized granules made from the remaining liquid of refined sugar production (leftover sugarcane juice). It is light brown in color with coarse-textured granules. Its flavor is similar to that of brown sugar, but raw sugar contains no molasses. True raw sugar can have contaminants and is purified as a result. Demerara, Barbados, and turbinado sugar are types of raw sugar.

Sugarcane Caña de azúcar *kah-NYAH deh ah-SOO-kahr*
   FRUIT & VEGETABLES A tall, thick grass rich in a sweet juice that when extracted and refined produces sugar and the by-product of molasses. The hard and fibrous grass has an inedible skin that must be peeled. Sugarcane is often used as skewers or stirrers in cocktails.

Sugar cubes Terrones de azúcar *teh-RROH-nehs deh ah-SOO-kahr*
   CONDIMENTS Sugar crystals that have been mixed with simple syrup and firmed into cubes.

Sulfites Sulfito *sool-FEE-toh*
   GENERAL The salt of sulfurous acid used as a preservative in food and beverages. It is said to cause allergic reactions in some people. It is added to wine to stop fermentation and prevent oxidation, and wines that contain sulfites must be labeled.

Sumac Zumaque *soo-MAH-keh*
   HERBS & SPICES A red berry that grows in clusters on small shrubs that is dried and ground to a powder and used as a spice. Used often in Middle Eastern cuisine, sumac imparts a red color and tart citrus flavor to meats and vegetables.

Sunchoke Aguaturma / Tupinambo *ah-gwah-TOOR-mah / too-pee-NAHM-boh*
   FRUIT & VEGETABLES See **Jerusalem artichoke**.

Sunflower oil Aceite de girasol *ah-SAY-teh deh hee-rah-ZOL*
   NUTS & OILS The oil extracted from sunflower seeds. Light yellow in color, it has a mild flavor. Its smoke point (450°F) makes it a great frying oil.

Sunflower seed Semilla de girasol *seh-MEE-yah deh hee-rah-SOHL*
HERBS & SPICES The seeds of the sunflower plant whose hulls are black with white stripes. The small beige-colored seeds can be dried or roasted and are sold plain or salted. Sunflower seeds are available hulled or in the shell.

Surf and Turf Mar y Montaña *mahr ee mohn-TAH-nya*
GENERAL A dish that includes both seafood and meat.

Sweat Sudar / Poner a sudar *soo-DAHR / poh-NEHR ah soo-DAHR*
COOKING METHOD / TECHNIQUE A cooking technique that softens vegetables without browning them. Vegetables are covered and cooked over low heat in a small amount of fat.

Sweet Dulce *DOOL-seh*
DESCRIPTOR One of the four basic tastes. It is described as tasting like sugar.

Sweet and sour sauce Salsa agridulce *SAHL-sah ah-gree-DOOL-seh*
CONDIMENTS A flavor balance between sweet and savory. Usually accomplished by mixing sugar or honey with vinegar or soy sauce to create a sauce, dressing, or marinade.

Sweetbreads Mollejas *moh-YEH-hahs*
MEAT Classified as offal, lamb, beef, or pork thymus glands and/or pancreas.

Sweetened condensed milk Leche condensada *LEH-cheh kohn-dehn-SAH-dah*
CONDIMENTS A mixture of whole milk and sugar that is heated until a little more than half of the water content is evaporated. This results in a sweet, thick syrup. If left unopened, the canned product can last for a couple of years.

Sweetener Edulcorante *eh-dool-koh-RAHN-teh*
CONDIMENTS A food additive that adds the basic taste of sweetness to a product. It can come from a natural source or be a man-made synthetic product (artificial sweetener).

Sweet pepper Pimiento / Ají *pee-mee-EHN-toh / ah-HEE*
FRUIT & VEGETABLES A mild pepper with a sweet or bitter sweet flavor. Most sweet peppers have a crisp, juicy flesh and come in colors ranging from green to red to yellow. Some examples are bell peppers, cubanelles, and sweet banana peppers.

Sweet potato Boniato / Batata roja / Patata dulce *boh-nee-AH-toh / bah-TAH-tah ROH-hah / pah-TAH-tah DOOL-seh*
FRUIT & VEGETABLES A large root vegetable that grows in tropical areas. Oval and elongated, it has a rough but edible brick-colored skin and a bright orange flesh. Sweet-flavored and moist-textured, it cooks similarly to a regular potato. A pale-colored variety exists but is not commonly seen. It is often confused with a yam, which is a different vegetable.

ENGLISH-SPANISH

S

Sweet potato, white Batata blanca / Boniato / Camote *bah-TAH-tah BLAHN-kah / boh-nyee-AH-toh / kah-MOH-teh*
FRUIT & VEGETABLES A variety of sweet potato with a thin, reddish skin and white flesh. It is a bit less sweet in flavor and not as dense as the traditional sweet potato.

Swiss chard Acelga *ah-SEHL-gah*
FRUIT & VEGETABLES A leafy green member of the beet family. Its hearty leaves are wrinkled and its stems are bright red. The vegetable has a slightly bitter flavor that mellows when cooked. If it is picked young, its tender leaves can be eaten raw, and its stems are edible when cooked.

Swiss cheese Queso Suizo *KEH-soh soo-EE-soh*
DAIRY Technically a Swiss-made cheese. Emmentaler is the one of the most well known Swiss cheeses. American Swiss cheese is any nutty-flavored cheese with holes in it.

Swordfish Pez espada *pehs ehs-PAH-dah*
FISH & SHELLFISH A large, saltwater fish recognized by its long, swordlike protrusion extending from its nose. Its flesh is dense and meaty yet mild in flavor. Due to its large size (average weight is 350 pounds) its meat is typically sold in steaks and chunks.

Syrup Jarabe / Sirope *hah-RAH-beh / see-ROH-peh*
CONDIMENTS A thick, viscous, and sticky liquid that is typically sweet.

T

Table Mesa *MEH-sah*
EQUIPMENT A piece of furniture with a flat top and four supporting legs.

Tablespoon Cucharada *koo-cha-RAH-dah*
MEASUREMENTS A culinary unit of measure equal to 3 teaspoons, 15 milliliters, or 1/2 fluid ounce.

Tahini Tahini *tah-EE-nee*
CONDIMENTS A thick paste made from ground sesame seeds.

Tallow Sebo *SEH-boh*
MEAT Rendered beef fat. Tallow is solid at room temperature.

Tamarillo / Tree tomato Tamarillo / Tomate de árbol *tah-mah-REE-yoh / to-MAH-teh deh AHR-bohl*
FRUIT & VEGETABLES An egg-shaped fruit, about two inches in length, that can be red, purple, or yellow in color. Its soft flesh is filled with edible seeds similar to those of a tomato. Its flavor is tangy and sweet. A tamarillo is almost always cooked as its skin tends to be bitter when raw.

Tamarind Tamarindo *tah-mah-REEN-doh*

HERBS & SPICES The brown pod that grows on the tamarind tree and contains small seeds and a tart pulp that becomes more sour when its dried. The pulp is used as a flavoring condiment for savory recipes.

Tangerine Mandarina *mahn-dah-REE-nah*

FRUIT & VEGETABLES A loose-skinned orange with a thick skin and sweet, juicy flesh. It is smaller than most oranges.

Tannin Tanino *tah-NEE-noh*

DESCRIPTOR An astringent substance found in seeds, stems, peels, and bark. It is an expected quality in wine and tea.

Tapioca (pearls) Tapioca (perlas) *tah-pee-OH-kah (PEHR-lahs)*

GRAINS & CEREALS The starch extracted from cassava (yuca) root used as a thickening agent. It comes in various forms with the two most common being flour (used like cornstarch) and pearls (must be soaked before using).

Taro root Taro *TAH-roh*

FRUIT & VEGETABLES The starchy root of the taro plant. Rough, brown, and hairy skin surrounds a cream-colored flesh that must be cooked before being eaten. It is neutral flavored, similar to a starchy potato. It has large green ornamental leaves (called callaloo in the Caribbean) that can be eaten if cooked.

Tarragon Estragón *ehs-trah-GOHN*

HERBS & SPICES An herb with soft, thin, and pointed green leaves. It has an anise-like flavor that is very popular in French cooking. It is one of the four classic fines herbes.

Tart Tarta *TAHR-tah*

BAKING & PASTRY A sweet or savory pastry with a straight-edged, shallow crust. It does not have a top crust. Fillings can be added before or after the crust is baked.

Tartar sauce Salsa tartara *SAHL-sah TAHR-tah-rah*

CONDIMENTS A chunky, mayonnaise-based sauce made with capers, pickles, onion, lemon juice, and seasonings. It is typically served with seafood.

Tartlet pan Molde de tarta *MOHL-deh deh TAHR-tah*

EQUIPMENT A metal pan used to mold and bake a tart shell.

Tasting menu Menu de degustación *meh-NOO deh deh-goos-tah-see-OHN*

GENERAL A set-price menu offering small portions of several dishes as a single meal. It is offered as a way of providing a sample of the full menu.

Tea Té *teh*

BEVERAGE A beverage made by rehydrating and steeping the dried leaves or buds of the tea plant in water. The various processing methods for the leaves determine the individual characteristics of each tea. Tea can be served hot or cold.

Teapot Tetera *teh-TEH-rah*
EQUIPMENT A vessel used for brewing tea. Typically it has a handle, a spout, and often a strainer to hold or catch loose tea leaves.

Teaspoon Cucharadita *koo-cha-rah-DEE-tah*
MEASUREMENTS A culinary unit of measure equal to $1/3$ teaspoon or 5 milliters.

Temper Templar *tehm-PLAHR*
COOKING METHOD / TECHNIQUE (1) To slowly increase the temperature of an ingredient (as with eggs and milk). (2) A technique used to stabilize chocolate by melting and cooling it. This results in a glossier and more workable (pliable) chocolate. It is necessary when chocolate will be used for decorating or candy making since without it chocolate will produce gray streaks on its surface after sitting for some time.

Temperature Temperatura *tehm-peh-rah-TOO-rah*
MEASUREMENTS The degree of hotness or coldness. Temperature is measured on the Celsius or Fahrenheit scale.

Tenderizer Masa para ablandar *MAH-sah PAH-rah ah-blahn-DAHR*
CONDIMENTS A powdered substance made up of enzymes used to break down tough meat fibers. Papaya contains an enzyme called papain that breaks down meat tissue. Many Latin American marinades contain papaya juice.

Tendon Tendón *tehn-DOHN*
MEAT An inelastic but flexible band that connects muscle to the bone.

Teriyaki sauce Salsa teriyaky *SAHL-sah teh-ree-YAH-kee*
CONDIMENTS A Japanese marinade consisting of soy sauce, sake, ginger, sugar, and seasonings that are boiled and reduced until it thickens to the desired viscosity. The marinade clings to the meat or vegetable, and because of the sugar, caramelizes the food as it cooks.

Terrine Terrina *teh-RREE-nah*
EQUIPMENT A long, rectangular, glazed ceramic or terra-cotta dish with tall, straight sides and a tight-fitting lid. It is used to shape and chill pâtés.
MEAT A mixture of ground meat or fish and fat that has been shaped in a terrine, cooked, and then chilled. It is also known as pâté.

Testicles Criadillas *kree-ah-DEE-yahs*
MEAT Male animal sex organs categorized as offal. Buffalo, boar, or bull testicles are eaten, typically breaded and deep-fried. They are popular in Mexico and Spain. They are also known as Rocky Mountain oysters.

Tetilla Queso Tetilla *KEH-soh teh-TEE-yah*
DAIRY A cow's milk cheese from Galicia in northwest Spain. It is one of the few cheeses of that region with a certificate of origin. It is a sweet and creamy-tasting, semisoft cheese with an inedible rind. It gets its name from its resemblance to the top of a nipple (*tetilla*).

Thermometer Termómetro *tehr-MOH-meh-troh*
EQUIPMENT An instrument that measures temperature.

Thyme Tomillo *toh-MEE-yoh*
HERBS & SPICES A member of the mint family, an herb with a woody stem and very small, oval leaves. It has a pungent woody and lemony flavor. Thyme is a member of the traditional bouquet garni. It is sold in bunches when fresh and is also available dried.

Tie Atar *ah-TAHR*
COOKING METHOD / TECHNIQUE To secure with a string. To bind or fasten pieces together.

Timer Marcador de tiempo *mahr-kah-DOHR deh tee-EHM-poh*
EQUIPMENT A timepiece instrument that measures time and cues its end.

Toast v. Brindis *BREEN-dees*
GENERAL The raising of one's glass in honor of someone or something.

n. Tostada *tohs-TAH-dah*
COOKING METHOD / TECHNIQUE A slice of bread that has been heated and as a result has dried and browned on both sides.

Toaster Tostadora *tohs-tah-DOH-rah*
EQUIPMENT A small electric kitchen appliance that toasts breads. It is typically constructed as a rectangular box with two to four slits on its top where slices of bread are inserted.

Tomatillo Tomatillo *toh-mah-TEE-yoh*
FRUIT & VEGETABLES A small, round, green fruit that is surrounded by a thin paper-like husk, which is inedible and must be removed. A member of the gooseberry family, the thin-skinned tomatillo is filled with small edible seeds in its center. Tart and tangy in flavor, its flesh is firm and can be eaten raw or cooked. It is very popular in Mexican cuisine.

Tomato Tomate *toh-MAH-teh*
FRUIT & VEGETABLES The fruit that grows on the tomato vine. Typically round, but also elongated or pear-shaped, a tomato has an edible, thin skin and its flesh is filled with small, edible seeds in its center. When immature, all tomatoes are green and tart and turn sweeter with their color changing to pink and orange then red. There are about seventy-five hundred varieties, each with its own color, shape, and flavor.

Tomato, cherry Tomate cherry *toh-MAH-teh cheh-RREE*
FRUIT & VEGETABLES A small, red or yellow tomato about one inch wide. It sweetness is due to its low acidity.

Tomato, dried Tomate seco *toh-MAH-teh SEH-koh*
FRUIT & VEGETABLES A tomato that has been dehydrated by a dehydrator or an oven. Dried tomatoes have a concentrated sweet flavor, with a wrinkled skin and chewy texture. They are available packed in oil or dried and kept in a plastic bag.

ENGLISH-SPANISH T

Tomato, hydroponic Tomate hidropónico *toh-MAH-teh ee-droh-POH-nee-koh*
FRUIT & VEGETABLES A greenhouse tomato grown in a liquid solution instead of soil.
Environmental factors such as light and temperature are controlled, as is exposure
to pests and weeds. This allows for tomatoes to be grown when soil and outside
temperature are unsuitable.

Tomato, plum Tomate pera *toh-MAH-teh PEH-rah*
FRUIT & VEGETABLES An egg-shaped tomato with significantly less seeds and pulp
than are in round tomatoes. Its higher proportion of flesh makes it suitable for making sauce. It is also known as a Roma tomato.

Tomato, sun-dried Tomate secado al sol *toh-MAH-teh seh-KAH-doh ahl sohl*
FRUIT & VEGETABLES A tomato that has been dehydrated by the sun. Sun-dried
tomatoes have a concentrated sweet flavor, with a wrinkled skin, and chewy texture.
They are available packed in oil or dried and kept in a plastic bag.

Tomato, vine-ripened Tomate en rama *toh-MAH-teh ehn RAH-mah*
FRUIT & VEGETABLES A tomato that is left to ripen on the vine.

Tomato, yellow Tomate amarillo *toh-MAH-teh ah-mah-REE-yoh*
FRUIT & VEGETABLES A variety of tomato that has a thin, yellow skin and a very sweet
flesh. Not widely available, it is usually grown from heirloom seeds.

Tomato paste Pasta de tomate *PAHS-tah deh toh-MAH-teh*
CONDIMENTS Cooked tomatoes that have been strained and reduced to a thick
paste. It can be found canned or in squeeze tubes.

Tomato sauce Salsa de tomate *SAHL-sah deh toh-MAH-teh*
CONDIMENTS A smooth or chunky sauce made from cooked tomatoes. It can be
plain or seasoned, thick or thin. It can be made fresh or purchased in a can.

Tongs Tenazas / Pinzas *teh-NAH-sahs / PEEN-sahs*
EQUIPMENT A tweeezer-like handheld kitchen tool used for picking up objects.
Tongs are often used in grilling.

Tongue Lengua *LEHN-gwah*
MEAT The large muscle found in an animal's mouth. Tongues from beef, veal, lamb,
and pork are eaten. A typical cow's tongue weighs about three pounds, the ones
from smaller animals weigh about one pound.

Tonic water Agua tónica *AH-gwah TOH-nee-kah*
BEVERAGE A sweetened, carbonated beverage that contains quinine, which gives it
its characteristic bitter flavor. It is used as a cocktail mixer.

Top Tapar *tah-PAHR*
COOKING METHOD / TECHNIQUE (1) To cover. (2) To provide a topping or layer.

Toss Remover *reh-moh-BEHR*
COOKING METHOD / TECHNIQUE To turn or shake food lightly.

Trim Recortar *reh-kohr-TAHR*

COOKING METHOD / TECHNIQUE To cut away unwanted parts.

Tripe Tripa / Menudo *TREE-pah / meh-NOO-doh*

MEAT A type of offal, most commonly beef stomach lining, but also lamb and pork. It is pale colored and has a netted honeycomblike-patterned texture. Tripe requires a long cooking time. It is available fresh, pickled, and canned.

Trout Trucha *TROO-chah*

FISH & SHELLFISH A freshwater fish that belongs to the salmon family. It has silvery skin and small bones. Its flesh is firm with a medium-fat content.

Truffle Trufa *TROO-fah*

FRUIT & VEGETABLES An edible fungus that grows three to twelve inches underground and near trees. Hunted out by pigs and dogs, it is considered a delicacy. There are two main types: black and white. The white is earthy and garlicky. The black is less pungent with earthy aromas. Truffles are served shaved atop hot food.

Truffle oil Aceite de trufa *ah-SAY-teh deh TROO-fah*

NUTS & OILS An oil made to provide the aroma and flavor of truffles. Most truffle oils do not contain truffles and are synthetically made with an olive oil base mixed with the chemical 2.4-dithiapentane. Truffle oil is significantly less expensive than actual truffles.

Truss Atar *ah-TAHR*

COOKING METHOD / TECHNIQUE To tie meat or poultry tightly into a compact shape with kitchen twine to help it cook evenly.

Tuna Atún *ah-TOON*

FISH & SHELLFISH A large saltwater fish found in warm waters. Its flesh ranges from pink to red in color and is moderate to high in fat. There are several varieties, some weighing as much as 1,000 pounds. The six types of tuna are (from largest to smallest) bluefin, southern bluefin, bigeye, yellow fin, albacore, and skipjack.

Turbot Rodaballo *roh-dah-BAH-yoh*

FISH & SHELLFISH A firm, lean flatfish with a mild-tasting white flesh. Found in cold northern European waters, it is often compared to Dover sole.

Turkey Pavo *PAH-boh*

MEAT A large, domesticated bird with a recognizable wattle that hangs below its chin. Traditionally cooked whole on Thanksgiving, turkey is also popular as a deli meat.

Turkey, breast Pechuga de pavo *peh-CHOO-gah deh PAH-boh*

MEAT The pectoral muscle that constitutes the white meat. It is low in fat and can get dry when cooked.

Turkey, leg Muslo entero de pavo *MOOS-loh ehn-TEH-roh deh PAH-boh*
MEAT The entire lower extremity of the bird from the hip to the foot that constitutes the dark meat.

Turkey, thigh Medio muslo de pavo *MEH-dee-oh MOOS-loh deh PAH-boh*
MEAT The upper portion of the bird's leg that constitutes the dark meat.

Turkey carcass Carcasa de pavo *kahr-KAH-sah deh PAH-boh*
MEAT The remains of the bird after the meat has been removed.

Turmeric Cúrcuma *KOOR-koo-mah*
HERBS & SPICES A spice made from the root of the turmeric plant that is boiled, dried, and then ground into a powder. Used primarily for the deep yellow color it imparts, it also gives off a mild, earthy, peppery flavor. It is a main ingredient in commercial curry powder and prepared mustard.

Turnip Nabo *NAH-boh*
FRUIT & VEGETABLES A small, round root vegetable that is white skinned except for its top half which is purple. The interior flesh is white with a slightly sweet taste. It is best to eat turnips when they are young, tender, and sweet as they get tough and starchy as they mature. Their skin needs to be peeled and they can be eaten cooked or raw.

Turn over Voltear *bohl-teh-AHR*
COOKING METHOD / TECHNIQUE (1) To fold over. (2) To move the position of something 180 degrees.

Tweezers Pinza *PEEN-sah*
EQUIPMENT (1) A pincer. (2) A small handheld tool used for grabbing or placing small objects.

U

Unleavened Ázimo *AH-see-moh*
BAKING & PASTRY Made without leavening. Baked goods that contain no leavening agents.

Unmold Desmoldar *dehs-mohl-DAHR*
COOKING METHOD / TECHNIQUE To remove a food from its mold or container.

Unsalted butter Mantequilla sin sal *mahn-teh-KEE-yah seen sahl*
DAIRY Butter that contains no salt. Because salt is a preservative, unsalted butter is more perishable.

Unsaturated fat Grasa insaturada *GRAH-sah een-sah-too-RAH-dah*
A triglyceride that contains one or more double bonds in its hydrocarbon fatty acid chain. A fat that is liquid at room temperature, it comes primarily from plant sources. Monounsaturated and polyunsaturated fats are types of unsaturated fats.

Up Arriba / Hacia arriba *ah-RREE-bah / AH-see-ah ah-RREE-bah*
DESCRIPTOR To move to a higher position. To face upward.

Utensils Utensilios *oo-tehn-SEE-lee-ohs*
EQUIPMENT Small tools or instruments used to handle food. Basic tableware utensils include forks, knives, and spoons.

V

Vanilla Vainilla *bah-ee-NEE-yah*
HERBS & SPICES The long, thin, brown pod that is the fruit of an orchid plant. Vanilla pods are handpicked when green, then boiled and dried, turning their characteristic brown color. They are usually split in half lengthwise and their seeds scraped off and used in recipes. Due to the labor-intensive harvesting, vanilla is the second most expensive spice next to saffron. There are three varieties: Bourbon-Madagascar (most common), Tahitian, and Mexican.

Vanilla extract Esencia de vainilla *eh-SEHN-see-ah deh bah-ee-NEE-yah*
CONDIMENTS A liquid that possesses the flavor and aroma of vanilla. Chopped vanilla beans are infused in a solution of alcohol and water, and then aged for a few months.

Veal Ternera *tehr-NEH-rah*
MEAT The meat from a calf one to three months old. Due to its young age, controlled milk-fed diet, and limited movement its meat is very tender and pale in color.

Veal, chop Chuleta de ternera *choo-LEH-tah deh tehr-NEH-rah*
MEAT An individual cut of veal from the loin area that includes a rib.

Veal, escalope Escalopa de ternera *ehs-kah-LOH-pah deh tehr-NEH-rah*
MEAT A boneless veal fillet that has been pounded thin.

Vegetable Vegetal / Hortaliza *beh-geh-TAHL / ohr-tah-LEE-sah*
FRUIT & VEGETABLES The edible root, tuber, stem, leaf, or flower of a plant.

Vegetable oil Aceite de vegetal *ah-SAY-teh deh beh-heh-TAHL*
NUTS & OILS A broad term to describe oil pressed from a plant source.

Vegetable peeler Pelador *peh-lah-DOHR*
EQUIPMENT A small kitchen tool used to remove the skin or peel of a fruit or vegetable. Vegetable peelers come in a variety of shapes and sizes and all have a small, razorlike blade attached to a handle.

Vegetable shortening Aceite solidificado / Manteca vegetal *ah-SAY-teh soh-lee-dee-fee-KAH-doh / mahn-TEH-kah beh-heh-TAHL*
CONDIMENTS A solid fat made from hydrogenated vegetable oil. The process converts the naturally occurring unsaturated fat to a saturated fat and in the process creates trans-fatty acids. Flavorless and colorless, it can be stored at room temperature. *See also* **Shortening**.

Vegetarian Vegetariano *beh-geh-tah-ree-AH-noh (nah)*
GENERAL A person who does not eat animal products.

Venison Ciervo / Venado *see-EHR-boh / beh-NAH-doh*
GAME The culinary name for deer meat both wild and farmed. Its flavor is similar to that of beef but it is much leaner, requiring care to be taken when cooking it so as to not dry out the meat.

Venison, saddle Silla de ciervo *SEE-yah deh see-EHR-boh*
GAME The connected two loins found on either side of the backbone. It is a very large cut of venison.

Vinaigrette Vinagreta *bee-nah-GREH-tah*
CONDIMENTS A mixture of vinegar and oil that has been seasoned. Often flavored with herbs, spices, and condiments like mustard and honey, it is used as a dressing on salads, vegetables, and cold meats and fish.

Vinegar Vinagre *bee-NAH-greh*
CONDIMENTS An acidic condiment made by converting fermented liquids (wine, beer, cider) into weak solutions of acetic acid through oxidation. Acetic acid is what gives vinegar its tart taste.

Vitamin Vitamina *bee-tah-MEE-nah*
GENERAL An organic substance required by the body in very small amounts for normal growth and activity. It cannot be synthesized entirely by the body and must be consumed through the diet or through supplements. There are a total of 13 vitamins categorized as either water or fat soluble.

Vodka Vodka *BOHD-kah*
BEVERAGE A distilled beverage. A clear liquid is obtained from multiple distillations of a fermented grain (rye, wheat, corn) or root vegetable (potato, beet). The distilled liquid is then filtered through charcoal to remove remaining impurities. The clear spirit is often flavored with fruit or spices.

W

Wafer cookie Barquillo *bahr-KEE-yoh*
BAKING & PASTRY A sweet, crisp, dry biscuit. It can be plain or flavored with chocolate or vanilla. Wafer cookies are sold as cookies and used to make ice cream cones.

Wakame Alga wakame *AHL-gah WAH-kah-mee*
FRUIT & VEGETABLES
An edible seaweed. Green in color, it has a briny flavor and a slippery texture. It is used in salads and to flavor soups.

Walnut Nuez *noo-EHS*
NUTS & OILS The dried fruit of the walnut tree. The hard, bumpy, round shell must be opened with the help of a nut cracker. The tan-colored nut is buttery and slightly tannic.

Walnut oil **Aceite de nuez** *ah-SAY-teh deh nwehs*
NUTS & OILS The oil extracted from walnuts. Light in color with a delicate nutty flavor, it is an expensive oil that is usually reserved for drizzling on dishes, as heating it
causes its flavor to diminish and brings out its bitterness.

Wasabi **Wasabi** *wah-SAH-bee*
HERBS & SPICES A Japanese horseradish root. It is used as a spice for its pungent,
mustard-like heat which is known to irritate the nasal passages. This long, white
root, rarely available fresh (which is grated when used), is most often found in paste
or powdered form that has been treated with green food coloring.

Water **Agua** *AH-gwah*
BEVERAGE A colorless, flavorless liquid necessary to sustain life. It is the base for
many liquids.

Water bath **Baño Maria** *BAH-nyoh mah-REE-ah*
COOKING METHOD / TECHNIQUE Both a cooking technique and a piece of equipment
that cooks food gently by the heat of steam. Traditionally a bain-marie is made up
of a large bowl or pot fitted atop a slightly smaller pot that contains a couple of
inches of water, and placed over low heat. The steam produced heats the top pot /
bowl and its contents. It is used to cook delicate foods as well as keep cooked foods
warm.

Water chestnut **Castaña de agua** *kahs-TAH-nyah deh AH-gwah*
FRUIT & VEGETABLES A root vegetable that grows underwater in flooded paddy
fields. Small, round, and with a brown skin that has to be peeled, it resembles a
chestnut. Its flesh is white and stays crunchy even when cooked. Water chestnuts
are available fresh or canned and can be eaten raw or cooked.

Watercress **Berro** *BEH-rroh*
FRUIT & VEGETABLES A leafy green vegetable that grows in an aquatic environment.
It has hearty but edible thin stems and small, dark green leaves. It has a crunchy
texture and a peppery flavor.

Watermelon **Sandía** *sahn-DEE-ah*
FRUIT & VEGETABLES Typically a large, elongated fruit that averages about fifteen
pounds. Its skin is green with white striations and its flesh is red and filled with black
seeds. Very juicy, sweet, and refreshing, it has a high water content. There is a seedless variety.

Wax paper **Papel encerado** *pah-PEHL ehn-seh-RAH-doh*
EQUIPMENT A moisture-proof, nonstick paper that has been covered with a thin
coating of wax on both sides. Microwave safe, it can be used in the oven when lining
baking pans so long as the batter fully covers it.

Well done Bien hecho *bee-EHN EH-cho*
COOKING METHOD / TECHNIQUE The doneness of meat described by its internal temperature, color, and juiciness. The meat should be gray brown throughout and its temperature should reach at least 160°F.

Wheat Trigo *TREE-goh*
GRAINS & CEREALS Cultivated grass grown around the world that is used to make flour for a large number of culinary uses. The wheat kernel contains gluten-forming amino acids that provide elasticity and produce very desirable results when baking. The grain is also fermented and used to make beer and distilled alcohol.

Wheat bran Salvado de trigo *sahl-BAH-doh deh TREE-goh*
GRAINS & CEREALS The rough outer coating of the wheat kernel. Wheat bran contains a high amount of fiber.

Wheat germ Germen de trigo *HEHR-mehn deh TREE-goh*
GRAINS & CEREALS The embryo of the kernel found inside a grain's endosperm (interior). It contains fat, vitamins, minerals, fiber, and protein.

Whey Suero *soo-EH-roh*
DAIRY The liquid portion of milk that separates from the solids (curds) when cheese is made or when milk sours.

Whisk v. Batir *bah-TEER*
COOKING METHOD / TECHNIQUE To beat or mix quickly while incorporating air into the mixture.

n. Agitador / Batidor manual *bah-hee-tah-DOHR / bah-tee-DOHR mah-noo-AHL*
EQUIPMENT A handheld kitchen tool used to beat, mix, or incorporate air into an ingredient. It is made of a number of thin wires that are curved to create a rounded balloon shape attached to a handle.

White peppercorn Pimienta blanca *pee-mee-EHN-tah BLAHN-kah*
HERBS & SPICES The ripe berry of the pepper plant that has had its skin removed and is then dried.

White sapote Sapote blanco *sah-POH-teh BLAHN-koh*
FRUIT & VEGETABLES A round fruit with a thin, green skin that turns yellow when mature. Its cream-colored flesh is very soft and sweet with the appearance of a tart vanilla pudding. It is not related to mamey or black sapote.

Whiting Pescadilla *pehs-kah-DEE-yah*
FISH & SHELLFISH A small, silver-skinned fish averaging about three pounds in weight. It has a firm, white flesh that has a mild flavor. It is typically available whole, fresh, salted, and smoked.

Whole grain Grano entero *GRAH-noh ehn-TEH-roh*
GRAINS & CEREALS A grain that has been minimally processed and contains all three edible parts—the bran, endosperm, and germ.

Whole wheat Trigo integral *TREE-goh een-teh-GRAHL*
GRAINS & CEREALS A wheat kernel that has been minimally processed and contains all three edible parts—the bran, endosperm, and germ.

Wild boar Jabalí *hah-bah-LEE*
GAME A large game animal that is a species of pig. Its meat is leaner but richer and stronger tasting.

Wild boar, saddle Silla de jabalí *SEE-yah deh hah-bah-LEE*
GAME The connected two loins found on either side of the backbone.

Wild rice Arroz silvestre *ah-RROHS seel-BEHS-treh*
GRAINS & CEREALS A long grass that grows in fresh, shallow water. Not a true rice, it is dark brown in color and a bit longer than long grain rice. It is sold dry. When cooked, it has a chewy texture and nutty flavor.

Wine Vino *BEE-noh*
BEVERAGES An alcoholic beverage made from the fermented juice of grapes. It can be categorized as still (nonsparkling), sparkling (effervescent), or fortified (reinforced with a spirit).

Wineglass Copa de vino *KOH-pah deh BEE-noh*
EQUIPMENT A special glass for drinking wine. It is recognizable by its long stem which holds a bowl and is supported by a foot. Some modern wineglasses are stemless.

Wine vinegar Vinagre al vino *bee-NAH-greh ahl BEE-noh*
CONDIMENTS A vinegar made from red or white wine. It can be aged in wooden casks, which results in its having a deeper flavor. It tends to be less acidic than cider or distilled vinegar.

Wishbone Espoleta *ehs-poh-LEH-tah*
MEAT A V-shaped bone found between the breast and the neck of a bird.

Wok Wok *wohk*
EQUIPMENT A special rounded-bottom cooking vessel (pot) used in Asian cuisine. A special ring may be necessary to put over a burner to keep it in place. Made of steel, it is used for many stovetop cooking methods, but is most popular for stir-frying.

Wonton wrappers Pasta wonton *PAHS-tah wohn-TOHN*
BAKING & PASTRY Small, square sheets of dough made from flour, egg, and water. Also known as wonton skins, they can be made fresh or purchased commercially. Purchased wrappers contain a small amount of cornstarch between the sheets to prevent them from sticking together.

Wooden spoon Cuchara de palo *koo-CHA-rah deh PAH-loh*
EQUIPMENT A spoon made from wood. A large version is used often as an all-purpose kitchen tool.

Worcestershire sauce Salsa inglesa *SAHL-sah een-GLEH-sah*
CONDIMENTS A dark brown, fermented liquid condiment made from vinegar, anchovies, molasses, tamarind, onion, garlic, sugar, salt, and spices. It has a deep savory flavor. Originally made in Worcestershire, England.

Wrap Envolver *ehn-bohl-BEHR*
COOKING METHOD / TECHNIQUE To envelope. To enclose or cover.

X

Xanthan gum Xantina *sahn-TEE-nah*
GENERAL Produced by the fermentation of sucrose, a starch that is used as a thickener. It also keeps solutions in emulsions and prevents them from separating.

Y

Yam Ñame *NYA-meh*
FRUIT & VEGETABLES A root vegetable tuber from a tropical vine. Large and elongated, it has a rough, brown skin and white flesh. Though often confused with (and mislabeled as) the sweet potato, the two can be easily substituted.

Yeast Levadura *leh-bah-DOO-rah*
BAKING & PASTRY A living, single-celled microorganism. As it grows, it converts its food (sugar) into carbon dioxide and alcohol. This process is called fermentation. It is used in bread baking and beer and wine production. Each of these processes has a specific yeast that functions best for its use. Baker's yeast and brewer's yeast are the two commercially available forms.

Yogurt Yogur *yoh-GOOR*
DAIRY A thick dairy product made from milk that has been curdled with a friendly bacteria. Slightly tart in flavor, many yogurts are flavored with fruit and other flavors. Sugar and gelatin are almost always added to improve the flavor and texture of yogurt.

Z

Za'atar Za'tar *sah-TAHR*
CONDIMENTS An herb and spice mixture used as a condiment. Popular in Middle Eastern cuisine, it is made from toasted sesame seeds mixed with dried oregano, thyme, marjoram, and salt. They are mixed with olive oil and made into a paste that is eaten with bread or spread on meats and vegetables.

ENGLISH-SPANISH X

Zamora Queso Zamora *KEH-soh sah-MOH-rah*

DAIRY A hard, sheep's milk cheese made in the province of Zamora in northeast Spain. It is a full-flavored cheese with a sharp, buttery, and nutty taste. Its rind is dark brown with the traditional zigzag pattern that is common with manchego. Protected by a Denominación de Origen, it is aged for six months during which it is rubbed olive oil and often turned.

Zest Piel / Cáscara *pee-EHL / KAHS-kah-rah*

FRUIT & VEGETABLES The skin of citrus fruit. Rich in essential oils, it is very fragrant and flavorful. Only the colored part of the skin is the zest; the white interior part is the bitter-tasting pith.

Zester Rallador / Acanalador *rah-yah-DOHR / ah-kah-nah-lah-DOHR*

EQUIPMENT A handheld kitchen tool used to remove the zest from citrus fruit. It is made up of a small, flat piece of metal perforated with small holes all along its top edge. The holes are placed against the skin of the fruit and the tool is pulled down with mild pressure. This results in small strips of citrus zest being peeled from the fruit.

Zucchini Calabacín *kah-lah-bah-SEEN*

FRUIT & VEGETABLES A variety of summer squash. A long, green fruit with an average length of about seven inches and a thin, edible skin. Its flesh is white in color and spongy in texture with small, edible seeds found along its center. Zucchini is mildly sweet in flavor.

SPANISH-ENGLISH

A

Abadejo *ah-bah-DEH-hoh* **Pollack / Haddock**
FISH & SHELLFISH A member of the cod family found in deep north Atlantic waters. A silver-skinned fish with a moderate amount of fat, it has a white flesh that is firm with a sweet flavor. It is used in making fish sticks and surimi (imitation crabmeat).

Abalón / Abulón *ah-bah-LOHN / ah-boo-LOHN* **Abalone**
FISH & SHELLFISH A mollusk found along the coastline of California, Mexico, and northern Spain. An abalone is a univalve whose shell is the source of mother-of-pearl. Fresh albalone is a delicacy but it can also be found canned, dried, and salted.

Ablandar *ah-blahn-DAHR* **Soften**
COOKING METHOD / TECHNIQUE To make less hard.

Aborrajado *ah-boh-rra-HAH-doh*
DISH (Colombia) Deep-fried sweet plantains with melted cheese.

Abrelata *ah-breh-LAH-tah* **Can opener**
EQUIPMENT An instrument used to open a can. It can be manual or electric.

Acanalador *ah-kah-nah-lah-DOHRa* **Zester**
EQUIPMENT See **Rallador**.

Acedera *ah-seh-DEH-rah* **Sorrel**
HERBS & SPICES A green leaf that is used as both a leaf vegetable and an herb. The leaves resemble spinach. Mature sorrel is more acidic and has a stronger flavor and tends to be used as an herb. When young, the tart leaves are added to salads or cooked like a leafy green.

Aceite *ah-SAY-teh* **Oil**
NUTS & OILS Fat extracted from a plant source that is liquid at room temperature. It is a very efficient medium for cooking as it boils at a much higher temperature than water.

Aceite de ajonjolí *ah-SAY-teh deh ah-hohn-hoh-LEE* **Sesame oil**
NUTS & OILS See **Aceite de sésamo**.

Aceite de almendra *ah-SAY-teh deh ahl-MENH-drah* **Almond oil**
NUTS & OILS A specialty oil made by pressing almonds.

Aceite de avellana *ah-SAY-teh deh ah-beh-YAH-nah* **Hazelnut oil**
NUTS & OILS Oil extracted from pressed hazelnuts. Due to its pronounced and intense flavor, it is often blended with a light and neutral oil.

Aceite de cacahuete *ah-SAY-teh deh kah-kah-WEH-teh* **Peanut oil**
NUTS & OILS See **Aciete de maní**.

Aceite de cártamo *ah-SAY-teh deh KAR-tah-moh* **Safflower oil**
NUTS & OILS Oil pressed from the seeds of the safflower. Flavorless and colorless, it is the oil with the highest amount of polyunsaturated fat and does not solidify when

chilled, and as a result is a popular choice for salad dressings. It has a high smoke point (450°F), making it a good frying oil.

Aceite de coco *ah-SAY-teh deh KOH-koh* **Coconut oil**

NUTS & OILS Oil extracted from the dried meat of the coconut. It is a highly saturated fat that is used for frying and in packaged foods.

Aceite de colza *ah-SAY-teh deh KOHL-zah* **Canola oil**

NUTS & OILS Neutral-tasting oil made from pressed rapeseeds. It has the lowest amount of saturated fat of any oil and almost as much monounsaturated fat as olive oil.

Aceite de girasol *ah-SAY-teh deh hee-rah-ZOL* **Sunflower oil**

NUTS & OILS Oil extracted from sunflower seeds. Light yellow in color, it has a mild flavor. Its smoke point (450°F) makes it a great frying oil.

Aceite de maíz *ah-SAY-teh deh mah-EES* **Corn oil**

NUTS & OILS A tasteless and colorless oil made from pressing corn kernels. It is a highly unsaturated fat with a high smoke point (410°F).

Aceite de maní / Aceite de cacahuete *ah-SAY-teh deh mah-NEE / ah-SAY-teh deh kah-kah-WEH-teh* **Peanut oil**

NUTS & OILS Oil pressed from peanuts that is then filtered and refined. It is mild in flavor and has a high smoke point (450°F), making it a great oil for deep frying. It is high in monounsaturated fat.

Aceite de nuez *ah-SAY-teh deh nwehs* **Walnut oil**

NUTS & OILS Oil extracted from walnuts. Light in color with a delicate nutty flavor, it is an expensive oil that is usually reserved for drizzling on dishes, as heating it causes its flavor to diminish and brings out its bitterness.

Aceite de oliva *ah-SAY-teh deh oh-LEE-bah* **Olive oil**

NUTS & OILS Oil extracted from the pressing of olives. Prized for its fruity and some-times spicy flavor, its color ranges from light yellow to dark green. It has the highest amount of monounsaturated fat of any oil.

Aceite de oliva extra-virgen *ah-SAY-teh deh oh-LEE-bah ehks-TRAH BEER-hehn* **Extra-virgin olive oil**

NUTS & OILS Olive oil obtained from the first cold pressing of olives and cannot contain more than 1 percent acidity by volume. Its color ranges from olive green to golden yellow and its flavor from fruity to spicy. It is considered the finest olive oil in the world.

Aceite de oliva ligero *ah-SAY-teh deh oh-LEE-bah lee-HEH-roh* **Light olive oil**

NUTS & OILS Olive oil that has gone through a filtration process resulting in a milder flavor, fragrance, and color, but with the same amount of fat and calories. The fil-tration process produces an oil with a higher smoke point. Due to its more neutral flavor, it is used in baking.

Aceite de palma *ah-SAY-teh deh PAHL-mah* **Palm oil**
NUTS & OILS Oil pressed from the fruit of the African palm. Often confused with palm kernel oil, which is oil taken from the seed inside the palm fruit, it has a distinctive flavor and red color that becomes clear when heated. Very high in saturated fat, it is thick and viscous at room temperature.

Aceite de pepita de uva *ah-SAY-teh deh peh-PEE-tah deh OO-bah* **Grapeseed oil**
NUTS & OILS Oil extracted from the seeds of grapes. Its neutral flavor and high smoke point make it good for sautéing or pan frying.

Aceite de sésamo / Aceite de ajonjolí *ah-SAY-teh deh SEH-sah-moh / ah-SAY-teh deh ah-hohn-ho-LEE* **Sesame oil**
NUTS & OILS The oil pressed from sesame seeds. There are two varieties: the cold-pressed oil, which is almost colorless and has a mild nutty flavor, and the toasted oil, which is made from toasted sesame seeds and has a dark, golden brown color and much stronger flavor.

Aceite de soya / Aceite de soja *ah-SAY-teh deh SOH-yah / ah-SAY-teh deh SOH-hah* **Soybean oil**
NUTS & OILS The oil pressed from soybeans. Light yellow in color, it is often labeled "vegetable oil." It is used abundantly in commercially made food products from salad dressings to mayonnaise. It is often hydrogenated and turned into margarine or shortening. Its high smoke point (450°F) makes it a great choice for frying.

Aceite de trufa *ah-SAY-teh deh TROO-fah* **Truffle oil**
NUTS & OILS An oil made to provide the aroma and flavor of truffles. Most truffle oils do not contain truffles and are synthetically made with an olive oil base mixed with the chemical 2.4-dithiapentane. Truffle oil is significantly less expensive than actual truffles.

Aceite de vegetal *ah-SAY-teh deh beh-heh-TAHL* **Vegetable oil**
NUTS & OILS A broad term used to describe oil pressed from a plant source.

Aceite solidificado / Manteca vegetal *ah-SAY-teh soh-lee-dee-fee-KAH-doh / mahn-TEH-kah beh-heh-TAHL* **Vegetable shortening**
NUTS & OILS A solid fat made from hydrogenated vegetable oil. When naturally occurring unsaturated fat is converted to a saturated fat the process creates trans-fatty acids. Flavorless and colorless, vegetable shortening can be stored at room temperature. *See also* Grasa.

Aceituna / Oliva *ah-say-TOO-nah / oh-LEE-bah* **Olive**
FRUIT & VEGETABLES A small, round fruit of the olive tree that contains a high amount of fat and has a seed or pit in its center. Many varieties exist and the flavor is dependent on the stage of ripeness when the olive is picked. All unripe olives are green and can stay green or turn a darker color when ripened. After being picked, they can be processed into oil or cured or brined for eating. Some are stuffed with pimientos, anchovies, or almonds.

Aceituna kalamata *ah-say-TOO-nah kah-lah-MAH-tah* **Kalamata olive**
FRUIT & VEGETABLES A dark purple black-colored Greek olive named after a city in Greece. It has a smooth skin and meaty flavor.

Aceituna negra / Oliva negra *ah-say-TOO-nah NEH-grah / oh-LEE-bah NEH-grah*
Black olive
FRUIT & VEGETABLES A ripe green olive that is either ripened on the tree or ripened artificially. The ripening process causes it to change to a black color.

Aceituna verde / Oliva verde *ah-say-TOO-nah BEHR-deh / oh-LEE-bah BEHR-deh* **Green olive**
FRUIT & VEGETABLES An olive harvested when still unripe and then cured. Green olives are often marinated with herbs or pitted and stuffed with pimientos, almonds, or anchovies.

Acelga *ah-SEHL-gah* **Swiss chard**
FRUIT & VEGETABLES A leafy, green member of the beet family. Its hearty leaves are green and wrinkled and its stems are bright red. It has a slightly bitter flavor that mellows when cooked. If it is picked young, its tender leaves can be eaten raw, and its stems are edible when cooked.

Acero inoxidable *ah-SEH-roh een-ohks-ee-DAH-bleh* **Stainless steel**
EQUIPMENT A steel metal that does not stain or rust as easily as regular steel.

Achicoria *ah-chee-koh-REE-ah* **Chicory**
FRUIT & VEGETABLES A relative of the endive, with leaves that are green and curly and white stalks. Its flavor is slightly bitter and it can be eaten raw or cooked.

Achiote *ah-chee-OH-teh* **Annatto seed**
HERBS & SPICES The seed of the annatto tree. This spice is used as much for coloring (bright orange red) as it is for flavor (earthy, slightly musky). It can be found in whole or powdered form. The annatto seed is sometimes referred to as achiote seed.

Achotillo *ah-choh-TEE-yoh* **Rambutan**
FRUIT & VEGETABLE *See* **Rambután**.

Ácido *AH-see-doh* **Acid**
GENERAL From the Latin *acidus* meaning sour, the taste associated with ingredients (vinegar, citrus fruit) possesing a pH below 7. Because acids break down cell walls, they can change the texture and appearance of food.

Ácido láctico *AH-see-doh LAHK-tee-koh* **Lactic acid**
GENERAL A tart and bitter-tasting acid. It forms when a particular bacteria combines with the milk-sugar lactose. It is responsible for the distinctive taste of soured milk and the tartness found in yogurt.

Acidular *ah-see-doo-LAHR* **Acidulate**
COOKING METHOD / TECHNIQUE To add an acid. Acidulated water is water that has had some vinegar or lemon juice added to it.

Aditivo *ah-dee-TEE-boh* **Additive**
GENERAL A substance added (intentionally or not) to food to preserve its flavor, nutrition, or quality, or to aid in its processing or preparation.

Aderezar / Aliñar *ah-deh-reh-ZAHR / ah-lee-NYAR* **Dress**
COOKING METHOD / TECHNIQUE To add a sauce or dressing to a salad, vegetable, fish, or meat.

Aderezo / Aliño *ah-deh-REH-zoh / ah-LEE-nyoh* **Dressing**
CONDIMENTS A sauce used to coat and flavor salads, vegetables, fish, or meat.

Adobar *ah-doh-BAHR* **Marinate**
COOKING METHOD / TECHNIQUE To soak food in a marinade to absorb its flavors or tenderize tough cuts of meat.

Adobo *ah-DOH-boh* **Marinade**
CONDIMENTS A liquid mixture containing an acid and other condiments and seasonings used to flavor meats, fish, and vegetables. The acid, usually in the form of citrus juice, vinegar, or wine, is helpful in tenderizing tough cuts of meat.
(Mexico) A dried chile-based marinade typically made with ancho chiles that have been rehydrated and pureed.

Adobo seco *ah-DOH-boh SEH-koh* **Rub**
CONDIMENTS A mixture of spices that is applied to and worked or massaged onto a piece of meat, fish, or vegetables.

Afilador de cuchillo *ah-fee-lah-DOHR deh koo-CHEE-yoh* **Knife sharpener**
EQUIPMENT An instrument used to fine-tune the sharp cutting edge of a knife by grinding the edge against a rough, hard surface at a specific angle (twenty degrees). It comes in manual and electric versions.

Alforfón *ahl-fohr-FOHN* **Buckwheat**
GRAINS & CEREALS Though technically an herb, buckwheat is categorized here under its common usage as a cereal grain. A relative of sorrel and rhubarb, its seeds are used to make a flour, the key ingredient to Russian blini and soba noodles.

Agallas *ah-GAH-yahs* **Fish gills**
FISH & SHELLFISH The respiratory organs found in aquatic organisims. Their main function is to take in oxygen from the water and release carbon dioxide.

Agar *ah-GAHR* **Agar**
HERBS & SPICES A setting agent or thickener derived from seaweed. Often referred to as Japanese gelatin, it differs from gelatin in that it sets at room temperature and is five times more powerful than gelatin, requiring less when being used. It is tasteless and serves as a vegetarian option to gelatin.

Agave *ah-GAH-veh* **Agave**
FRUIT & VEGETABLES A succulent (water-retaining) plant that grows in Mexico, Central America, and the southwestern United States. Poisonous when raw, it develops

a mildly sweet flavor when cooked. The sap collected from the plant is used to make tequila. Agave nectar is also used as a sugar substitute.

Agitador / Batidor manual *ah-hee-tah-DOHR / bah-tee-DOHR mah-noo-AHL* **Whisk**

EQUIPMENT A handheld kitchen tool used to beat, mix, or incorporate air into an ingredient. It is made of a number of thin wires that are curved to create a rounded, balloon shape attached to a handle.

Agrio / Cortado *AH-gree-oh / kohr-TAH-doh* **Sour**

DESCRIPTOR One of the four basic tastes. It is described as a sharp, tart taste.

Agua *AH-gwah* **Water**

BEVERAGE A colorless, flavorless liquid necessary to sustain life. The base for many liquids.

Aguacate *ah-gwah-KAH-teh* **Avocado**

FRUIT & VEGETABLES A fruit with a buttery texture, nutty flavor, and flesh that goes from pale yellow to green. It matures on the tree, but ripens off the tree. The Hass variety, which is small and dark, is most commonly used in the United States.

Agua de rosas *AH-gwah deh ROH-sahs* **Rosewater**

CONDIMENTS A distillation of rose petals. It has a distinctive flavor and highly floral aroma that is used in recipes, especially baked goods.

Agua de soda *AH-gwah deh SOH-dah* **Soda water**

BEVERAGE Carbonated water that is effervescent and fizzy. Depending on the bottler, it may contain minerals producing a distinct flavor. It is also known as club soda or seltzer water.

Agua destilada *AH-gwah dehs-tee-LAH-dah* **Distilled water**

BEVERAGE Water that has been purified through distillation.

Agua fresca *AH-gwah FREHS-kah*

BEVERAGE (Mexico) A flavored water that has been infused with flowers, fruit, or leaves. It is a refreshing drink that is served cold and over ice.

Aguapanela *ah-gwah-pah-NEH-lah*

BEVERAGE (Colombia) A drink made by infusing water with panela until the sugar is completely dissolved. One of the most popular beverages in Colombia, it is served hot or cold with lemon or lime usually squeezed in it.

Aguardiente *ah-gwahr-dee-EHN-teh*

BEVERAGE A distilled alcoholic beverage made from sugarcane consumed in many South American countries. Similar to Italian grappa, it has a high alcoholic content. It can be flavored or left plain. Aguardiente literally translates as "firewater."
(Colombia) An anis-flavored spirit made from sugarcane. It is typically drunk as a shot and almost never mixed in a cocktail.

Agua salada *AH-gwah sah-LAH-dah* **Brine**
COOKING METHOD / TECHNIQUE *See* **Salmuera**.

Agua tonica *AH-gwah TOH-nee-kah* **Tonic water**
BEVERAGE A sweetened, carbonated beverage that contains quinine, which gives it its characteristic bitter flavor. It is used as a cocktail mixer.

Aguaturma / Tupinambo *ah-gwah-TOOR-mah / too-pee-NAHM-boh* **Jerusalem artichoke / Sunchoke**
FRUIT & VEGETABLES A tuber from the sunflower plant similar in appearance to fresh ginger. The thin skin is light brown and bumpy, and the white flesh is crunchy and sweet with a faint nutty flavor. It can be eaten raw, or cooked with or without its skin.

Ahumado / Ahumar *ah-oo-MAH-doh / ah-oo-MAHR* **Smoked / Smoke**
COOKING METHOD / TECHNIQUE The process of flavoring, cooking, or curing a food by exposing it to smoke generated by the burning of a specific wood and/or herbs.

Aioli *ah-ee-OH-lee*
CONDIMENTS (Spain) A sauce that resembles a thin mayonnaise. It is an emulsification of an egg yolk and olive oil that is flavored with a generous amount of garlic.

Ajedrea *ah-heh-DREH-ah* **Savory**
HERBS & SPICES A strong-flavored herb that tastes like a blend of thyme, mint, and rosemary. It is similar in appearance to rosemary but the leaves are a bit more delicate.

Ají *ah-HEE* **Bell pepper / Sweet pepper**
FRUIT & VEGETABLES *See* **Pimiento**.

Ajiaco *ah-hee-AH-koh*
DISH (Colombia) A chicken stew made with corn on the cob that has been cut crosswise into small chunks and three different types of potatoes.
(Cuba) A thick and hearty root vegetable stew that is flavored with shredded beef as well as dried beef (tasajo).

Ají de gallina *ah-HEE deh gah-YEE-nah*
DISH (Peru) Thin strips of chicken sautéed and served smothered in a spicy cheese sauce made from small, yellow chile peppers blended with cheese, milk, bread, and walnuts.

Ají rojo *ah-HEE ROH-hoh* **Red bell pepper**
FRUIT & VEGETABLE *See* **Pimiento rojo**.

Ají verde *ah-HEE BEHR-deh* **Green bell pepper**
FRUIT & VEGETABLE *See* **Pimiento verde**.

Ajo *AH-hoh* **Garlic**
FRUIT & VEGETABLES A member of the lily family that also includes onions, leeks, and chives. It is a bulb that grows underground and is made up of sections individually wrapped in a paperlike skin called cloves. The entire bulb is called a head. It has a pungent, spicy flavor that is strong when raw, but mellows as it cooks, even

becoming sweet if cooked slowly for a long period of time. Used as an aromatic seasoning in many dishes, garlic is available fresh, dried, or in powdered form.

Ajo blanco con uvas *AH-hoh BLAHN-koh kohn OO-bahs*
DISH (Spain) A chilled, raw soup similar to gazpacho but made without tomatoes. Almonds and garlic are pureed and mixed with bread to which olive oil, vinegar, and water are added to make a soup. It is garnished with chopped green grapes.

Ajo en polvo *AH-hoh ehn POHL-boh* **Garlic powder**
CONDIMENTS Dehydrated garlic that has been ground to a fine powder.

A la asturiana *ah lah ah-stoo-ree-AH-nah*
COOKING METHOD / TECHNIQUE (Spain) Dishes that use hard cider in their preparation.

A la francesa *ah lah frahn-SEH-sah*
COOKING METHOD / TECHNIQUE **v.** In the French style. To cut a vegetable or meat into lengthwise strips.
n. A preparation for a cut of raw meat that is still attached to a rib bone. The protruding bone is throughly cleaned and stripped of all meat and fat.

A la gallega *ah lah gah-YEH-gah*
COOKING METHOD / TECHNIQUE (Spain) Dishes containing paprika and oil.

A la parrilla / Asar a la parrilla *ah lah pah-RREE-yah / ah-SAHR ah lah pah-RREE-yah* **Grilled**
COOKING METHOD / TECHNIQUE Cooked on a metal grate that is placed over hot coals or a heat source.

A la riojana *ah lah ree-oh-HAH-nah*
COOKING METHOD / TECHNIQUE (Spain) Dishes that use roasted red peppers from the Rioja region in their preparation. Chilendron is another name for this.

Albahca *ahl-BAH-kah* **Basil**
HERBS & SPICES A member of the mint family, an herb that is key to Mediterranean cooking, especially Italian cuisine. It is also often used in Asian cooking. There are a few varieties but the most popular is sweet basil, which has a slight anise and licorice flavor.

Albardillar *ahl-bahr-dee-YAHR* **Barding**
COOKING METHOD / TECHNIQUE Adding or placing fat over lean pieces of meat, especially game, to make them moist and tender.

Albaricoque *ahl-bah-ree-KOH-keh* **Apricot**
FRUIT & VEGETABLES A relative of the peach that has been grown for over four thousand years. Its thin, furry, orange skin can be cut through without difficulty, exposing a seed that falls out easily.

Albedo *ahl-BEH-doh* **Pith**
FRUIT & VEGETABLES The soft, white, bitter-tasting membrane that lies between the peel and the flesh of a citrus fruit.

Albóndigas *ahl-BOHN-dee-gahs* **Meatballs**
MEAT Ground meat that is seasoned, shaped into balls, and cooked. Bread crumbs and egg are often added to bind and keep the meatballs from falling apart.

Albondigón *ahl-bohn-dee-GOHN*
DISH (Peru) Meat loaf.

Albumina *ahl-boo-MEE-nah* **Albumin**
DAIRY The protein found in egg whites. When spelled albumen with an "e," it is another word for egg white.

Alcachofa *ahl-kah-CHOH-fah* **Artichoke**
FRUIT & VEGETABLES An unopened flower bud that needs to be trimmed when mature but can be eaten in its entirety when young. The mature variety can be boiled or steamed and care must be taken when getting close to the heart, as its surrounded by an inedible fur (the "choke") that must be removed. The stem can be eaten if peeled and has a flavor very similar to that of the heart. Other vegetables have the word "artichoke" in their name, but the true artichoke is the globe artichoke.

Alcaparra *ahl-kah-PAH-rrah* **Caper**
HERBS & SPICES The sun-dried flower bud of a bush native to the Mediterranean. The dried buds are pickled. Packed in a brined solution or salted, they have a sharp, salty, vinegary flavor.

Alcapurrias *ahl-kah-pooh-RREE-ahs*
DISH (Puerto Rico) A stuffed fritter. The dough can be made from mashed yuca or plantain and the stuffing consists of ground meat or seafood.

Alcaravea *ahl-kah-rah-VEH-ah* **Caraway**
HERBS & SPICES A seed whose flavor is very similar to that of anise. It comes from a plant that is a member of the parsley family.

Alcohol *ahl-KOHL* **Alcohol**
BEVERAGE Ethyl/ethanol alcohol is the type of alcohol found in alcoholic beverages. It is produced by distilling fermented sugars obtained from fruit or grains. Pure ethyl alcohol boils at 173°F and freezes at -173°F.

Alegría *ah-leh-GREE-ah*
DISH (Colombia) A sweet similar to a cocada.

Aleta *ah-LEH-tah* **Fish fin**
FISH & SHELLFISH A flat and wing-shaped piece of anatomy on a fish. It helps it steer and provides stability.

Alfajores *ahl-fah-HOH-rehs*
BAKING & PASTRY (Argentina) A sandwich cookie. Dulce de leche is sandwiched between two shortbread cookies that are dusted with powdered sugar, coated with chocolate, or left plain.
(Peru) A layered dessert of thin sugar cookies and caramel (manjar blanco).

Alfandoque *ahl-fahn-DOH-keh*
DISH (Colombia) A dessert made from panela and peanuts.

Alfombrilla de bambú *ahl-fohm-BREE-yah deh bahm-BOO* **Bamboo mat**
EQUIPMENT *See* Tejido de bambú.

Alforfón *ahl-fohr-FOHN* **Buckwheat**
GRAINS & CEREALS Though technically an herb, buckwheat is categorized here under its common usage as a cereal grain. A relative of sorrel and rhubarb, its seeds are used to make a flour, the key ingredient to Russian blini and soba noodles.

Alga hijiki *AHL-gah hee-GEE-kee* **Hijiki**
FRUIT & VEGETABLES A long, thin Japanese seaweed that is boiled and dried after it has been harvested from the ocean. It must be reconstituted before being used. Often prepared as a salad or used in recipes, it has a salty licoricelike flavor.

Alga kombu *AHL-gah KOHM-boo* **Kombu**
FRUIT & VEGETABLES Long, wide pieces of seaweed that are dried and sold as long strips or sheets. Cultivated off the coasts of China, Japan, and Korea and popular in Japanese cuisine, it is one of the main ingredients in dashi.

Alga nori *AHL-gah NOH-ree* **Nori**
FRUIT & VEGETABLES The Japanese name for very thin sheets of dried seaweed. Its color ranges from green to black and it tastes of seawater and marine life. Usually eaten in dried form, it is used as a wrapper for sushi. It typically comes in square shapes but can be cut into any desired form.

Algarroba *ahl-gah-RROH-bah* **Carob / Locust beans**
FRUIT & VEGETABLES (1) The pod of the carob tree that is sweet and possesses a flavor similar to chocolate. The seeds found in pods are dried, roasted, and ground into a powder that is used as a flavoring in baked goods. Because of its low fat content, carob is often used as a chocolate substitute. (2) The seeds found inside the carob pod. They are the source of locust bean gum, which is used as a thickener in processed foods.

Alga wakame *AHL-gah WAH-kah-mee* **Wakame**
FRUIT & VEGETABLES An edible seaweed. Green in color, it has a briny flavor and a slippery texture. It is used in salads and to flavor soups.

Algas marinas *AHL-gahs mah-REE-nahs* **Seaweed**
FRUIT & VEGETABLES Marine algae. Used as food primarily in Asian cuisine, it is typically found in dried form.

Aliñar *ah-lee-NYAR* **Dress**
COOKING METHOD / TECHNIQUE *See* Aderezar.

Aliño *ah-LEE-nyoh* **Dressing**
CONDIMENTS *See* Aderezo.

Almeja *ahl-MEH-hah* **Clam**
FISH & SHELLFISH A bivalve that burrows into sediment. It comes in three different sizes: littleneck (small), cherrystone (medium), and chowder (large).

Almejas a la marinera *ahl-MEH-hahs ah lah mah-ree-NEH-rah*
DISH (Spain) Clams cooked in a white wine sauce flavored with onions, garlic, paprika, parsley, and dried red chile pepper.

Almendra *ahl-MEHN-drah* **Almond**
NUTS & OILS The kernel of the almond tree encased in a hard, inedible shell. Almonds are available in markets blanched (without their thin brown skin) or with their skin on.

Almendras molidas *ahl-MENH-drahs moh-LEE-dahs* **Almonds, ground**
NUTS & OILS Almonds that have been pulverized into a coarse powder. This is achieved with a food processor or mortar and pestle. When almonds are ground, a small amount of sugar is typically added to absorb some of the oil and prevent a paste from forming.

Almendras troceadas *ahl-MENH-drahs troh-seh-AH-dahs* **Almonds, sliced**
NUTS & OILS Almonds that have been sliced thinly lengthwise.

Almibar *ahl-MEE-bahr* **Simple syrup**
BAKING & PASTRY A solution of sugar and water that is heated until the sugar melts. An irreversible process that removes the graininess of the sugar crystals, it can be made into various densities to meet different needs (thin, medium, heavy). The more sugar that is used, the more viscous the syrup.

(Almibar) a punto de escarchado *(ahl-MEE-bahr) ah POON-toh deh ehs-kar-CHAH-doh* **Soft-crack stage**
BAKING & PASTRY The temperature at which a small amount of sugar syrup separates into hard but flexible threads when immersed in cold water (270°F–290°F/ 132°C–143°C).

(Almibar) a punto de perla *(ahl-MEE-bahr) ah POON-toh deh PEHR-lah* **Soft-ball stage**
BAKING & PASTRY The temperature at which a small amount of sugar syrup forms soft pliable balls when immersed in cold water (234°F–240°F/112°C–116°C).

Almidón *ahl-mee-DOHN* **Starch**
GENERAL A complex carbohydrate (polysaccharide) found in plant products.

Almojabana *ahl-moh-hah-BAH-nah*
DISH (Colombia) A small, round cheese bread made from cornmeal and a white farmer cheese.
(Puerto Rico) A rice fritter flavored with cheese

Almuerzo / Comida *ahl-MWEHR-soh / koh-MEE-dah* **Lunch**
GENERAL The midday meal. For many countries this is the main meal of the day.

Al pastor *ahl pahs-TOHR*
DISH Meat that is cooked over an open flame and usually by rotisserie.
COOKING METHOD & TECHNIQUE (Mexico) A style of cooking.

Alta cocina *AHL-tah koh-SEE-nah* **Haute cuisine**
GENERAL Food prepared and served in an elegant and highly technical manner.
Haute cuisine is French for "high cooking."

Alubia *ah-LOO-bee-ah* **Bean**
FRUIT & VEGETABLES *See* Judía.

Alubia de ojo *ah-LOO-bee-ah deh OH-hoh* **Black-eyed pea**
FRUIT & VEGETABLES A small, beige bean with a black spot said to have come to
America through the slave trade. It is very popular in the southern United States.

Al vacío *ahl bah-SEE-oh* **Sous vide**
COOKING METHOD / TECHNIQUE A cooking technique that seals food in a vacuum-
packed bag and cooks it for an extended period of time at a controlled temperature.

Amaranto *ah-mah-RAHN-toh* **Amaranth**
GRAINS & CEREALS A plant high in protein. Both its seeds and leaves can be eaten,
and most commonly the seeds are ground into a flour, which does not contain gluten, and used to make breads. The greens can be cooked or eaten raw in a salad.

Amargo *ah-MAHR-goh* **Bitter**
DESCRIPTOR One of the five basic tastes. It is perceived to be acrid and unpleasant.

Amasar *ah-mah-SAHR* **Knead**
COOKING METHOD / TECHNIQUE To knead bread dough, blending its ingredients and
working the gluten strands, to add strength to the dough. It can be done manually
or by a machine. The process consists of stretching and folding the dough onto itself
until a smooth and elastic dough forms.

Amontillado *ah-mohn-tee-YAH-doh*
BEVERAGE (Spain) A medium-dry sherry pale tan in color. Although less dry than
fino, it is also consumed as an apéritif.

Anacardo *ah-nah-KAHR-doh* **Cashew**
NUTS & OILS The kidney-shaped nut that grows on the cashew tree. The shell is very
toxic and must be carefully removed. The nut is made up of almost 50 percent fat.

Ancas de rana *AHN-kahs deh RAH-nah* **Frog's legs**
GAME The hind legs of a frog. They are its only edible part and their flavor and texture are often compared to those of a tender chicken breast.

Anchoa *ahn-CHOH-ah* **Anchovy**
FISH & SHELLFISH A small, silvery blue fish from the Mediterranean coastline. Anchovies are filleted, salt-cured, and canned. Some are also smoked. They are salty and
tend to be used sparingly. *See* Boquerón.

Añejo *ahn-NYE-hoh* **Mature**
DESCRIPTOR Ripe. Fully developed. Aged.

Angélica *ahn-HEH-lee-kah* **Angelica**
HERBS & SPICES An aromatic herb that is a member of the parsley family and thrives in northern, cold climates. Its stems and leaves are commonly used in baking, often blanched and candied for decorating cakes and pastries. The roots and seeds of the plant are also used for making liqueurs.

Anguila *ahn-GEE-lah* **Eel**
FISH & SHELLFISH A long, dark gray, snakelike-looking fish that is found in both fresh and salt water. Its thick skin is tough and rubbery and must be removed before its flesh, which is meaty and often smoked, is cooked.

Angulas *ahn-GOO-lahs* **Baby eels**
FISH & SHELLFISH (Spain) The offspring of eels. Born near Bermuda, they migrate to the waters north of Spain and are caught at the mouth of rivers. They are very small, about the size of a small blade of grass, and have a mild taste.

Angulas a la bilbaina *ahn-GOO-lahs ah lah beel-bah-EE-nah*
DISH (Spain) Baby eels in garlic sauce. This is the traditional way of serving the eels. They come piping hot in an earthenware dish and guests are given wooden forks for eating in order to prevent burning their mouths with a metal utensil.

Anís *ah-NEES* **Anise**
HERBS & SPICES An herbaceous plant that is a member of the parsley family and has a distinctive sweet licorice flavor. Its leaves and seeds are used in both sweet and savory preparations. This is the flavor found in liqueurs such as anisette (*anis* in Spanish), aguardiente, and pastis.

Anís estrellado *an-NEES ehs-treh-YAH-doh* **Star anise**
HERBS & SPICES A dried, star-shaped spice that comes from an evergreen tree grown in China and Japan. It has a licorice aniselike flavor that is used to flavor sweet and savory dishes as well as to infuse tea. It is available in whole or ground form.

Annón / Chirimoya *ah-NOHN / chee-ree-MOH-yah* **Cherimoya**
FRUIT & VEGETABLES A round, green-skinned fruit with a scalelike pattern. Its flesh is milky and creamy with embedded black seeds. Its flavor is a blend of banana and papaya.

Anticuchos *ahn-tee-KOO-chohs*
DISH (Peru) Skewers of marinated and grilled beef hearts. While served at restaurants, they are commonly sold by street vendors.

Antioxidante *ahn-tee-ohks-ee-DAHN-teh* **Antioxidant**
GENERAL A substance that inhibits oxidation. From a culinary point of view, oxidation results in browning and in food becoming rancid. Ascorbic acid (vitamin C) is a natural antioxidant that is used often in food preparation.

Antojito *ahn-toh-HEE-toh*
DISH (Mexico) A snack usually made from a corn-based product such as a tortilla.

Apelación / Denominación *ah-peh-lah-see-OHN / deh-noh-mee-nah-see-OHN*
Appellation
DESCRIPTOR A geographical designation applied to a grape-growing area controlled by governmental rules. The rules address issues such as grape varieties and yields per acre and vary by country and even by region. The goal of an appellation is to produce a high-quality product.

Aperitivo *ah-peh-ree-TEE-boh* **Appetizer**
GENERAL Technically the first course served at the table. It should be bite-size and is meant to stimulate the appetite. The term is often wrongly interchanged with hors d'oeuvre.
BEVERAGE An alcoholic beverage served in small quantities before a meal to stimulate the appetite.

Apimentado *ah-pee-mehn-TAH-doh* **Blackened**
COOKING METHOD / TECHNIQUE Coated with ground black pepper and spices.

Apio *AH-pee-oh* **Celery**
FRUIT & VEGETABLES A green, fibrous, ribbed stalk that grows in bunches. The stalks get more tender and lighter in color toward the center of the bunch.

Apio-nabo *AH-pee-oh NAH-boh* **Celeriac**
FRUIT & VEGETABLES The root of a special type of celery plant. It has a brown and knobby exterior and a beige-colored interior that browns easily and must be soaked in acidulated water. Also known as celery root, it has a mild celery flavor.

Aplasta papas *ah-PLAHS-tah PAH-pahs* **Potato masher**
EQUIPMENT A handheld kitchen tool used to crush cooked potatoes or other soft ingredients into a mash. A long handle is attached to a metal wire formed into a zigzag shape or a flat, blunt sheet of metal.

Aplastar *ah-plahs-TAHR* **Crush**
COOKING METHOD / TECHNIQUE To break, pound, or grind into small fragments or powder. Tools used to obtain this result include a mortar and pestle, rolling pin, meat pounder, and the bottom of a heavy pan.

Arandano negro *ah-RAHN-dah-noh NEH-groh* **Blueberry**
FRUIT & VEGETABLES A small, round, blackish blue fruit that grows on a bush. Its translucent flesh is sweet while its dark skin can be tart.

Arandano rojo *ah-RAHN-dah-noh ROH-hoh* **Cranberry**
FRUIT & VEGETABLES A round, bright red berry with a tart flavor. Cranberries are available fresh (in bags), frozen, and dried. There are many processed products derived from cranberries such as juice, jelly, and canned sauce.

Arañitas *ah-rah-NYEE-tahs*
DISH (Puerto Rico) Plantain cakes made from shredded green plantains.

Arenque *ah-REHN-keh* **Herring**
FISH & SHELLFISH Small fish that swim in large pools and are found in cold salt water. Oily and silver-colored, they grow no larger than a pound in weight. Young herrings are often used as a substitute for sardines. Fresh herring can be baked, grilled, or sautéed and is often also cured or pickled.

Arepa *ah-REH-pah*
DISH (Colombia) A unleavened corn cake that is cooked on a griddle until its exterior turns golden. Typically eaten plain, but at times served with a topping or filling, it is a very traditional snack food.
(Venezuela) An unleavened corn cake that is typically about six inches round. It can be eaten plain but usually contains a filling such as cheese or meat. After the corn cake is cooked, it is split and the filling added.

Arequipe *ah-reh-KEE-peh*
CONDIMENT (Colombia) A thick caramel sauce made from sweetened cow's milk very similar to dulce de leche.

Aroma *ah-ROH-mah* **Aroma**
DESCRIPTOR A sense of smell that is usually associated with a pleasant odor.

Aromáticos *ah-roh-MAH-tee-kohs* **Aromatics**
GENERAL Plant products—vegetables, herbs, and spices—that contribute vivid aromas and flavors to food preparation.

Arriba / Hacia arriba *ah-RREE-bah / AH-see-ah ah-RREE-bah* **Up**
GENERAL To move to a higher position. To face upward.

Arrollado de chancho *ah-rroh-YAH-doh deh CHAN-choh*
DISH (Chile) Pork loin that is marinated in garlic and spices, barded (covered in pork fat), and then roasted.

Arroz *ah-RROHS* **Rice**
GRAINS & CEREALS The seeds of the rice plant that are processed and used as an edible cereal grain. The small kernels come in different sizes (long, medium, and short) and categories (white, brown) based on the rice variety and how much processing they have undergone. A staple in many cuisines, it is high in starch. Rice must be cooked by boiling or steaming before it is eaten.

Arroz a banda *ah-RROHS ah BAHN-dah*
DISH (Spain) A paella-style rice dish made with only fish stock and colored with saffron.

Arroz a la mexicana *ah-RROHS ah lah meh-hee-KAH-nah*
DISH (Mexico) Rice cooked in tomato puree, which results in rice with a red hue.

Arroz arborio *ah-RROHS ahr-BOH-ree-oh* **Arborio rice**
GRAINS & CEREALS A short grain rice with a very high starch content. Named after the Italian town of Arborio, it is used to make risotto as its high starch content is helpful in creating a creamy risotto.

Arroz basmati *ah-RROHS bahs-MAH-tee* **Basmati rice**
GRAINS & CEREALS A long grain rice that is grown on the foothills of the Himalayas. It is light textured and very fragrant and is used often in Indian and Middle Eastern cuisine.

Arroz blanco *ah-RROHS BLAHN-koh* **White rice**
GRAINS & CEREALS Rice that has had its husk, bran, and germ removed.

Arroz chaufa *ah-RROHS CHOW-fah*
DISH (Peru) The Peruvian version of Chinese fried rice.

Arroz con coco *ah-RROHS kohn KOH-koh*
DISH (Colombia) Coconut rice, a typical dish from Caribbean coastal communities.

Arroz con dulce *ah-RROHS kohn DOOL-seh*
DISH (Puerto Rico) Sweet rice pudding.

Arroz con gandules *ah-RROHS kohn gahn-DOO-lehs*
DISH (Puerto Rico) Rice and pigeon peas seasoned with smoked ham, pork, chorizo, olives, red peppers, and sofrito. It is Puerto Rico's national dish.

Arroz congri *ah-RROHS kohn-GREE*
DISH (Cuba) Red beans and rice. Raw rice is cooked in a pot of cooked red beans that were flavored with small pork chunks. The rice absorbs the bean liquid, and the final product is a dry combination of rice and beans with small chunks of pork.

Arroz con leche *ah-RROHS kohn LEH-cheh* **Rice Pudding**
DISH Traditionally served cold, a small amount of uncooked rice is boiled until most of the starch is leached out. It is then simmered in milk. The result is a very tender grain in a dense pudding.

Arroz con pollo *ah-RROHS kohn POH-yoh*
DISH Yellow rice with chicken. It is traditionally made with short grain rice (Valencia rice) that is tinted with saffron or yellow food coloring (bijol).

Arroz con pollo a la chorrera *ah-RROHS kohn POH-yoh ah lah cho-RREH-rah*
DISH (Cuba) A soupy version of yellow rice and chicken.

Arroz de grano corto *ah-RROHS deh GRAH-noh KOHR-toh* **Short grain rice**
GRAINS & CEREALS Rice that is short, stubby, and almost round. It contains a high amount of starch.

Arroz de grano largo *ah-RROHS deh GRAH-noh LAHR-goh* **Long grain rice**
GRAINS & CEREALS Rice that is four to five times as long as it is wide. It can be white or brown. Its grains separate easily after being cooked.

Arroz frito *ah-RROHS FREE-toh* **Fried rice**
DISH A Chinese dish made with day-old rice stir-fried in a wok with other ingredients and seasonings such as eggs, vegetables, scallions, and soy sauce. Diced chicken, pork, or shrimp is often also added.

Arroz integral *ah-RROHS een-teh-GRAHL* **Brown rice**
GRAINS & CEREALS Rice that contains the entire rice grain with the exception of the inedible husk. Light brown in color, it has a nutty flavor and chewy texture.

Arroz jazmín *ah-RROHS hahs-MEEN* **Jasmine rice**
GRAINS & CEREALS A long grain rice with a nutty flavor and very fragrant aroma. Its texture is similar to that of basmati rice. It is also known as fragrant Thai rice.

Arroz negro *ah-RROHS NEH-groh*
DISH (Spain) Short grain rice cooked with squid. The squid's ink sacs are used for flavoring and to tint the rice a black color. Arroz negro literally translates as "black rice."

Arroz para sushi *ah-RROHS PAH-rah SOO-shee* **Sushi rice**
GRAINS & CEREALS White, short grained, sticky rice with a high starch content. The rice is boiled or steamed and mixed with a mixture of rice vinegar, sugar, and salt before being used to form sushi. It is washed before it is cooked to remove excess starch.

Arroz silvestre *ah-RROHS seel-VEHS-treh* **Wild rice**
GRAINS & CEREALS A long grass that grows in fresh shallow water. Not a true rice, it is dark brown in color and a bit longer than long grain rice. When cooked, it has a chewy texture and nutty flavor.

Arroz y habichuelas *ah-RROHS ee ah-bee-CHEWH-lahs*
DISH (Puerto Rico) Rice and red beans.

Arrurruz *ah-rroo-RROOS* **Arrowroot**
GRAINS & CEREALS The starchy tuber of the tropical arrowroot plant. The root is ground into a flour that is used primarily as a thickener. A unique characteristic of the thickener is that it remains clear when heated; it also does not impart a raw chalky taste if undercooked. The flour should be mixed with a small amount of water before being added to hot liquid in order to maximize it effectiveness.

Asado *ah-SAH-doh*
COOKING METHOD / TECHNIQUE *See* **Asar**.
DISH (Argentina) An Argentinean barbecue event.

Asado a la brasa *ah-SAH-do ah lah BRAH-sah* **Barbecue**
COOKING METHOD / TECHNIQUE Cooking meat and poultry slowly and indirectly through hot coals or wood. The meat is covered and often basted with a sauce to keep it moist. *See also* **Barbacoa**.

Asado al sartén *ah-SAH-doh ahl sahr-TEHN* **Pan roasted**
COOKING METHOD / TECHNIQUE A two-part cooking technique that begins by searing food in an ovenproof skillet over high heat and then transferring the skillet to the

oven to finish cooking. It allows food to achieve a golden brown sear and maintain its moisture while it cooks internally.

Asador *ah-sah-DOHR* **Barbecue**
EQUIPMENT A covered outdoor oven with a grate in its center. It can be heated by electricity, gas, coals, or wood. Some barbecues are fitted with a spit / rotisserie.

Asadura / Despojo *ah-sah-DOO-rah / dehs-POH-hoh* **Offal**
MEAT Internal organs and flesh that is not muscle and that is used in cooking or for making sausage. It is the British word for variety meats.

Asafetida *AH-sah feh-TEE-dah* **Asafoetida**
HERBS & SPICES An herbaceous fennel-like plant that grows mainly in Iran and India. When raw, it has a pungent garlic smell but mellows when cooked, imparting flavors and aromas reminiscent of sautéed onion and garlic. It can be found in both powdered and lump form.

Asar / Asado *ah-SAHR / ah-SAH-do* **Roasting**
COOKING METHOD / TECHNIQUE A dry cooking method that subjects food to heat in an oven or another heat source. It causes a browning reaction on the surface of the food resulting in the intensification of flavor.

Asar a fuego directo *ah-SAHR ah foo-EH-goh dee-REHK-toh* **Broil**
COOKING METHOD / TECHNIQUE To cook food directly under a heat source.

Asar en parrilla *ah-SAHR ehn pah-REE-yah* **Charbroil**
COOKING METHOD / TECHNIQUE To cook food directly over dry heat. The food is typically placed on a metal grate that leaves grill marks on it.

Astringente *ahs-treen-HENH-teh* **Astringent**
DESCRIPTOR The dry, puckering mouthfeel typically caused by tannins.

Asustar / Submergir en agua con hielo *ah-soos-TAHR / soob-mehr-HEER ehn AH-gwah kohn ee-EH-loh* **Shock**
COOKING METHOD / TECHNIQUE To stop the cooking of a food by plunging it in an ice bath.

Atar *ah-TAHR* **Tie / Truss**
COOKING METHOD / TECHNIQUE (1) To secure with a string. To bind or fasten pieces together. (2) To tie meat or poultry tightly into a compact shape with kitchen twine to help the meat cook evenly.

Atole *ah-TOH-leh*
BEVERAGE (Mexico) A thick, milky beverage made with corn masa. The masa is mixed with milk, strained, and often flavored with sugar and cinnamon.

Atún *ah-TOON* **Tuna**
FISH & SHELLFISH A large saltwater fish found in warm waters. Its flesh ranges from pink to red in color and is moderate to high in fat. There are several varieties, some weighing as much as a 1,000 pounds. The six types of tuna are (from largest to smallest) bluefin, southern bluefin, big eye, yellow fin, albacore, and skipjack.

Avellana *ah-beh-YAH-nah* **Hazelnut**
NUTS & OILS The nut that grows on the hazel tree. It is a small, round nut inside a hard, brown shell that must be cracked open. The nut has a thin, brown skin that is slightly bitter and should be removed. Hazelnuts are used in both savory and sweet recipes and can be ground, chopped, or left whole.

Avena *ah-BEH-nah* **Oats**
GRAINS & CEREALS A cereal grass that bears a kernel, which must be removed from its husk in order to be edible for human consumption. It can be cooked and served in a manner similar to rice.

Avena molida *ah-BEH-nah moh-LEE-dah* **Oatmeal**
GRAINS & CEREALS Toasted and hulled whole oats that have been cut, crushed, or steamed and flattened with rollers. Oatmeal is used as a thickener, a flavoring, or simply cooked as a breakfast cereal.

Aves *AH-behs* **Poultry**
MEAT Domesticated fowl—chickens, turkeys, geese, and ducks—raised for food. The flesh and/or eggs are eaten.

Aves caseras *AH-behs kah-SEH-rahs* **Game birds**
GAME Hunted wild birds suitable for human consumption. The sizes of the birds range from small (partridge, dove) to medium (pheasant) to large (goose, turkey).

Avestruz *ah-behs-TROOS* **Ostrich**
GAME A large bird whose meat is often compared to very lean beef. The size of an ostrich egg is equivalent to sixteen chicken eggs and is cooked in similar ways.

Azafrán *ah-sah-FRANH* **Saffron**
HERBS & SPICES A spice made from the dried yellow-orange stigmas of the purple crocus. Because each flower has only three stigmas and because they must be picked by hand, this spice is the world's most expensive spice by weight. It is used for its sweet, grassy flavor and yellow coloring.

Ázimo *AH-see-moh* **Unleavened**
BAKING & PASTRY Made without leavening. Baked goods that contain no leavening agents.

Azúcar *ah-SOO-kahr* **Sugar**
CONDIMENTS A simple carbohydrate derived from sugarcane and sugar beets. Sugar refers to crystallized sucrose (table sugar). It provides a sweet taste, tenderizes baked goods, and is responsible for the browning reaction of caramelization.

Azúcar Demerara *ah-SOO-kahr deh-meh-RAH-rah* **Demerara sugar**
CONDIMENTS A form of raw sugar made from sugarcane juice that has been dehydrated. The large, brown-colored sugar crystals get their name from the Demerara area of Guyana where the technique is said to have originated.

Azúcar en bruto *ah-SOO-kahr ehn BROO-toh* **Raw sugar**
CONDIMENTS See **Azucar sin refinar.**

Azúcar en polvo *ah-SOO-kahr ehn POHL-voh* **Powdered sugar**
CONDIMENTS Granulated white sugar that has been ground to a fine powder. It is ground to different degrees of fineness from XXX to 10X, the more X's the finer the grain. A small amount of cornstarch is added to prevent it from clumping. It is used in recipes for its quick dissolving property and is dusted over desserts for garnish. It is also known as confectioner's sugar and icing sugar.

Azúcar glas *ah-SOO-kahr glahs* **Confectioners' sugar**
CONDIMENTS *See* **Azucar en polvo**.

Azúcar moreno *ah-SOO-kahr moh-REH-noh* **Brown sugar**
CONDIMENTS White sugar mixed with molasses.

Azúcar moreno claro *ah-SOO-kahr moh-REH-noh KLAH-roh* **Light brown sugar**
CONDIMENTS Granulated white sugar mixed with molasses. About 3.5 percent of the product weight is molasses, which results in a light brown color and distinctive caramel flavor. Its moist texture is due to the water-attracting qualities of molasses.

Azúcar moreno oscuro *ah-SOO-kahr moh-REH-noh ohs-KOO-roh* **Dark brown sugar**
CONDIMENTS White sugar combined with molasses (6.5 percent of the mixture is molasses). The sugar has a high moisture content due to the water-loving nature of molasses. It is dark brown in color and deep caramel in flavor.

Azúcar sin refinar / Azúcar en bruto *ah-SOO-kahr seen reh-fee-NAHR / ah-SOO-kahr ehn BROO-toh* **Raw sugar**
CONDIMENTS Crystallized granules made from the remaining liquid of refined sugar production (left-over sugarcane juice). It is light brown in color with coarse-textured granules; its flavor is similar to that of brown sugar, but it contains no molasses. True raw sugar can have contaminants and is purified as a result. Demerara, Barbados, and turbinado sugar are types of raw sugars.

B

Baboso *bah-BOH-soh* **Slimy**
DESCRIPTOR Description of something having a thick, viscous substance on it (slime).

Bacalao *bah-kah-LAH-oh* **Cod**
FISH & SHELLFISH A white and firm saltwater fish from the north Atlantic. It is lean and has a mild flavor. In Spain and Latin America it is typically found as salt cod, fillets preserved through drying and salting. Very popular throughout Spain, especially the interior areas that do not have access to the sea, it has to be soaked for twenty-four to thirty-six hours before being used in order to remove the salt.

Bacalao a la Vizcaína *bah-kah-LAH-oh ah lah bees-kah-EE-nah*
DISH (Spain) Reconstituted salt cod simmered in a sweet red pepper sauce that is flavored with onions, garlic, bacon, ham, and dried chile pepper. An egg yolk is used to emulsify the sauce. It is considered one of the most popular dishes of the Basque region.

Bacalao al pil-pil *bah-kah-LAH-oh ahl peel peel*
   DISH (Spain) A traditional dish from the Basque region of Spain. Rehydrated salt cod is poached in a garlic-infused olive oil for several minutes before being placed in an earthenware dish. The olive oil used for poaching is then slowly drizzled into the dish while the dish is gently swayed so as to emulsify the oil with the natural fish juice. The result is cod served a creamy garlicky fish sauce.

Bacalao salado *bah-kah-LAH-oh sah-LAH-doh* **Salt cod**
   FISH & SHELLFISH (Spain) Salted and dried cod. It is sold whole or in portions.

Bajo en grasa *BAH-hoh ehn GRAH-sah* **Low fat**
   GENERAL Not deriving a large amount of calories from fat. According to U.S. labeling guidelines, it refers to food that has three grams of fat or less per serving.

Banano *bah-NAH-noh* **Banana**
   FRUIT & VEGETABLE *See* Plátano.

Bañar *bah-NYAR* **Coat**
   COOKING METHOD / TECHNIQUE *See* Cubrir.

Bañar con huevo / Baño de huevo / Glaseado de huevo *bah-NYAR kohn WEH-voh / bah-NYO deh WEH-voh / glah-seh-AH-doh deh WEH-voh* **Egg wash**
   COOKING METHOD / TECHNIQUE A mixture of egg or egg yolk with a small amount of water or milk. It is brushed on a baked good before baking to give it a golden brown color and shine.

Bandeja de hornear *bahn-DEH-hah deh ohr-neh-AHR* **Baking sheet**
   EQUIPMENT A flat, firm sheet of metal that typically has an upward curved edge.

Bandeja Paisa *bahn-DEH-hah PAH-ay-sah*
   DISH (Colombia) A large dish with a lot of variety including grilled steak, fried pork skin, chorizo, red beans, rice, a fried egg on top of the dish, and an arepa to accompany it. All items are served on the same dish. It is a typical dish from Medellín.

Baño de huevo *BAH-nyoh deh WEH-voh* **Egg wash**
   COOKING METHOD / TECHNIQUE *See* Bañar con huevo.

Baño Maria *BAH-nyoh mah-REE-ah* **Bain-marie**
   EQUIPMENT A piece of equipment that cooks food gently by the heat of steam. Traditionally it is made up of a large bowl or pot fitted atop a slightly smaller pot that contains a couple of inches of water and placed over low heat. The steam produced heats the top pot / bowl and its contents. *See also* **Water bath** and **Double boiler**.
   COOKING METHOD / TECHNIQUE The technique using a bain-marie to cook delicate foods, that can burn or curdle easily, by the heat of steam as well as keep cooked foods warm.

Barbacoa *bahr-bah-KOH-ah* **Barbecue**
   EQUIPMENT (Mexico) An underground pit oven or barbecue. It can also refer to the food cooked in the pit that is typically wrapped in banana, avocado, or maguey leaves. *See also* Asado a la brasa.

Barnizar *bahr-nee-SAHR* **Glaze**
COOKING METHOD / TECHNIQUE *See* Glasear.

Barquillo *bahr-KEE-yoh* **Ice cream cone / Cookie**
BAKING & PASTRY (1) A thin-wafer cookie that is molded into a cone shape and used as an edible container that holds ice cream. (2) A sweet, crisp, dry biscuit. It can be plain or flavored with chocolate or vanilla. Wafer cookies are sold as cookies and used to make ice cream cones.

Barramundi *bah-rrah-MOON-dee* **Barramundi**
FISH & SHELLFISH A firm, white, flaky saltwater fish from the Pacific West region. Popular in Australia, it is now being raised in aquaculture.

Barril *bah-RREEL* **Cask**
EQUIPMENT A large wooden barrel typically made of oak used to store or age wine or spirits.

Base de migas *BAH-seh deh MEE-gahs* **Cookie-crumb crust**
BAKING & PASTRY A pasty dough or crust made up of crushed cookies bound by a fat such as melted butter.

Batata blanca / Camote *bah-TAH-tah BLAHN-kah / kah-MOH-teh* **White sweet potato**
FRUIT & VEGETABLES A variety of sweet potato with a thin, reddish skin and white flesh. It is a bit less sweet in flavor and not as dense as the traditional sweet potato.

Batata roja *bah-TAH-tah ROH-hah* **Sweet potato**
FRUIT & VEGETABLE *See* Boniato.

Batido *bah-TEE-doh* **Milk shake**
BEVERAGE A beverage made from milk, ice cream, and a flavoring (fruit, chocolate, or syrup) that is pureed in a blender. Popular flavors vary by region. In Cuba, tropical fruits such as mamey or mango as well as trigo (wheat) are common. In Brazil, avocado is a popular flavor.

Batter
BAKING & PASTRY *See* Pasta para rebozar.

Batidora *bah-tee-DOH-rah* **Mixer**
EQUIPMENT An electric kitchen tool used to whip or beat ingredients. It can be handheld or stationary. The handheld version is used for smaller tasks and has a small motor with two whisks connected to it. The larger stationary machine stands on its own and has a dedicated work bowl with various attachments used to mix ingredients.

Blender
EQUIPMENT *See* Liquadora.

Batidor de varilla *bah-tee-DOHR deh bah-REE-yah* **Hand mixer (electric)**
EQUIPMENT A small handheld electric appliance used to whip, beat, and mix ingredients. Two beaters are connected to a handle base that contains the motor. The beaters are submerged into the ingredients before the motor is started.

Batidor manual *bah-tee-DOHR mah-noo-AHL* **Whisk**
EQUIPMENT *See* Agitador.

Batir *bah-TEER* **Whisk / Cream**
COOKING METHOD / TECHNIQUE (1) To beat or mix quickly while incorporating air into a mixture. (2) To beat or mix two or more ingredients until they are smooth and well incorporated with no sign of individual particles. This process also helps to incorporate air into the mixture.

Baya de enebro *BAH-yah deh eh-NEH-broh* **Juniper berry**
HERBS & SPICES Dark purple–colored berries that resemble blueberries. They have a strong herbaceous flavor with lots of tannin and are used often with game meats in European cooking. They are typically used dried because they are very bitter when raw.

Bayas *BAH-yahs* **Berries**
FRUIT & VEGETABLES Small, round, edible fruit that tend to be juicy sweet and sometimes tart. They have small edible seeds but do not have a pit.

Bebida *beh-BEE-dah* **Beverage**
BEVERAGE A liquid prepared and consumed by humans. Alcohol and/or other substances such as caffeine can form part of a beverage.

Beicon / Bacon / Tocino *BEH-ee-kohn / BEH-ee-kohn / toh-SEE-noh* **Bacon**
MEAT Traditionally, smoked and cured pork belly. However, other cuts of pork can be used as well.

Bellota *beh-YOH-tah* **Acorn**
NUTS & OILS The nut of the oak tree, consumed mostly by wildlife.

Berberecho *behr-beh-REH-choh* **Cockle**
FISH & SHELLFISH A small bivalve with a tricolor ribbed shell. It can be eaten raw or cooked.

Berenjena *beh-rehn-HEH-nah* **Eggplant**
FRUIT & VEGETABLES A member of the nightshade family, a pear-shaped fruit with a smooth skin that is typically dark purple but can also be white. Although it is technically a fruit, an eggplant is typically prepared as a savory ingredient. Its beige-colored flesh has a spongy texture and is filled with very small, edible, brown seeds. Its flesh takes on a meaty and creamy texture when cooked. Eggplants can vary substantially in thickness and length.

Bergamota *behr-gah-MOH-tah* **Bergamot**
HERBS & SPICES A small, sour citrus fruit whose peel and essence is used to flavor Earl Grey tea.

Berro *BEH-rroh* **Watercress**
FRUIT & VEGETABLES A leafy green vegetable that grows in an aquatic environment. It has hearty but edible, thin stems and small dark green leaves. It has a crunchy texture and a peppery flavor.

Besuguera *beh-soo-GEH-rah* **Fish poacher**
EQUIPMENT A long, thin cooking vessel used to poach fish. It has a tight-fitting lid and an internal rack onto which the fish is laid. A flavored liquid is added and the fish is placed onto the rack before the covered poacher is placed in the oven or over heat.

Beta-carotina *BEH-tah kah-roh-TEE-nah* **Beta-carotene**
GENERAL A powerful antioxidant, it is the precursor (will turn into) to vitamin A. Found only in plant products, it is not toxic if consumed in excess as the body will eliminate it.

Bicarbonato de sodio *bee-kahr-boh-NAH-toh deh SOH-dee-oh* **Baking soda**
CONDIMENTS An alkali that functions as a leavener for baked goods when combined with an acid and moisture. It is typically used when a recipe has an acidic component. It is also known as sodium bicarbonate.

Bien hecho *bee-EHN EH-cho* **Well done**
COOKING METHOD / TECHNIQUE The doneness of meat described by its internal temperature, color, and juiciness. The meat should be gray brown throughout and its temperature should reach at least 160°F.

Birría *bee-RREE-ah*
DISH (Mexico) Meat (usually lamb or goat) marinated with chiles and slow roasted in the oven with maguey leaves and broth. This produces very tender meat and an intensely flavored chile sauce.

Bistec empanizado *bees-TEHK ehm-pah-nee-SAH-doh*
DISH (Cuba) Steak that has been pounded thin, breaded, and fried.

Bitter *BEE-tehr* **Bitters**
CONDIMENTS An alcoholic beverage made with herbs, roots, bark, and other parts of a plant and used to flavor cocktails. It has a high alcohol content and bitter taste. It is also consumed as a digestif.

Bivalvo *bee-VAHL-voh* **Bivalve**
FISH & SHELLFISH A mollusk that contains two shells hinged together such as a clam, oyster, or mussel.

Bizcocho *bees-KOH-choh* **Cookie**
BAKING & PASTRY *See* Galleta.

Blanditas *blahn-DEE-tahs*
BAKING & PASTRY (Mexico) The whitest, thinnest tortillas. They are very refined and expensive.

Bocadillo *boh-kah-DEE-yoh* **Guava paste**
FRUIT & VEGETABLE *See* Pasta de guayaba.

Sandwich
GENERAL *See* Sándwich.

Bogavante *boh-gah-BAHN-teh* **Lobster**
FISH & SHELLFISH *See* Langosta.

Bok choy *bohk choy* **Bok choy**
FRUIT & VEGETABLES A vegetable that grows in bunches with a white crunchy stalk and dark green leaves. Its flavor is very mild. It is often used in Asian cooking.

Bol *bohl* **Mixing Bowl**
EQUIPMENT *See* Cuenco.

Bowl
EQUIPMENT *See* Plato hondo.

Bolas de masa *BOH-lahs deh MAH-sah* **Dumplings**
DISH Balls of dough that are steamed, fried, or baked. They can be sweet or savory and are often stuffed with a filling.

Boleto seco *boh-LEH-toh SEH-koh* **Porcini, dried**
FRUIT & VEGETABLES Wild mushroom of the *boletus edulis* species. Light brown in color, porcini have smooth and meaty caps can range in diameter from one to ten inches. They have an intense earthy flavor and are difficult to find fresh but are available dried year-round.

Boliche *boh-LEE-cheh*
DISH (Cuba) Pot roast made with eye round that has been marinated with sour orange juice and garlic.

Bolillos *boh-LEE-yohs* **Roll**
BAKING & PASTRY *See* Panecillo.

Bolis *BOH-lees*
DISH (Colombia) Frozen fruit bars.

Bolsa pastelera *BOHL-sah pahs-teh-LEH-rah* **Pastry bag**
EQUIPMENT A cone-shaped bag with an opening on either end. A semisoft ingredient is added through the large end and squeezed out of the small opening, which can be fitted with special tips that produce decorative piping. Pastry bags come in various materials including cloth and disposable plastic.

Bombilla *bohm-BEE-yah*
EQUIPMENT (Argentina/Chile) One of two parts of a mate set used to drink yerba mate tea. It is a straw with a scoop and sieve on the end that is submerged.

Boniato / Batata roja / Patata dulce *boh-nee-AH-toh / bah-TAH-tah ROH-hah / Pah-TAH-tah DOOL-seh* **Sweet potato**

FRUIT & VEGETABLES A large root vegetable that grows in tropical areas. Oval and elongated, it has a rough but edible brick-colored skin and a bright orange flesh. Sweet-flavored and moist-textured, it cooks similarly to a regular potato. There is a pale-colored variety but it is not commonly seen. It is often confused with a yam, which is a different vegetable.

Bonito *boh-NEE-toh* **Bonito**

FISH & SHELLFISH A variety of tuna (skip jack) that is a member of the mackerel family. It is often preserved for canning or drying (dried into bonito flakes).

Boquerón *boh-keh-ROHN*

FISH & SHELLFISH (Spain) Anchovy or smelt.

Boquerones en vinagre *boh-keh-ROH-nehs ehn bee-NAH-greh*

DISH (Spain) Anchovies marinated in white wine vinegar and garlic for a few days. They are served cold.

Borraja *boh-RRAH-hah* **Borage**

HERBS & SPICES An herb with blue five-point flowers and green leaves. Popular in Europe, it is eaten both raw and cooked. If raw, it must be finely chopped in order to make sure its hairy texture isn't overwhelming.

Botana *boh-TAH-nah* **Snack**

GENERAL *See* Tentempié.

Bouquet garni *boo-KEH gahr-NEE* **Bouquet garni**

HERBS & SPICES A bunch of herbs that have been tied together with string or bundled in a pouch made of cheesecloth. The traditional combination is parsley, thyme, and bay leaf but any herb combination can be made.

Boysenberry *boy-sehn-BEH-rree* **Boysenberry**

FRUIT & VEGETABLES A berry that looks like a large purple raspberry and has a slight sweet tart flavor. It was made by crossing a raspberry, blackberry, and loganberry in the early 1920s.

Brazo gitano *BRAH-soh hee-TAH-noh*

DISH (Spain) A cake roll filled with custard and pine nuts. The roll is dusted with powdered sugar and cinnamon. Brazo gitano literally translates as "arm of a gypsy."

Brecol *breh-KOHL* **Broccoli**

FRUIT & VEGETABLES A vegetable made up of clusters of dark green buds held by edible stems. A relative of the cabbage and cauliflower family, it resembles cauliflower.

Brecol chino *breh-KOHL CHEE-noh* **Chinese broccoli**

FRUIT & VEGETABLES A vegetable with wide, green leaves connected to a steam, often with small white flower heads attached. The entire vegetable is eaten. It has a slight bitter taste and is used often in stir-fry dishes. It is also known as Chinese kale.

Brema común *BREH-mah koh-MOON* **Bream**
 FISH & SHELLFISH A general term for a species of fish found all over the world in both
 fresh and salt waters. Bream have a firm, white flesh that is low in fat. Popular varieties include sea bream (Japan), *dorada* (Spain), *daurade* (France), and porgy (United
 States).

Brindis *BREEN-dees* **Toast**
 GENERAL To raise one's glass in honor of someone or something.

Brocha *BROH-cha* **Brush**
 EQUIPMENT A handheld instrument containing bristles that is used to spread liquid,
 paste, or powder.

Brocheta / Palillo / Pincho *broh-CHE-tah / pah-LEE-yoh / PEEN-cho* **Skewer**
 EQUIPMENT A long, thin wooden or metal stick with a pointed end used to pierce
 food. Food can be cooked on a skewer or it can be used as a serving tool.

Brocheta de metal *broh-CHE-tah deh meh-TAHL* **Metal skewer**
 EQUIPMENT A rod or stick made of stainless steel used to pierce through food and
 hold it while the food is cooked. It is typically used when grilling food.

Brote *BROH-teh* **Sprout**
 FRUIT & VEGETABLES A baby shoot, a new plant growth. It has a tender texture and
 mild flavor.

Brote de bambú *BROH-teh deh bahm-BOO* **Bamboo shoot**
 FRUIT & VEGETABLES The ivory-colored shoot of an edible bamboo species. It is cut
 as soon as it appears above ground to ensure its tenderness. Bamboo shoots are
 typically found canned but can also be found fresh.

Brote de judía mungo *BROH-teh deh hoo-DEE-ah MOON-goh* **Mung bean
sprout**
 FRUIT & VEGETABLES The germinated sprout of the mung bean, which has a long,
 thin, off-white stem with yellow tips and a crunchy texture and herbaceous, nutty
 flavor. Used as a vegetable, they are served raw or cooked.

Brote de alfalfa *BROH-teh deh ahl-FAHL-fah* **Alfalfa sprout**
 FRUIT & VEGETABLES Thin, long stems produced by sprouted alfalfa seeds that are
 often used in salads and sandwiches.

Budín *boo-DEEN* **Pudding**
 BAKING & PASTRY *See* Pudín.

Buey *boo-WAY* **Crab**
 FISH & SHELLFISH *See* Cangrejo.

Búfalo *BOO-fah-loh* **Buffalo**
 GAME An animal also known as a bison. Its meat is lower in fat than that of beef yet
 very tender. The flavor is very mild. Buffalo milk is used to make cheese.

Bufé *boo-FEH* **Buffet**

GENERAL A meal where food is set out on tables and guests help themselves or are served a helping before sitting down to eat.

Bulgur *BOOL-guhr* **Bulgur**

GRAINS & CEREALS Wheat kernels that have had the bran removed and then are boiled and dried. Often confused with cracked wheat, bulgur is used often in the Middle East.

Buñuelo *boo-ny-WEH-loh* **Doughnut / Fritter**

DISH (1) Traditionally, ring-shaped fried dough topped with sugar, chocolate, or sugarglaze, or filled with jelly, custard, or pastry cream. (2) A sweet or savory fried ball of dough. The batter can be plain or mixed with ground meat, shredded vegetables, or a flavorful condiment. In Cuba, the dough is made from boiled malanga and/or yucca that have been peeled, mashed, and bound with an egg.

Buñuelo de bacalao *boo-ny-WEH-loh deh bah-kah-LAH-oh*

DISH (Spain) Fried puffs made from a dough of salt cod, mashed potato, and egg yolk.

Buñuelos de viento *boo-ny-WEH-lohs deh bee-ehn-toh*

DISH (Spain) Dough that is similar to that of pâte choux. Small balls of dough are deep-fried and dusted with powdered sugar. They are similar to doughnuts. Buñuelos de viento literally translates as "puffs of wind."

Burrito *boo-RREE-toh*

DISH (Mexico) A hot flour tortilla filled with meat or beans and sometimes cheese. The burrito is then rolled, covered with foil, and baked until warmed through.

Butifarra *boo-tee-FAH-rrah*

DISH (Cuba) The broad term for fresh sausage.

(Peru) A ham sandwich served in a round roll with a spicy sauce made with chile peppers and lime.

Butifarra Catalana *boo-tee-FAH-rrah kah-tah-LAH-nah*

DISH (Spain) A spicy fresh pork sausage from Cataluna.

C

Caballa *kah-BAH-yah* **Mackerel**

FISH & SHELLFISH A firm and fatty saltwater fish with a pleasantly strong flavor. Sold whole when small or in fillets or steaks, they spoil quickly as a result of their high fat content and are often smoked to help preserve them. The most popular types are king mackerel and Spanish mackerel.

Cabrito *kah-BREE-toh* **Goat, young**

DISH Meat from a young goat.

(Mexico) A young goat cooked in an underground pit (barbacoa) and flavored with maguey or avocado leaves.

Cacahuete / Maní *kah-kah-WEH-teh / mah-NEE* **Peanut**
FRUIT & VEGETABLES Technically a legume, a dried seed enclosed in an inedible shell / pod. Two nuts are enclosed in a beige-colored, soft shell that has a netted texture. They have a very thin, dark red papery skin that is edible. There are several varieties, the two most popular being the Spanish peanut and the Virginia peanut. Peanuts can be purchased shelled or in the shell.

Cacao en polvo *kah-KAH-oh ehn POHL-boh* **Cocoa powder**
CONDIMENTS Dried ground cocoa beans that have had their cocoa butter removed. Dutch cocoa is cocoa powder that has been treated with an alkali to neutralize its acidity.

Cacerola / Cazuela / Sartén *kah-seh-ROH-lah / kah-soo-EH-lah / sahr-TEHN* **Pan**
EQUIPMENT A wide, shallow cooking vessel typically made from a metal. *See also* **Olla**.

Cacerola de gratinado *kah-seh-ROH-lah deh grah-tee-NAH-doh* **Gratin dish**
EQUIPMENT A special ovenproof dish used to hold food that is to be gratinéed (set under the broiler) and immediately brought to the table.

Cacerola de suflé *kah-seh-ROH-lah deh soo-FLEH* **Soufflé dish**
EQUIPMENT A special round, ovenproof ceramic dish that has a flat bottom and tall straight sides. Traditionally the exterior is fluted. Soufflé dishes come in various sizes.

Cachaça *kah-CHA-sah* **Cachaça**
BEVERAGE A Brazilian distilled alcoholic beverage made from fresh sugarcane juice. The caipirinha is the most popular cachaça-based cocktail.

Cachapas *kah-CHA-pahs*
DISH (Venezuela) Pancakes made from a batter of fresh corn. They are typically served with a topping such as butter or shredded white cheese.

Cadera *kah-DEH-rah* **Rump**
MEAT Meat from the back or hind leg. Another name for round cut.

Café *kah-FEH* **Coffee**
BEVERAGE A caffeinated beverage made by extracting the flavor of ground coffee beans.

Café cubano *kah-FEH koo-BAH-noh* **Cuban coffee**
BEVERAGE Strong espresso coffee that has a sweet sugar-foam floating on top of the coffee. The foam is made by creaming sugar with a few drops of espresso coffee then pouring the coffee over the creamed sugar. It is served in small, one-ounce quantities.

Café de achicoria *kah-FEH deh ah-chee-koh-REE-ah* **Chicory coffee**
BEVERAGE A blend of ground coffee beans and ground chicory root. The root comes from a special variety of chicory that has been dried and roasted.

Café descaffeinado *kah-FEH dehs-kah-feh-ee-NAH-doh* **Coffee, decaffeinated**
BEVERAGE Coffee that has had the caffeine removed. This can be achieved through steaming and removing the caffeine-containing outer layer of the coffee bean or chemically removing it with the addition of a solvent.

Caféina *kah-feh-EE-nah* **Caffeine**
GENERAL A stimulant found naturally in some foods. It affects the nervous system, heart, and kidneys and also dilates blood vessels.

Café instantáneo *kah-FEH eens-tahn-TAH-neh-oh* **Coffee, instant**
BEVERAGE Powdered coffee made by heat drying freshly brewed coffee.

Café solo *kah-FEH SOH-loh* **Espresso**
BEVERAGE *See* Espresso.

Cafetera *kah-feh-TEH-rah* **Coffee maker**
EQUIPMENT An appliance that makes coffee.

Cajeta *kah-HEH-tah*
CONDIMENTS (Mexico) Caramel sauce made from goat's milk similar to dulce de leche.

Calabacín *kah-lah-bah-SEEN* **Zucchini**
FRUIT & VEGETABLES A long, green fruit with an average length of about seven inches and a thin, edible skin. Its flesh is white in color and spongy in texture with small, edible seeds found along its center. A variety of summer squash, it is mildly sweet in flavor.

Calabacín amarillo *kah-lah-bah-SEEN ah-mah-REE-yoh* **Yellow squash**
FRUIT & VEGETABLES A variety of summer squash with a crook neck and soft, edible, yellow skin. Its white flesh contains small, edible seeds and turns translucent when cooked.

Calabaza *kah-lah-BAH-zah* **Pumpkin**
FRUIT & VEGETABLES A large, round, orange fruit that is a winter squash and member of the gourd family. Hard, inedible skin surrounds a sweet, dense flesh that must be cooked before being eaten. A cluster of seeds are found within a membrane web in the center of the fruit and can be eaten when husked and roasted. Canned pumpkin puree is available year-round.

Squash
FRUIT & VEGETABLES A fruit from the gourd family. There are two main varieties: summer squash and winter squash. Summer squashes have a thin, edible skin and seeds with a flesh that is sweet with a high water content. Winter squashes have a hard, thick, inedible skin and seeds and a dense but sweet flesh that must be cooked before eating.

Calabaza almizclera *kah-lah-BAH-zah ahl-mees-KLEH-rah* **Butternut squash**
FRUIT & VEGETABLES A peanut-shaped winter squash that has pale beige skin and bright orange flesh. It has an average weight of two and a half pounds.

Calabaza bellota *kah-lah-BAH-zah beh-YOH-tah* **Acorn squash**
FRUIT & VEGETABLES A round, winter squash with a dark green skin and orange flesh. All winter squashes have hard, thick, inedible skin and seeds that can be removed before or after being cooked.

Calabaza bonetera *kah-lah-BAH-zah boh-neh-TEH-rah* **Pattypan squash**
FRUIT & VEGETABLES A small, flat, round summer squash. Its thin and edible skin can be yellow, green, or white. It is cooked and treated the same way as other summer squashes.

Calabaza de espaguetti *kah-lah-BAH-zah deh eh-spah-GEH-tee* **Spaghetti squash**
FRUIT & VEGETABLES An oblong winter squash measuring about one foot in length with a hard skin that is yellow, orange, or white with green stripes. Its yellow flesh must be cooked to be eaten and separates easily into thin strands that resemble spaghetti pasta.

Calamar / Chipirón *kah-lah-MAHR / chee-pee-ROHN* **Squid**
FISH & SHELLFISH A marine animal with ten legs. The white-colored flesh is sweet but becomes tough and chewy if not cooked properly. After the insides have been eviscerated, the body can be stuffed or sliced into rings and then cooked. The ink sac inside is extracted and used as a coloring and flavoring in a number of recipes.

Calamares en su tinta *kah-lah-MAH-rehs ehn soo TEEN-tah*
DISH (Spain) Squid, large or small, that are stuffed with a mixture of ham and chopped squid tentacles and cooked in a sauce made with the ink from its sac, red wine, and fish broth.

Calçot *kahl-KOHTS*
DISH (Spain) A special type of young green onion that is native to Spain and cooked on the grill until charred. It is eaten whole, plain or dipped in tomato sauce.

Caldera / Olla para caldo *kahl-DEH-rah / oh-YAH PAH-rah KAHL-doh* **Stockpot**
EQUIPMENT A large pot with sides as tall as the pot is wide that allows the liquid to simmer without much reduction. Stockpots come in various sizes ranging from six to thirty-six quarts.

Caldereta *kahl-deh-REH-tah* **Fish stew**
FISH & SHELLFISH A dish prepared by slowly simmering fish and vegetables in a liquid until the liquid thickens up. The slow moist cooking method allows for the meat to tenderize and the flavors to blend.

Caldo *KAHL-doh* **Broth**
CONDIMENTS A liquid obtained from simmering vegetables with meat, poultry, or fish in water.

Caldo blanco *KAHL-doh BLAHN-koh* **Chicken stock**
MEAT *See* **Caldo de pollo**.

Caldo de pollo / Caldo blanco *KAHL-doh deh POH-yoh / KAHL-doh BLAHN-koh*
Chicken stock
MEAT The strained liquid resulting from simmering chicken bones, vegetables, and water. It is used as a base for soups, stews, and sauces.

Caldo gallego *KAHL-doh gah-YEH-goh*
DISH (Spain) A hearty white bean soup from Galicia in northern Spain. White beans are simmered with ham, bacon, and beef chuck and flavored with potatoes, turnips, and kale.

Caldo líquido *KAHL-doh LEE-kee-doh* **Stock**
CONDIMENTS The flavored liquid resulting from the simmering of vegetables, herbs, and animal bones for a long period of time. The liquid is reduced until the flavors are concentrated and the liquid thickens. Stock is used as a base for sauces, soups, and stews.

Caldo oscuro *KAHL-doh ohs-KOO-roh* **Beef stock**
MEAT A strained liquid of simmered browned beef bones and aromatic vegetables.

Caliente *kah-lee-EHN-teh* **Hot**
DESCRIPTOR A descriptive measure of a high temperature.

Callos a la gallega *KAH-yohs ah lah gah-YEH-gah*
DISH (Spain) A hearty dish made with tripe and chickpeas and flavored with paprika and cumin.

Caloría *kah-loh-REE-ah* **Calorie**
GENERAL The unit of measure for food energy. The four sources of calories are carbohydrates, proteins, fats, and alcohol.

Camara frigorífica *KAH-mah-rah free-goh-REE-fee-kah* **Refrigerator**
EQUIPMENT *See* **Nevera**.

Camarón *kah-mah-ROHN* **Shrimp**
FISH & SHELLFISH A crustacean found in both fresh and salt water. Shrimp live on the water's floor and feed by filtering food matter. There are two main classifications: larger warm-water shrimp and smaller cold-water shrimp. They come in a variety of colors (pink, light brown, gray) and sizes. The cooked flesh is meaty, sweet, and succulent. Though the terms prawns and shrimp are used interchangeably, and the crustaceans are of the same order, they are different species.

Camarones al ajillo *kah-mah-ROH-nehs ahl ah-HEE-yoh*
DISH (Cuba) Shrimp cooked in a garlic and oil sauce.

Cambur *kahm-boor* **Banana**
FRUIT & VEGTABLE *See* **Plátano**.

Camote *kah-MOH-teh* **White sweet potato**
FRUIT & VEGETABLE *See* **Batata blanca**.

Camu camu *KAH-moo KAH-moo*
FRUIT & VEGETABLES (Peru) A cherry-looking fruit from the camu camu tree. The flesh is extremely tart and must be pureed and mixed with water or milk and sugar in order to be eaten. It has a dark red color that imparts a pink hue to drinks and food.

Caña de azúcar *kah-NYAH deh ah-SOO-kahr* **Sugarcane**
FRUIT & VEGETABLES A tall, thick grass rich in a sweet juice that when extracted and refined produces sugar and the by-product of molasses. Hard and fibrous grass, it has an inedible skin that must be peeled. Sugarcane is often used as skewers or stirrers in cocktails.

Canchas *KAHN-chas*
FRUIT & VEGETABLES (Peru) Toasted corn kernels that are often used as a garnish on ceviche or eaten as a snack. A special variety of corn indigenous to Peru is used. Canchas look like large, half-popped popcorn kernels.

Canela *kah-NEH-lah* **Cinnamon**
HERBS & SPICES The dried inner bark of the evergreen tree. The brick red–colored spice can be purchased as sticks or ground powder. It has a pungent bittersweet flavor that is used in both sweet and savory dishes.

Canelazo *kah-neh-LAH-soh*
BEVERAGE (Colombia) An alcoholic beverage made of aguapanela mixed with cinnamon and aguardiente.

Cangrejo / Buey / Jaiba / Centollo *kahn-GREH-hoh / boo-WEH / HAY-ee-bah / sehn-TOH-yoh* **Crab**
FISH & SHELLFISH A crustacean found in fresh or salt water. Of the more than four-thousand varieties that exist, all have two claws in addition to their legs. Crabmeat is sweet and can be served cold or hot after it has been cooked and removed from its shell. It is available fresh, canned, or frozen.

Cangrejo azul *kahn-GREH-hoh ah-SOOL* **Blue crab**
FISH & SHELLFISH A crustacean that is found along the Atlantic Coast and the Gulf of Mexico. It has blue claws and a blue green shell and can be both hard- or soft-shelled.

Cañitas al brandy *kah-NYEE-tahs ahl BRAHN-dee* **Brandy snaps**
BAKING & PASTRY Thin, crisp cookies baked in the oven until golden brown. They remain pliable when hot and are shaped into tubes or baskets stuffed or filled with cream and/or fruit. They may or may not contain brandy but are made with a good amount of butter, sugar, and corn syrup, which allow them to be shaped when hot.

Cantaloup *kahn-tah-LOOP* **Cantaloupe**
FRUIT & VEGETABLES A fruit whose skin is netted with a greenish gray color and has orange flesh. The cantaloupes found in the United States are really muskmelons; true cantaloupes are found in Europe.

Cantarela *kahn-tah-REH-lah* **Chanterelle**

FRUIT & VEGETABLES A funnel-shaped wild mushroom that is yellow orange in color with gills that run beneath its cap. It has a nutty flavor and chewy, meaty texture. It can be found fresh, dried, or canned.

Cantimpalo *kahn-teem-PAH-loh*

MEAT (Spain) A highly regarded variety of chorizo from the area of Cantimpalo. The paprika-cured pork sausage is thick in diameter and contains big chunks of meat.

Caparazón / Concha *kah-pah-rah-SOHN / KOHN-cha* **Shell**

FISH & SHELLFISH The hard outer covering of many marine animals. For certain animals it is their skeletal system.

Caparrón *kah-pah-RROHN* **Red kidney bean**

FRUIT & VEGETABLE See **Judía roja**.

Capeado *kah-peh-AH-doh* **Crusted**

COOKING METHOD / TECHNIQUE See **Rebozado**.

Caracol *kah-rah-KOHL* **Snail**

MEAT A land or water mollusk that has a spiral shell. Eaten for thousands of years, it is considered a delicacy.

Caracola *kah-rah-KOH-lah* **Conch**

FISH & SHELLFISH A mollusk found in a single spiral shell in southern warm waters. The muscle can be eaten raw but must be tenderized by being pounded or finely chopped if cooked.

Carageena *kah-rah-GEE-nah* **Carrageenan**

GENERAL A thickener and stabilizer that gels like gelatin and is able to do so at room temperature. Derived from a seaweed, it is a vegetarian alternative to gelatin.

Carambola / Fruta estrella *kah-rahm-BOH-lah / FROO-tah ehs-TREH-yah* **Carambola**

FRUIT & VEGETABLES A tropical fruit with a waxy skin that has five prominent protrusions. When sliced crosswise, it takes the shape of a star, which is why it is also referred to as star fruit. When ripe, it has a yellow orange skin and flesh that contains a small dark seed. It is juicy with a fresh, slightly tart flavor.

Caramelizado *kah-rah-meh-lee-ZAH-doh* **Caramelized**

COOKING METHOD / TECHNIQUE The browning that occurs when heating food that contains carbohydrates.

Caramelizar *kah-rah-meh-lee-ZAHR* **Caramelize**

COOKING METHOD / TECHNIQUE To heat sugar until it melts and turns a dark golden brown color.

Caramelo *kah-rah-MEH-loh* **Caramel**

BAKING & PASTRY Melted sugar that has been heated until it turns into an amber-colored syrup. A small amount of water can be added to thin the mixture. When the liquid cools it becomes hard and brittle. Butter or cream can be added to it to make a soft caramel.

Caramelo / Dulces *kah-rah-MEH-loh / DOOL-sehs* **Candy**
BAKING & PASTRY The generic term for a sweet confection. It can be hard or soft and made with or without chocolate.

Caraota negra *kah-rah-OH-tah NEH-grah* **Black bean**
FRUITS & VEGETABLES *See* **Frijol negro**.

Carapulcra *kah-rah-POOL-krah*
DISH (Peru) A pork and chicken stew that contains chile peppers, peanuts, cumin, and dried potatoes (freeze dried) that are toasted on a skillet before being added to the stew.

Carbohidrato *kahr-boh-ee-DRAH-toh* **Carbohydrate**
GENERAL A nutrient needed to sustain life and the most common source of energy. Sugar, starch, and fiber are all carbohydrates.

Cardamomo *kahr-dah-MOH-moh* **Cardamom**
HERBS & SPICES A member of the ginger family, a light green pod filled with small black seeds. When the whole pod is used, it should be lightly crushed in order to help extract the flavor of the seeds. The aroma and flavor are warm, sweet, and strong. A little of this spice goes a long way unless you are using the ground variety, which is much weaker.

Careta de cerdo *kah-REH-tah deh SEHR-doh* **Pig cheeks**
MEAT The cheeks of a hog, also known as hog jowls. They are typically smoked and cured and used for flavoring dishes.

Carimanolas *kah-ree-mah-NOH-lahs*
DISH (Colombia) Yuca fritters made from a mash of the root vegetable. They are often served with tomato sauce.

Carne *KAHR-neh* **Meat**
MEAT An animal's flesh consumed as food. It can be its muscle or an organ.

Carne de cerdo / Carne de puerco *KAHR-neh deh SEHR-doh / KAHR-neh deh poo-EHR-koh* **Pork**
MEAT Meat from domesticated pigs that are less than a year old. The meat can be fresh or cured.

Carne de cerdo, chuleta *KAHR-neh deh SEHR-doh , choo-LEH-tah* **Pork, chop**
MEAT The cut of meat from the loin section that is cut perpendicular to the spine and typically has a rib bone attached.

Carne de cerdo, costillas *KAHR-neh deh SEHR-doh, kohs-TEE-yahs* **Pork, spareribs**
MEAT The meat that comes from the lower portion of the ribs, the part closest to the underbelly of the pig. Very flavorful, and popular for barbecuing, they have less

meat and more fat than baby back ribs that come from the loin section. St. Louis–style ribs are trimmed spare-ribs.

Carne de cerdo, escalopa KAHR-neh deh SEHR-doh, ehs-kah-LOH-pah **Pork, escalope**

MEAT A very thin slice of boneless pork that has been pounded.

Carne de cerdo, filete KAHR-neh deh SEHR-doh, fee-LEH-teh **Pork, cutlet**

MEAT A thin, boneless slice of pork.

Carne de cerdo, lomo KAHR-neh deh SEHR-doh, LOH-moh **Pork, loin**

MEAT The cut of meat located on the top (back) of the pig between the leg and the shoulder. Found on either side of the spine / rib cage, it is a very tender and lean cut that will dry out if overcooked.

Carne de cerdo, paletilla / Pernil KAHR-neh deh SEHR-doh, pah-leh-TEE-yah / pehr-NEEL **Pork, shoulder**

MEAT The meat from the upper portion of the front leg of the pig. Very flavorful and a bit fatty, it is also known as pork butt. See also **Paleta**.

Carne de cerdo, pierna KAHR-neh deh SEHR-doh, pee-EHR-nah **Pork, leg**

MEAT A cut that is taken from the back legs of the pig. Ham comes from this cut.

Carne de cerdo, pierna deshuesada KAHR-neh deh SEHR-doh, pee-EHR-nah dehs-weh-SAH-dah **Pork, boneless leg**

MEAT Meat of the pork leg that has had the bone removed.

Carne de cerdo, solomillo KAHR-neh deh SEHR-doh, soh-loh-MEE-yoh **Pork, tenderloin**

MEAT The meat taken from the loin section of the pig. The most tender cut of pork, this thin, elongated muscle is usually sold in pairs.

Carne de cerdo troceada KAHR-neh deh SEHR-doh troh-seh-AH-dah **Pork, diced**

MEAT Any cut of pork that has been cut into small pieces before or after cooking.

Carne de puerco KAHR-neh deh poo-EHR-koh **Pork**

MEAT See **Carne de cerdo**.

Carne de res / Vacuno KAHR-neh deh rehs / bah-KOO-noh **Beef**

MEAT Cattle raised for its meat. The term refers to the animal's muscles, which are portioned into cuts and graded on quality by the USDA (prime, choice, select).

Carne de res, arrachera KAHR-neh deh rehs, ah-rrah-CHEH-rah **Skirt steak**

MEAT See **Entraña**.

Carne de res, asado de tira / Costilla cargada KAHR-neh deh rehs, ah-SAH-doh deh TEE-rah / kohs-TEE-yah kahr-GAH-dah **Short ribs**

MEAT The cut of meat that comes from the short plate of cattle. Specifically, it is found in the bottom portion of the ribs, close to the belly. It is a very flavorful but fatty cut of meat filled with connective tissue. It is the same cut as the St. Louis–style sparerib in pork.

Carne de res, bife ancho *KAHR-neh deh rehs, BEE-feh AHN-choh* **Rib eye**
MEAT *See* **Filete de lomo alto.**

Carne de res, bife ancho con costilla / Lomo vetado con costilla / Churrasco redondo *KAHR-neh deh rehs, BEE-feh AHN-choh kohn kohs-TEE-yah / LOH-moh beh-TAH-doh kohn kohs-TEE-yah / choo-RRAHS-koh reh-DOHN-doh* **Porterhouse**
MEAT Cut from the rear and end of the short loin. A large cut of beef with the bone still attached. Similar to the T-bone, it consists of both the tenderloin and strip steak. (A porterhouse steak is a large T-bone taken from the rear of the short loin.)

Carne de res, bife angosto *KAHR-neh deh rehs, BEE-feh ahn-GOHS-toh* **Sirloin**
MEAT *See* **Solomillo.**

Carne de res, bife angosto con lomo *KAHR-neh deh rehs, BEE-feh ahn-GOHS-toh kohn LOH-moh* **T-Bone**
MEAT *See* **Chuleta con solomillo.**

Carne de res, bife chico *KAHR-neh deh rehs, BEE-feh CHEE-koh* **Sirloin**
MEAT *See* **Solomillo.**

Carne de res, bistec de cadera / Colita de cuadril / Punta de picana / Empuje *KAHR-neh deh rehs, bees-TEHK deh kah-DEH-rah / koh-LEE-tah deh kwah-DREEL / POON-tah deh pee-KAH-nah / ehm-POO-heh* **Rump steak**
MEAT A steak cut from the top round (tail end) section. The most tender part of the round. Lean and moderately tough, it is best when braised.

Carne de res, cadera *KAHR-neh deh rehs, kah-DEH-rah* **Top Round**
MEAT *See* **Tapa plana.**

Carne de res, chuleta con solomillo / Bife angosto con lomo / Entrecot *KAHR-neh deh rehs, choo-LEH-tah kohn soh-loh-MEE-yoh / BEE-feh ahn-GOHS-toh kohn LOH-moh / ehn-treh-KOHT* **T-Bone**
MEAT Cut from the middle section of the short loin. Consists of a T-shaped bone with meat on either side—a strip steak and a tenderloin.

Carne de res, churrasco redondo *KAHR-neh deh rehs, choo-RRAHS-koh reh-DOHN-doh* **Porterhouse**
MEAT *See* **Bife ancho con costilla.**

Carne de res, colita de cuadril *KAHR-neh deh rehs, koh-LEE-tah deh kwah-DREEL* **Rump steak**
MEAT *See* **Bistec de cadera.**

Carne de res, corte de solomillo *KAHR-neh deh rehs, KOHR-teh deh soh-loh-MEE-yoh* **Fillet steak**
MEAT *See* **Filete.**

Carne de res, costilla cargada *KAHR-neh deh rehs, kohs-TEE-yah kahr-GAH-dah* **Short ribs**
MEAT *See* **Asado de tira.**

Carne de res, empuje *KAHR-neh deh rehs, ehm-POO-heh* **Rump steak**
MEAT *See* **Bistec de cadera.**

Carne de res, entraña / Arrachera *KAHR-neh deh rehs, ehn-TRAH-nya / ah-rrah-CHEH-rah* **Skirt Steak**

MEAT Cut taken from the plate or belly of cattle. Specifically, it is the diaphram muscle. Flat and long, it is flavorful but a bit fatty and tough. It is the cut most often used to make fajitas.

Carne de res, entrecot *KAHR-neh deh rehs, ehn-treh-KOHT* **T-Bone**

MEAT *See* **Chuleta con solomillo**.

Carne de res, espadilla *KAHR-neh deh rehs, ehs-pah-DEE-yah* **Chuck**

MEAT An inexpensive cut of meat located between the neck and shoulder. It is a tough cut that must be cooked slowly to be tenderized. It is a popular cut for making hamburgers.

Carne de res, falda / Vacio / Tapabarriga *KAHR-neh deh rehs, FAHL-dah / bah-SEE-oh / tah-pah-bah-RREE-gah* **Flank**

MEAT A flat and fibrous cut of beef from the belly muscle of the cow. It is almost always marinated before cooking because, while very flavorful, it is tough and needs tenderizing.

Carne de res, filete / Corte de solomillo *KAHR-neh deh rehs, fee-LEH-teh / KOHR-teh deh soh-loh-MEE-yoh* **Fillet steak**

MEAT An individual portion of the tenderloin. Also referred to as filet mignon.

Carne de res, filete de lomo alto / Bife ancho / Lomo vetado *KAHR-neh deh rehs, fee-LEH-teh deh LOH-moh AHL-toh / BEE-feh AHN-choh / LOH-moh beh-TAH-doh* **Rib eye**

MEAT Cut from the rib section. A very tender steak available with or without the bone.

Carne de res, lomo *KAHR-neh deh rehs, LOH-moh* **Whole tenderloin**

MEAT *See* **Solomillo entero**.

Carne de res, lomo liso *KAHR-neh deh rehs, LOH-moh LEE-soh* **Sirloin**

MEAT *See* **Solomillo**.

Carne de res, Lomo vetado *KAHR-neh deh rehs, LOH-moh beh-TAH-doh* **Rib eye**

MEAT *See* **Filete de lomo alto**.

Carne de res, lomo vetado con costilla *KAHR-neh deh rehs, LOH-moh beh-TAH-doh kohn kohs-TEE-yah* **Porterhouse**

MEAT *See* **Bife ancho con costilla**.

Carne de res, planchuela *KAHR-neh deh rehs, plahn-choo-EH-lah* **Short plate**

MEAT *See* **Tapa de asado**.

Carne de res, plateada *KAHR-neh deh rehs, plah-teh-AH-dah* **Short plate**

MEAT *See* **Tapa de asado**.

Carne de res, punta de ganso *KAHR-neh deh rehs, POON-tah deh GAHN-soh* **Top round**

MEAT *See* **Tapa plana**.

Carne de res, punta de picana *KAHR-neh deh rehs, POON-tah deh pee-KAH-nah* **Rump steak**

  MEAT *See* Bistec de cadera.

Carne de res, solomillo / Bife angosto / Lomo liso / Bife chico *KAHR-neh deh rehs, soh-loh-MEE-yoh / BEE-feh ahn-GOHS-toh / LOH-moh LEE-soh / BEE-feh CHEE-koh* **Sirloin**

  MEAT The cut of beef located between the short loin and round. Typically cut into steaks, it is a flavorful cut with a firm texture.

Carne de res, solomillo entero / Lomo *KAHR-neh deh rehs, soh-loh-MEE-yoh ehn-TEH-roh / LOH-moh* **Whole tenderloin**

  MEAT Considered the most tender cut of beef. Located in the loin section of the cattle (the middle of its back), this muscle does very little work and remains tender.

Carne de res, tapa de asado / Plateada / Planchuela *KAHR-neh deh rehs, TAH-pah deh ah-SAH-doh / plah-teh-AH-doh / plahn-choo-EH-lah* **Short plate**

  MEAT A cut from the belly area below the ribs, it is best when slow cooked by moist heat.

Carne de res, tapa de cuadril *KAHR-neh deh rehs, TAH-pah deh kwah-DREEL* **Top round**

  MEAT *See* Tapa plana.

Carne de res, Tapa plana / Tapa de cuadril / Punta de ganso / Cadera *KAHR-neh deh rehs, TAH-pah PLAH-nah / TAH-pah deh kwah-DREEL / POON-tah deh GAHN-soh / kah-DEH-rah* **Top round**

  MEAT The top portion of the round (tail end) section of the cattle.

Carne de res, tapabarriga *KAHR-neh deh rehs, tah-pah-bah-RREE-gah* **Flank**

  MEAT *See* Falda.

Carne de res, vacío *KAHR-neh deh rehs, bah-SEE-oh* **Flank**

  MEAT *See* Falda.

Carne molida *KAHR-neh moh-LEE-dah* **Ground beef**

  MEAT A cut of beef that has been ground. Depending on the cut used, fat may be incorporated into it.

Carne molida en forma *KAHR-neh moh-LEE-dah ehn FOHR-mah* **Meat patty**

  MEAT Ground meat that has been shaped into a round, flat disk.

Carnero *kahr-NEH-roh* **Mutton**

  MEAT The meat of a domesticated sheep that is over two years old. It has a stronger flavor and tougher flesh than those of a younger lamb.

Carne seca *KAHR-neh SEH-kah* **Beef jerky**

  MEAT Dried beef, also known as *tasajo*.

Carnitas *kahr-NEE-tahs*

  DISH (Mexico) Seasoned and fried tender pork that is shredded.

Carozo *kah-ROH-soh* **Pit**

FRUIT & VEGETABLES The seed or stone of a fruit located in the center of its flesh.

Carpa *KAHR-pah* **Carp**

FISH & SHELLFISH A freshwater fish native to Asia. Its most popular use in the United States is as the main ingredient in gefilte fish.

Carta *KAHR-tah* **Menu**

GENERAL (1) A list of dishes to be served. (2) A list of options to choose from in order to create a meal.

Cáscara *KAHS-kah-rah* **Zest**

FRUIT & VEGETABLE *See* **Piel**.

Caseína *kah-seh-EE-nah* **Casein**

DAIRY The principal protein found in milk. It coagulates or thickens when mixed with rennin, forming cheese.

Castaña *kahs-TAH-nyah* **Chestnut**

NUTS & OILS A nut encased in a hard, dark shell that must be removed along with its bitter inner skin before being eaten. It can be eaten raw but that is not common in the United States. Typically a chestnut is roasted, boiled, pureed, or candied resulting in a nut with a soft texture and sweet flavor.

Castaña de agua *kahs-TAH-nyah deh AH-gwah* **Water chestnut**

FRUIT & VEGETABLES A root vegetable that grows underwater in flooded paddy fields. Small, round, and with a brown skin that has to be peeled. It resembles a chestnut. Its flesh is white and stays crunchy even when cooked. Available fresh or canned, it can be eaten raw or cooked.

Cau cau criollo *KAH-oo KAH-oo kree-OH-yoh*

DISH (Peru) A dish consisting of cooked tripe (intestine) served in a sauce made from onion, garlic, yellow chile peppers, turmeric, and boiled potatoes. The dish can also be made with seafood and would then go by the name seafood cau cau (cau cau de marisco).

Causa *KAH-oo-sah*

DISH (Peru) A cold potato salad flavored with lemon, chile peppers, and olive oil, served layered with chicken, shrimp, or canned tuna. Avocado and mayonnaise are also added to the layers.

Cava *KAH-vah*

BEVERAGE (Spain) A sparkling wine from Spain that is made by the Champagne method. It is named after the cellars in which the wine is produced.

Cayena *kah-YEH-nah* **Cayenne pepper**

FRUIT & VEGETABLES A bright red, hot chile pepper available in both fresh and dried form. When dried and crushed, it is referred to as crushed red pepper. When dried and ground, it is referred to as cayenne pepper.

Caza *KAH-sah* **Game**
  GAME Hunted wild animals that are safe for human consumption. Popular examples are duck, boar, rabbit, and venison.

Cazabe *kah-SAH-beh* **Cassava**
  FRUIT & VEGETABLE *See* **Yuca**.

Cazerola para asar *kah-seh-ROH-lah PAH-rah ah-SAHR* **Roasting pan**
  EQUIPMENT A wide, shallow pan used to roast meats and/or vegetables. It may or may not have handles and is often fitted with a rack to lift the food off the bottom of the pan ensuring even air circulation.

Cazón *kah-SOHN*
  FISH & SHELLFISH (Mexico) A sand shark. Its flesh is very firm and meaty in texture.

Cazuela *kah-soo-EH-lah* **Pan**
  EQUIPMENT *See* **Cacerola**.

Cazuela cacerola *kah-soo-EH-lah kah-seh-ROH-lah* **Casserole dish**
  EQUIPMENT A deep, ovenproof dish that goes from oven to table. It can be round, square, or rectangular and may have handles and a lid.

Cebada *seh-BAH-dah* **Barley**
  GRAINS & CEREALS An ancient grain used often for animal fodder. When malted, it can make beer or whiskey.

Cebada perlada *seh-BAH-dah pehr-LAH-dah* **Pearl barley**
  GRAINS & CEREALS Barley that has had its husk and bran layer removed, resulting in a softer texture and whiter color. It cooks faster than regular barley.

Cebolla *seh-BOH-yah* **Onion**
  FRUIT & VEGETABLES The bulb of an onion plant that has an inedible, papery outer skin and a juicy interior flesh made up of concentric layers. There are many varieties of onion ranging in color, size, and flavor. Prized for its aromatic aroma and flavor, it can be eaten raw but is used sparingly due to its pungent and sharp flavor. Cooking mellows an onion's flavor and brings out its sweetness.

Cebolla española *seh-BOH-yah ehs-pah-NYOH-lah* **Spanish onion**
  FRUIT & VEGETABLES A large, round onion that comes in three colors: yellow, red, and white. The yellow variety is sweet and the red is used raw when thinly sliced.

Cebolla roja *seh-BOH-yah ROH-hah* **Red onion**
  FRUIT & VEGETABLES A medium-size onion with a reddish purple–colored skin. It has an intense sweet flavor that decreases when it is cooked. It is also known as Italian onion or purple onion.

Cebolla verde *seh-BOH-yah BEHR-deh* **Green onion**
  FRUIT & VEGETABLES An immature onion. It has a white base that is beginning to turn into a bulb and a straight green top, both of which are edible. The white portion has a stronger flavor. It is also referred to as a scallion although it is not exactly the same.

Cebolleta *seh-boh-YEH-tah* **Scallion**

FRUIT & VEGETABLES A member of the onion family with a mild onion flavor lacking a fully developed bulb. It has a stronger-flavored white base close to the roots and milder-tasting green tops. Long and straight, the entire scallion can be eaten raw or cooked. It is also known as spring onion or green onion.

Cebollino *seh-boh-YEE-noh* **Chive**

HERBS & SPICES A member of the onion family. This green herb is a long, thin stem with a mild onion flavor. It produces small flowers that can be eaten but are mostly used for garnish.

Cebollita en vinagre *seh-boh-YEE-tahs ehn bee-NAH-greh* **Cocktail onion**

CONDIMENTS A pickled sweet pearl onion that maintains a crunchy texture. It is used as a garnish in cocktails.

Cecina *seh-SEE-nah*

MEAT (Spain) Dried, cured beef. It is also called *jamón de toro*.

Cedazo *seh-DAH-soh* **Sieve**

EQUIPMENT *See* **Criba**.

Cena *SEH-nah* **Dinner**

GENERAL The evening meal. In the United States it is the main meal of the day; in other countries it may be a light supper eaten after 9:00 p.m.

Centeno *sehn-TEH-noh* **Rye**

GRAINS & CEREALS A cereal grass whose grain is harvested and milled into flour. Low in gluten, it is a key ingredient in pumpernickel bread. Rye is also used for making whiskey.

Centollo *sehn-TOH-yoh* **Crab**

FISH & SHELLFISH *See* **Cangrejo**.

Centrifugadora de ensalada / Escurridora de ensalada *sehn-tree-foo-gah-DOH-rah deh ehn-sah-LAH-dah / ehs-koo-ree-DOH-rah deh ehn-sah-LAH-dah* **Salad spinner**

EQUIPMENT A kitchen tool that uses centrifugal force to dry its contents, primarily salad greens. A plastic basket containing the food is placed inside a bowl. When the top is sealed, the basket spins and shoots out excess water, which collects in the bowl.

Cepillo de fregar *seh-PEE-yoh deh freh-GAHR* **Scrubbing brush**

EQUIPMENT A brush made with short stiff bristles that are rubbed against dirty surfaces for cleaning.

Cepillo para repostería *seh-PEE-yoh PAH-rah reh-pohs-teh-REE-ah* **Pastry brush**

EQUIPMENT A thin-bristled brush used for a variety of pastry tasks such as wiping off excess flour or brushing egg wash onto pastry.

Cerdo / Puerco / Chancho *SEHR-doh / PWEHR-koh / CHAHN-choh* **Pork**
MEAT Meat from domesticated pigs that are less than a year old. It can be fresh or cured. *See also* **Carne de cerdo.**

Cereal *SEH-reh-ahl* **Cereal**
GRAINS & CEREALS A plant from the grass family that produces an edible seed. Rice, corn, wheat, and oats are popular examples of cereal.

Cereza *seh-REH-sah* **Cherry**
FRUIT & VEGETABLES A small, round fruit surrounding a seed that ranges in color from bright red to purplish black to golden. It can be either sweet or sour. The sour variety is too tart to be eaten raw and is used for baking or confections.

Cernedor *sehr-neh-DOHR* **Sifter**
EQUIPMENT A handheld kitchen tool used for sifting.

Cerner *sehr-NEHR* **Sift**
COOKING METHOD / TECHNIQUE *See* **Tamizar.**

Cerveza *sehr-VEH-sah* **Beer**
BEVERAGE It is made from a mixture of malted cereals, hops, yeast, and water. The alcoholic beverage most consumed in the world.

Cesta de bambú *SEHS-tah deh bahm-BOO* **Bamboo steamer**
EQUIPMENT *See* **Olla de bambú.**

Ceviche / Cebiche *seh-BEE-cheh*
FISH & SHELLFISH (Peru) Bite-size pieces of fish (typically corvina) that are marinated in lime juice and flavored with chiles. The acid from the citrus juice cures the fish. The fish is never heated. As opposed to the one from Mexico, Peruvian ceviche does not contain tomatoes. Typically topped with raw onions and toasted corn and served with boiled sweet potatoes and a local seaweed called yuyo, it is a staple throughout the coastal region of Peru.

Chaira *CHAH-ee-rah* **Honing steel**
EQUIPMENT A metal rod that is coated with a special fine abrasive. A knife is passed over it at a specific angle to align the material on the blade's edge but it does not reshape or sharpen it.

Chairo *CHAH-ee-roh*
DISH (Peru) A soup made from chalona (dried beef), chuno (freeze-dried potatoes), red chile pepper, and camote (sweet potatoes).

Chalona *chah-LOH-nah*
Meat (Peru) Salt-cured lamb meat that is left to dry in the sun for up to a month. Alpaca meat was traditionally used for this.

Chalota *chah-LOH-tah* **Shallot**
FRUIT & VEGETABLE *See* **Escalonia.**

Chalupa *chah-LOO-pah*
DISH *See* **Sope.**

Champaña / Champán *cham-PAH-nya / cham-PAHN* **Champagne**
BEVERAGE A sparkling wine from the northeast region of France called Champagne. Its color can range from light yellow to blush rose. Its sweetness varies from bone dry to very sweet.

Champiñón *cham-pee-ny-OHN* **Mushroom**
FRUIT & VEGETABLES *See* **Seta.**

Champiñón portobello *cham-pee-ny-OHN pohr-toh-BEH-loh* **Portobello mushroom**
FRUIT & VEGETABLES *See* **Seta portobello.**

Champiñón salvaje *cham-pee-ny-OHN sahl-BAH-heh* **Wild mushrooms**
FRUIT & VEGETABLES *See* **Seta salvaje.**

Champurrado *cham-poo-RRAH-doh*
BEVERAGE (Mexico) A chocolate version of atole popular in Oaxaca where chocolate is melted into the atole. It is also called atole de chocolate.

Champús *cham-POOS*
BEVERAGE (Colombia) A smoothie-style drink made from a base of corn-infused water that has been sweetened with panela. The base is flavored with pineapple and lulo fruit and then pureed with ice.

Chancho *CHAN-choh* **Pork**
MEAT *See* **Cerdo.**

Changua *chan-GOO-ah*
DISH (Colombia) A light soup often drunk for breakfast. Similar in consistency to an egg drop soup, it is made with milk, water, and egg and flavored with cilantro.

Changurro *chahn-GOO-rroh*
DISH *See* **Shangurro.**

Charquí *cha-ree-KEE*
COOKING METHOD / TECHNIQUE (Peru) (1) A technique for drying meat that salts it before dehydrating it. (2) The name given to the meat that is dried by this technique.

Chaucha *cha-OO-cha* **Green bean**
FRUIT & VEGETABLE *See* **Judía verde.**

Chayote *cha-YOH-teh* **Chayote**
FRUIT & VEGETABLES A pear-shaped fruit with a pale green, slightly wrinkled, edible skin. Its white flesh is bland tasting but some say it resembles a cucumber. It has a soft seed in its center that is not eaten. Chayote can be eaten cooked or raw and can be treated similarly to a summer squash.

SPANISH-ENGLISH C

Cherna *CHEHR-nah* **Grouper**
FISH & SHELLFISH A firm, white fish from the warm Atlantic or Gulf waters. A member of the sea bass family, it has skin with a very strong flavor that should be removed before cooking.

Chicha *CHEE-cha*
BEVERAGE (Colombia) A strong alcoholic beverage made from fermented corn. It is drunk all over Colombia and typically served in dried coconut shells.

Chicha morada *CHEE-cha moh-RAH-dah*
BEVERAGE (Peru) A nonalcoholic beverage made from an infusion of purple corn and water. The infusion is chilled before chopped fruit, lemon, and sugar are added.

Chicharro *CHEE-chah-rroh* **Split green pea**
FRUIT & VEGETABLE *See* **Guisante verde partido**.

Chicharrón *chee-cha-RROHN* **Cracklings**
MEAT Crisp, browned pork skin that has been fried or roasted. It can have meat still attached to it.

Chicozapote *chee-koh-sah-POH-teh* **Sapodilla**
FRUIT & VEGETABLES The small, egg-shaped fruit (two to four-inches in diameter) that grows on the sapodilla tree whose bark produces a white gum called chicle, the base for chewing gum. Its skin is brown and scruffy and its flesh is pale beige. Sweet and juicy with a couple of seeds in its center, the fruit does not ripen until picked from the tree.

Chifas *CHEE-fahs*
GENERAL (Peru) A Chinese restaurant in Peru.

Chilaquiles *chee-lah-KEE-lehs*
DISH (Mexico) A tortilla casserole. Day-old tortillas are fried, drained, and then tossed in a warm chili sauce. The entire mixture is then covered with crumbled queso fresco, crema, onion, and cilantro.

Chile / Guindilla *CHEE-leh / geen-DEE-yah* **Chile**
HERBS & SPICES A pod of a plant of the *Capsicum* genus. There are more than two hundred varieties greatly ranging in length and width. The chile originated in the Americas and has long been associated with Mexican cuisine. It is widely known for the heat it imparts which varies from mild to blistering hot. *See also* **Pimiento italiano; Cayena**.

Chile anaheim / Guindilla anaheim *CHEE-leh ah-nah-eh-EEM / geen-DEE-yah ah-nah-eh-EEM* **Anaheim chile**
HERBS & SPICES A long and narrowly shaped, slightly sweet and mild chile that comes in green and red varieties. One of the most commonly used varieties in the United States, it and can be purchased fresh or dried and is frequently stuffed.

Chile ancho / Guindilla ancho *CHEE-leh AHN-choh / geen-DEE-yah AHN-choh*
Ancho chile

HERBS & SPICES The sweetest of the dried chiles. Its heat is mild and its color is a deep, reddish brown. It gets its name from its broad width (*ancho* means wide in Spanish). It is a dried poblano.

Chile chilaca / Guindilla chilaca *CHEE-leh chee-LAH-kah / geen-DEE-yah chee-LAH-kah* **Chilaca chile**

HERBS & SPICES A very long and thin, fresh chile pepper measuring up to nine inches in length. Richly flavored with medium heat, it is dark green in color and turns dark brown when ripe. When dried, it is a pasilla chile or chile negro.

Chile chipotle / Guindilla chipotle *CHEE-leh chee-POHT-leh / geen-DEE-yah chee-POHT-leh* **Chipotle chile**

HERBS & SPICES A dried and smoked jalapeño. Dark brown with wrinkled skin and a smoky, slightly sweet flavor, chipotles are available dried or canned in adobo.

Chile habanero / Guindilla habanero *CHEE-leh ah-bah-NEH-roh / geen-DEE-yah ah-bah-NEH-roh* **Habanero chile**

HERBS & SPICES A very hot chile that has a slight fruity flavor. Small and round, it is typically green in color but turns orange when ripe.

Chile jalapeño / Guindilla jalapeño *CHEE-leh hah-lah-peh-NYOH / geen-DEE-yah hah-lah-peh-NYOH* **Jalapeño chile**

HERBS & SPICES A small hot chile pepper that averages about two inches in length. Its smooth skin is green when unripe and turns red if left to mature on the vine. Its seeds and veins, which hold most of the heat, can be easily removed. It is available fresh or canned. Dried, smoked jalapeños are called chipotle peppers.

Chile mulato / Guindilla mulato *CHEE-leh moo-LAH-toh / geen-DEE-yah moo-LAH-toh* **Mulato chile**

HERBS & SPICES A type of dried poblano chile that is darker and sweeter than other varieties. Dark brown, wrinkled, and measuring about four inches long, it has a mild spice and a chocolate, licorice flavor.

Chilendrón *chee-lehn-DROHN*

DISH (Spain) The term given to foods cooked with roasted red peppers (pimientos). Chicken, pork, and lamb are commonly used. This style of cooking is typical in the region of Aragon.

Chile pasilla / Guindilla pasilla *CHEE-leh pah-SEE-yah / geen-DEE-yah pah-SEE-yah* **Pasilla chile**

HERBS & SPICES A long, thin, dried chile measuring about seven inches in length. Black and wrinkled, it is sometimes referred to as chile negro (black chile). Richly flavored but mildly hot, it is the dried version of the chilaca chile.

Chile poblano / Guindilla poblano *CHEE-leh pohb-LAH-noh / geen-DEE-yah pohb-LAH-noh* **Poblano chile**
HERBS & SPICES A dark green, mild chile whose flavor is more intense the darker its skin is. It gets its name from Puebla, Mexico, where it originates. Measuring about two by four inches, it is very commonly roasted and stuffed. When dried, it is called ancho or mulato chile.

Chile serrano / Guindilla serrano *CHEE-leh seh-RRAH-noh / geen-DEE-yah seh-RRAH-noh* **Serrano chile**
HERBS & SPICES A small, thin chile pepper averaging about three inches in length. Hot and spicy, it has smooth skin that turns red or orange when ripe. Because of its meaty flesh, it does not dry well and is available only fresh, canned, or pickled.

Chile tailandés / Guindilla tailandés *CHEE-leh tah-ee-lahn-DEHS / geen-DEE-yah tah-ee-lahn-DEHS* **Thai chile**
HERBS & SPICES The small, thin-skinned but very spicy chile commonly found in Thailand and other Southeast Asian countries. Green when unripe, it turns a bright red color when it matures.

Chile pasilla Oaxaca / Guindilla pasilla Oaxaca *CHEE-leh pah-SEE-yah wah-HAH-kah / geen-DEE-yah pah-SEE-yah wah-HAH-kah* **Pasilla Oaxaca**
HERBS & SPICES The smoked pasilla chile. It is hotter than the chipotle chile.

Chilmole *cheel-MOH-leh*
DISH (Mexico) Black recado made with charred and ashy chiles.

Chiltoma *cheel-TOH-mah* **Bell Pepper**
FRUIT & VEGETABLE See **Pimiento**.

Chimichanga / Chivichanga *chee-mee-CHAN-gah / chee-bee-CHAN-gah*
DISH (Mexico) Long, thin burritos that are panfried until crisp.

Chimichurri *chee-mee-CHOO-rree*
CONDIMENTS (Argentina) A chunky sauce used as a condiment for grilled meats. It is made of chopped parsley, olive oil, herbs, and seasoning.
(Nicaragua) A raw sauce made from chopped fresh parsley, fresh oregano, garlic, olive oil, and red chile pepper. It is very similar to the Argentinean version except this one has a spicy component.

Chinchulines *cheen-choo-LEE-nehs*
MEAT (Argentina) Chitterlings. These are small intestines categorized as offal.

Chipachole *chee-pah-CHOH-leh*
DISH (Mexico) Tomato-based spicy soup flavored with chipotle chiles

Chipirón *chee-pee-ROHN* **Squid**
FISH & SHELLFISH See **Calamar**.

Chirimoya *chee-ree-MOH-yah* **Cherimoya**
FRUIT & VEGETABLE See **Annón**.

Chirivía *chee-ree-BEE-ah* **Parsnip**
FRUIT & VEGETABLES A beige-colored root vegetable that looks like a carrot but is sweeter and stronger flavored. Its very thin skin should be peeled off. A parsnip is used in the same as a carrot and can be eaten raw or cooked.

Chistorra *chees-TOH-rrah* **Pepperoni**
MEAT The Italian American name for a spicy cured dried sausage made from pork and beef.

Chivo *CHEE-boh* **Goat**
MEAT A four-legged, cloven-hoofed animal that is a bovine related to sheep. The meat of mature animals has a strong flavor and is tough, while that of young animals, called kids, is tender.

Chocolate *choh-koh-LAH-teh* **Chocolate**
BAKING & PASTRY Food made from seed of cacao tree. The seeds are removed from their pods, fermented, dried, and roasted. They are then cracked and the chocolate liquor is separated from the cocoa butter in the nibs. The chocolate liquor is used to make various chocolate products.

Chocolate blanco *choh-koh-LAH-teh BLAHN-koh* **White chocolate**
BAKING & PASTRY A confection of sugar, cocoa butter, and milk solids. It cannot be classified as real chocolate because it contains no chocolate liquor.

Chocolate con leche *choh-koh-LAH-teh kohn LEH-che* **Milk chocolate**
BAKING & PASTRY Chocolate that has dry milk powder and sugar added to it. It must contain 12 percent milk solids and 10 percent chocolate liquor.

Chocolate de cobertura *choh-koh-LAH-teh deh koh-behr-TOO-rah* **Couverture chocolate**
BAKING & PASTRY Extremely glossy and high-quality coating chocolate. It must contain a minimum of 32 percent cocoa butter as the more it contains the higher the sheen, the firmer the snap, and creamier the flavor of the chocolate. It is typically found only in specialty shops.

Chocolate de repostería *choh-koh-LAH-teh deh reh-pohs-teh-REE-ah* **Baking chocolate**
BAKING & PASTRY Pure, unadulterated chocolate (chocolate liquor) mixed with some cocoa butter in order to make a solid. It is also known as bittersweet chocolate.

Chocolate mexicano *choh-koh-LAH-teh meh-hee-KAH-noh* **Mexican chocolate**
BAKING & PASTRY Grainy-textured dark chocolate that has cinnamon and sugar added. Ground almonds can also be included. It is used for making hot chocolate or as an ingredient in mole poblano.

Chocolate negro / chocolate oscuro *choh-koh-LAH-teh NEH-groh / choh-koh-LAH-teh ohs-KOO-roh* **Dark chocolate**
BAKING & PASTRY Chocolate made by adding fat and sugar to chocolate liquor (nibs of the cacao bean). The amount of fat and sugar varies, resulting in a range of intensity in chocolate flavor among dark chocolate. Milk is never added.

SPANISH-ENGLISH C

Chocolate semidulce *choh-koh-LAH-teh seh-mee-DOOL-seh* **Semisweet chocolate**
  BAKING & PASTRY Unsweetened dark chocolate that has had sugar, lecithin, and vanilla added to it. It must contain at least 50 percent chocolate liquor, but the amount of sugar added is not regulated, resulting in a high disparity in flavor among brands.

Choricero *choh-ree-SEH-roh*
  FRUIT & VEGETABLE *See* **Pimiento choricero**.

Chorizo *choh-REE-soh* **Chorizo**
  MEAT Highly seasoned pork sausage popular in Mexico and Spain. Fresh pork is used in the Mexican variety, while smoked pork is used for the Spanish. The spices and flavorings used vary according to the region in which they are made. Both types are used to flavor recipes; the Spanish variety can be eaten raw.

Chuleta *choo-LEH-tah* **Chop**
  MEAT An individual portion of meat taken from the rib section with an attached rib bone. *See also individual types of meat.*

Chunchurría *choon-choo-RREE-ah*
  MEAT (Colombia) Pork, beef, or lamb small intestine, which may be grilled or fried.

Chuno *CHOO-noh*
  FRUIT & VEGETABLES (Peru) A freeze-dried potato made from frost-resistant potatoes. It is traditionally obtained by freezing the potato at night and then exposing it to sunlight during the day so as to dehydrate it. Chunos last for at least a year and can be made into a flour.

Chuno, blanco *CHOO-noh, BLAHN-koh*
  FRUIT & VEGETABLES (Peru) A dried chuno potato that is washed in water, resulting in a "cleaned" potato.

Chuno, negro *CHOO-noh, NEH-groh*
  FRUIT & VEGETABLES (Peru) A dried chuno potato that is left as is and not washed in water.

Chupe de camarones *CHOO-peh deh kah-mah-ROH-nehs*
  DISH (Peru) A shrimp stew. The light base is made with shrimp stock and milk and contains shrimp, potatoes, and chile peppers.

Chupito / Dedal *choo-PEE-toh / deh-DAHL* **Shot**
  BEVERAGE A small drink of liquor. It typically contains one fluid ounce, but there is no standard size.

Churrasco *choo-RRAHS-koh* **Grilled steak**
  MEAT (Argentina) Skirt steak.
  (Nicaragua) Tenderloin.
  (Puerto Rico) Flank or skirt steak.

Churrasquería / Churrascaría *choo-rrahs-keh-REE-ah / choo-rrahs-kah-REE-ah*
Steakhouse
  GENERAL A restaurant that primarily serves meat (beef).

Churros *CHOO-rrohs*
  BAKING & PASTRY (Mexico) Long, thin doughnuts that have ridges on the exterior. Sprinkled heavily with sugar, they are typically eaten with or dipped into hot chocolate or coffee. (Spain) Pastries made with a deep-fried batter of flour and water and doused with granulated sugar after they have been fried. Typically shaped into small logs or knots, they are eaten for breakfast or as a snack and are often dipped into hot chocolate.

Chutney *CHOOT-nee* **Chutney**
  CONDIMENTS A condiment made from cooked fruit. It can be chunky or smooth, mild or hot. Vinegar and spices are added for flavor.

Cidra *SEE-drah* **Citron**
  FRUIT & VEGETABLES A large, round, yellow citrus fruit. The pulp is very tart. The peel is used for its lemony flavoring and aroma.

Ciervo / Venado *see-EHR-voh / beh-NAH-doh* **Venison**
  GAME The culinary name for deer meat. Its flavor is similar to that of beef but is much leaner, requiring care to be taken when cooking it so as to not dry out the meat.

Ciervo, silla *see-EHR-boh , SEE-yah* **Venison, saddle**
  GAME The connected two loins found on either side of the backbone, it is a very large cut of venison.

Cigala *see-GAH-lah* **Langoustine**
  FISH & SHELLFISH A deep-sea crustacean that looks like a small lobster and can grow up to eight inches long. The colder the waters it comes from, the more flavor it has. It is also known as Norway lobster.

Cilantro / Perejil chino *see-LAHN-troh / peh-reh-HEEL CHEE-noh* **Cilantro**
  HERBS & SPICES The green leaves and stem from the coriander plant used as an herb. Both the leaves and stronger-flavored stems can be eaten. Sold in bunches, it has a bright pungent flavor. It is also known as Chinese parsley.

Cinta *SEEN-tah* **Ribbon**
  GENERAL (1) A thin or thick line. (2) A strip of material used for tying or trimming.

Ciruela *see-roo-EH-lah* **Plum**
  FRUIT & VEGETABLES A small, round fruit, about three inches in diameter, that grows on the plum tree. The edible, thin skin is typically purple red in color but can also be yellow. The yellow flesh is juicy with a sweet tart flavor. A single seed is found in the center of the fruit. Dried plums are called prunes.

Ciruela pasa *see-roo-EH-lah PAH-sah* **Prune**
  FRUIT & VEGETABLES A dried plum. It has a very dark purple, wrinkled skin with a chewy texture, and an intense sweetness.

Cítrico *SEE-tree-koh* **Citrus**
FRUIT & VEGETABLES A family of fruit that thrive in tropical to temperate climates. Juice laden, they have a tart flavor due to the high amounts of citric acid found in the pulp. Oranges, limes, lemons, and grapefruit are the most common types.

Clara de huevo *KLAH-rah deh WEH-voh* **Egg white**
DAIRY The inside of an egg that makes up two-thirds of the egg's weight. It is transparent in its raw state and turns opaque white when cooked. It is primarily made of albumin protein.

Clarificar *klah-ree-FEE-kahr* **Clarify**
COOKING METHOD / TECHNIQUE To clear a cloudy liquid.

Claro *KLAH-roh* **Light**
DESCRIPTOR Pale in color.

Clavo *KLAH-voh* **Clove**
HERBS & SPICES The dried unopened flower bud of the evergreen clove tree. Nail-shaped and dark brown in color, it is sold whole or ground. The spice has a warm flavor that is used to flavor sweet and savory dishes.

Clementina *kleh-mehn-TEE-nah* **Clementine**
FRUIT & VEGETABLES A small mandarin orange with a thin skin that easily peels off. Usually seedless, it has a very sweet flavor.

Cocada *koh-KAH-dah*
DISH (Colombia) A very sweet confection of shredded coconut shaped into small balls held together with sugar syrup.
(Mexico) A sweet coconut custard.

Cocer a fuego lento *koh-SEHR ah foo-EH-goh LEHN-toh* **Simmer**
COOKING METHOD / TECHNIQUE To cook food gently in a liquid that is heated to just below the boiling point (about 185°F). Small bubbles will just begin to rise and break the surface.

Cocer a media *koh-SEHR ah MEH-dee-ah* **Coddle**
COOKING METHOD / TECHNIQUE A cooking method that slowly cooks food in individual covered containers placed in simmering water. It is often used with eggs.

Cochinillo *koh-chee-NEE-yoh* **Suckling pig**
MEAT A young pig, about two to six weeks old, that is roasted whole. Its weight ranges between ten and twenty-five pounds.

Cochinillo asado *koh-chee-NEE-yoh ah-SAH-doh*
MEAT (Spain) A whole roasted suckling pig traditionally cooked in a wood-burning oven.

Cocido *koh-SEE-doh*
DISH (Spain) A Castilian boiled dinner that takes about a day or two to make. It contains chickpeas, chicken, beef, bacon, sausage, meatballs, and vegetables. It is eaten in stages; the broth is served first, then the meats and vegetables.

Cocido madrileño *koh-SEE-doh mah-dree-LEH-nyo*
DISH (Spain) The cocido made in Madrid, which contains chorizo and meatballs.

Cocido valenciano *koh-SEE-doh bah-lehn-see-AH-noh*
DISH *See* **Puchero**.

Cocinar / Cocinando *koh-see-NAHR / koh-see-NAHN-doh* **Cooking**
COOKING METHOD / TECHNIQUE The process of preparing food by selecting, measuring, and cooking ingredients.

Cocinar a fuego lento *koh-see-NAHR ah foo-EH-goh LEHN-toh* **Slow cook**
COOKING METHOD / TECHNIQUE To cook food with low and steady moist heat.

Cocinar al vapor *koh-see-NAHR ahl bah-POHR*
COOKING METHOD / TECHNIQUE To cook food with the heat produced by converting water to steam.

Coco *KOH-koh* **Coconut**
NUTS & OILS The dried nut of the coconut palm tree. The very hard and inedible outer husk is green when immature and brown and hairy when ripe. The hollow nut holds a thin coconut juice in its center, which is consumed as a refreshing beverage. The white coconut meat, which is attached to the husk, is cut or grated loose. It can be found fresh or dried.

Cocochas *koh-KOH-chahs*
FISH & SHELLFISH *See* **Kokotxas**.

Cóctel *KOHK-tehl* **Cocktail**
BEVERAGE An alcoholic beverage made by combining a spirit with a mixer (juice or soda).

Cóctel de frutas *KOHK-tehl deh FROO-tahs* **Fruit cocktail**
FRUIT & VEGETABLES A mixture of various fruit that have been chopped up into bite-size pieces. They can be tossed with a sweet syrup or left plain with a small amount of lemon juice tossed in to prevent the fruit from turning brown.

Codillo ahumado *koh-DEE-yoh ah-oo-MAH-doh* **Hock**
MEAT The portion of an animal's leg located between the foot and the thigh. It does not have much meat but it does have a large amount of bone and connective tissue, which is good for flavoring and thickening food.

Codorniz *koh-dohr-NEES* **Quail**
GAME A very small game bird averaging less than half a pound in weight. Its pale flesh has a marked flavor that is not as intense as that of a wild game bird but is not as bland as that of a domesticated chicken.

Cohombro de mar *koh-OHM-broh deh mahr* **Sea cucumber**
FISH & SHELLFISH A long-bodied marine animal that lives on the ocean floor. Highly gelatinous, it is often used in soups. Typically found dried, it must be soaked for a day until it doubles in size.

Col *kohl* **Cabbage**
FRUIT & VEGETABLES A leafy green vegetable that is a relative of cauliflower, broccoli, and Brussels sprouts. Its color can range from white to green to red, and its leaves can be flat or curly. Cabbage can grow as a compact head or a loose group of leaves.

Colada *koh-LAH-dah*
BEVERAGE (Cuba) A container with approximately one and a half cups of Cuban coffee that is sold in disposable takeaway cups and shared with a group.

Colador *koh-lah-DOHR* **Strainer**
EQUIPMENT A kitchen tool with a netted, meshed, or perforated bottom used to strain or filter food items or sift dry ingredients. Colanders come in a variety of sizes and net / mesh densities.

Colador / Coladera *koh-lah-DOHR / koh-lah-DEH-rah* **Colander**
EQUIPMENT A perforated bowl used as a tool to drain liquids.

Colar *koh-LAHR* **Strain**
COOKING METHOD / TECHNIQUE (1) To filter. To remove impurities. (2) To sift and separate ingredients.

Col china *kohl CHEE-nah* **Chinese cabbage**
FRUIT & VEGETABLES A cabbage with thin, green, wavy leaves connected to wide white stalks, both of which are eaten. Thinner and crisper than other cabbage varieties, it is also known as Napa cabbage.

Coles de Bruselas *KOH-lehs deh broo-SEH-lahs* **Brussels sprouts**
FRUIT & VEGETABLES A member of the cabbage family that look like miniature cabbage heads. They grow on stalks with many small heads lined up in rows.

Col fermentada *kohl fehr-mehn-TAH-dah* **Sauerkraut**
CONDIMENTS A dish made from shredded cabbage fermented in brine.

Coliflor *koh-lee-FLOHR* **Cauliflower**
FRUIT & VEGETABLES A cruciferous vegetable made up of a bunch of florets attached to a stalk. Typically white in color, it can also be green or purple, which turns light green when cooked.

Colinabo *koh-lee-NAH-boh* **Kohlrabi**
FRUIT & VEGETABLES A member of the turnip family with a white or purple bulb and thin stems and dark green leaves. The bulb is used more than the leaves, although both are edible. It has a mild sweet flavor reminiscent of a turnip and its texture is similar to that of a potato.

Colita de cuadril *koh-LEE-tah deh kwah-DREEL*
MEAT (Argentina) A cut of meat equivalent to tri-tip or sirloin bottom.

Col lombarda *kohl lohm-BAHR-dah* **Red cabbage**
FRUIT & VEGETABLES A tight head of cabbage with dusty blue red–colored leaves. It will turn blue if exposed to an alkaline solution, but will become a bright red when an acid like vinegar is added. It can be eaten raw or cooked.

Colmenilla *kohl-meh-NEE-yah* **Morel**
FRUIT & VEGETABLES An edible wild mushroom although some are cultivated. Its cap is cone shaped and filled with spongelike holes and ranges in size from one to four inches long. Its flavor is earthy and nutty and is more intense in the darker mushrooms. Morels are available fresh, dried, or canned.

Colorantes alimenticios *koh-loh-RAHN-tehs ah-lee-mehn-TEE-see-ohs* **Food coloring**
CONDIMENTS Edible dyes used to color food. Available in liquid, paste, or powder form, food coloring is used most often in a baking to tint frosting and icings.

Col rizada *kohl ree-ZAH-dah* **Kale**
FRUIT & VEGETABLES A member of the cabbage family that has dark green leaves with very curly edges that are attached at its base but do not form a tight head. The hearty, cabbage-flavored leaves have a thick center stem that should be removed before they are cooked or eaten. The leaves can be treated like spinach.

Col savoy *kohl sah-BOY* **Savoy cabbage**
FRUIT & VEGETABLES A tight head of cabbage with crinkled leaves that have a netted texture. Its mild flavor and crisp leaves make it one of the best varieties for eating. Its outer leaves are green with veins that turn progressively white as they get closer to the center of the head.

Col verde *kohl BEHR-deh* **Green cabbage**
FRUIT & VEGETABLES The most common variety of cabbage, with a tight head and thick, hearty, green leaves. It is used to make coleslaw.

Comal *koh-MAHL*
EQUIPMENT (Mexico) A flat, round cooking vessel made of cast iron or steel used to make tortillas or toast ingredients. It is often kept permanently on the stovetop.

Combinar *kohm-bee-NAHR* **Combine**
COOKING METHOD / TECHNIQUE To mix or incorporate two substances.

Comedor *koh-meh-DOHR* **Dining room**
GENERAL The room in a house or restaurant where tables are set and guests sit to eat.

Comida *koh-MEE-dah* **Meal**
GENERAL Food eaten at a set time.

Comida basura *koh-MEE-dah bah-SOO-rah* **Junk food**
GENERAL Food that has little or no nutritional value.

Comida Lenta *koh-MEE-dah LEHN-tah* **Slow Food**
GENERAL A movement started by Italian journalist Carlo Petrini that promotes the preservation of culture and local cuisine. It began as a response to the opening of the fastfood chain, McDonalds, in Rome.

Comida orgánica *koh-MEE-dah ohr-GAH-nee-kah* **Organic**
GENERAL Food grown without the use of synthetic pesticides, fertilizers, antibiotics, or chemicals.

Comino *koh-MEE-noh* **Cumin**
HERBS & SPICES A flat, dark brown seed that resembles caraway. It must be ground before being used and delivers a strong, nutty, and lemony flavor. It is often used in Cuban and Mexican cooking.

Compota *kohm-POH-tah* **Compote**
BAKING & PASTRY A dessert of slowly cooked whole or chopped fruit in simple syrup and spices. It can be served chilled or warm.

Concha *KOHN-cha* **Shell**
FISH & SHELLFISH See **Caparazón.**

Condimentar *kohn-dee-mehn-TAHR* **Season**
COOKING METHOD / TECHNIQUE See **Sazonar.**

Condimento *kohn-dee-MEHN-toh* **Condiment**
CONDIMENTS A savory accompaniment to food. It can be a sauce or spice mixture. See also **Sazón.**

Condimento para encurtido *kohn-dee-MEHN-toh PAH-rah ehn-koor-TEE-doh*
Pickling spice
HERBS & SPICES A spice blend used in the pickling marinade liquid. Blends differ but spices are usually left whole and include peppercorns, bay leaves, cloves, mustard seeds, and coriander seeds among others.

Conejo *koh-NEH-hoh* **Rabbit**
GAME An animal whose flavor and flesh is similar to that of chicken and can be cooked and prepared in a similar manner.

Confitura *kohn-fee-TOO-rah* **Preserve**
COOKING METHOD / TECHNIQUE See **Mermelada.**

Conforme a la ley judaica *kohn FOHR-meh ah lah LEH-ee hoo-dee-AH-kah*
GENERAL See **Kosher.**

Congelador *kohn-heh-lah-DOHR* **Freezer**
EQUIPMENT An electric appliance with a temperature-controlled compartment that maintains the temperature below the freezing point of water. All items placed in the compartment become frozen. Freezers come in various sizes, and some form part of a unit with a refrigerator.

Congelar *kohn-heh-LAHR* **Freeze**
COOKING METHOD / TECHNIQUE (1) To turn into ice. (2) To convert from a liquid to a solid by decreasing the temperature of an item below freezing.

Conservar *kohn-sehr-BAHR* **Can**
COOKING METHOD / TECHNIQUE See **Enlatar.**

Copa de vino *KOH-pah deh BEE-noh* **Wineglass**

EQUIPMENT A special glass for drinking wine. It can be recognized by its long stem which holds a bowl and is supported by a foot. Some modern wineglasses are stemless.

Copita *koh-PEE-tah* **Snifter**

EQUIPMENT A shortstemmed, wide-bottomed glass used to drink brandy. Its narrow top traps the brandy's aroma in the glass.

Copos de avena *KOH-pohs deh ah-BEH-nah* **Rolled oats**

GRAINS & CEREALS Whole oats that have been steamed and flattened under heavy rollers. Rolled oats cook more quickly than whole oats. They are used in baked goods and for breakfast cereal.

Copos de bonito *KOH-pohs deh boh-NEE-toh* **Dried bonito flakes**

FISH & SHELLFISH Dried fermented and smoked skipjack tuna, which is also known as bonito. The dried fish is pink in color and shaved as needed. The shavings can be purchased in bags and are the main ingredient in dashi.

Copos de coco *KOH-pohs deh KOH-koh* **Coconut flakes**

CONDIMENTS Dried, shredded coconut that can be sweetened or unsweetened. It is available canned or in bags.

Copos de maíz *KOH-pohs deh mah-EES* **Cornflakes**

GRAINS & CEREALS A breakfast cereal made from milled corn. Its small, irregularly shaped, thin flakes are light yellow in color.

Copos de pimiento rojo *KOH-pohs deh pee-mee-EHN-toh ROH-hoh* **Red pepper flakes**

HERBS & SPICES A combination of various red chile peppers that are dried and crushed. Because the seeds are included in the mix the flakes are hot and spicy.

Copos de salvado *KOH-pohs deh sahl-BAH-doh* **Bran flakes**

GRAINS & CEREALS A dry, ready-to-eat whole grain cereal irregularly shaped into small, thin sheets or flakes.

Copus *KOH-poohs*

DISH (Peru) A meal prepared from a variety of meats (turkey, goat, hen) cooked in an underground pit and covered with blankets of clay. It is served with fried plantains and *camotes* (sweet potatoes).

Coquinas *koh-KEE-nahs*

FISH & SHELLFISH (Spain) Very small clams found in Spain.

Coquito *koh-KEE-toh*

BEVERAGE (Puerto Rico) An eggnog-style holiday beverage made with coconut milk and rum. It is typically served in small shot glasses.

Corazón *koh-rah-SOHN* **Heart**

MEAT Organ meat that is made up almost entirely of muscle. Its very low fat content means it can become tough if cooked improperly or for too long. It can come from cattle, calves, chickens, or lambs.

Cordero *kohr-DEH-roh* **Lamb**

MEAT Meat from domesticated sheep that are less than one year old. The flesh is tender with a pronounced meaty flavor.

Cordero, chuleta *kohr-DEH-roh, choo-LEH-tah* **Lamb, chop**

MEAT An individual cut of lamb that still has the rib bone attached.

Cordero, corona *kohr-DEH-roh, koh-ROH-nah* **Lamb, crown**

MEAT Two racks of lamb ribs that are cooked, placed upright, and curved to form a circular shape. Paper truffles are traditionally placed over the top of each rib bone.

Cordero, corte de paletilla *kohr-DEH-roh, KOHR-teh deh pah-leh-TEE-yah* **Lamb, shoulder steak**

MEAT An individual sliced portion of the lamb shoulder.

Cordero, costillar *kohr-DEH-roh, kohs-tee-YAHR* **Lamb, rack**

MEAT The cut taken from the rib section. About eight rib bones and their meat are attached to each other. It is typically served in one piece.

Cordero, costillas *kohr-DEH-roh, kohs-TEE-yahs* **Lamb, French trimmed**

MEAT Lamb chops that have had all the meat and fat trimmed off the rib bone.

Cordero, paletilla *kohr-DEH-roh, pah-leh-TEE-yah* **Lamb, shoulder**

MEAT The cut located right below the neck. It is an economical cut that is flavorful but can get tough and chewy if not cooked properly. The entire shoulder is typically sold boneless and can be cooked as a roast.

Cordero, pierna *kohr-DEH-roh, pee-EHR-nah* **Lamb, leg**

MEAT An entire hind leg from the lamb.

Coriandro *koh-ree-AHN-droh* **Coriander**

HERBS & SPICES A plant related to the parsley family that is used for its seeds and leaves. The seeds are small and tan, have a lemony flavor, and can be found whole or ground. The leaves, known as cilantro, have a pungent flavor that is not at all similar to the flavor of the seeds.

Cortadito *kohr-tah-DEE-toh*

BEVERAGE Espresso coffee that has shot of hot milk added.

Cortado *kohr-TAH-doh* **Break**

COOKING METHOD / TECHNIQUE A situation where at least two substances from an emulsion separate.

Sour

DESCRIPTOR *See* **Agrio**.

Cortado al bies *kohr-TAH-doh ahl BEE-ehs* **Bias cut**
COOKING METHOD / TECHNIQUE A diagonal slice or cut made with a knife.

Cortador de melón / Vaciador de melon *kohr-tah-DOHR deh meh-LOHN / bah-see-ah-DOHR deh meh-LOHN* **Melon baller**
EQUIPMENT A handheld kitchen tool with a small, round, hollow half circle connected to a handle. It is used to scoop out balls of melon flesh.

Cortador de pastel *kohr-tah-DOHR deh pahs-TEHL* **Cookie cutter / Pastry wheel**
EQUIPMENT (1) A plastic or metal tool used to cut shapes from rolledout cookie dough. It comes in various shapes and sizes. (2) A small handheld kitchen tool made up of a slightly sharp, round disk attached to a handle. Resembling a small pizza cutter, it is used to cut sheets of pastry or cookie dough. The edge of the disk can be plain or fluted to give a decorative appearance.

Cortar *kohr-TAHR* **Curdle**
COOKING METHOD / TECHNIQUE To separate as when a dairy product separates into curds and whey. The curds form as a result of proteins that coagulate from exposure to heat or an acid.

Cut
COOKING METHOD / TECHNIQUE To separate into parts with a knife.

Cortar / Trocear / Picar *kohr-TAHR / troh-seh-AHR / pee-KAHR* **Chop**
COOKING METHOD / TECHNIQUE To cut food into irregularly shaped bite-size pieces.

Cortar en dados *kohr-TAHR ehn DAH-dohs* **Dice**
COOKING METHOD / TECHNIQUE To cut food into cubes. They can be small, medium, or large measuring 1/8 to 1/4 inch.

Cortar en filete *kohr-TAHR ehn fee-LEH-teh* **Fillet**
COOKING METHOD / TECHNIQUE See Filetiar.

Cortar en forma libro *kohr-TAHR ehn FOHR-mah LEE-broh* **Butterfly**
COOKING METHOD / TECHNIQUE To cut a food item so as to split its thickness in half. Once the item is split, it is opened like a book. This technique is used most often on thick pieces of meat or fish.

Corte rombiodales *KOHR-teh rohm-bee-oh-DAH-lehs* **Diagonal cut**
COOKING METHOD / TECHNIQUE A slanted, square pattern of cuts.

Corteza *kohr-TEH-sah* **Crust**
BAKING & PASTRY (1) The hardened outer layer of a baked good. (2) A hard crisp covering added to an ingredient such as a meat, vegetables, or fruit.

Corvina *kohr-BEE-nah* **Bass**
FISH & SHELLFISH See Lubina.

Costilla *kohs-TEE-yah* **Rib**
MEAT (1) A cut of meat to which muscle and/or flesh is attached. (2) A bone that protrudes from the vertebrae.

SPANISH-ENGLISH C

Crema *KREH-mah* **Cream**

DAIRY A pasteurized dairy product consisting primarily of the fat found in milk. The fat content can vary from 18 percent (light) to 36 percent (heavy).

(Mexico) Cream similar to sour cream with a much thinner consistency and richer flavor.

Crema agria / Nata agria *KREH-mah AH-gree-ah / NAH-tah AH-gree-ah* **Sour cream**

DAIRY A dairy product made by adding lactic acid–producing bacteria and a small amount of rennet to cream. The added bacteria thickens the cream and gives it a tart and sour taste.

Crema batida *KREH-mah bah-TEE-dah* **Whipped cream**

DAIRY Cream that has been beaten by hand or machine until light and airy.

Crema catalana *KREH-mah kah-tah-LAH-nah*

DISH (Spain) A vanilla custard with a thin but crisp candied-sugar topping.

Crema de cacao *KREH-mah deh kah-KAH-oh* **Cocoa butter**

CONDIMENTS Vegetable fat extracted from cocoa beans. It is used to add smoothness and flavor to foods.

Crema de coco *KREH-mah deh KOH-koh* **Coconut cream**

CONDIMENTS A liquid made by simmering four parts shredded coconut with one part water or milk and then straining it. It is different from cream of coconut, which is sweetened.

Crema de coco endulsada *KREH-mah deh KOH-koh ehn-dool-SAH-dah* **Cream of coconut**

CONDIMENTS A thick sweet mixture of coconut paste and sugar. It is a main ingredient in piña coladas.

Crema de limón *KREH-mah deh lee-MOHN* **Lemon curd**

CONDIMENTS A thick and creamy mixture made predominately from lemon juice and egg yolks that have been sweetened with sugar. It is simmered until it thickens and can be used in desserts or as a spread.

Crema de mantequilla *KREH-mah deh mahn-teh-KEE-yah* **Buttercream**

DAIRY A sweet and creamy icing. In its simplest form it is made by whipping butter with powdered sugar.

Crema de tarwi *KREH-mah deh TAHR-wee*

DISH (Peru) A cream-based soup made with the root vegetable tarwi

Crema doble / Nata doble *KREH-mah DOH-bleh / NAH-tah DOH-bleh* **Double cream**

DAIRY Cream with a milk fat content of approximately 48 percent. It is most often found in Europe and Britain.

Crema espesa / Nata espesa *KREH-mah ehs-PEH-sah / NAH-tah ehs-PEH-sah*
Heavy cream
DAIRY Cream with a milk fat content of 36 to 40 percent.

Crema extra espesa / Nata extra espesa *KREH-mah EKS-trah ehs-PEH-sah / NAH-tah EKS-trah ehs-PEH-sah* **Clotted cream**
DAIRY Cream made from unpasteurized milk that is heated until a layer of cream forms on the surface. The cream is then removed and cooled. Typically used as a spread, it is a specialty of Devonshire, England.

Crema fresca / Nata fresca *KREH-mah FREHS-kah / NAH-tah FREHS-kah* **Crème fraîche**
DAIRY Developed by the French, this is a high-fat soured cream made from unpasteurized cream that thickens with the naturally present bacterial cultures at room temperature. The variety found in the United States is slightly different and is made with pasteurized cream that has bacteria added to it. Its high fat content prevents it from breaking at a high temperature.

Crema inglesa *KREH-mah een-GLEH-sah* **Crème anglaise**
BAKING & PASTRY A very thin custard used as a dessert sauce. It is made with sugar, egg yolks, milk, and vanilla.

Crema montada / Nata montada *KREH-mah mohn-TAH-dah / NAH-tah mohn-TAH-dah* **Whipping cream**
DAIRY Cream that contains 30 to 36 percent milk fat.

Crema pastelera *KREH-mah pahs-teh-LEH-rah* **Pastry cream**
BAKING & PASTRY A thick, sweet custard made from milk, eggs, flour, and sugar. It is used to fill cakes, tarts, éclairs, pies, and other pastries.

Crema semidesnatada / Nata semidesnatada *KREH-mah seh-mee-dehs-nah-TAH-dah / NAH-tah seh-mee-dehs-nah-TAH-dah* **Light cream**
DAIRY Cream that contains 18 to 30 percent milk fat. The lightest form of cream, it is often used to lighten coffee.

Cremor tartaro *kreh-MOHR TAHR-tah-roh* **Cream of tartar**
CONDIMENTS A crystallized acid found in the interior of wine barrels. This white powder is used when an acidic ingredient is needed in a recipe. It is used in baking to help the leavening process and improves the stability and volume of whipped egg whites.

Crepe / Crepa *krehp / KREH-pah* **Crepe**
BAKING & PASTRY Paper-thin pancakes that are rolled or folded and topped with a sauce. They can be sweet or savory and are often stuffed with a filling.

Criadillas *kree-ah-DEE-yahs* **Testicles**
MEAT Male animal sex organs categorized as offal. Buffalo, boar, or bull testicles are eaten, typically breaded and deep-fried. They are popular in Mexico and Spain. They are also known as Rocky Mountain oysters.

Criba / Cedazo / Tamiz *KREE-bah / seh-DAH-soh / tah-MEES* **Sieve**
EQUIPMENT A kitchen tool made up of a mesh or net used to strain particles or liquid. It comes in various shapes, sizes, and mesh densities.

Cristalería *krees-tah-leh-REE-ah* **Glassware**
EQUIPMENT Tableware made with glass. This most often refers specifically to drinking vessels.

Crocante *kroh-KAHN-teh* **Crunchy**
DESCRIPTOR The noisy crackling sound made when chewing. Also the term used to describe a food item that produces a crackling sensation.

Croquetas *kroh-KEH-tahs* **Croquettes**
DISH Ground meat, fish, or cheese mixed with a thick cream sauce (béchamel), then shaped into small logs, breaded, and fried.
(Cuba) Made from a thick béchamel sauce that is flavored with pureed ham, codfish, or chicken. Shaped into long cylinders, it is coated with cracker meal and deep-fried.
(Spain) Deep-fried fritters. The filling (meat, fish, or cheese) is blended with béchamel sauce, shaped into a log, breaded, and deep-fried. A very popular tapa.

Crudo *KROO-doh* **Raw**
DESCRIPTOR (1) Having not been exposed or treated with heat. (2) A food's natural state.

Crujiente *kroo-hee-EHN-teh* **Crispy**
DESCRIPTOR The brittle texture typically of a thin product that is firm but easily broken.

Crustaceo *kroos-TAH-seh-oh* **Crustacean**
FISH & SHELLFISH One of two types of shellfish. Crustaceans are made up of a jointed external skeleton that is also referred to as a shell. Crab, shrimp, and lobster are examples. *See also* **Marisco.**

Cuajar *kwah-HAHR* **Set**
COOKING METHOD / TECHNIQUE To become firm. It is a term used often with custards, eggs, and cheese.

Cubito de caldo / Pastilla de caldo *koo-BEE-toh deh KAHL-doh / pahs-TEE-yah deh KAHL-doh* **Stock cube**
CONDIMENTS Dehydrated beef, chicken, or vegetable stock compressed and shaped into a square. They are also known as bouillon cubes.

Cubrir / Bañar *koo-BREER / bah-NYAHR* **Coat**
COOKING METHOD / TECHNIQUE To cover food with another ingredient usually by rolling, dipping, or pressing.

Dredge
COOKING METHOD / TECHNIQUE *See* **Rebozar.**

Cuchara *koo-CHA-rah* **Spoon**

EQUIPMENT A utensil used for eating and serving. It is made of a small, round bowl attached to a handle.

Cuchara calada / Cuchara con ranuras *koo-CHA-rah kah-LAH-dah / koo-CHA-rah kohn rah-NOO-rahs* **Slotted spoon**

EQUIPMENT A spoon with holes or slits in its bowl. It is used to lift ingredients while allowing liquid to pass or drip through.

Cuchara con ranuras *koo-CHA-rah kohn rah-NOO-rahs* **Slotted spoon**

EQUIPMENT *See* **Cuchara calada**.

Cucharada *koo-cha-RAH-dah* **Tablespoon**

MEASUREMENTS A culinary unit of measure equal to 3 teaspoons, 15 milliliters, or $1/2$ fluid ounce.

Cuchara de palo *koo-CHA-rah deh PAH-loh* **Wooden spoon**

EQUIPMENT A spoon made from wood. A large version is used often as an all-purpose kitchen tool.

Cucharadita *koo-cha-rah-DEE-ta* **Teaspoon**

MEASUREMENTS A culinary unit of measure equal to $1/3$ teaspoon or 5 milliliters.

Cucharas de medir *koo-CHA-rahs deh meh-DEER* **Measuring spoons**

EQUIPMENT A kitchen tool used to measure small quantities of dry or liquid ingredients. Measuring spoons are sold in sets that range in size from $1/8$ teaspoon to 1 tablespoon.

Cucharrón *koo-cha-RROHN* **Ladle**

EQUIPMENT A large, deep-bowled spoon with a long handle used to serve soup or other liquids.

Cuchillo *koo-CHEE-yoh* **Knife**

EQUIPMENT A sharp-edged, handheld tool used to cut food. It consists of a handle attached to a blade and comes in a variety of sizes and materials.

Cuchillo de carnicero *koo-CHEE-yoh deh kahr-nee-SEH-roh* **Cleaver**

EQUIPMENT A cutting tool with a large rectangular blade. It is used by butchers for its ability to cut through bones. The flat side of the blade can be used for pounding.

Cuchillo de chef *koo-CHEE-yoh deh chehf* **Chef's knife**

EQUIPMENT An all-purpose knife with a blade six to twelve inches long. The tip is curved allowing for a rocking motion to occur when chopping or handling the knife. It is also known as a French knife.

Cuchillo de vegetal *koo-CHEE-yoh deh beh-heh-TAHL* **Paring knife**

EQUIPMENT A small knife with a blade three inches long. It is used for specific detailed tasks such as hulling strawberries, deveining shrimp, and creating intricate garnishes.

Cuchillo serrado *koo-CHEE-yoh seh-RRAH-doh* **Serrated knife**
   EQUIPMENT A knife with a sawlike blade used to slice through very delicate foods such as terrines or cakes or foods with a tough crust or skin such as breads or sausages. It can cut through food without squeezing it or applying undo pressure. Also referred to as cuchillo de sierra.

Cuenco / Bol *koo-EHN-koh / bohl* **Mixing bowl**
   EQUIPMENT A work bowl used to mix or toss ingredients. It comes in sizes ranging from three-quarters quart to over eight quarts and materials such as ceramic, glass, and stainless steel.

Curado *koo-RAH-doh* **Cured**
   COOKING METHOD / TECHNIQUE Preserved with smoke, salt, or an acid (pickling).

Cúrcuma *koor-KOO-mah* **Turmeric**
   HERBS & SPICES A spice made from the root of the turmeric plant that is boiled, dried, and then ground into a powder. Used primarily for the deep yellow color it imparts, it also gives off a mild, earthy, peppery flavor. It is a main ingredient in commercial curry powder and prepared mustard.

Curry en polvo *KOO-ree ehn POHL-voh* **Curry powder**
   HERBS & SPICES A blend of about twenty spices. Popular in India and the Caribbean, the combination of spices varies regionally, but most blends contain coriander, tumeric, cumin, and nutmeg. The spices can be ground and mixed fresh or purchased commercially. Curry's flavor can be sweet and/or hot. Hot curry is known as Madras curry.

Cuscus *COOS-coos* **Couscous**
   GRAINS & CEREALS A very small, round-shaped pasta made from semolina flour. Most packaged varieties of couscous are precooked and require only a small amount of boiling liquid poured over the grains to steam them for about five minutes. It is a staple starch of north African countries.

Cuscus israeli *COOS-coos ees-rah-eh-LEE* **Israeli couscous**
   GRAINS & CEREALS Closer to orzo than couscous, a small, round wheat pasta that is much larger than regular couscous. It is often used as a substitute for rice.

Cuy chactado *kwee chak-TAH-doh*
   DISH (Peru) A deep-fried guinea pig.

D

Daiquirí *dah-ee-kee-REE* **Daiquiri**
   BEVERAGE A rum-based cocktail made with lime juice, fruit, and sugar. A frozen daiquiri is made by pureeing the mixture with ice cubes in a blender.

Danesa *dah-NEH-sah* **Danish**
BAKING & PASTRY An open-faced flaky breakfast pastry that is filled with fruit, cream cheese, and/or nuts. The pastry is made from a slightly sweetened yeast dough that is flavored with vanilla.

Datil *DAH-teel* **Date**
FRUIT & VEGETABLES The brown, oval-shaped fruit of the date palm, which is found abundantly in the Middle East. It has a sweet flesh that surrounds a single narrow seed. The fruit must be picked unripe and allowed to mature off the tree. It can be found in fresh or dried form. Dates can be eaten as is, or pitted and stuffed.

Dedal *deh-DAHL*
BEVERAGE *See* Chupito.

Deglasar *deh-glah-SAHR* **Deglaze**
COOKING METHOD / TECHNIQUE To loosen brown bits of food that have stuck to the bottom of a sauté pan by pouring in a liquid and scraping the bottom of a pan. The result is a very flavorful base that is used for a sauce or within a recipe.

Dejar caer *deh-HAHR kah-EHR* **Drop**
COOKING METHOD / TECHNIQUE To let fall.

Denominación *deh-noh-mee-nah-see-OHN* **Appellation**
See Apelación.

Derretido *deh-rreh-TEE-doh* **Melted**
COOKING METHOD / TECHNIQUE Having changed the physical property of food from the solid to the liquid state by applying heat.

Derretir *deh-rreh-TEER* **Melt**
COOKING METHOD / TECHNIQUE To change the physical property of food from the solid state to the liquid state by heating.

Render
COOKING METHOD / TECHNIQUE To melt animal fat.

Desaguar / Desague / Escurrir *deh-sah-GWAHR / deh-SAH-gweh / ehs-koo-REER* **Drain**
COOKING METHOD / TECHNIQUE To remove excess liquid or fat from an item by using a colander or placing the item on top of a paper towel to absorb excess moisture or fat.

Desayuno *deh-sah-YOO-noh* **Breakfast**
GENERAL The first meal of the day typically eaten in the morning.

Descascarar / Descortezar *dehs-kahs-kah-RAHR / dehs-kohr-teh-SAHR* **Shuck**
COOKING METHOD / TECHNIQUE To remove shellfish from their shell. To peel off the husks from corn.

Descorazonar *dehs-koh-rah-soh-NAHR* **Core**
COOKING METHOD / TECHNIQUE *See* Quitar el corazón.

Desgrasar *dehs-grah-SAHR* **Degrease**
COOKING METHOD / TECHNIQUE To remove fat from a liquid. This can be done by skimming the fat off with a spoon, patting the fat that floats to the top with a paper towel, or chilling the liquid until the fat floats to the top, solidifies, and then is removed.

Deshidratar *dehs-ee-drah-TAHR* **Dehydrate**
COOKING METHOD / TECHNIQUE To remove the moisture content from food by slowly heating it. Drying can be done by the sun, air, or in the oven.

Deshuesado y listo *dehs-weh-SAH-doh ee LEES-toh* **Boned and rolled meat**
MEAT A piece of meat with all bones removed, tightly rolled, and tied with twine (cooking string).

Deshuesar *dehs-weh-SAHR* **Bone**
COOKING METHOD / TECHNIQUE To remove the bone from a piece of meat, poultry, or fish.

Desinflar *dehs-een-FLAHR* **Deflate / Degas**
COOKING METHOD / TECHNIQUE To reduce an object's volume through the removal of air.

Desminuzar *dehs-mee-noo-SAHR* **Mince**
COOKING METHOD / TECHNIQUE *See* Picar.

Desmoldar *dehs-mohl-DAHR* **Unmold**
COOKING METHOD / TECHNIQUE To remove a food from its mold or container.

Desnatar / Quitar nata *dehs-nah-TAHR / kee-TAHR NAH-tah* **Skim**
COOKING METHOD / TECHNIQUE To remove the cream (fat) from milk.

Despellejar / Pelar *dehs-peh-yeh-HAHR / peh-LAHR* **Skin**
COOKING METHOD / TECHNIQUE To peel or strip the skin or outer layer of an ingredient.

Despepitador *dehs-peh-pee-tah-DOHR* **Pitter**
EQUIPMENT A handheld kitchen tool used to remove the seed or pit from olives or cherries. A prong pushes the seed out of the center of the fruit.

Despepitador de manzana *dehs-peh-pee-tah-DOHR deh mahn-SAH-nah*
Apple corer
EQUIPMENT A kitchen tool used to cut and remove the center of an apple. There are several variations of this tool but the classic one is a long cylinder tube that is serrated on one end and has a handle on the other.

Desplumar *dehs-ploo-MAHR* **Pluck**
COOKING METHOD / TECHNIQUE (1) To remove feathers. (2) To pull off quickly.

Despojo *dehs-POH-hoh* **Offal**
MEAT *See* Asadura.

Destilación *dehs-tee-lah-see-OHN* **Distillation**
COOKING METHOD / TECHNIQUE The process of purifying a liquid by boiling it, collecting its vapors, and cooling the vapors until they turn into liquid form.

Desvenar *dehs-veh-NAHR* **Devein**
COOKING METHOD / TECHNIQUE To remove the intestinal tract from a shrimp, which is located along its back.

Dextrosa *deks-TROH-sah* **Dextrose**
CONDIMENTS The commercial name for glucose when it is derived from cornstarch. Glucose is the most basic form of sugar and is found in almost all carbohydrates. It is also known as corn sugar.

Digestión *dee-hehs-tee-OHN* **Digestion**
GENERAL The breakdown of food inside the body into small components that can be absorbed into the bloodstream.

Digestivo *dee-hehs-TEE-boh* **Digestive**
BEVERAGE An alcoholic beverage taken after a meal to aid in digestion.

Diluir / Diluido *dee-loo-EER / dee-loo-EE-doh* **Dilute**
COOKING METHOD / TECHNIQUE To decrease a flavor's intensity through the addition of water or another liquid.

Disolver *dee-sohl-BEHR* **Dissolve**
COOKING METHOD / TECHNIQUE To cause a solid to disappear into a liquid.

Doblar *doh-BLAHR* **Fold**
COOKING METHOD / TECHNIQUE A technique used to combine two ingredients of different weights, the lighter of which has typically been aerated. The lighter ingredient is slowly incorporated into the heavier one by gently scooping up the heavy ingredient and turning it onto the lighter one until the mixture is well blended. This technique maintains the volume and light texture of the mixture.

Dorada *doh-RAH-dah* **Gilthead sea bream**
FISH & SHELLFISH A fish of the bream species. Prized in Europe for its great taste and versatility, it is considered to be the best tasting of the breams.

Dorar *doh-RAHR* **Brown**
COOKING METHOD / TECHNIQUE To develop a brown color on meat or vegetables by cooking them quickly over high heat. This also develops the flavors.

Dulce *DOOL-seh* **Sweet**
DESCRIPTOR One of the four basic tastes. It is described as tasting like sugar.

Candy
BAKING & PASTRY *See* Caramelo.

Dulce de leche *DOOL-seh deh LEH-cheh*
CONDIMENTS (Argentina) A thick sweetened milk sauce similar in taste to caramel. It is used as a flavoring, pastry filling, and topping.

Dulce de maduro *DOOL-seh deh mah-DOO-roh*
DISH (Colombia) A dessert made with mashed ripe plantains, panela, and cinnamon.

Durazno *doo-RAHS-noh* **Peach**
 FRUIT & VEGETABLE *See* **Melocotón.**

Durian *doo-ree-AHN* **Durian**
 FRUIT & VEGETABLES The fruit of the durian tree that is known as much for its succulent texture and sweet flavor as it is for its offensive odor. The size and shape of a football, it has skin that is brown and covered with spikes. Outlawed by commercial airliners, it can be found in the United States canned or frozen.

E

Edulcorante *eh-dool-koh-RAHN-teh* **Sweetener**
 CONDIMENTS A food additive that adds the basic taste of sweetness to a product. It can come from a natural source or be a man-made synthetic product (artificial sweetener).

Ejote *eh-HOH-teh* **Green bean**
 FRUIT & VEGETABLE *See* **Judía verde.**

Eglefino *ehg-leh-FEE-noh* **Haddock**
 FISH & SHELLFISH *See* **Abadejo.**

Elote / Mazorca *eh-LOH-teh / mah-SOHR-kah* **Corn on the cob**
 FRUIT & VEGETABLES *See* **Maíz.**

Embutidos *ehm-boo-TEE-dohs*
 MEAT (Spain) Cured meats and sausages.

Empanada *ehm-pah-NAH-dah* **Pie**
 BAKING & PASTRY *See* **Pye.**
 DISH (Argentina/Chile) A baked pastry filled with meat, cheese, or hundreds of other fillings. Usually savory, it is eaten as a snack.
 (Cuba) A turnover stuffed with guava or beef.
 (Spain) The tem used in northern Spain (especially the region of Galicia) for a savory nine-inch pie filled with meat, fish, or vegetables.

Empanadilla *ehm-pah-nah-DEE-yah*
 DISH (Spain) A bite-size empanada (the suffix "-illa" refers to something small). Shaped like turnovers, empanadillas are stuffed with a variety of fillings and eaten as a tapa.

Empanizar *ehm-pah-nee-SAHR* **Bread**
 COOKING METHOD / TECHNIQUE To coat an ingredient with bread crumbs, flour, or another ground grain. Often the food is dipped in egg or a liquid to help the crumbs adhere before being fried or baked. This process creates a crispy exterior while maintaining a moist interior.

Empapar / Remojar / Poner en remojo *ehm-pah-PAHR / reh-moh-HAHR / poh-NEHR ehn reh-MOH-hoh* **Soak**

COOKING METHOD / TECHNIQUE (1) To immerse in a liquid. (2) To cause something to be wet.

Emulsión *eh-mool-see-OHN* **Emulsion**

COOKING METHOD / TECHNIQUE A mixture made up of an emulsifier and two ingredients that normally would not blend with each other. The mixture can be thick or thin and can stay blended permanently or temporarily.

Emulsionante / Emulsivo *eh-mool-see-oh-NAHN-teh / eh-mool-SEE-voh* **Emulsifier**

COOKING METHOD / TECHNIQUE A substance that binds together two ingredients that normally do not blend with each other.

Enchiladas *ehn-chee-LAH-dahs*

DISH (Mexico) A dish made from lightly fried corn tortillas that are dipped in a chile sauce, stuffed with meat, and rolled.

Enchiladas de mole *ehn-chee-LAH-dahs deh MOH-leh*

DISH (Mexico) Enchiladas sauced with mole poblano or mole rojo.

Enchiladas suizas *ehn-chee-LAH-dahs soo-EE-sahs*

DISH (Mexico) Enchiladas made with a creamy tomatillo sauce, sprinkled with cheese, and then baked until the cheese is melted.

Enchiladas verdes *ehn-chee-LAH-dahs BEHR-dehs*

DISH (Mexico) Enchiladas made with a sauce of tomatillos, green chiles such as poblanos, and cilantro.

Enchilado de camarones *ehn-chee-LAH-doh deh kah-mah-ROH-nehs*

DISH (Cuba) Shrimp stewed in a sweet and tangy tomato sauce.

Enchilado de langosta *ehn-chee-LAH-doh deh lahn-GOHS-tah*

DISH (Cuba) Lobster stewed in a sweet and tangy tomato sauce.

Encutir *ehn-koo-TEER* **(to) Pickle**

COOKING METHOD / TECHNIQUE To preserve or marinate in vinegar or a brine mixture.

Endibia *ehn-DEE-bee-ah* **Endive**

FRUIT & VEGETABLES A relative of chicory, which can be eaten raw or cooked. There are three main varieties used in cooking: Belgian endive, curly endive, and escarole.

Endibia bélgica *ehn-DEE-bee-ah BEHL-hee-kah* **Belgian endive**

FRUIT & VEGETABLES A type of endive that is made up of a tightly packed head of leaves shaped like a small torpedo. The long, white leaves have pale yellow tips. The plant is grown in complete darkness to prevent the leaves from turning green. Slightly bitter in flavor, it can be eaten raw or cooked.

Eneldo *eh-NEHL-doh* **Dill**
HERBS & SPICES An herb with a slender stem and feathery green leaves that resemble fennel tops. It has a very delicate flavor reminiscent of anise that is lost when heated. It is available in fresh and dried form.

Enfriar *en-free-AHR* **Chill**
COOKING METHOD / TECHNIQUE To cool down. This can be done a in refrigerator or on ice.

Enfrijoladas *ehn-free-hoh-LAH-dahs*
DISH (Mexico) Enchiladas made with lightly fried tortillas that are dipped in a bean sauce.

Engrasar *ehn-grah-SAHR* **Grease**
COOKING METHOD / TECHNIQUE To coat or slather a baking dish or pan with a fat so as to make it a nonstick surface.

Enlatar / Envasar / Conservar *ehn-lah-TAHR / ehn-bah-SAHR / kohn-sehr-VAHR* **Can**
COOKING METHOD / TECHNIQUE To preserve food by processing and sealing in an airtight container.

Enmolades *ehn-moh-LAH-dehs*
DISH (Mexico) Enchiladas made with lightly fried tortillas dipped in black mole.

Enriquecer *ehn-ree-keh-SEHR* **Enrich**
COOKING METHOD / TECHNIQUE (1) To increase the flavor intensity or nutrient content of a dish through the addition of an ingredient. (2) To increase the viscosity or thickness of a liquid through the addition of cream or a fat.

Enrollar *ehn-roh-YAHR* **Roll**
COOKING METHOD / TECHNIQUE To cause something to take on a cylindrical shape.

Ensalada *ehn-sah-LAH-dah* **Salad**
FRUIT & VEGETABLES A mixture of raw or cooked food—meat, seafood, fruit, or vegetables—tossed with a moist dressing. It typically includes salad greens but does not have to.

Ensalada de San Isidro *ehn-sah-LAH-dah deh sahn ee-SEE-droh*
DISH (Spain) A salad made with lettuce, tomato, onion, and canned tuna and drizzled with a red wine vinaigrette. It can include asparagus, chopped egg, cucumbers, and olives but the base ingredients are always the same.

Entomatada *ehn-toh-mah-TAH-dah*
DISH (Mexico) Enchiladas made with lightly fried tortillas that are dipped in tomato sauce.

Entrada / Primer plato *ehn-TRAH-dah / pree-MEHR PLAH-toh* **First course**
GENERAL The first course of a meal. It can also be called the appetizer.

Entremeses *ehn-treh-MEH-sehs* **Hors d'oeuvre**

GENERAL Small, bite-size appetizers served before a meal and often accompanied by cocktails. They can be hot or cold but are almost always savory. They can be served before or after taking a seat at the dinner table.

Enturbiar / Machacar *ehn-too-bee-AHR / mah-cha-KAHR* **Muddle**

COOKING METHOD / TECHNIQUE To crush or mash ingredients with the blunt end of a long stick (known as a muddler). This technique is often used when making mixed drinks that are flavored with fresh herbs.

Envasar *ehn-bah-SAHR* **Can**

COOKING METHOD / TECHNIQUE *See* Enlatar.

Envolver *ehn-bohl-BEHR* **Wrap**

COOKING METHOD / TECHNIQUE (1) To envelope. (2) To enclose or cover.

Envuelve plástico *ehn-BWEHL-veh PLAHS-tee-koh* **Plastic wrap**

EQUIPMENT Thin plastic film used to wrap food and containers. It has the ability to cling to itself or other surfaces without adhesive, making it a very useful wrapper. It can create an airtight environment if sealed correctly.

Epazote *eh-pah-SOH-teh* **Epazote**

HERBS & SPICES A wild herb with a flavor similar to that of coriander that is popular in Mexican cooking. It has a strong pungent flavor that is used in small quantities. Often used to flavor beans and stews, it is said to be a remedy for intestinal discomfort. It is most commonly found dried.

Eperlano *eh-pehr-LAH-noh* **Smelt**

FISH & SHELLFISH A very small (average length seven inches) fish that lives in salt water but travels to fresh water to spawn (breed). It has a shimmering silver skin with a rich and oily flesh. It is sold and eaten whole.

Equipo de pastelería *eh-KEE-poh deh pahs-teh-leh-REE-ah* **Bakeware**

EQUIPMENT Equipment used to make baked goods.

Erizo *eh-REE-soh* **Sea urchin**

FISH & SHELLFISH A marine animal found in a small, round shell with hard protruding prickly spines. Its orange-colored roe is considered a delicacy and is typically eaten right out of the shell.

Escabeche / En vinagre *ehs-kah-BEH-cheh / ehn bee-NAH-greh*

COOKING METHOD / TECHNIQUE A cooking method that marinates fried or poached fish in a vinegar or citrus marinade. The fish is cooled before it is marinated and is served chilled or at room temperature. Originally made as a preservation technique for fish, it is now also used on chicken, pork, and rabbit. It is popular in Spain, Cuba, Panama, Puerto Rico, and Peru.

Escaldar *ehs-kahl-DAHR* **Blanch / Scald**
  COOKING METHOD / TECHNIQUE (1) To quickly cook and cool food by plunging it in boiling water and then cooling it in an ice water bath. This is typically performed on fruit and vegetables to loosen the skins, brighten the color, and enhance the flavor. (2) To heat milk just below boiling (about 180°F). Before pasteurization it was done to destroy damaging bacteria and enzymes found in the milk. Currently it is done to raise the temperature of milk and/or infuse a flavor such as vanilla bean or cinnamon stick.

Escalfar *ehs-kahl-FAHR* **Poach**
  COOKING METHOD / TECHNIQUE To cook food gently in simmering liquid. The liquid can be water or a seasoned mixture that imparts flavor to the ingredient.

Escalonia / Chalota *ehs-kah-LOH-nee-ah / chah-LOH-tah* **Shallot**
  FRUIT & VEGETABLES A relative of the onion that looks more like a garlic. The small bulb is made up of individual segments covered entirely by a thin, papery skin. Its flesh is white with a tinge of pink or gray, and it has a sweet mild onion-like flavor.

Escama *ehs-KAH-mah* **Scale**
  FISH & SHELLFISH Small, hard plates that grow on the skin of fish and provides protection.

Escamoso *ehs-kah-MOH-soh* **Flaky**
  DESCRIPTOR Used to describe pastry whose texture is made up of dry, flat, thin layers of sheets stacked upon each other.

Escarchar *ehs-kahr-CHAR* **Frost**
  COOKING METHOD / TECHNIQUE To cover a baked good with icing or frosting.

Escarola *ehs-kah-ROH-lah* **Curly endive**
  FRUIT & VEGETABLES A member of the endive family that is often confused with chicory. It is a loose head of green, slightly furry leaves that curl at the tips. The leaves have a slight bitter taste.

Escudella *ehs-koo-DEH-yah*
  DISH (Spain) The cocido made in the Catalan region. It contains butifarra catalana sausage.

Escurrir *ehs-koo-REER* **Drizzle**
  COOKING METHOD / TECHNIQUE To pour a liquid over food in a thin stream.

  Drain
  COOKING METHOD / TECHNIQUE See Desaguar.

Escurridora de ensalada *ehs-koo-ree-DOH-rah deh ehn-sah-LAH-dah* **Salad spinner**
  EQUIPMENT See Centrifugadora de ensalada.

Esencia *eh-SEHN-see-ah* **Extract**
CONDIMENT A concentrated flavor derived from food by distillation. Most commonly found in liquid form but also available in powder or gel.

Esencia de almendra *eh-SEHN-see-ah deh ahl-MEHN-drah* **Almond extract**
CONDIMENTS A flavoring produced by combining almond oil with ethyl alcohol. Use the proper amount of the best-quality extract you can find as the flavor is intense. Also referred to as *extracto de almendra*.

Esencia de vainilla *eh-SEHN-see-ah deh bah-ee-NEE-yah* **Vanilla extract**
CONDIMENTS A liquid that possesses the flavor and aroma of vanilla. Chopped vanilla beans are infused in a solution of alcohol and water and then aged for a few months. Also referred to as *extracto de vainilla*.

Espadilla *ehs-pah-DEE-yah* **Beef, chuck**
MEAT An inexpensive cut of meat located between the neck and shoulder. It is a tough cut that must be cooked slowly to be tenderized. It is a popular cut for making hamburgers.

Espaguetis *ehs-pah-GEH-tees* **Spaghetti**
GRAINS & CEREALS Long, thin, round pasta made from wheat. It is Italian in origin.

Espalmar *ehs-pahl-MAHR* **Pound**
COOKING METHOD / TECHNIQUE To flatten an ingredient by striking it with a heavy object.

Espárrago *ehs-PAH-rrah-goh* **Asparagus**
FRUIT & VEGETABLES A member of the lily family that has an herbaceous sweet flavor and gets significantly tougher as it matures. There are four types of asparagus. Green (*verde*) is the most common type; white (*blanco*), popular in Europe, grows underground and as such does not develop chlorophyll; purple (*morado*) remains purple when fresh or lightly sautéed but turns green with prolonged cooking; and wild (*silvestre*) is tender and very thin.

Espátula *ehs-PAH-too-lah* **Spatula**
EQUIPMENT A handheld kitchen utensil that serves as a multipurpose tool. The material (rubber, metal, wood, plastic) it is made with determines is function, which includes scraping bowls, turning fish, folding ingredients, and stirring mixtures.

Espátula de goma *ehs-PAH-too-lah deh GOH-mah* **Rubber spatula**
EQUIPMENT A spatula with a rubber head. Its flexible nature makes it ideal for folding ingredients and mixing and scraping mixtures out of mixing bowls

Especia *ehs-PEH-see-ah* **Spice**
HERBS & SPICES The dried bark, bud, fruit, root, stem, or seed of a plant or treeused for flavoring. Spices are available whole or ground.

Espina *ehs-PEE-nah* **Fish bone**
FISH & SHELLFISH The small, thin bone of a fish.

Espinaca *ehs-pee-NAH-kah* **Spinach**
FRUIT & VEGETABLES A delicate leafy green plant that can be eaten raw or cooked. Oxalic acid present in the leaves produces a slight bitter taste and leaves the mouth with a powdery coated sensation. Depending on the variety the dark green leaves can be curled at the edges and take on a range of shapes.

Espoleta *ehs-poh-LEH-tah* **Wishbone**
MEAT A V-shaped bone found between the breast and the neck of a bird.

Espolvorear *ehs-pohl-boh-reh-AHR* **Dust**
COOKING METHOD / TECHNIQUE *See* **Polvorear.**

Esponja *ehs-POHN-hah* **Sponge**
EQUIPMENT A soft, porous spongy material that absorbs liquid and is used for washing and cleaning.

Espresso / Café solo *ehs-PREH-soh / kah-FEH SOH-loh* **Espresso**
BEVERAGE A strong, dark coffee made by forcing hot water through finely ground and packed coffee beans. It is served in small quantities in a special cup called a demitasse.

Espumadera *ehs-poo-mah-DEH-rah* **Skimming spoon**
EQUIPMENT A kitchen utensil used to remove an item from the surface of a liquid. It is a spoon with mesh netted bowl.

Espumadera oriental *ehs-poo-mah-DEH-rah oh-ree-ehn-TAHL* **Spider**
EQUIPMENT A type of strainer or skimmer used in Asian kitchens. A long handle is attached to the wide bowl of a spoon that is shallow and has a hollow netted texture that resembles a spiderweb.

Espumar / Quitar espuma *ehs-poo-MAHR / kee-TAHR ehs-POO-mah* **Skim**
COOKING METHOD / TECHNIQUE To remove foam from the surface.

Esqueixada de bacalao / Ensalada de bacalao desmigado *ehs-keh-eeks-AH-dah deh bah-kah-LAH-oh / ehn-sah-LAH-dah deh bah-kah-LAH-oh dehs-mee-GAH-doh*
DISH (Spain) A popular Catalan dish, a cold salad made with salted cod, onion, tomato, black olives, and an abundant amount of extra-virgin olive oil.

Estabilizante *ehs-tah-bee-lee-SAHN-teh* **Stabilizer**
GENERAL An additive used to keep solutions emulsified and in solution. A stabilizer prevents ingredients from separating.

Estante *ehs-TAHN-teh* **Rack**
EQUIPMENT A framework for holding an object or food item.

Estofar *ehs-toh-FAHR* **Braise**
COOKING METHOD / TECHNIQUE A slow cooking method used to develop flavors and tenderize tough cuts of meat, although the method is also used on vegetables. The food is first browned in fat, then a liquid is added and the mixture is covered tightly

with a lid. The food is left to cook in the oven or on the range at a low temperature for a long period of time.

Estopilla / Paño de muselina *ehs-toh-PEE-yah / PAH-nyoh deh moo-seh-LEE-nah* **Cheesecloth**

EQUIPMENT A lightweight cotton cloth used in cooking that will stay intact when wet and will not impart a flavor. It is used for straining liquids, lining molds, and creating packets of herbs.

Estragón *ehs-trah-GOHN* **Tarragon**

HERBS & SPICES An herb with soft, thin, and pointed green leaves. It has an aniselike flavor that is very popular in French cooking. It is one of the four fines herbes.

Estufa *ehs-TOO-fah* **Stove**

EQUIPMENT A kitchen appliance that cooks food and includes the range (burners) and the oven.

Etileno *eh-tee-LEH-noh* **Ethylene**

GENERAL An odorless, colorless, and tasteless gas that is naturally present in many fruit and vegetables. It is a plant hormone that increases as the fruit matures and accelerates the aging process. Avocados, apples, bananas, peaches, and melons produce a large amount of ethylene and can help speed the ripening process of other fruit.

Eviscerar *eh-bee-seh-RAHR* **Eviscerate**

COOKING METHOD / TECHNIQUE To remove an animal's internal organs.

Exprimidor *eks-pree-mee-DOHR* **Juicer**

EQUIPMENT A manual or electric kitchen tool used to extract liquid from a fruit or vegetable. Juicers vary in size, with some being small handheld devices and others counter-mounted small electric appliances.

Exprimidor de cítricos *eks-pree-mee-DOHR deh SEE-tree-kohs* **Lemon squeezer**

EQUIPMENT A handheld kitchen tool used to extract the juice from a lemon or lime. It comes in different shapes and sizes but must be made with an acid-resistant material.

Extender *eks-tehn-DEHR* **Roll out**

COOKING METHOD / TECHNIQUE To flatten. To extend or straighten by applying force with a roller or rolling pin.

Extracto *eks-TRAK-toh* **Extract**

CONDIMENTS *See* Esencia.

Extraer *eks-trah-EHR* **Extract**

COOKING METHOD / TECHNIQUE To remove. To draw out. To pull out.

Extraer el jugo *eks-trah-EHR ehl HOO-goh* **Juice**

COOKING METHOD / TECHNIQUE To extract the liquid (juice) found in a fruit or vegetable.

SPANISH-ENGLISH **E**

F

Fabada asturiana *fah-BAH-dah ahs-too-ree-AH-nah*
DISH (Spain) A hearty bean stew that hails from Asturias in northern Spain. White beans are stewed with blood sausage, chorizo, ham hocks, and bacon and flavored with olive oil, garlic, and paprika.

Faina *fah-ee-NAH*
DISH (Argentina) A thin bread made with chickpea flour.

Faisan *fah-ee-SAHN* **Pheasant**
GAME A medium-size game bird averaging three and a half pounds. It needs care when being cooked to prevent the flesh from drying out. It is often covered in fat (barded)to retain moisture.

Fajita *fah-HEE-tah* **Fajita**
DISH A Tex-Mex creation; a distant cousin of the taco. Grilled meat is sautéed with onion and peppers and then wrapped in a soft flour or corn tortilla. Originally, it was made with skirt steak but is now also made with chicken or shrimp. Typical accompaniments include sour cream, pico de gallo, and guacamole.

Fecha de caucidad *FEH-chah deh kow-see-DAHD* **Expiration date**
GENERAL A date stamped on a food package informing the consumer when the product will most likely not be usable.

Fecha de vencimiento *FEH-chah deh behn-see-mee-EHN-toh* **Expiration date**
GENERAL *See* Fecha de caucidad.

Fenogreco *feh-noh-GREH-koh* **Fenugreek**
HERBS & SPICES Popular in Indian cooking, a plant that is used for its leaves and seeds. Its round, yellow seeds of the same name are more commonly used and are available in whole or ground form. Used often for curries and pickling, it is also a main ingredient in artificial maple syrup flavoring.

Fermentación *fehr-mehn-tah-see-OHN* **Fermentation**
COOKING METHOD / TECHNIQUE A chemical change that occurs in food and beverages wherein enzymes from yeast or bacteria cause alcohol and carbon dioxide to form. It results in a change in appearance, texture, and flavor.

Fermento *fehr-MEHN-toh* **Leavening**
BAKING & PASTRY *See* Levadura.

Fiambre *fee-AHM-breh* **Processed meat**
MEAT Precooked or cured meats that are thinly sliced and served cold or at room temperature. Also known as cold cuts, they include ham, turkey, roast beef, bologna, and salami.

Fibra *FEE-brah* **Fiber**
(1) The indigestible portion of plant-based foods. (2) The striations found in an animal's muscles.

Fideos *fee-DEH-ohs* **Noodles**
GRAINS & CEREALS Pasta made with flour, water, and eggs or egg yolk. The flour can be made from wheat, rice, buckwheat, or another grain. Always flat, noodles can be thin or thick, long or short, or shaped into a square. They are available fresh or dried.

Fideos al huevo *fee-DEH-ohs ahl WEH-voh* **Egg noodles**
GRAINS & CEREALS See Pasta al huevo.

Fideos asiáticos *fee-DEH-ohs ah-see-AH-tee-kohs* **Asian noodles**
GRAINS & CEREALS Long, flat noodles made from a dough of wheat, rice, or soy flour, water, and sometimes egg.

Fideos de alforfón *fee-DEH-ohs deh ahl-fohr-FOHN* **Soba noodles**
GRAINS & CEREALS A thin, dark tan, Japanese noodle made with buckwheat flour.

Fideos de arroz *fee-DEH-ohs deh ah-RROHS* **Rice noodles**
GRAINS & CEREALS Long, thin noodles made from rice flour and water. Pale white when dried, they become translucent when cooked.

Fideos de celofán *fee-DEH-ohs deh seh-loh-FAHN* **Bean thread noodles**
GRAINS & CEREALS Dried translucent noodles made from the starch of green mung beans. They are also known as cellophane noodles or glass noodles.

Fideos de trigo *fee-DEH-ohs deh TREE-goh* **Wheat noodles**
GRAINS & CEREALS Noodles made from wheat flour.

Fideos muy finos de arroz *fee-DEH-ohs moo-EE FEE-nohs deh ah-RROS* **Rice vermicelli**
GRAINS & CEREALS Very thin and long noodle strands made from rice flour. They are also known as rice sticks.

Fideua *fee-DEH-oo-ah*
DISH (Spain) Paella made with a small, thin pasta (fideo) instead of rice.

Filete *fee-LEH-teh* **Fillet**
MEAT A boneless piece of fish or meat.

Filete de pescado *fee-LEH-teh deh pehs-KAH-doh* **Fish fillet**
FISH & SHELLFISH A single, boneless piece of fish that is cut from the top or side of the fish.

Filetiar / Cortar en filete *fee-leh-tee-AHR / cohr-TAHR en fee-LEH-teh*
COOKING METHOD / TECHNIQUE To cut off a boneless piece of fish or meat.

Filtrar *feel-TRAHR* **Filter**
COOKING METHOD / TECHNIQUE To pass through a strainer, cheesecloth, or paper so as to remove impurities or unwanted ingredients.

Finas hierbas *FEE-nahs ee-EHR-bahs* **Fines herbes**
HERBS & SPICES A classic combination of fresh chervil, chives, parsley, and tarragon that are finely chopped. Fines herbes are often used in French cooking.

Fino *FEE-noh*
> BEVERAGE (Spain) The most common type of sherry consumed in Spain. Very dry and pale in color, it is consumed as an apéritif.

Flamear *flah-meh-AHR* **Flambé**
> COOKING METHOD / TECHNIQUE French for "flaming," the technique of lighting food on fire after sprinkling it with a liquor just before serving.

Flamenquines *flah-mehn-KEE-nehs*
> DISH (Spain) A roll of ham and pork bound by béchamel sauce, breaded, and deep-fried (similar to a croquette). This can also refer to any dish that is native to the region of Andalusia.

Flan *flahn*
> DISH Traditional-style baked egg custard made in a caramelized mold. *See* **Natilla**.

Flan de coco *flahn deh KOH-koh*
> DISH Baked-egg custard made with sweetened coconut in a caramelized mold.

Flautas *flah-OW-tahs*
> DISH (Mexico) Stuffed and rolled tortillas that are deep-fried until golden brown and crispy.

Fleso *FLEH-soh* **Flounder**
> FISH & SHELLFISH A flat, saltwater, white flesh fish. It has a delicate flavor and a brownish tan skin that allows it to camouflage itself in the ocean.

Fletán *fleh-TAHN* **Halibut**
> FISH & SHELLFISH A very large, white, and firm-fleshed fish that comes from the waters of the north Pacific and Atlantic oceans. Low-fat and-mild flavored, it is available in steaks and fillets.

Flor de calabaza *flohr deh kah-lah-BAH-sah* **Squash blossom**
> FRUIT & VEGETABLES The flower from the summer or winter squash. Yellow or orange in color, it tastes vaguely like squash. Often stuffed and fried, squash blossoms can be sautéed or left raw and used in a salad or as a garnish.

Flor comestible *FLOH-rehs koh-mehs-TEE-bleh* **Flowers, edible**
> FRUIT & VEGETABLES Flowers that are not sprayed with pesticides and have a desirable flavor and appearance. They are used for garnish, steeping in oil, or making teas or other beverages.

Foja *FOH-hah* **Grouse**
> GAME A small game bird similar to a chicken in size.

Fonda *FOHN-dah*
> GENERAL (Mexico) A food stand or stall.

Formar *fohr-MAHR* **Form / Shape**
> COOKING METHOD / TECHNIQUE (1) To put together. (2) To shape. To give form to. To make something fit a certain way.

Frambuesa *frahm-boo-EH-sah* **Raspberry**

FRUIT & VEGETABLES A member of the berry family that is very small in size (less than one inch in length) with a bumpy exterior texture. It is cone shaped with a hollow center and an opening on one end of the berry. Sweet and tart in flavor, it is traditionally a deep pink red but there are other color varieties—golden and black.

Frambuesa dorada *frahm-boo-EH-sah doh-RAH-dah* **Golden raspberry**

FRUIT & VEGETABLES One of the three main varieties of raspberry (the others are red and black). It is a delicate fruit with a sweet and slightly tart flavor.

Fregadero *freh-gah-DEH-roh* **Sink**

EQUIPMENT A basin with running water used for washing hands and objects.

Freidora *freh-ee-DOH-rah* **Deep-fat fryer**

EQUIPMENT A small appliance used for deep-frying foods. It is a deep container with an adjustable electric thermometer that controls the temperature of the oil it contains.

Freír *freh-EER* **Fry / Deep-fry**

COOKING METHOD / TECHNIQUE To cook food in hot fat. The food can be completely submerged (deep-fry), partially submerged (panfry), or quickly cooked in a small amount of fat (sauté).

Freír a la sartén *freh-EER ah lah sahr-TEHN* **Panfry**

COOKING METHOD / TECHNIQUE To cook food in a small amount of fat in a skillet making sure the fat does not submerge the food.

Fresa *FREH-sah* **Strawberry**

FRUIT & VEGETABLES A red, pointed-end fruit with small, edible, yellow seeds surrounding its skin. It is juicy, sweet, and fragrant when ripe. Strawberries are available fresh or frozen.

Fricasé de pollo *free-kah-SEH deh POH-yoh*

DISH Braised marinated chicken pieces simmered in a tomato-based sauce that is flavored with onions, capers, dry wine, and potatoes.

Frigorífico *free-goh-REE-fee-koh* **Refrigerator**

EQUIPMENT See Nevera.

Frijol *free-HOHL* **Dried bean**

FRUIT & VEGETABLES See Legumbre.

Frijoles borrachos *free-HOH-lehs boh-RRAH-chohs*

DISH (Mexico) Beans cooked with beer as well as water.

Frijoles charros *free-HOH-lehs CHAH-rrohs*

DISH (Mexico) Pinto beans made with pork, onion, poblano chiles, tomatoes, and cilantro.

Frijol colorado *free-HOHL koh-loh-RAH-doh* **Pinto bean**

FRUIT & VEGETABLE See Judía pinta.

Frijol negro / Caraota negra *free-HOHL NEH-groh / kah-rah-OH-tah NEH-grah*
Black bean
> FRUIT & VEGETABLES Small, shiny beans with a creamy and meaty flesh that can be purchased dried or canned. Very popular in Latin American cuisines, they are served as a soup or side dish.

Frijol negro chino *free-HOHL NEH-groh CHEE-noh* **Chinese black bean, dried**
> FRUIT & VEGETABLES Small, fermented soybeans that turn black and soft as a result of the process. They are preserved in salt and take on a complex pungent and salty flavor. Mostly used as a condiment, they are typically finely chopped before added to a dish. They are also known as fermented black beans.

Frijoles refritos *free-HOH-les reh-FREE-tohs* **Refried beans**
> DISH Cooked beans that have been mashed and fried in lard or other fat. A traditional dish in Mexican and Tex-Mex cuisine, it is typically made with pinto beans but black or red beans can be used as well.

Frío *FREE-oh* **Cold**
> DESCRIPTOR Having a low temperature.

Frita *FREE-tah*
> DISH (Cuba) A hamburger-style sandwich made with ground pork mixed with ground chorizo. It is served on a round bun and topped with very thin shoestring fries and sautéed diced onions.

Frito *FREE-toh* **Fried**
> COOKING METHOD / TECHNIQUE A food that has been cooked in hot fat.

Fructosa *frook-TOH-sah* **Fructose**
> CONDIMENTS A simple carbohydrate that is sweeter than sucrose (table sugar) but loses its sweetness when heated. It can safely be consumed by diabetics and comes in powdered or liquid form. It cannot be evenly substituted with granulated table sugar.

Fruit *FROO-tah* **Fruta**
> FRUIT & VEGETABLE Part of a flowering plant whose purpose is to disseminate seeds. The flesh sweetens and its skin may change to a brighter color as it ripens and matures.

Fruta confitada *FROO-tah kohn-fee-TAH-dah* **Candied fruit**
> BAKING & PASTRY See **Fruta cristalizada**.

Fruta cristalizada / Fruta confitada / Fruta escarchada / Fruta glaseada
FROO-tah krees-tah-lee-SAH-dah / FROO-tah kohn-fee-TAH-dah / FROO-tah ehs-kahr-CHAH-dah / FROO-tah glah-seh-AH-dah **Candied fruit**
> BAKING & PASTRY Pieces of fruit that have been dipped in sugar syrup and then dried. Granulated sugar can also be dusted over them before they are dried for added texture.

Fruta de jack *FROO-tah deh yahk* **Jackfruit**
FRUIT & VEGETABLES A very large, oval-shaped tropical fruit with green, spiky skin that can grow up to one hundred pounds in weight. Its faintly sweet flesh is cream colored with seeds dispersed throughout it. It is used in savory dishes when unripe and sweet recipes when mature.

Fruta de la pasión / Granadilla *FROO-tah deh lah pah-see-OHN / grah-nah-DEE-yah* **Passion fruit**
FRUIT & VEGETABLES A small egg-shaped tropical fruit whose skin is typically dark brown but can also be yellow. Similar in structure to a pomegranate, inside it has a white pith that surrounds seeds covered in yellow flesh that are sweet with some sour and tart notes. The seeds can be eaten whole or pressed through a strainer to extract the juice.

Fruta del pan *FROO-tah dehl pahn* **Breadfruit**
FRUIT & VEGETABLES A large, green-skinned fruit native to the Caribbean. The cream-colored flesh is eaten when the fruit is unripe or before it becomes too sweet. It can be made sweet or savory by frying, grilling, baking, or stewing.

Fruta escarchada *FROO-tah ehs-kahr-CHAH-dah* **Candied fruit**
BAKING & PASTRY *See* **Fruta cristalizada.**

Fruta estrella *FROO-tah ehs-TREH-yah* **Star fruit**
FRUIT & VEGETABLES *See* **Carambola.**

Fruta glaseada *FROO-tah glah-seh-AH-dah* **Candied fruit**
BAKING & PASTRY *See* **Fruta cristalizada.**

Fruta seca *FROO-tah SEH-kah* **Dried fruit**
FRUIT & VEGETABLES Fruit that has been severely dehydrated resulting in a concentrated and intense sweet flavor. The fruit is dried by the sun or by a special oven.

Fruto seco *FROO-toh SEH-koh* **Nut**
NUTS & OILS A large, dried, oily, and edible seed of a plant that is enclosed in a shell.

FuFu de plátano *foo-FOO deh PLAH-tah-noh*
DISH (Cuba) Fried green or sweet plantains that are mashed and mixed with pork cracklings.

G

Galangal *gah-LAHN-gahl* **Galangal**
HERBS & SPICES A root tuber that has a hot peppery, citrus flavor used for seasoning. It is similar in appearance to fresh ginger with a thin skin that needs to be peeled. Its flesh is creamy white in color. Available fresh or dried, it is used as a substitute for ginger.

Galleta *gah-YEH-tah* **Cracker**
GRAINS & CEREALS A salted or savory thin biscuit or wafer.

Galleta / Bizcocho *gah-YEH-tah / bees-KOH-choh* **Cookie**
BAKING & PASTRY A small, sweet cake made with flour, sugar, eggs, and a high ratio of fat. Its texture can be crispy, crunchy, soft, or cakey.

Galleta / Tortita *gah-YEH-tah / tohr-TEE-tah* **Biscuit**
GRAINS & CEREALS A sweet or savory quick bread leavened with baking powder or baking soda. It can also refer to a thin sweet cookie.

Galleta de arroz *gah-YEH-tah deh ah-RROHS* **Rice cracker**
GRAINS & CEREALS A thin cracker made from rice flour that does not contain gluten.

Galón *gah-LOHN* **Gallon**
MEASUREMENTS A liquid measure of volume the equivalent of 16 cups or 8 pints or 4 quarts.

Gamba *GAHM-bah* **Prawn**
FISH & SHELLFISH A crustacean. A prawn can refer to either species of the lobster family that has sweet tasting meat and looks like a small Maine lobster or a large shrimp. Although the terms prawns and shrimp are used interchangeably, they are different species.

Gambas al ajillo *GAHM-bahs ahl ah-HEE-yoh*
DISH (Spain) Garlic shrimp. Small shrimp are placed in a small earthenware dish, drizzled with a hefty amount of olive oil, chopped, garlic, and dried red chile pepper, and cooked over a hot flame.

Gambas con garbardina *GAHM-bahs kohn gahr-bahr-DEE-nah*
DISH (Spain) Batter-coated, deep-fried shrimp. Gambas con garbardina literally translates as "shrimp in coats."

Gandinga *gahn-DEEN-gah*
DISH (Puerto Rico) Stewed pork innards.

Garam masala *GAH-rahm mah-SAH-lah* **Garam masala**
HERBS & SPICES A mixture of dry-roasted and ground spices that is traditional in northern India. The combination varies according to personal preference but typically contains about twelve different spices. It passes on an earthy and warm flavor to dishes. The spice blends can be made at home or purchased commercially.

Garbanzo *gahr-BAHN-soh* **Chickpea**
FRUIT & VEGETABLES A round, beige-colored legume that has a firm texture and nutty flavor. Garbanzos can be found dried or canned.

Garnacha *gahr-NAH-chah*
DISH *See* Sope.

Garrotxa *gah-RROCH-ah* **Garrotxa**
DAIRY A goat's milk cheese named after the town where it is made in the northeast section of Spain. It is a semisoft cheese with a nutty flavor and a soft and slightly moldy blue gray rind.

Gasificar *gah-see-fee-KAHR* **Aerate**
COOKING METHOD / TECHNIQUE To incorporate air.

Gastronomía *gahs-troh-noh-MEE-ah* **Gastronomy**
GENERAL The art and science of preparing good food.

Gazpacho andaluz *gahs-PAH-choh ahn-dah-LOOS*
DISH (Spain) A chilled, raw soup made from pureed tomatoes, green peppers, onion, cucumber, and garlic. Bread is often added when pureeing to help thicken the soup. Customarily small bowls containing the chopped vegetables of the soup and croutons are passed around for the diner to sprinkle on top of the soup.

Gazpachuelo *gahs-pah-CHWEH-loh*
DISH (Spain) A fish soup flavored with vinegar and mayonnaise. Although the name sounds like gazpacho, it has nothing to do with the chilled tomato soup.

Gelatina *geh-lah-TEE-nah* **Gelatin**
CONDIMENTS A thickener or setting agent derived from the collogan found inside an animal's bones. It melts when it is heated and solidifies into a jellylike texture when it is cooled. It is odorless, tasteless, and colorless and is available in sheets or powdered form.

Germen *HEHR-mehn* **Germ**
GRAINS & CEREALS The embryo or seed of a cereal grain. Located in the kernel, it contains many nutrients including vitamins, fiber, and fatty acids. It is a component of a whole grain but can be removed and sold independently.

Germen de trigo *HEHR-mehn deh TREE-goh* **Wheat germ**
GRAINS & CEREALS The embryo of the kernel found inside the grain's endosperm (interior). It contains fat, vitamins, minerals, fiber, and protein.

Ginebra *hee-NEH-brah* **Gin**
BEVERAGE A grain alcohol that is redistilled and flavored with juniper berries and other botanicals. It is a very dry spirit with a sharp and distinct flavor.

Gineo *hee-NEH-oh* **Banana**
FRUIT & VEGETABLE See **Plátano.**

Glasa *GLAH-sah* **Glaze (reduced sauce)**
COOKING METHOD / TECHNIQUE A thick or thin sauce that is used to coat food and adds color, shine, and flavor. It can be sweet or savory.

Glaseado *glah-seh-AH-doh* **Royal icing**
BAKING & PASTRY Icing or frosting made of powdered sugar, egg whites, and a drop of lemon juice. It hardens quickly into an opaque white frosting and is often used in cake and cookie decorations.

Glaseado de huevo *glah-seh-AH-doh deh WEH-voh* **Egg wash**
COOKING METHOD / TECHNIQUE See **Bañar con huevo.**

Glasear / Barnizar / Glaseado *glah-seh-AHR / bahr-nee-SAHR / glah-seh-AH-doh*
Glaze
COOKING METHOD / TECHNIQUE To brush on or coat a food with a sweet or savory sauce that will set on the food and produce a shine.

Glicerina *glee-seh-REE-nah* **Glycerin**
GENERAL The common name for glycerol. A component of a triglyceride, it is obtained from fats. It is a thick, colorless liquid used to add sweetness to and retain moisture in foods.

Glucosa *gloo-KOH-sah* **Glucose**
GENERAL Generally referred to as dextrose, a simple sugar that is not as sweet as table sugar. It does not crystallize and is used often in commercial food preparation.

Gluten *GLOO-tehn* **Gluten**
GENERAL A combination of the proteins glutenin and gliadin, which are found in cereal grains, most commonly wheat. The two proteins must be hydrated in order to activate gluten which is responsible for creating a strong network structure in baked goods.

GMS (Glutamato Monósodico) *GLOO-tah-mah-toh moh-noh-SOH-dee-koh*
MSG (Monosodium Glutamate)
CONDIMENTS A sodium salt of glutamic acid, one of the twenty-two amino acids. Naturally found in kombu seaweed, it is also commercially synthesized and sold in the form of a white powder. Although flavorless, it has the ability to enhance the flavor of savory foods and provide the unique taste sensation "umami."

Gordita *gohr-DEE-tah*
DISH *See* **Sope.**

Gota *GOH-tah* **Drop**
COOKING METHOD / TECHNIQUE A very small amount of liquid released onto a plate or container.

Gramo *GRAH-moh* **Gram**
MEASUREMENTS A metric measure of mass equivalent to $1/1,000$ kilogram or 0.0022 pound.

Granada *grah-NAH-dah* **Pomegranate**
FRUIT & VEGETABLES A round, red fruit the size of an orange with a small projection jutting from its stem end. The thick skin encloses a large amount of red fleshy seeds that are contained within a beige-colored spongy membrane. The seeds are the only edible part of the fruit and have a tart and tannic flavor and underlying sweetness.

Granadilla *grah-nah-DEE-yah* **Passion fruit**
FRUIT & VEGETABLES *See* **Fruta de la pasión.**

Granadina *grah-nah-DEE-nah* **Grenadine**
CONDIMENTS A dark red, artificially sweetened, pomegranate-flavored syrup used to color and flavor drinks. It was originally made from real pomegranates.

Grano *GRAH-noh* **Grain**
GRAINS & CEREALS The dried edible portion of the cereal plant. Examples of plants from which grains are removed include corn, wheat, rice, oats, and barley. The word "grain" is often used interchangeably with cereal.

Grano entero *GRAH-noh ehn-TEH-roh* **Whole grain**
GRAINS & CEREALS A grain that has been minimally processed and contains all three edible parts: the bran, endosperm, and germ.

Gran reserva *grahn reh-SEHR-bah* **Gran reserve**
BEVERAGES A term given to wine that has been aged for at least five years. It is also intended to be given to wines made in exceptional years, but this is up to the discretion of the winemaker.

Grasa *GRAH-sah* **Fat / Grease**
GENERAL A macronutrient necessary for human survival that contains nine calories per gram. From a culinary standpoint it refers to triglycerides that are both in the solid and liquid state, but technically fats are solid and oils are liquid. Its functions are varied and include adding flavor, richness, color, and tenderness to foods.
MEAT Rendered animal fat.

Grasa / Aceite solidificado *GRAH-sah / ah-seh-EE-teh soh-lee-dee-fee-KAH-doh* **Shortening**
GENERAL Broadly, any cooking fat that is solid at room temperature.

Grasa insaturada *GRAH-sah een-sah-too-RAH-dah* **Unsaturated fat**
GENERAL A triglyceride that contains one or more double bonds in its hydrocarbon fatty acid chain. It is a fat that is liquid at room temperature and comes primarily from plant sources. Monounsaturated and polyunsaturated fats are types of unsaturated fat.

Grasa saturada *GRAH-sah sah-too-RAH-dah* **Saturated fat**
GENERAL A triglyceride primarily containing saturated fatty acids. These hydrocarbon chains have no double bonds and are filled to capacity with carbon atoms making them very stable. It is solid at room temperature and found primarily in animal fats.

Gratinado *grah-tee-NAH-doh* **Au gratin**
COOKING METHOD / TECHNIQUE The technique of creating a golden brown crust by broiling a topping of cheese and/or bread crumbs mixed with butter.

Grosella *groh-SEH-yah* **Currant**
FRUIT & VEGETABLES A small berry related to the gooseberry. There are three different varieties, which come in three different colors: black, red, white. The black currant must be cooked and is used to make cassis liqueur. The red and white can be eaten raw.

Guama *goo-AH-mah*
  DISH (Colombia) A fruit that looks like an oversize vanilla bean. The inedible pod holds a number of seeds that are covered in a white, cotton-looking flesh that is eaten. The large seeds found within the flesh are inedible.

Guarapo *gwah-RAH-poh*
  BEVERAGE (Cuba) Sugarcane juice. This is served over ice as a refreshment.

Guardar *gwar-DAHR* **Store**
  COOKING METHOD / TECHNIQUE To set aside for future use.

Guarnición *gwar-nee-see-OHN* **Garnish**
  COOKING METHOD / TECHNIQUE A final decorative and edible component to a dish. It should be visually appealing and reflect the flavor and/or composition of the dish.

Guasca *GWAHS-kah*
  DISH (Colombia) An herb similar in appearance to basil with its flavor more reminiscent of that of rosemary. It is typically used dried to flavor ajiaco soup.

Guayaba *gwah-YAH-bah* **Guava**
  FRUIT & VEGETABLES A small, oval-shaped, tropical fruit with a bumpy skin that ranges in color from yellow green when unripe to dark purple when mature. The red flesh can be eaten only when the fruit is ripe and it is often used to make juice or preserves. It is available fresh and canned and is very popular in Mexico and the Caribbean.

Guindilla *geen-DEE-yah* **Chile**
  HERBS & SPICES See Chile and entries under specific types.

Guisante *gee-SAHN-teh* **Pea / Green pea**
  FRUIT & VEGETABLES (1) A member of the legume family, which means it has an edible seed found inside a pod. Some pods are edible and others are not, requiring the seeds (peas) to be removed. (2) An immature bean inside a pod. It must be removed from its pod and eaten fresh before its natural sugars turn into starch, dramatically altering its flavor. It is also known as an English pea or garden pea. Peas are available fresh, canned, frozen, or dried.

Guisante amarillo partido *gee-SAHN-teh ah-mah-REE-yoh pahr-TEE-doh* **Split yellow pea**
  FRUIT & VEGETABLES A dried yellow sweet pea that has been mechanically split to cook faster.

Guisante dulce *gee-SAHN-teh DOOL-seh* **Sugar snap pea**
  FRUIT & VEGETABLES A pea with an edible pod. Slightly rounded, it resembles a cross between an English pea and a snow pea.

Guisante verde partido / Chicharro *gee-SAHN-teh BEHR-deh pahr-TEE-doh / CHEE-chah-rroh* **Split green pea**
  FRUIT & VEGETABLES A dried green sweet pea that has been mechanically split to cook faster.

Guisar *gee-SAHR* **Stew**

COOKING METHOD / TECHNIQUE To simmer a food in a thick, flavored liquid for a long time. This tenderizes tough cuts of meat and allows flavors to blend.

Guiso *GEE-soh* **Stew**

DISH A dish made by slowly cooking a meat and/or vegetables in a liquid for a long period of time.

H

Haba *AH-bah* **Fava bean**

FRUIT & VEGETABLES Also known as a broad bean, a large bean that comes in a pod and is inedible unless very young. Once removed from the pod, fresh fava beans must be blanched to remove their tough skin. They can be purchased fresh, dried, or canned.

Habichuela *ah-bee-choo-EH-lah* **Bean**

FRUIT & VEGETABLE See **Judía**.

Hacer tiras *ah-SEHR TEE-rahs*

COOKING METHOD / TECHNIQUE See **Trituar**.

Hallaca *ah-YAH-kah*

DISH (Venezuela) A mixture of raisins, olives, and seasonings that is combined with beef, pork, and/or chicken then stuffed in a cornmeal mixture. It is all wrapped in a banana leaf and steamed. Similar to Mexican tamales, these are served during the Christmas holidays.

Hamburguesa *ahm-boor-GEH-sah* **Hamburger**

MEAT A ground beef patty that is cooked to a desired doneness and sandwiched between two round buns.

Harina *ah-REE-nah* **Flour**

GRAINS & CEREALS The finely ground kernel of a cereal grain. It can contain the entire kernel or just parts of it.

Harina blanca *ah-REE-nah BLAHN-kah* **White flour**

GRAINS & CEREALS The flour made only from the endosperm (starchy part) of the wheat kernel.

Harina de arroz *ah-REE-nah deh ah-RROHS* **Rice flour**

GRAINS & CEREALS Dried, uncooked, white rice that has been ground to a fine powder. It does not contain gluten. Rice flour is used for making baked goods.

Harina de avena *ah-REE-nah deh ah-BEH-nah* **Oat flour**

GRAINS & CEREALS Toasted and hulled whole oats that have been ground into a powder. It does not contain gluten.

Harina de fuerza *ah-REE-nah deh foo-EHR-sah* **Bread flour**

GRAINS & CEREALS An unbleached wheat flour that is high in gluten protein and used for bread making. It is made from 99 percent hard wheat flour.

Harina de garbanzos *ah-REE-nah deh gahr-BAHN-sohs* **Chickpea flour**
GRAINS & CEREALS The flour made from ground dried chickpeas.

Harina de maíz *ah-REE-nah deh mah-EES* **Cornmeal**
GRAINS & CEREALS Dried corn kernels ground to a specific texture—fine, medium, or coarse. Depending on the type of corn used, its color can be yellow, white, or blue.

Harina de papa *ah-REE-nah deh PAH-pah* **Potato flour**
GRAINS & CEREALS The flour made from boiled then dried potatoes that are ground into a powder. Used as a thickener, it is gluten free. It is also known as potato starch.

Harina de repostería *ah-REE-nah deh reh-pohs-teh-REE-ah* **Cake flour**
GRAINS & CEREALS A soft wheat flour that is low in protein and high in starch content. It produces tender cakes with a fine crumb.

Harina de trigo duro *ah-REE-nah deh TREE-goh DOO-roh* **Durum flour**
GRAINS & CEREALS Durum is one of the three major types of wheat that is high in protein but is inelastic and does not rise well. For this reason it is not used for bread making but is the flour of choice for pasta making since it can be boiled for a long period of time without falling apart.

Harina de trigo integral *ah-REE-nah deh TREE-goh een-teh-GRAHL* **Whole wheat flour**
GRAINS & CEREALS The flour made from the milling of the wheat's whole grain.

Harina leudada *ah-REE-nah leh-oo-DAH-dah* **Self-rising flour**
GRAINS & CEREALS All-purpose flour that has had baking powder and salt added to it.

Harina sin mezcla *ah-REE-nah seen MEHS-klah* **All-purpose flour**
GRAINS & CEREALS A flour that is a blend of low-gluten soft wheat and high-gluten hard wheat. Because of this combination, it can be used for many purposes in the kitchen. All-purpose flour is milled solely from the inner part of the wheat (the endosperm). It does not contain germ or bran. It is also referred to as AP flour.

Harinoso *ah-ree-NOH-soh* **Mealy**
DESCRIPTOR The description of a texture that is slightly dry and crumbly.

Heladera *eh-lah-DEH-rah* **Refrigerator**
EQUIPMENT *See* Nevera.

Helado / Nieve *eh-LAH-doh / nee-EH-beh* **Ice cream**
BAKING & PASTRY A frozen dessert made with cream, milk (fresh or powdered), and a sweetener (sugar, honey, or an artificial sweetener). A flavoring such as chocolate, caramel, or nuts can be added. Commercial ice creams usually contain stabilizers and thickeners to help improve and maintain their texture.

Hervir *ehr-BEER* **Boil**
COOKING METHOD / TECHNIQUE To cook by raising the temperature of water to 212°F.

Híbrido *EE-bree-doh* **Hybrid**
DESCRIPTOR A result of crossbreeding.

Hielo *ee-EH-loh* **Ice**
BEVERAGE The frozen state of water.

Hielo seco *ee-EH-loh SEH-koh* **Dry ice**
GENERAL Solid carbon dioxide that is used for long-term chilling. It turns into a gas, not a liquid, and as such will not produce water. It will produce burns if it comes in contact with skin.

Hierbabuena *ee-ehr-bah-boo-EH-nah* **Peppermint**
HERBS & SPICES *See* **Yerba buena**.

Hierba de limón *ee-EHR-bah deh lee-MOHN* **Lemongrass**
HERBS & SPICES A tall grass used as an herb. The section closest to the root contains the most citrus lemon flavor and is cylindrical in shape with layers resembling a scallion. Lemongrass must be crushed or chopped in order to allow its flavor to be infused into the dish. It is available fresh or dried.

Hierba *ee-EHR-bah* **Herb**
HERBS & SPICES The fresh or dried leaves of a plant used in small amounts to add flavor to food. They offer very little nutritional value.

Hierbas de Provenza *ee-EHR-bahs deh proh-BEHN-sah* **Herbes de Provence**
HERBS & SPICES A mixture of dried herbs commonly used in the South of France. Lavender is a key ingredient and others include basil, rosemary, sage, fennel seed, thyme, and bay leaf. It is used on meats and vegetables.

Hígado *EE-gah-doh* **Liver**
MEAT A large organ that is prized for its rich taste and creamy texture. It is best consumed from young animals as liver from older ones can be tough and stronger flavored. Most liver consumed comes from calves, cattle, geese, and poultry. Depending on the animal source, it is available fresh or frozen, whole or sliced.

Hígado de pato *EE-gah-do deh PAH-toh* **Duck liver**
MEAT An organ meat that is very fatty and rich tasting. It is used in making the French delicacy foie gras.

Higo *EE-goh* **Fig**
FRUIT & VEGETABLES The fruit from the fig tree. On average it has a two-inch diameter and ranges in color from golden yellow to dark purplish–black. The interior of the fresh fig is red with lots of small edible seeds. Both the skin and flesh can be eaten and are very sweet. Figs are available fresh or dried and are eaten raw or cooked.

Higo chumbo / Tuna *EE-goh CHOOM-boh / TOO-nah* **Prickly pear**
FRUIT & VEGETABLES The small, oval-shaped fruit of the cactus plant that grows off the cactus pad (nopal). Its prickly textured skin is inedible and ranges in color from green to bright pink. Its flesh is slightly tart, sweet, and juicy. Prickly pears can be eaten raw or cooked.

Hinojo *ee-NOH-hoh* **Fennel**
FRUIT & VEGETABLES An aromatic plant with a licorice and anise-like flavor. Its base is a white bulb that is used as a vegetable and can be eaten raw or cooked. It has a number of green stems protruding from the bulb that have thin feathery green leaves similar in taste and texture to dill. The leaves have a very delicate flavor and should not be cooked.

Hogao *oh-GAH-oh*
DISH (Colombia) A stir-fry of onion, tomato, and cilantro, the flavor base to many dishes.

Hoja de curry *OH-hah deh KOO-ree* **Curry leaf**
HERBS & SPICES The leaf of the curry tree. Fresh, dark green curry leaves are small (about three inches) and have a short shelf life. They freeze well but will lose flavor. They are available in dried form, but the flavor is inferior.

Hoja de laurel *OH-hah deh lah-oo-REHL* **Bay leaf**
HERBS & SPICES An herb native to the Mediterranean. There are two varieties: the long, thin, and more flavorful California bay leaf and the more oval and subtle Turkish leaf. Also known as laurel leaves, bay leaves can be purchased dried or fresh, which are more difficult to find.

Hojaldre *oh-HAHL-dreh* **Puff pastry**
BAKING & PASTRY Light, flaky pastry made from chilled layers of butter sandwiched between sheets of dough. The unleavened pastry rises by the steam let go by the butter and separates into many thin layers.

Hoja de maíz / Hoja de tamal *OH-hah deh mah-EES / OH-hah deh tah-MAHL*
Corn husk
FRUIT & VEGETABLES The inedible, papery outer layer surrounding corn kernels. Fresh husks are green while dried ones are beige in color and must be soaked in hot water for about twenty minutes to soften before being used. They are primarily used to wrap tamales.

Hoja de plátano *OH-hah deh PLAH-tah-noh* **Banana leaf**
FRUIT & VEGETABLES The large, flexible leaves of a banana plant. A leaf's spine needs to be removed in order to make it pliable and is then cut to the appropriate size for cooking, where it imparts a unique smoky flavor. Banana leaves are used in Latin American and Asian cooking to wrap or cover food. In the United States they are often found frozen.

Hoja de parra *OH-hah deh PAH-rrah* **Grape leaf**
FRUIT & VEGETABLES The large, edible, green leaves of a grapevine that are often used in Greek and Middle Eastern cooking for wrapping foods. Sold in jars, they are typically rolled up and kept in a brine solution to keep them preserved.

Hoja de roble (roja o verde) *OH-hah deh ROHB-leh (ROH-hah oh BEHR-deh)*
Oak leaf lettuce (red or green)
FRUIT & VEGETABLES A looseleaf lettuce whose leaves are attached at the base of its head. Its flavorful, soft, wavy leaves are predominantly green with splashes of red.

Hoja santa *OH-hah SAHN-tah*
HERBS & SPICES (Mexico) An herb whose flavor is a cross between the aniselike flavor of fennel and the spiciness of black pepper.

Hoja de tamal *OH-hah deh tah-MAHL* **Corn husk**
FRUIT & VEGETABLE *See* **Hoja de maíz**.

Honear a ciegas *ohr-neh-AHR ah see-EH-gahs* **Blind bake**
COOKING METHOD / TECHNIQUE To bake an empty pie crust before adding the filling. Often the crust is pierced with a fork and/or lined with parchment paper and topped with baking beans to prevent the pastry from rising and help it bake evenly.

Hongo *OHN-goh* **Mushroom**
FRUIT & VEGETABLES *See* **Seta**.

Horchata *ohr-CHA-tah*
BEVERAGE (Mexico) A cold beverage made by infusing ground rice and almonds into water and flavoring it with cinnamon and lime zest. It is finished by being sweetened with sugar and poured over ice.

Hormigas culonas *ohr-MEE-gahs koo-LOH-nahs*
DISH (Colombia) Large fried ants eaten in the region of Santander.

Hornear / Hornada *ohr-neh-AHR / ohr-NAH-dah* **Baking**
COOKING METHOD / TECHNIQUE To cook in an oven with dry heat to produce baked goods.

Hornear a ciegas *ohr-neh-AHR ah see-EH-gahs* **Blind bake**
COOKING METHOD / TECHNIQUE To bake an empty pie crust before adding the filling. Often the crust is pierced with a fork and/or lined with parchment paper and topped with baking beans to prevent the pastry from rising and help it bake evenly.

Horno *OHR-noh* **Oven**
EQUIPMENT A kitchen appliance powered by gas or electricity. It consists of an enclosed chamber that roasts or bakes food through the circulation of hot air.

Hortaliza *ohr-tah-LEE-sah* **Vegetable**
FRUIT & VEGETABLES *See* **Vegetal**.

Huachinango *wah-chee-NAHN-goh* **Red snapper**
FISH & SHELLFISH *See* **Pargo**.

Huancaína *wahn-kah-EE-nah*
DISH (Peru) A spicy cheese sauce served over boiled potatoes or with vegetables. Its main ingredients are yellow chile peppers (ají amarillo), farmer's cheese, evaporated milk, and/or eggs.

Hueso de caña *WEH-soh deh KAH-nya* **Marrowbone**
MEAT A beef bone, typically from the thigh, that contains marrow.

Hueso *WEH-soh* **Bone**
GENERAL Porous connective tissue that forms the skeleton of animals.

Pit
FRUIT & VEGETABLES *See* **Carozo**.

Hueso de medular / Hueso de caña *WEH-soh deh meh-doo-LAHR / WEH-soh deh KAH-nyah* **Marrowbone**
MEAT A beef bone, typically from the thigh, that contains marrow.

Huevas *WEH-vahs* **Roe**
FISH & SHELLFISH Female fish eggs.

Huevas de salmón *WEH-vahs deh sahl-MOHN* **Salmon roe**
FISH & SHELLFISH The eggs from a female salmon. Large, round, and glistening orange in color with a light texture, they explode in your mouth.

Huevo *WEH-voh* **Egg**
DAIRY A reproductive body with an oval-shaped, thin, protective shell protecting a yellow yolk surrounded by a clear, protein-rich membrane. The most common egg used for eating comes from a hen but can also come from a female duck, goose, or quail. The shell can be either brown or white, which is due to the hen's breed and has no impact on the egg's taste or nutritional content. Although the shell is not commonly eaten, every part of the egg is edible. *See also* **Yema**; **Clara de heuevo**.

Huevo cocido *WEH-voh koh-SEE-doh* **Hard-boiled egg**
COOKING METHOD / TECHNIQUE An egg in its shell that has been submerged into boiling water long enough for the yolk and white to firm up. It takes about eight minutes for the egg to become solidified. Hard-boiled eggs can be kept in their shells in the refrigerator for up to a week.

Huevo de codorniz *WEH-voh deh koh-dohr-NEES* **Quail egg**
DAIRY A very small egg about one inch in diameter. Its shell is beige with brown spots. Its flavor is very similar to a chicken egg and it can be cooked and prepared in the same way.

Huevo de pato *WEH-voh deh PAH-toh* **Duck egg**
DAIRY The egg from a duck similar in taste to that of a chicken egg but slightly larger in size.

Huevo en vinagre *WEH-voh ehn bee-NAH-greh* **Pickled egg**
DAIRY A hard-boiled egg that has been marinated and preserved in a vinegar solution.

Huevos a la flamenca *WEH-vohs ah lah flah-MEHN-kah*
DISH (Spain) Individual portions of baked eggs with ham, chorizo, and asparagus cooked and served in earthenware ramekins.

Huevos a la mexicana *WEH-vohs ah lah meh-hee-KAH-nah*

DISH (Mexico) Eggs scrambled with chiles, tomatoes, and onions.

Huevos estrellados con patatas fritas *WEH-vohs ehs-treh-YAH-dohs kohn pah-TAH-tahs FREE-tahs*

DISH (Spain) A simple but classic dish of eggs fried in olive oil and placed over a bed of french fried potatoes. The eggs are then cut up over the potatoes and the yolks run all over the dish.

Huevos rancheros *WEH-vohs rahn-CHEH-rohs*

DISH (Mexico) Fried eggs placed over a soft corn tortilla and topped with a spicy, chunky tomato sauce. The yolks are usually left exposed and are not covered by the sauce.

Huitlacoche / Cuitlacoche *weet-lah-KOH-cheh* **Huitlacoche**

CONDIMENTS Corn fungus that attacks kernels and causes them to swell to almost ten times their natural size. Earthy, smoky, and sweet-flavored, it has a dark grayish color with shades of white that resembles mold. Used in a similar fashion and where mushrooms would be used, it is considered a delicacy in Mexico. Sometimes referred to as Mexican truffle, in the United States it is available canned or frozen.

Humo *OO-moh* **Smoke**

GENERAL A vapor emitted when a material combusts. It is commonly a by-product of fire.

I

Ibérico *ee-BEH-ree-koh* **Iberian**

DAIRY Relating or belonging to the Iberian peninsula, which is comprised of Spain and Portugal.

Idiazabal *ee-dee-ah-SAH-bahl* **Idiazabal**

DAIRY An unpasteurized sheep's milk cheese from the Basque region of Spain. It is a pressed cheese that may be lightly smoked during the aging process giving it a nutty and slightly smoky flavor. The cheese is formed in rounds and shares manchego's characteristic zigzag pattern on its rind.

Inca Kola *EEN-kah KOH-lah*

BEVERAGE (Peru) The iconic drink of Peru. A nonalcoholic fizzy soda that is yellow in color and has an artificially sweet bubble gum flavor.

Incorporar *een-kohr-poh-RAHR* **Incorporate**

COOKING METHOD / TECHNIQUE To mix two or more ingredients until well blended.

Infundir *een-foon-DEER* **Infuse**

COOKING METHOD / TECHNIQUE To extract the flavor of a food by soaking it in a hot liquid.

Infusión *een-foo-see-OHN* **Infusion**
  COOKING METHOD / TECHNIQUE The flavor that has been extracted from a food by
  having soaked it in a hot liquid.

Irradiar / Irradiado *ee-rrah-dee-AHR / ee-rrah-dee-AH-doh* **Irradiate / Irradiated**
  GENERAL To extend the shelf life of food by exposing it to low doses of X-rays or
  gamma rays in order to eliminate the presence of microorganisms. The process is
  approved by the FDA and all foods that have undergone this process must bear an
  international symbol.

Isla flotante *EES-lah floh-TAHN-teh* **Floating island**
  DISH A dessert comprising islands of meringue floating in a sea of crème anglaise.
  Lightly beaten egg whites are poached in sweetened hot milk and set aside while
  the milk is used to make the crème anglaise.

J

Jabalí *hah-bah-LEE* **Wild boar**
  GAME A large game animal that is a species of pig. Its meat is leaner but richer and
  stronger tasting.

Jabalí, silla *hah-bah-LEE, SEE-yah* **Wild boar, saddle**
  GAME The connected two loins of the boar found on either side of the backbone.

Jaiba *HAY-ee-bah* **Crab**
  FISH & SHELLFISH *See* **Cangrejo.**

Jalea *hah-LEH-ah* **Jelly**
  CONDIMENTS A spreadable product made from fruit juice, sugar, and pectin. The
  pectin, which is responsible for thickening the product, can be naturally occurring
  in the fruit or added in powdered form.

Jamaica *hah-MAH-ee-kah*
  HERBS & SPICES (Mexico) A dried hibiscus flower that is infused in water to make an
  agua fresca. Bright red in color, it has a tart taste.

Jamón *hah-MOHN* **Ham**
  MEAT Cooked or fresh meat from the pig's hind leg. The meat is taken from the hip
  down to the middle shank and is cured to some degree. Often it is also smoked after
  it is cured. It is available boneless or with the bone in.

Jamón iberico *hah-MOHN ee-BEH-ree-koh*
  MEAT (Spain) Iberian ham. A cured ham produced only in Spain from black Iberian
  pigs that naturally seek out and eat almost only acorns. The finest jamón iberico is
  called jamón de bellotas.

Jarabe / Sirope *hah-RAH-beh / see-ROH-peh* **Syrup**
  CONDIMENTS A thick, viscous, and sticky liquid that is typically sweet.

Jarabe de arce *hah-RAH-beh deh AHR-seh* **Maple syrup**
CONDIMENTS The sap from the maple tree that has been boiled and reduced until a thick liquid forms.

Jarabe de maíz *hah-RAH-beh deh mah-EES* **Corn syrup**
CONDIMENTS A sweet, dense, sticky syrup made by processing cornstarch with acids. There are two varieties: light and dark. The light is clarified to remove color and the dark has caramel flavoring and coloring added.

Jarras de medir *HAH-rrahs deh meh-DEER* **Measuring cups**
EQUIPMENT *See* **Tazas de medir.**

Jengibre *hehn-HEE-breh* **Ginger**
HERBS & SPICES The tuber root of the ginger plant. The light brown and very bumpy skin must be peeled off before it is used. The flesh is pale yellow in color and very fibrous, which is why it tends to be grated and its juice extracted for use. It has a strong peppery and soapy flavor that is very aromatic. A staple in Asian cooking, it is used in both sweet and savory recipes. It can be found in powdered form, but it is inferior in taste to the fresh.

Jenjibre en conserva *hehn-HEE-breh ehn kohn-SEHR-bah* **Candied ginger**
BAKING & PASTRY Peeled pieces of ginger that have been boiled in sugar syrup, dusted with granulated sugar, and then dried.

Jengibre encurtido *hehn-HEE-breh ehn-koor-TEE-doh* **Pickled ginger**
CONDIMENTS Thikly sliced ginger that has been marinated in a vinegar solution. Often artificially colored pink, it is served and eaten after sushi.

Jerez dulce *geh-REHS DOOL-seh* **Cream sherry**
BEVERAGE (Spain) A very sweet sherry. It has a syrupy texture and deep amber color and is drunk with dessert.

Jícama / Nabo dulce *HEE-kah-mah / NAH-boh DOOL-seh* **Jicama**
FRUIT & VEGETABLES A large root vegetable that averages one and a half pounds in weight. Its white flesh is crunchy with a texture and flavor similar to those of a water chestnut; its thin brown skin is inedible. Jícama can be eaten raw or cooked.

Jitomate *hee-toh-MAH-teh*
FRUIT & VEGETABLES (Mexico) The term used in central Mexico for the common tomato used in everyday cooking.

Judía / Alubia / Frijol / Pororo / Grano / Habichuela / Ejote / Vainita / Chaucha *hoo-DEE-ah / ah-LOO-bee-ah / free-HOHL / poh-ROH-roh / GRAH-noh / ah-bee-choo-EH-lah / eh-HOH-teh / bah-ee-NEE-tah / cha-OO-cha* **Bean**
FRUIT & VEGETABLE A seed from a pod. Beans can be fresh or dried. If fresh, they can be unripe (the entire pod and bean is eaten) or ripe (the beans must be removed from the pods).

Judía amarilla *hoo-DEE-ah ah-mah-REE-ah* **Wax bean**
FRUIT & VEGETABLES A light yellow variety of green bean.

Judía cannellini *hoo-DEE-ah kah-neh-LEE-nee* **Cannellini bean**
FRUIT & VEGETABLES A white, kidney-shaped bean. Prized for its smooth texture, it can be found canned or dried.

Judía china *hoo-DEE-ah CHEE-nah* **Chinese bean**
FRUIT & VEGETABLES A green bean that averages at least one foot in length. Picked before they are mature, Chinese beans grow abundantly in Southeast Asia. Treated as regular green beans, they are often cut into smaller pieces. They are also known as yard-long bean.

Judía francesa *hoo-DEE-ah frahn-SEH-sah* **French bean**
FRUIT & VEGETABLES A tender, young green bean that can be eaten with its pod.

Judía lima *hoo-DEE-ah LEE-mah* **Lima bean**
FRUIT & VEGETABLES Named after Lima, Peru, where they were discovered more than one hundred years ago, a plump, pale green, kidney-shaped bean that has a mild but meaty flavor. When fresh, lima beans are found in pods that must be removed before cooking. They are available frozen or canned. They are also called butter beans.

Judía navy *hoo-DEE-ah NAH-bee* **Navy bean**
FRUIT & VEGETABLES A small, pea-size, dried bean that is white in color, mild flavored, dense, and creamy.

Judía pinta / Frijol colorado *hoo-DEE-ah PEEN-tah / free-HOHL koh-loh-RAH-doh* **Pinto bean**
FRUIT & VEGETABLES A small, light pink, dried bean coated with black spots. Popular in southwest United States and northern Mexico, it is the bean commonly used for refried beans.

Judía roja / Caparrón *hoo-DEE-ah ROH-hah / kah-pah-RROHN* **Red kidney bean**
FRUIT & VEGETABLES A firm medium-size bean that is shaped like a kidney. It has a dark red skin, a meaty flesh, and a full- bodied flavor.

Judía verde / Chaucha *hoo-DEE-ah BEHR-deh / cha-OO-cha* **Green bean**
FRUIT & VEGETABLES The immature or unripe fruit of a bean plant. Small seeds are found inside an edible pod. Some varieties have a fibrous string that needs to be pulled off, but many do not. Also referred to as common beans, green beans are available fresh, frozen, and canned.

Jugo *HOO-goh* **Juice**
BEVERAGE The liquid extracted from a fruit or vegetable.

Juliana / Cortar a la Juliana *hoo-lee-AH-nah / kohr-TAHR ah lah hoo-lee-AH-nah* **Julienne**
DESCRIPTOR n. Food that has been cut into thin strips. The length of the food is not important.
COOKING METHOD / TECHNIQUE v. To cut food into thin strips.

Jurel *hoo-REHL* **Scad**

FISH & SHELLFISH A saltwater fish that grows to be about one foot in length. Belonging to the same family as pompanos and jack mackerels, it has very large eyes and silver-colored skin.

K

Kaki / Palo santo *KAH-kee / PAH-loh SAHN-toh* **Persimmon**

FRUIT & VEGETABLES The fruit, resembling an orange tomato, that grows on the persimmon tree and comes in two varieties. The more common hachiya is astringent unless fully ripened and has a soft and creamy texture. Like those of the tomato, both the skin and flesh are eaten either raw or cooked. The other variety, fuyu, is not tart but is also not commonly available.

Ketchup *KEH-choop* **Ketchup**

CONDIMENTS A tangy tomato-based condiment made with sugar, vinegar, and other spices. Often used as an ingredient in recipes, it is typically used as a topping on hamburgers and french fries.

Kiebre *kee-EH-breh* **Hare**

GAME A relative of a rabbit. Its flesh is stronger in flavor and darker in color than that of a rabbit. It is available domesticated or wild and needs to be tenderized or cooked by a moist heat method to prevent the meat from becoming tough.

Kiwi *KEE-wee* **Kiwi**

FRUIT & VEGETABLES A small, egg-shaped fruit with brown furry skin that is not eaten. The flesh is bright green with a small white center dotted with edible, tiny black seeds. It has a juicy texture and a sweet tart flavor that is slightly astringent.

Kokotxas / Cocochas *koh-KOH-chahs*

FISH & SHELLFISH (Spain) The meat that surrounds the gills of the fish. Kokotxas is considered a delicacy.

Kosher / Conforme a la ley judaica *KOH-shehr / kohn-FOHR-meh ah lah LEH-ee hoo-dee-AH-kah* **Kosher**

GENERAL Conforming to Jewish dietary laws. Kosher laws state what foods can be eaten and in what combination they can be eaten. They also apply to the kitchen / facility in which the food is prepared.

Kumquat *KOOM-kwaht* **Kumquat**

FRUIT & VEGETABLES *See* **Naranja china**.

L

Lámina *LAH-mee-nah* **Sheet**

GENERAL A thin, expansive, and unbroken surface area of a material.

SPANISH-ENGLISH K

Langosta / Bogavante *lahn-GOHS-tah / boh-gah-BAHN-teh* **Lobster**
  FISH & SHELLFISH A crustacean found all over the world in both cold and warm waters, ranging in weight from one to six pounds. Two main types exist: Maine lobster, which is found in cold waters, has claws, and a sweet, tender flesh; and spiny or rock lobster, which is found in warm waters, has no claws, and firmer meat that is found only in the tail. They can be found live and fresh or dead and frozen.

Lata *LAH-tah* **Can**
  EQUIPMENT An airtight metal container used to store beverages and food.

Lavanda *lah-BAHN-dah* **Lavender**
  HERBS & SPICES A member of the mint family, a plant that produces a purple flower that is used in both savory and sweet recipes for its floral aroma and flavor. When dried, the flower serves as a key ingredient in herbes de Provence. It also produces a nectar that bees use to make honey. The flowers are often candied and used as a garnish in baked goods.

Lavaplatos *lah-bah-PLAH-tohs* **Dishwasher**
  EQUIPMENT (1) An electric machine that washes dishes and utensils. (2) A person that washes dishes in restaurants or other commercial setting.

Leche *LEH-cheh* **Milk**
  DAIRY A creamy white liquid produced by the mammary glands of mammals. The most common source is a cow, but milk from goats, sheep, and water buffalo is also consumed.

Leche condensada *LEH-cheh kohn-dehn-SAH-dah* **Condensed milk / Sweetened condensed milk**
  DAIRY (1) A combination of whole milk and sugar that is heated until 60 percent of the water content is evaporated and the mixture is reduced to a sweet, thick consistency. (2) A mixture of whole milk and sugar that is heated until a little more than half of the water content is evaporated. This results in a sweet, thick syrup. If left unopened, the canned product can last for a couple of years.

Leche de cabra *LEH-cheh deh KAH-brah* **Goat's milk**
  DAIRY The milk extracted from a goat. Available fresh or canned, it can be drunk or made into cheese.

Leche de coco *LEH-cheh deh KOH-koh* **Coconut milk**
  CONDIMENTS A liquid made by simmering equal amounts of shredded coconut with water and then straining it.

Leche desnatada *LEH-cheh dehs-nah-TAH-dah* **Skim milk**
  DAIRY Nonfat milk. Milk that has had its cream (fat) removed.

Leche de soya *LEH-cheh deh SOH-yah* **Soy milk**
  BEVERAGE A nondairy beverage made from cooked ground soybeans that is milky in texture. It is naturally high in protein and low in fat.

Leche de tigre *LEH-cheh deh TEE-greh*

DISH (Peru) The name given to the leftover juice produced from the ceviche ingredients.

Leche en polvo *LEH-cheh ehn POHL-voh* **Milk powder / Powdered milk**

DAIRY (1) Milk that has had all its liquid evaporated. It has a longer shelf life than regular milk and does not need to be refrigerated. It comes in nonfat and whole milk varieties. (2) Dehydrated milk. It can come from whole milk, nonfat milk, or buttermilk. It is also known as dry milk.

Leche evaporada *LEH-cheh eh-bah-poh-RAH-dah* **Evaporated milk**

DAIRY Milk that has been heated to between 110° and 140°F until it has lost half of its water. Its tan color and slight caramel flavor are a result of the caramelization that occurred to the milk sugar during the heating process. It has a creamy texture and mouthfeel. Available in cans, it has a long shelf life if kept unopened.

Leche frita *LEH-cheh FREE-tah*

DISH (Spain) A thick custard that is cooled and cut into squares, dredged in egg and bread crumbs, and pan-fried until golden brown and crisp. It is dusted with powdered sugar and cinnamon before serving. Leche frita literally translates as "fried milk."

Leche mazada *LEH-cheh mah-SAH-dah* **Buttermilk**

DAIRY Nonfat or low-fat milk that has bacteria added to it. It has a thick consistency and tangy flavor. Acidic in nature, it has a low pH.

Lechón *leh-CHOHN*

MEAT (Cuba) Typically, a whole pig but can refer to a cut of pork.

Lechona *leh-CHOH-nah*

DISH (Colombia) A whole roasted pig whose belly is stuffed with yellow rice, peas, and onions and cooked in an outdoor brick oven.

Lechuga *leh-CHOO-gah* **Lettuce**

FRUIT & VEGETABLES A plant that produces edible, leafy greens. Grown throughout the world, lettuce falls under one of four main families: crisphead, romaine, loose-leaf, and butterhead. Typically eaten raw, lettuce is the base of most salads. Its flavor is described as grassy, and its texture is crisp.

Lechuga iceberg *leh-CHOO-gah EES-behrg* **Iceberg lettuce**

FRUIT & VEGETABLES Thin, light green leaves that are wrapped into a tight head of lettuce. Its neutral flavor and crisp texture is due to its high water content. It is also known as crisphead lettuce.

Lechuga lollo rojo *leh-CHOO-gah LOH-yoh ROH-hoh* **Lollo rosso lettuce**

FRUIT & VEGETABLES Looseleaf lettuce with very curly red leaves. The core is pale green in color. The leaves are tender but crisp.

Lechuga trocadero *leh-CHOO-gah troh-kah-DEH-roh* **Butterhead lettuce**
FRUIT & VEGETABLES Small loose heads of a light green lettuce. Its leaves are tender and have a buttery texture. Bibb and Boston lettuce belong to this family.

Lecitina *leh-see-TEE-nah* **Lecithin**
GENERAL A member of the lipid family, a diglyceride that falls under the category of phospholipid. It acts as an emulsifier, which is an agent that binds two ingredients that do not normally mix, creating a smooth and homogenized mixture. It is found abundantly in egg yolks.

Legumbre / Frijol seco *leh-GOOM-breh / free-HOHL SEH-koh* **Dried bean**
FRUIT & VEGETABLES The seeded pods of a legume that have been dried. Common examples are black beans, chickpeas, and pinto beans.

Lengua *LEHN-gwah* **Tongue**
MEAT The large muscle found in the mouth of an animal. Beef, veal, lamb, and pork tongue are cooked and eaten. A typical beef tongue weighs about three pounds; tongue from smaller animals weighs about one pound.

Lenguado *lehn-GWAH-doh* **Sole, common or Dover**
FISH & SHELLFISH A flat fish that dwells in the bottom of the ocean and averages about one foot in length. Its skin is brown gray in color. It has a mild buttery flavor and firm texture. It is very popular in Europe.

Lenguas de gato *LEHN-gwahs deh GAH-toh*
DISH (Spain) A wafer-thin cookie typically served as an accompaniment to a dessert or with ice cream. Lenguas de gato literally translates as "cat's tongue."

Lenteja *lehn-TEH-hah* **Lentil**
FRUIT & VEGETABLES The seed of the lentil plant that grow in pods. They come in a variety of colors (brown, green, yellow, and red) that are determined by the presence or absence of a husk. They are dried as soon as they are ripe and do not need to be soaked before cooking. A legume, lentils contain a high amount of protein and are often used as a meat substitute.

Levadura *leh-bah-DOO-rah* **Yeast**
BAKING & PASTRY A living, single-celled microorganism. As it grows, it converts its food (sugar) into carbon dioxide and alcohol. This process is called fermentation. Yeast is used in bread baking and beer and wine production. Each of these processes has a specific yeast that functions best for its use. Baker's yeast and brewer's yeast are the two commercially available forms.

Levadura / Fermento *leh-bah-DOO-rah / fehr-MEHN-toh* **Leavening**
BAKING & PASTRY A substance used in batters and doughs that reacts with moisture, heat, and acidity to trigger a reaction causing the creation of a gas. This gas lightens the batter or dough allowing it to rise and gain volume.

Levadura en polvo *leh-bah-DOO-rah ehn POHL-boh* **Baking powder**
BAKING & PASTRY A leavener made up of baking soda, an acid, and a moisture absorber. It is typically used when the recipe does not have an acidic component or does not have enough of one. It has a limited shelf life.

Levadura seca *leh-bah-DOO-rah SEH-kah* **Dry yeast**
BAKING & PASTRY Small dehydrated granules of yeast. The lack of moisture causes the living microorganism (yeast) to be in a dormant state. The organism is revived when the yeast granules are rehydrated.

Levístico *leh-BEES-tee-koh* **Lovage**
HERBS & SPICES A plant whose dark green leaves and seeds are used as an herb and spice. Its flavor and aroma are similar to those of celery and often used as a substitute for celery seed. Levistico is very popular in southern Europe, especially the Liguria region of Italy.

Libra *LEE-brah* **Pound**
MEASUREMENTS A unit of measure of weight the equivalent of 16 ounces.

Libro de cocina *LEE-broh deh koh-SEE-nah* **Cookbook**
GENERAL *See* Recetario.

Lichi *LEE-chee* **Lychee**
FRUIT & VEGETABLES The small, round, tropical fruit that grows on the lychee tree. About the size of a cherry, it has a rough and hard, red outer skin that is inedible but easy to remove. The juicy flesh is creamy white and surrounds a single large seed. Mildly sweet in flavor, it is available fresh, canned, or frozen.

Licor *lee-KOHR* **Liquor / Liqueur**
BEVERAGE (1) A spirit, a drinkable, distilled beverage containing ethanol. (2) A spirit that has been sweetened and flavored with items such as seeds, spices, flowers, or roots.

Ligar / Unir *lee-GAHR / oo-NEER* **Bind**
COOKING METHOD / TECHNIQUE To add an ingredient to a mixture to make it all stick together. Eggs, mayonnaise, bread crumbs, and mustard are common binders.

Ligero *lee-GEH-roh* **Light**
DESCRIPTOR (1) Of little weight or density. (2) Having few calories.

Lima / Limón verde *LEE-mah / lee-MOHN BEHR-deh* **Lime**
FRUIT & VEGETABLES A small, round fruit of the lime tree that grows in tropical regions. About three inches in diameter, it has a thin, green skin that turns yellow as it ripens. Its seedless flesh is pale green and juicy with a tart citrus flavor.

Lima kaffir *LEE-mah kah-FEER* **Kaffir lime**
FRUIT & VEGETABLES The small, bumpy, green-skinned citrus fruit that grows on the kaffir tree. The fruit's rind and the tree's leaves have the most flavor and aroma and are used to add flavor to food. Most often found dried, the leaves can be purchased fresh and have a more intense flavor.

Limón *lee-MOHN* **Lemon**
FRUIT & VEGETABLES The small, egg-shaped citrus fruit that grows on a lemon tree. Its flesh and skin are both yellow in color and edible. The juicy flesh has a bright flavor that is tart and acidic. The skin is full of natural oils and can be grated and used for flavoring. It is best to remove the white pith that separates the skin from the flesh as it is bitter.

Limonada *lee-moh-NAH-dah* **Lemonade**
BEVERAGE A beverage made by mixing lemon juice, water, and sugar.

Limón en conserva *lee-MOHN ehn kohn-SEHR-bah* **Preserved lemon**
CONDIMENTS Lemons that are conserved in a salt and acid solution. Spices are often added to infuse the flavor. It is common in Middle Eastern cuisine.

Limón verde *lee-MOHN BEHR-deh* **Lime**
FRUIT & VEGETABLES See **Lima**.

Limpiar *leem-pee-AHR* **Clean (to)**
COOKING METHOD / TECHNIQUE To remove dirt or marks.

Lípido *LEE-pee-doh* **Lipid**
GENERAL A fatty substance that falls under one of three categories: triglyceride, phospholipid, and cholesterol. Lipids cannot dissolve in water and include both fats and oils.

Liquadora / Batidora *lee-kwah-DOH-rah / bah-tee-DOH-rah* **Blender**
EQUIPMENT A small electric appliance used to blend, crush, and puree ingredients. It typically consists of a tall pitcher with sharp rotary blades at its base connected to an electric stand.

Litro *LEE-troh* **Liter**
MEASUREMENTS A metric unit of measure of volume, slightly more than 1 quart, approximately equivalent to 4 fluid cups.

Llenar *yeh-NAHR* **Fill**
COOKING METHOD / TECHNIQUE (1) To add to. (2) To make full.

Lodo *LOH-doh* **Slurry**
COOKING METHOD / TECHNIQUE A cooking technique that mixes a dry starch (flour, cornstarch) with a room-temperature liquid in order to dissolve the starch before adding it to a hot liquid. This is done to prevent the starch from clumping. The mixture is used as a thickener and must be cooked for a few minutes after it has been added.

Lomo *LOH-moh* **Loin**
MEAT A tender cut of meat from either side of the backbone or spine of the animal. It is typically used for steaks or chops.

Lomo saltado *LOH-moh sahl-teh-AH-doh*

DISH (Peru) A dish made from stir-fried beef mixed with french fries and served with rice. The beef is thinly sliced and sautéed with onions, tomatoes, and chile peppers. The french fries can be served on the side or mixed in with the stir-fry.

Longaniza *lohn-gah-NEE-sah*

MEAT (Mexico) Unlinked sausage meat. Made with cuts of meat that are inferior to those used to make chorizo, it is cheaper than chorizo but used for the same purposes.

(Spain) Long pork sausage that is flavored with paprika and crushed rosemary.

Loto *LOH-toh* **Lotus root**

FRUIT & VEGETABLES Edible root of the aquatic lotus plant. Cylindrical in shape, it measures about three inches in diameter. A cross section of the root shows the white colored flesh filled with sponge-like holes. The root has a crisp textured flesh surrounded by a thin, reddish-colored skin that must be removed before being eaten. Its flavor is similar to that of a water chestnut. Available fresh, canned, and dried.

Lubina / Corvina *loo-BEE-nah / kohr-BEE-nah* **Bass**

FISH & SHELLFISH A white, flaky fish with a fine texture and mild sweet flesh. It can grow to be three feet long and twenty pounds in weight.

Lúcuma *LOO-koo-mah*

FRUIT & VEGETABLES (Peru) A medium-size, egg-shaped fruit whose exterior looks like a small papaya. It has a yellow green skin and yellow flesh that tastes like a mix of sweet potato and caramel. It has a semisoft but dense texture. The fruit is native to Peru.

Lucio *loo-see-OH* **Pike**

FISH & SHELLFISH A freshwater fish with a long and thin body. Lean with firm flesh and lots of bones, it is often used for fish mousse or stuffing.

Lulada *loo-LAH-dah*

BEVERAGE (Colombia) A drink made with lulo fruit and lime.[[Add entry for Lulo fruit or explain in this definition]]

Lulo *LOO-loh* **Lulo fruit**

FRUIT & VEGETABLES A tangy tropical fruit that looks like a yellow tomato with a strong citrus flavor. The interior yellow flesh is filled with inedible seeds that must be strained. Lulo is one of the most popular fruits in Colombia.

M

Macerar *mah-seh-AHR* **Macerate**

COOKING METHOD / TECHNIQUE To steep or soak a food in a liquid in order to infuse the food with the flavor of the liquid.

Machacar / Hacer puré *mah-chah-KAHR / ah-SEHR poo-REH* **Mash**
   COOKING METHOD / TECHNIQUE To compress or squish food and reduce it to a pulp.

Muddle
   COOKING METHOD / TECHNIQUE *See* **Enturbiar.**

Mache *mahsh* **Mâche**
   FRUIT & VEGETABLES Narrow and dark green leaves, which are very delicate and tender, used in salads for their slight nutlike flavor. It is also known as corn salad or lamb's lettuce.

Macis *MAH-sees* **Mace**
   HERBS & SPICES A spice taken from the nutmeg tree. It is the dried, red covering of the nutmeg seed and as such its flavor is very similar to that of a nutmeg. Its color is a bit more red and vivid than nutmeg's and is used when imparting color is important in a dish. It is sold in powdered form.

Mahimahi *mah-hee-mah-hee* **Mahimahi**
   FISH & SHELLFISH A saltwater fish found in warm waters. Medium-size, it averages about twenty pounds. Firm and flavorful with a moderate amount of fat makes it a good grilling fish. It is also known as dolfinfish, but its Hawaiian name (mahimahi) is more commonly used to avoid confusion with the dolphin mammal.

Mahón *mah-OHN* **Mahon**
   DAIRY Named after the town where it originated on the island of Minorca, Spain, a firm, cow's milk cheese with a nutty flavor that sharpens as it ages. It has an orange-colored rind that is achieved from its being rubbed with butter, oil, and paprika.

Maíz *mah-EES* **Corn**
   FRUIT & VEGETABLES A cereal grain that grows on stalks. Yellow, white, or sometimes blue kernels are attached to a cob and surrounded by layers of papery husks. The sweet-tasting kernels can be cooked and eaten directly off the cob or cut off before cooking.

Maíz, baby *mah-EES BAY-bee* **Baby corn**
   FRUIT & VEGETABLES The immature ears of corn that are picked right after the silks of the corn are formed. They can be purchased raw or canned and are mostly imported from Asia.

Maizena *mah-ee-SEH-nah* **Cornstarch**
   GRAINS & CEREALS The flour made from the interior of the dried corn kernel (endosperm). Used as a thickening agent, it must be combined with a small amount of cool water before being added to a hot liquid in order to prevent it from clumping.

Maíz para palomitas *mah-EES PAH-rah pah-loh-MEE-tahs* **Popcorn**
   GRAINS & CEREALS A special type of dried corn kernels that pop open when heated. The moisture found inside the kernels turns to steam when heated and cannot escape the hard impermeable husks until enough pressure builds up and explodes the kernels open (palomitas).

Majorero *mah-hoh-REH-roh* **Majorero**

DAIRY From the island of Fuerteventura in the Canary Islands, a cheese made from the milk derived from the island's goats, which is unusually high in fat. Firm, pale, and white in color, its flavor is buttery and nutty yet mildly tart.

Malta *MAHL-tah* **Malt**

GRAINS & CEREALS The name given to the process of sprouting a grain underwater then removing and drying it once it has germinated. The dried grain is then ground into a powder and used to flavor foods and beverages. The grain's resulting flavor is deeper and sweeter than it was originally.

BEVERAGE A nonalcoholic soft drink made from malted barley, hops, and water. Very dark in color and sweet in taste, it has a flavor reminiscent of molasses. Typically served over ice, it is popular in Latin America especially in the Caribbean.

Mamey *mah-MAY* **Mamey**

FRUIT & VEGETABLES A medium-size, oval fruit with a slightly coarse, brown skin similar in thickness to the avocado skin. The flesh is a vivid orange red and very soft and sweet when ripe. Its flavor is a cross between a sweet potato and a cherry. Eaten raw, it is often used to make ice cream and milk shakes.

Mamoncillo *mah-mohn-SEE-yoh*

FRUIT & VEGETABLES (Colombia) A small, green fruit that grows in clusters. It has a hard, inedible skin that is easily peeled away. Its flesh is light pink in color with a soft texture that surrounds a large, inedible seed. It is tart yet sweet in flavor and is usually eaten by sucking on the flesh and then spitting out the seed.

Manchamanteles *mahn-chah-mahn-TEH-lehs*

DISH (Mexico) One of the seven Oaxacan moles that is deep red in color and fruity in flavor. Manchamanteles literally translates as "tablecloth stainer."

Manchego *mahn-CHEH-goh* **Manchego**

DAIRY A Spanish, sheep cheese produced in La Mancha, a region in central Spain just south of Madrid. It is a semifirm cheese with a creamy and slight sharp flavor. Aged for three months to a year in natural caves, it comes in ten-inch round wheels that have a recognizable zigzag pattern embossed on their rind. Considered Spain's most popular cheese, it is protected by Denomiación de Origen.

Mandarina *mahn-dah-REE-nah* **Mandarin / Tangerine**

FRUIT & VEGETABLES (1) A citrus fruit that resembles an orange but is much smaller. The skin is loosely attached to the flesh and easily peels off. There are several varieties, each with its own trait, but all have a sweet flavor. (2) A loose-skinned orange with a thick skin and sweet, juicy flesh. It is smaller than most oranges.

Mandioca *mahn-dee-OH-kah* **Cassava**

FRUIT & VEGETABLES *See* Yuca.

Mandolina *mahn-doh-LEE-nah* **Mandoline**
EQUIPMENT A kitchen tool used to precisely slice and cut food into juliennes or matchsticks. It consists of a thin, rectangular-shaped box with a sharp blade found in its center that adjusts to alter the thickness of the cuts.

Mango *MAHN-goh* **Mango**
FRUIT & VEGETABLES A tropical fruit that is oblong and green-skinned when unripe, but turns yellow and red and fragrant as it matures. A very large oval seed is found in its center with the flesh attached. The flesh must be cut apart from the seed and the skin is inedible. The flesh is golden yellow with a dense texture that is juicy and sweet. There are more than a hundred different varieties. Some varieties are more fibrous than others.

Mangostán *mahn-goh-STAHN* **Mangosteen**
FRUIT & VEGETABLES A fruit that grows in Southeast Asia and has no relation to the mango. It looks like a small, round eggplant. Its interior flesh is soft, cream-colored, and divided into segments. Its flavor is refreshingly tart and sweet.

Maní *mah-NEE* **Peanut**
FRUIT & VEGETABLE *See* Cacahuete.

Manjar blanco *mahn-HAHR BLAHN-koh*
CONDIMENTS (Colombia) A thick version of arequipe.
(Peru) A sweetened milk caramel similar to dulce de leche.

Manojo *mah-NOH-hoh* **Bunch / Handful**
MEASUREMENTS An inexact measurement generally adding up to a handful. A measure of how much the hand can grasp.

Manteca *mahn-TEH-kah* **Lard**
CONDIMENTS Rendered pork fat that is used for both cooking and baking. Prized for its high smoke point and distinct flavor, it is fat taken from the area surrounding the pig's kidneys which is considered the best.

Manteca vegetal *mahn-TEH-kah beh-heh-TAHL* **Vegetable shortening**
CONDIMENTS *See* Aceite solidificado.

Mantequilla *mahn-teh-KEE-yah* **Butter**
DAIRY Cream that is beaten (or churned) until it solidifies. Butter can be salted or unsalted. U.S. law states that butter must be 80 percent fat; the remaining ingredients are water and milk solids.

Mantequilla clarificada *mahn-teh-KEE-yah klah-ree-fee-KAH-dah*
Clarified butter
DAIRY Butter that has been melted and its milk solids removed. It has a higher smoke point than regular butter and a milder flavor. Also known as drawn butter, in eastern India it is referred to as ghee.

Mantequilla de cacahuete *mahn-teh-KEE-yah deh kah-kah-WEH-teh*
Peanut butter

CONDIMENTS *See* **Mantequilla de maní**.

Mantequilla de maní *mahn-teh-KEE-yah deh mah-NEE* **Peanut butter**

CONDIMENTS A paste made from grinding roasted peanuts and often mixing them with salt. Some commercial varieties contain sugar and other additives to prevent the naturally present oils from separating.

Mantequilla marrón *mahn-teh-KEE-yah mah-RROHN* **Brown butter**

DAIRY Butter that has been heated until the milk solids caramelize and become brown. This must be done slowly to prevent the butter from burning. It results in a butter with a deep nutty flavor. Brown butter is used as a sauce, a condiment, and in pastry making.

Mantequilla sin sal *mahn-teh-KEE-yah seen sahl* **Unsalted butter**

DAIRY Butter that contains no salt. Because salt is a preservative, this butter is more perishable.

Manzana *mahn-SAH-nah* **Apple**

FRUIT & VEGETABLES One of the oldest cultivated fruits. The apple has over a thousand varieties that vary in color, texture, and flavor. Apples can be eaten raw or cooked and are used in both savory and sweet recipes. They are are available year-round but are best in the fall.

Manzanilla *mahn-sah-NEE-yah* **Chamomile**

HERBS & SPICES A dried flower used for making tea. The tea is both herbal and non-caffeinated.

BEVERAGE (Spain) An extremely dry variety of fino sherry. It is produced only in the coastal town of Sanlucar de Barrameda. Because the vineyards are close to the ocean, it gives the sherry a unique salty taste.

Máquina de hacer helado *MAH-kee-nah deh ah-SEHR eh-LAH-doh* **Ice cream maker**

EQUIPMENT A manual or electric kitchen tool used for making ice cream. When ice cream is made manually, a cream mixture is put in a canister and constantly stirred while being frozen to prevent ice crystals from forming. The electric version stirs the container for you. Ice cream makers come in various sizes and price points, but all work on the same principal.

Máquina de hacer pasta *MAH-kee-nah deh ah-SEHR PAHS-tah* **Pasta machine**

EQUIPMENT A kitchen tool used to roll out and cut sheets of pasta dough. Pasta machines come in manual and electric versions. The most common type passes the dough between two rollers, flattening it out to the desired thickness.

Marcador de tiempo *mahr-kah-DOHR deh tee-EHM-poh* **Timer**

EQUIPMENT A timepiece instrument that measures time and cues its end.

Marcar *mahr-KAHR* **Score**

COOKING METHOD / TECHNIQUE To make small shallow gashes in a food or ingredient.

Margarina *mahr-gah-REE-nah* **Margarine**
CONDIMENTS A butter substitute developed in 1869 by a French chemist as an affordable alternative to butter. Modern margarine is made with vegetable oil that has been hydrogenated until it becomes spreadable. Food coloring, emulsifiers, and preservatives are often used to make it look and taste like butter.

Margarita *mahr-gah-REE-tah* **Margarita**
BEVERAGE A popular cocktail in Mexico made with tequila, triple sec, and lime juice. It is served straight up, on the rocks, or frozen. The rim of the glass is typically dipped in lime juice and coated with salt.

Maria Luisa *mah-REE-ah loo-EE-sah* **Lemon verbena**
HERBS & SPICES An herb with long, thin, soft green leaves that have a very pronounced lemon flavor. It is used to flavor dishes as well as make tea and lemon oil.

Marimitako *mahr-mee-TAH-koh*
DISH (Spain) A very simple fish stew made with green and red peppers, onions, tomatoes, and potatoes.

Mariquitas *mah-ree-KEE-tahs*
DISH (Cuba) Fried plantain chips.

Marisco / Crustaceo / Molusco *mah-REES-koh / kroos-tah-SEH-oh / moh-LOOS-koh* **Shellfish**
FISH & SHELLFISH An aquatic animal that contains a shell. Two main types are crustaceans (*crustaceos*) and mollusks (*moluscos*).

Mariscos *mah-REES-kohs* **Seafood**
FISH & SHELLFISH Any fish, shellfish, or marine life served as food.

Mar y Montaña *mahr ee mohn-TAH-nya* **Surf and Turf**
DISH A dish that includes both seafood and meat.

Masa *MAH-sah* **Dough / Pastry**
BAKING & PASTRY A stiff mixture made primarily of flour and water. It has a pliable texture that can be worked, scooped, and/or kneaded by hand. It is the precursor to breads, cakes, cookies, pie crust, and pasta.
(Mexico) The term given to dough used to make tamales, tortillas, and other corn-based products. It is made from dried corn kernels that have been cooked then soaked in limewater. The wet corn is then ground into a dough.

Masa agria *MAH-sah AH-gree-ah* **Sourdough**
BAKING & PASTRY A yeast starter made with flour, water, sugar yeast, and a special bacteria called lactobacilli. This bacterial culture produces lactic and acetic acid giving the starter a distinctive sour and tart flavor. Sourdough bread is leavened with this yeast starter.

Masa filo *MAH-sah FEE-loh* **Phyllo dough**
BAKING & PASTRY Tissue-thin sheets of unleavened dough. It is used to make sweet and savory recipes. Popular in Greek cuisine, it is available frozen or fresh.

Masa harina *MAH-sah ah-REE-nah*

GRAINS & CEREALS (Mexico) A commercially manufactured flour made from dried corn kernels that have been treated to make masa, then further ground and dried to make a flour. When mixed with a liquid such as chicken broth, it becomes tamal dough (masa).

Masamorra *mah-sah-MOH-rrah*

BEVERAGE (Colombia) A light beverage that is an infusion of water and corn. Often milk is added to give it body, and panela or guava paste is added to give it flavor.

Masa para ablandar *MAH-sah PAH-rah ah-blahn-DAHR* **Tenderizer**

CONDIMENTS A powdered substance made up of enzymes used to break down tough meat fibers. Papaya contain an enzyme called papain that breaks down meat tissue. Many Latin American marinades contain papaya juice.

Masticar *mahs-tee-KAHR* **Chew**

GENERAL To crush food with your teeth.

Matambre *mah-tah-AHM-breh*

DISH (Argentina) A dish made by stuffing a pounded flank steak with vegetables, eggs, and spices and rolling it. After it has cooked, the meat is cut into thick, cross-wise slices. Matambre translates as "hunger killer" or "shoe leather".

Mate *MAH-teh*

BEVERAGE An infusion made from the dried leaves of the yerba mate plant. Bitter in flavor, it can be sweetened with sugar. It is the national drink of Argentina and is also consumed in other South American countries, especially Chile and Brazil.

Mayonesa *mah-yoh-NEH-sah* **Mayonnaise**

CONDIMENTS An emulsion of vegetable oil, egg yolk, and lemon juice or vinegar. It is a thick and creamy condiment used as a spread or in recipes.

Mazamorra morada *mah-sah-MOH-rrah moh-RAH-dah*

DISH (Peru) A typical Peruvian jellylike dessert that gets its texture and viscosity from the starch of the indigenous purple corn. It is purple in color and looks like loose, jarred grape jelly with pieces of fruit mixed in.

Mazapán *mah-sah-PAHN* **Marzipan**

CONDIMENTS Almond paste that has added sugar. Its pliable nature makes it ideal for shaping and molding into forms. Food coloring is often added when making decorative shapes.

Mazorca *mah-SOHR-kah* **Corn on the cob**

FRUITS & VEGETABLES *See* Maíz.

Medida *meh-DEE-dah* **Measurement**

COOKING METHOD / TECHNIQUE A unit of measure such as inch, ounce, cup, or gram.

SPANISH-ENGLISH M

Medio hecho *MEH-dee-oh EH-choh* **Medium**
COOKING METHOD / TECHNIQUE The doneness of meat described by its internal temperature, color, and juiciness. The meat should be pink and firm in the center and its temperature should reach 140°F-150°F.

Medir *meh-DEER* **Measure**
MEASUREMENTS To assign a value to an attribute such as length, volume, or weight.

Mejillón *meh-hee-YOHN* **Mussel**
FISH & SHELLFISH A bivalve mollusk found in both salt and fresh water. Its oblong shell is blue black in color with streaks of yellow. Its flesh is dark tan, firm, and meaty. It is available fresh (live) or canned (plain or smoked).

Mejorana *meh-hoh-RAH-nah* **Marjoram**
HERBS & SPICES A member of the mint family that looks and tastes like oregano with a mild sweet flavor. Available fresh and dried, it is used often in Europe.

Melaza *meh-LAH-sah* **Molasses**
CONDIMENTS A thick, dark brown syrup that is a by-product of sugar refining. The result of the boiled-down juice extracted from sugarcane or sugar beets, it has a deep caramel flavor that can be bitter.

Melocotón / Durazno *meh-loh-koh-TOHN / doo-RAHS-noh* **Peach**
FRUIT & VEGETABLES The fruit of the peach tree that has a characteristic fuzzy skin ranging in color from white to blush red. Its flesh, orange yellow or blush white in color, is dense, juicy, and sweet and surrounds one seed / pit.

Melón *meh-LOHN* **Melon**
FRUIT & VEGETABLES A fruit that grows on a vine.There are two categories of melons. The muskmelon is round with netted or smooth skin. Its seeds are contained in the center of the fruit and its flesh is dense but juicy and sweet as it ripens. The watermelon is oblong with a smooth, green skin and a red juicy flesh that is dotted with black seeds.

Melón de miel *meh-LOHN deh MEE-ehl* **Honeydew**
FRUIT & VEGETABLES A member of the muskmelon family, a round fruit with a smooth and pale green skin that is inedible. The flesh is slightly darker than its peel and can be very juicy and sweet. It is similar to a cantaloupe in that it contains a number of small seeds in its center that must be removed before eating.

Membrillo *mehm-BREE-yoh* **Quince**
FRUIT & VEGETABLES The yellow pear-shaped fruit that grows on the quince tree. Its flavor is very tart and astringent and is therefore best when cooked so the flavor mellows out. Due to its naturally high amount of pectin, quince is often used to make jam and preserves. It is often paired with Manchego cheese.

Memela *meh-MEH-lah*
DISH *See* **Sope.**

Menta *MEHN-tah* **Mint**

HERBS & SPICES An herb that has sturdy, green leaves that deliver a fresh flavor with a cool aftertaste. Its essential oil is extracted and used as a flavoring. Mint is used in both sweet and savory recipes as well as a number of cocktails. There are more than twenty-five species of this plant. Two main varieties are peppermint and spearmint. Yerba buena is a hybird of the mint family that is used throughout Latin America.

Menu de degustación *MEH-noo deh deh-goos-tah-see-OHN* **Tasting menu**

GENERAL A set-price menu offering small portions of several dishes as a single meal. It is offered as a way of providing a sample of the full menu.

Menudo *meh-NOO-doh* **Tripe**

DISH *See* **Tripa**.

(Mexico) Hearty tripe soup.

Merengue *meh-REHN-geh* **Meringue**

BAKING & PASTRY A mixture of egg whites and sugar whipped until peaks are formed. The texture of the peaks ranges from soft to stiff. Meringue can be eaten uncooked and used as a dessert topping or baked in a low oven until completely dry.

Merienda *meh-ree-EHN-dah* **Snack**

GENERAL An informal meal. A small amount of food eaten in between meals.

Merluza *mehr-LOO-sah* **Hake**

FISH & SHELLFISH A saltwater fish that is a relative of the cod and found in northern Pacific and Atlantic waters. It is a delicate-flavored white fish that has a firm texture. It is very popular in Spain.

Merluza a la sidra *mehr-LOO-sah ah lah SEE-drah*

DISH (Spain) Hake cooked in hard cider.

Mermelada / Confitura *mehr-meh-LAH-dah / con-fee-TOO-rah* **Preserve / Jam / Marmalade**

CONDIMENTS (1) A spreadable product made from fruit puree that has been sim-mered with water and sugar until the plant's natural pectins thicken the mixture. It is used as a spread or in desserts. (2) A spread made from fruit cooked with sugar and pectin where chunks of fruit are still in tact and pieces of rind are mixed in. Citrus fruit are most commonly used.

Mero *MEH-roh* **Jewfish**

FISH & SHELLFISH A member of the sea bass family, the largest member of the grouper species averaging 75 to 150 pounds in weight. It can be found in the warm waters of the Atlantic and Gulf of Mexico and parts of the Pacific. Also known as black bass, it is a firm, white fish with a mild flavor. Its name was offically changed to goliath grouper in 2001.

Mesa *MEH-sah* **Table**

EQUIPMENT A piece of furniture with a flat top and four supporting legs.

Mesclador de masa *mehs-klah-DOHR deh MAH-sah* **Pastry cutter**
EQUIPMENT A handheld kitchen tool used to cut or blend butter into flour. It is made up of a number of curved thin rods attached to a rounded handle.

Mesclun *MEHS-kloon* **Mesclun**
FRUIT & VEGETABLES A mix of small tender salad greens. The combination and type of greens vary.

Metate *meh-TAH-teh*
EQUIPMENT (Mexico) A kitchen tool that is a rectangular grinding stone made of lava rock. It has a thick rod (mano) that is laid onto the stone and rolls over the item to be ground.

Mezcal *mehs-KAHL*
BEVERAGE (Mexico) A distilled spirit made from the roasted heart (center) of a mature maguey plant (the same plant used to make tequila). It differs from tequila in that is has a smoky flavor. It can be made from plants found in any part of Mexico, as opposed to tequila, which must come from plants specifically found near the town of Tequila in Jalisco.

Mezcaleros *mehs-kah-LEH-rohs*
EQUIPMENT (Mexico) Very small, earthenware mugs used for drinking shots of tequila.

Mezcla de cinco especias en polvo *MEHS-klah deh SEEN-koh eh-SPEH-see-ahs ehn POHL-voh* **Five-spice powder**
HERBS & SPICES A mixture of five ground spices—cinnamon, cloves, fennel seed, star anise, and Szechuan peppercorns—used in Chinese cooking.

Mezclar *mehs-KLAHR* **Blend**
COOKING METHOD / TECHNIQUE To mix two or more substances together until well combined.

Mezzaluna *meh-sah-LOO-nah* **Mezzaluna**
EQUIPMENT A half-moon-shaped, curved blade with a handle on either side of the blade. It chops food by rocking the blade's edge over the ingredient to be cut.

Michelada *mee-cheh-LAH-dah*
BEVERAGE (Mexico) A beer cocktail. Small amounts of lime juice, Worcestershire sauce, hot sauce, and salt are added to beer and served over ice.

Microonda *mee-kroh-OHN-dah* **Microwave oven**
EQUIPMENT A kitchen appliance that cooks food by using microwave radiation to heat water molecules within the food. It cooks food quickly but does not cause browning or caramelization.

Miel *mee-EHL* **Honey**
CONDIMENTS A thick, sweet syrup made from flower nectar by bees. The type of flower used determines the color and flavor of the liquid. It offers the same amount of sweetness as table sugar but with added flavor and texture/mouthfeel. It is used

for cooking, baking, as a spread, and as a beverage sweetener. At times it is sold with its honeycomb and is available pasteurized so that it will not crystallize.

Miel de azahar *mee-EHL deh ah-sah-AHR* **Orange blossom honey**
CONDIMENTS Honey derived from the nectar of the orange blossom.

Miel de trébol *mee-EHL deh TREH-bohl* **Clover honey**
CONDIMENTS Honey made from the nectar of the clover flower.

Migas *MEE-gahs* **Bread crumbs**
DISH *See* **Pan rallado.**
(Spain) A dish of cubed day-old bread sautéed in olive oil and bacon fat and seasoned with garlic, paprika, and cumin. It may or may not contain diced ham and bacon. It typically served as an accompaniment to fried eggs. Migas literally translates as "bread crumbs."

Migadas *Mee-GAH-dahs*
DISH *See* **Sope.**

Mijo *MEE-hoh* **Millet**
GRAINS & CEREALS A cereal grain rich in protein that is more popular for its use in animal feed than for human consumption, although it gets distributed to needy regions of the world. Prepared in the same manner as rice, it has a bland flavor and serves as a good canvas for other foods.

Milanesas *mee-lah-NEH-sahs*
DISH (Argentina) Meat or chicken that has been breaded and fried.

Mililitro *mee-lee-LEE-troh* **Milliliter**
MEASUREMENTS A metric unit of measure that calculates length and is equivalent to $1/1,000$ meter.

Mineral *mee-neh-RAHL* **Mineral**
GENERAL A nonliving substance that is naturally occurring and has a specific chemical composition. It is required by the body in very small amounts.

Mofongo *moh-FOHN-goh*
DISH (Puerto Rico) A mash made from fried plantains, pork cracklings, onions, garlic, and herbs and spices. (If the plantain is very green it may be boiled before frying.) Typically shaped into patties, monfongo can also be stuffed with beef, chicken, or seafood.

Moho *MOH-oh* **Mold**
GENERAL A variety of fungus that grows on food. It causes food spoilage and appears as fuzzy, blue green spots. Some fungus can be desirable such as the one used in cheese making.

Mojito *moh-HEE-toh* **Mojito**
BEVERAGE A rum-based cocktail made by muddling lime wedges, mint, and sugar and topping it with rum and club soda. It is served in a tall glass over ice and garnished with a mint sprig. Cuba is the birthplace of the mojito.

SPANISH-ENGLISH M

Mojo *MOH-hoh*
DISH (Cuba) A garlic, sour orange, and olive oil sauce used as a marinade, condiment, or dipping sauce.

Molcajete y tejolete / Mortero *mohl-kah-HEH-teh ee teh-loh-HEH-teh / mohr-TEH-roh* **Mortar and pestle**
EQUIPMENT A two-piece kitchen tool made up of à bowl and thick blunt stick used to crush and mash ingredients. The bowl (*molcajete*) is the mortar and the stick (*tejolete*) is the pestle. Each piece is made from the same material, usually wood, marble, ceramic, or rock.

Molde *MOHL-deh* **Mold**
EQUIPMENT A container used to shape food into a specific form. Ingredients are put inside the container and then cooked or cooled in it in order to take on the container's shape. Molds come in various shapes and sizes.

Molde Bundt *MOHL-deh boont* **Bundt pan**
EQUIPMENT A tube pan with a rounded bottom with ridges. A typical Bundt pan holds twelve cups of batter.

Molde circular *MOHL-deh seer-koo-LAHR* **Ring mold**
EQUIPMENT A circular metal form about three inches tall and three to six inches wide. It does not have a top or bottom and is used to shape ingredients into a circle.

Molde de flan *MOHL-deh deh flahn* **Flan pan**
EQUIPMENT Any type of pan used to cook flan. Typically round, it can be large or small and can be made of various materials.

Molde de pan *MOHL-deh deh pahn* **Loaf pan**
EQUIPMENT A deep, rectangular pan used for making meat loaf and pound cake. It comes in a range of sizes, but the most common is nine inches long by five inches wide by three inches deep.

Molde de pastel *MOHL-deh deh pahs-TEHL* **Pie pan**
EQUIPMENT An ovenproof container used for baking a pie. It comes in a variety of shapes, sizes, and materials but all pie pans have sloping sides.

Molde desmontable *MOHL-deh dehs-mohn-TAH-bleh* **Springform cake pan**
EQUIPMENT A round baking pan whose sides and bottom can be detached. A spring or latch mechanism secures or unmolds the straight edges of the pan from the flat bottom. It is used with tarts and cakes that would be difficult to remove from a traditional pan. It is available in various sizes.

Molde de tarta *MOHL-deh deh TAHR-tah* **Tartlet pan**
EQUIPMENT A metal pan used to mold and bake a tart shell.

Molde para pastel *MOHL-deh PAH-rah pahs-TEHL* **Cake pan**
EQUIPMENT A mold used for baking cakes. Traditional shapes of a cake pan are round, square, and rectangular but there are specialty forms such as heart-shaped and tube pans. The materials used vary and can be metal based or silicone.

Mole *MOH-leh*

DISH (Mexico) One of Mexico's most famous sauces. There are hundreds of variations that originate from one of seven master moles. A common characteristic is the long list of aromatic ingredients that blend to make the sauce. Chocolate is one of the most infamous ingredients, but not all moles contain chocolate.

Moler *moh-LEHR* **Grind**

COOKING METHOD / TECHNIQUE To break down food to very small particles. This can be accomplished with an electric grinder, meat grinder, mortar and pestle, or food processor.

Molinillo *moh-lee-NEE-yoh* **Peppermill**

EQUIPMENT A handheld kitchen tool used to grind peppercorns.

(Mexico) A special device to create froth in traditional drinks such as champurrado.

Molinillo / Pasapuré *moh-lee-NEE-yoh / pah-sah-poo-REH* **Food mill**

EQUIPMENT A mechanical kitchen tool that breaks down food into a puree and separates skins and seeds from flesh. It is typically used only with fruit and vegetables that are very soft or have been cooked.

Molinillo / Trituradora *moh-lee-NEE-yoh / tree-too-rah-DOH-rah* **Grinder**

EQUIPMENT A manual or electric kitchen tool used to grind food.

Mollejas *moh-YEH-hahs* **Gizzards / Sweetbreads**

MEAT (1) Organs found in the digestive tract of birds that grind up food. Often sold with whole birds, they are packaged in small bags and placed in the bird's cavity, but they can also be purchased separately. They must be cooked with by a slow moist heat method in order to tenderize the tough meat. (2) Classified as offal, lamb, beef, or pork thymus glands and/or pancreas.

(Argentina) The thymus gland of lamb, beef, or pork.

Molusco *moh-LOOS-koh* **Mollusk**

FISH & SHELLFISH One of two main categories of shellfish (the other is crustacean). An invertebrate whose soft body lives inside a shell that is either made up of two pieces and hinged (bivalve) or forms one solid piece (univalve). *See also* **Marisco**.

Mondongo *mohn-DOHN-goh*

DISH (Mexico) Hearty tripe soup flavored with reconstituted and pureed dried red chiles.

(Puerto Rico) Pork tripe stew.

Montar *mohn-TAHR* **Mount**

COOKING METHOD / TECHNIQUE To add small, cold pieces of butter to a sauce and stir constantly until the butter is completely melted and incorporated into the sauce. This is done right before serving to add body and shine to the sauce.

Mora *MOH-rah* **Blackberry**

FRUIT & VEGETABLES A purple black berry that is very tart when immature. Blackberries grow on bushes and have small, plump, round clusters that make up their flesh.

Mora logan *MOH-rah LOH-gahn* **Loganberry**
FRUIT & VEGETABLES A berry that looks like a hybrid between a raspberry and black-berry. It has the form of a blackberry with the color of a raspberry and the flavor of both. Like other berries, it can be eaten raw or used as an ingredient in desserts or jams.

Morcilla *mohr-SEE-yah* **Blood sausage**
MEAT Pork sausage made with the blood of the pig. It can contain other ingredients such as bread crumbs, rice, nuts, and spices. It is generally eaten fried.
(Spain) Blood sausage.

Morcilla rellena *mohr-SEE-yah reh-YEH-nah*
MEAT (Colombia) Blood sausage.

Morcillo *mohr-SEE-yoh* **Shank**
MEAT The meat from the lower part of the leg, typically beef, veal, lamb, or pork. It is very flavorful but also very tough due to the high amount of connective tissue it contains. It must be cooked over low heat for a long time to be tenderized.

Moros y Christianos *MOH-rohs ee krees-tee-AH-nohs*
DISH (Cuba) A combination dish of black beans and rice. Raw rice is cooked in a pot of cooked black beans that were flavored with small pork chunks. The rice absorbs the bean liquid and the final product is a dry combination of rice and beans with small chunks of pork. Literally translating to Moors (black beans) and Christians (white rice), the recipe's name makes historical reference to the period when Spain was invaded and then occupied by the North African Moors for over 800 years.

Mortero *mohr-TEH-roh* **Mortar and Pestle**
EQUIPMENT *See* **Molcajete y tejolete.**

Mostaza *mohs-TAH-sah* **Mustard**
CONDIMENTS The paste made from powdered mustard seed mixed with wine, beer or vinegar, water, and spices. The piquant condiment is used as a spread or in recipes.

Mostaza a la antigua *mohs-TAH-sah ah lah ahn-TEE-gwah* **Whole grain mustard**
CONDIMENTS A prepared mustard made with mustard seeds that are not ground but left whole and mixed with the other ingredients.

Mostaza americana *mohs-TAH-sah ah-meh-ree-KAH-nah* **American mustard**
CONDIMENTS Often referred to as yellow mustard, a paste made from powdered white mustard seeds, water, vinegar, and spices. Turmeric is the spice that gives it its characteristic bright yellow color.

Mostaza de Dijon *mohs-TAH-sah deh dee-JOHN* **Dijon mustard**
CONDIMENTS A pale yellow mustard that is sharp in flavor. Made from mustard seeds, white wine, and unfermented grape juice (verjuice) instead of vinegar, this recipe was first created in Dijon, France, in 1856.

Mostaza francesa *mohs-TAH-sah frahn-SEH-sah* **French mustard**

CONDIMENTS A prepared mustard made from ground mustard seeds, water, and vinegar. Brown mustard seeds, which are zestier than the white variety, are used.

Mostaza inglesa picante *mohs-TAH-sah een-GLEH-sah pee-KAHN-teh* **Hot English mustard**

CONDIMENTS A prepared mustard made from white and brown mustard seeds mixed with vinegar, water, and other spices. It is bright yellow in color and very spicy hot.

Mujol *moo-HOHL* **Mullet roe**

FISH & SHELLFISH The female fish eggs from mullet fish. They are available fresh or salt-cured. Botargo is the Italian version and Karasumi the Japanese.

Muy poco hecho *moo-EE POH-koh EH-choh* **Rare**

COOKING METHOD / TECHNIQUE The doneness of meat described by its internal temperature, color, and juiciness. The meat should be cold and red in the center and its temperature should reach 125°F–130°F.

N

Nabo *NAH-boh* **Turnip**

FRUIT & VEGETABLES A small, round, root vegetable that is white skinned except for its top half which is purple. The interior flesh is white with a slightly sweet taste. It is best to eat a turnip when it is young, tender, and sweet as it gets tough and starchy as it matures. Its skin needs to be peeled and it can be eaten cooked or raw.

Nabo dulce *NAH-boh DOOL-seh* **Jicama**

FRUIT & VEGETABLE See **Jícama**.

Nabo sueco *NAH-boh soo-EH-koh* **Rutabaga**

FRUIT & VEGETABLE See **Rutabaga**.

Nacho *NAH-choh* **Nacho**

DISH A dish often associated with Tex-Mex cuisine made of layers of tortilla chips and melted cheese and topped with a dollop of sour cream, sliced jalapeños, chopped tomatoes, and sliced black olives.

Ñame *NYA-meh* **Yam**

FRUIT & VEGETABLES A root tuber vegetable from a tropical vine. Large and elongated, it has a rough, brown skin and white flesh. Often confused with (and mislabeled as) the sweet potato, a yam can be easily substituted for it.

Naranja *nah-RAHN-hah* **Orange**

FRUIT & VEGETABLES The citrus fruit of the orange tree. The orange-colored flesh is divided into segments by a white pith, which is surrounded by an orange skin that is fragrant and full of natural oils. The juicy flesh is sweet tasting and slightly tart.

Naranja agria *nah-RAHN-hah AH-gree-ah* **Seville orange**
  FRUIT & VEGETABLES An orange with thick skin that is pale yellow orange in color. A bitter fruit, it is not an eating orange as it has a very sour flesh and a high acid content. The juice is used often in marinades, and the skin is used in making bitters.

Naranja china / Naranja enana / Kumquat *nah-RAHN-hah CHEE-nah / nah-RAHN-hah eh-NAH-nah / KOOM-kwaht* **Kumquat**
  FRUIT & VEGETABLES A tiny orange whose flavor is both sweet and tart. Both the skin and flesh is eaten. Kumquats can be found raw, cooked, or pickled.

Naranja enana *nah-RAHN-hah eh-NAH-nah* **Kumquat**
  FRUIT & VEGETABLES See **Naranja china**.

Naranja sanguina *nah-RAHN-hah sahn-GWEE-nah* **Blood orange**
  FRUIT & VEGETABLES A sweet yet tart orange with a bright red flesh.

Nata *NAH-tah* **Cream**
  DAIRY See **Crema**.

Nata agria *NAH-tah AH-gree-ah* **Sour cream**
  DAIRY See **Crema agria**.

Nata doble *NAH-tah DOH-bleh* **Double cream**
  DAIRY See **Crema doble**.

Nata espesa *NAH-tah ehs-PEH-sah* **Heavy cream**
  DAIRY See **Crema espesa**.

Nata extra espesa *NAH-tah EKS-trah. ehs-PEH-sah* **Clotted cream**
  DAIRY See **Crema extra espesa**.

Nata fresca *NAH-tah FREHS-kah* **Crème fraîche**
  DAIRY See **Crema fresca**.

Nata montada *NAH-tah mohn-TAH-dah* **Whipping cream**
  DAIRY See **Crema montada**.

Nata semidesnatada *NAH-tah seh-mee-dehs-nah-TAH-dah* **Light cream**
  DAIRY See **Crema semidesnatada**.

Natilla *nah-TEE-yah* **Custard**
  BAKING & PASTRY A pudding style-dessert made in the oven or on the stovetop. Typically flavored with vanilla, it is served on its own or as part of a tart or pie.
  DISH (Cuba) A vanilla custard made on the stovetop and traditionally served cold with a dusting of cinnamon.

Nectarina *nehk-tah-REE-nah* **Nectarine**
  FRUIT & VEGETABLES A fruit with smooth, red skin with yellow streaks that belongs to the same species as the peach. Its flesh is white or yellow and is sweet and juicy with a single seed in its center that can be loose or clinging to the flesh.

Nevera / Refrigerador / Heladera / Frigorífico / Camara frigorífica
*neh-BEH-rah / reh-free-geh-rah-DOHR / eh-lah-DEH-rah / free-goh-REE-fee-koh /
KAH-mah-rah free-goh-REE-fee-kah* **Refrigerator**

EQUIPMENT A large electric cooling appliance that keeps its contents at a constant temperature that is below room temperature. Typically shaped like a box, the thermally insulated appliance comes in different sizes and is often connected to a freezer.

Nevero *neh-BEH-roh*

GENERAL (Mexico) An ice cream vendor.

Nieve *nee-EH-beh* **Ice cream**

BAKING & PASTRY *See* **Helado**.

Níspero *NEES-peh-roh* **Loquat**

FRUIT & VEGETABLES A yellow, pear-shaped fruit. Its flesh is crisp and juicy and its texture is similar to that of an apple. Its has a tart flavor and can be eaten raw or used as an ingredient in desserts. High in pectin, it is good for making jam.

Nixtamal *neeks-tah-MAHL*

FRUIT & VEGETABLES Field corn (dried hominy) that is cooked in an alkaline solution (limewater) and hulled. The hulled nixtamal corn is then ground and turned into masa.

Nopales *noh-PAH-lehs* **Cactus**

FRUIT & VEGETABLES The oval, dark green leaves of the nopal cactus. Tart in flavor, the leaves' thorns are cut off before they are sliced and cooked. They are available fresh and canned.

Nubes *NOO-behs* **Marshmallow**

CONDIMENTS A confection made from corn syrup, water, gelatin, gums, and flavorings. Cylindrical in shape, it can be large or small and is often white in color. Its spongy texture changes to molten and gooey when heated.

Nuez *noo-EHS* **Walnut**

NUTS & OILS The dried fruit of the walnut tree. The hard, bumpy, round shell must be opened with the help of a nut cracker. The tan-colored nut is buttery and slightly tannic.

Nuez de Brasil *noo-EHS deh brah-SEEL* **Brazil nut**

NUTS & OILS A giant tree found in the Amazon that produces a large seed of the same name. The seed is often mistakenly referred to as a nut.

Nuez macadamia *noo-EHS mah-kah-DAH-mee-ah* **Macadamia nut**

NUTS & OILS The nut of the macadamia tree which is native to Australia. Buttery sweet in flavor, it is round and beige colored. It is almost always sold shelled since its shell is very hard and difficult to crack.

Nuez moscada *noo-EHS mohs-KAH-dah* **Nutmeg**
  HERBS & SPICES The seed found inside the fruit of the nutmeg tree. It is covered with a meshlike membrane that when dried and ground becomes the spice mace. The remaining one-inch-long seed is dried and when grated has a warm, sweet flavor. The brown-colored spice can be purchased whole or ground.

O

Oblea *oh-BLEH-ah*
  BAKING & PASTRY (Colombia) A thin wafer cookie, usually about nine inches wide. It is often smeared with arequipe and eaten as a snack.

Oca *OH-kah* **Goose**
  MEAT A web-footed animal much larger than a duck. It can be wild or domesticated and while its meat is eaten, it is most popular for its creamy, rich liver that results from force feeding.

Ocopa *oh-KOH-pah*
  DISH (Peru) A dish very similar to papas a la huancaina except the sauce contains peanuts and an herb called huacatay that imparts a vivid green color.

Okra / Quingombó *OH-krah / keen-gohm-BOH* **Okra**
  FRUIT & VEGETABLES Thin, long, green pods from the okra plant that are harvested when still unripe and used as a vegetable although technically a fruit. When cooked, okra lets go of a sticky substance that serves as a thickener. It has an herbaceous green flavor. It is most popularly used in gumbo.

Oliva *oh-LEE-bah* **Olive**
  FRUIT & VEGETABLES *See* **Aceituna**.

Oliva negra *oh-LEE-bah NEH-grah* **Black olive**
  FRUIT & VEGETABLES *See* **Aceituna negra**.

Oliva verde *oh-LEE-bah BEHR-deh* **Green olive**
  FRUIT & VEGETABLES *See* **Aceituna verde**.

Olla *OH-yah* **Saucepan**
  EQUIPMENT A round cooking vessel with one long or two short handles and a tight-fitting lid. It comes in sizes ranging from one-half quart to four quarts and can be deep or shallow. Materials it is made of include stainless steel, aluminum, and copper among others.

Olla / Cacerola *OH-yah / kah-seh-ROH-lah* **Pot**
  EQUIPMENT A deep cooking vessel with one or two handles and a lid used on the stovetop. It is the common name for most cooking vessels.

Olla de bambú al vapor / Cesta de bambú *OH-yah deh bahm-BOO ahl BAH-pohr / SEHS-tah deh bahm-BOO* **Bamboo steamer**

EQUIPMENT A round, stackable steamer made from bamboo wood and used in Asian food preparation. Wooden bamboo sticks make up the grates that form the bottom and it has solid bamboo sides.

Olla de presión *OH-yah deh preh-see-OHN* **Pressure cooker**

EQUIPMENT A special pot with a sealed airtight lid that regulates the internal pressure of the vessel and does not allow steam or heat to escape. The buildup of steam and pressure inside the pot results in food cooked at a significantly higher temperature. It results in a substantial reduction of cooking time.

Olla para caldo *oh-YAH PAH-rah KAHL-doh* **Stockpot**

EQUIPMENT See Caldera.

Olla para cocinar al vapor / Vaporera *OH-yah PAH-rah koh-see-NAHR ahl BAH-pohr / bah-poh-REH-rah* **Steamer**

EQUIPMENT A device or cooking vessel used to create steam and cook food with the heat generated.

Olluco *oh-YOO-koh*

FRUIT & VEGETABLES (Peru) A yellow tuber vegetable, similar in appearance to a yellow potato, whose texture remains crunchy when cooked.

Olluquito con charqui *oh-yoo-KEE-toh kohn CHAHR-kee*

DISH (Peru) A stew of *olluco* and *charqui* lamb that is served over rice.

Oloroso *oh-loh-ROH-soh*

BEVERAGE (Spain) A medium sweet sherry, very fragrant and deep amber in color. Due to its sweet flavor, it is drunk with dessert.

Onza *OHN-sah* **Ounce**

MEASUREMENTS Unit of measure of weight equivalent to $1/16$ pound or 28.35 grams.

Oporto / Vino porto *oh-POHR-toh / BEE-noh POHR-toh* **Port**

BEVERAGE A sweet, fortified wine typically made from red grapes, although there is a white variety. Similar types of wines are produced in other areas of the world, but only those made in the Duoro region of Portugal can be called port.

Orégano *oh-REH-gah-noh* **Oregano**

HERBS & SPICES A member of the mint family, an herb with small, green leaves, purple flowers, and a pungent flavor that is used in many dishes in the Mediterranean and Latin America. There is a Mexican and Mediterranean variety of which the former is stronger. Oregano is available fresh or dried.

Orégano brujo *oh-REH-gah-noh BROO-hoh*

HERBS & SPICES (Puerto Rico) Wild oregano that grows all over the island of Puerto Rico.

Oreja de cerdo *oh-REH-hah deh SEHR-doh* **Pig's ear**

MEAT The cooked ear of a pig. Due to the high amount of collagen contained in the ear, it becomes incredibly gelatinous when cooked for a long time over low heat. Very popular in Spain, it is served as part of a stew called a cocido or simply roasted and served as a tapa.

Orgánico *ohr-GAH-nee-koh*

GENERAL *See* **Comida orgánica**.

Orujo *oh-ROO-hoh*

BEVERAGE *See* **Aguardiente**.

Ostra *OHS-trah* **Oyster**

FISH & SHELLFISH A bivalve that lives in salt water with a rough, gray, and rocklike shell. Its interior pale beige flesh is soft and succulent with a salty, briny flavor. The size and flavor of an oyster vary according to the variety. Oysters can be eaten raw or cooked.

P

Pabellón criollo *pah-beh-YOHN kree-OH-yoh*

DISH (Venezuela) The national dish of Venezuela made up of shredded beef (carne mechada), white rice, black beans (caraotas negras), and fried sweet plantains (tajadas).

Pacana *pah-KAH-nah* **Pecan**

NUTS & OILS The nut that grows on the pecan tree. About one inch in length, the smooth brown shell holds the lighter-colored nut which is recognizable by its ribbed texture. The kernel has a characteristic buttery flavor that is used in both sweet and savory recipes.

Pachamanca *pah-chah-MAHN-kah*

DISH (Peru) A meal similar to a barbecue where a variety of meats and vegetables are slowly cooked on an underground bed of hot stones.

Paella *pah-EH-yah*

DISH (Spain) A rice dish made in a paellera. Many variations exist based on the region in which they are made. The original is said to come from Valencia, the area of Spain responsible for much of the rice production. All paellas are made with short grain rice and are cooked over heat, not in an oven.

Paella a la valenciana *pah-EH-yah ah lah bah-lehn-see-AH-nah*

DISH (Spain) The original paella that uses ingredients that are commonly found in Valencia such as land snails, rabbit, lima beans, and string beans.

Paellera *pah-eh-YEH-rah*

EQUIPMENT (Spain) The cooking vessel used to make paella. It is a wide and shallow pot that does not have a lid.

Paleta *pah-LEH-tah* **Shoulder**

MEAT The cut of meat taken from the front leg of an animal. Depending on the animal, it can run from the neck down to the leg. It is very flavorful but very tough due to the high amount of its connective tissue.

Paleta de helado *pah-LEH-tah deh eh-LAH-doh* **Ice cream scoop**

EQUIPMENT A kitchen tool and utensil used to serve ice cream. Depending on the type of scoop used, the ice cream can be formed into a spherical ball or a long egg shape. Scoops come in various sizes.

Palillo *pah-LEE-yoh* **Skewer**

EQUIPMENT *See* **Brocheta**.

Palillos chinos *pah-LEE-yohs CHEE-nohs* **Chopsticks**

EQUIPMENT Long, thin eating or cooking utensils used throughout Asia. Made up of two even-length sticks typically made from wood, bamboo, or plastic, they range in length from five to twelve inches.

Pallar *pah-YAH-reh* **Lima bean**

FRUIT & VEGETABLES *See* **Judía lima**.

Palmitas *pahl-MEE-tahs* **Hearts of palm**

FRUIT & VEGETABLES Pale, white tubes ranging in width from one-half inch to two inches. They are found in the inner core of the bark of a special palm tree, and the tree must be killed for the vegetables to be harvested. Their flavor is reminiscent of that of an artichoke and they are available canned or fresh. Popular in Brazil, they are typically tossed in salads.

Paloma / Pichón *pah-LOH-mah / pee-CHON* **Pigeon**

GAME A small game bird popular in Europe. It is also known as wood pigeon.

Paloma torcaz *pah-LOH-mah tohr-KAHS* **Squab**

GAME A young, usually about four weeks old, domesticated pigeon that has never flown. Its dark red–colored flesh is very tender. Most squabs weigh less than one pound.

Palomilla, bistec de *pah-loh-MEE-yah, bees-TEHK deh* **Palomilla steak**

DISH (Cuba) An inexpensive cut of beef, usually from the round, that has been pounded very thin and panfried. Typically it is served with a lime wedge.

Palo santo *PAH-loh SAHN-toh* **Persimmon**

FRUIT & VEGETABLES *See* **Kaki**.

Pambazo *pahm-BAH-soh*

DISH (Mexico) A sandwich made with a slathering of black bean spread and filled with ground or sliced beef, avocado, lettuce, and tomato.

Pan *pahn* **Bread**

GRAINS & CEREALS A baked good made with flour, salt, water, and sometimes a leavener. It can be baked, steamed, or fried.

SPANISH-ENGLISH P

Panceta de cerdo *pahn-SEH-ta deh SEHR-doh* **Pork belly**
  MEAT A cut of meat taken from the belly of the pig. It is made up of layers meat and flesh. When the cut is cured it becomes bacon. *See* Cerdo.

Pandebono *pahn-deh-BOH-noh*
  GRAINS & CEREALS (Colombia) Rolls made from corn flour, cassava starch, cheese, and egg. Pandebono literally translates as "good bread."

Pan de centeno entero / Pan negro *pahn deh sehn-TEH-noh / pahn NEH-groh* **Pumpernickel**
  GRAINS & CEREALS A dark bread made with rye flour and a sourdough starter, which produces a slightly sour taste. It was traditionally baked very slowly to achieve the dark color and deep flavor, but nowadays molasses is sometimes added to achieve the same results more quickly.

Pan de jamón *pahn de HAH-mohn*
  GRAINS & CEREALS (Venezuela) A soft, sweet bread stuffed with ham, olives, and raisins and typically eaten during the Christmas holidays.

Pan de maíz *pahn de mah-EES*
  GRAINS & CEREALS (Colombia) Corn bread.

Pan de molde *pahn de MOHL-deh* **Sandwich bread**
  GRAINS & CEREALS A pullman loaf of bread that is made with white flour and baked in a long narrow pan. Its slices are square and have four flat crusts.

Pandequeso *pahn-deh-KEH-soh*
  GRAINS & CEREALS (Colombia) Cheese bread rolls.

Pandeyuca *pahn-deh-YOO-kah*
  GRAINS & CEREALS (Colombia) Bread rolls made from yuca flour.

Panal de miel *pah-NAHL deh mee-EHL* **Honeycomb**
  CONDIMENTS A wax structure made by honeybees to store their honey. It is made up of a number of six-sided individual compartments. The bees produce their own wax to construct it.

Panecillo / Bolillo *pah-neh-SEE-yoh / boh-LEE-yoh* **Roll**
  GRAINS & CEREALS A small, round piece of bread. It is used as a side dish or for making sandwiches.

Panela *pah-NEH-lah*
  CONDIMENTS (Colombia) A hardened piece of sugar (sucrose) created from the remnants of evaporated sugarcane juice. It is brown in color and formed into a solid disk. A stone is typically used to break apart pieces of panela.

Panetela *pah-neh-TEH-lah* **Pound cake**
  BAKING & PASTRY A sweet loaf cake traditionally made with a pound each of flour, butter, sugar, and eggs.

Panetela borracha *pah-neh-TEH-lah boh-RRAH-chah*
DISH (Cuba) Pound cake that is soaked in simple syrup. It is called panetela borracha especial if a liquor is added.

Pan francés *pahn frahn-SEHS* **French bread**
GRAINS & CEREALS A crusty and light-textured bread made from a fat-free yeast dough. The texture of the crust is achieved by spraying the dough with water during the baking process. Its typical shape is the baguette, which is long and thin and has slits running along its topside. During baking these slits allow steam to escape and a light crust to form.

Paño de muselina *PAH-nyoh deh moo-seh-LEE-nah* **Cheesecloth**
EQUIPMENT *See* **Estopilla.**

Pan negro *pahn NEH-groh* **Pumpernickle**
GRAINS & CEREALS *See* **Pan de centeno.**

Panqueque *pahn-KEH-keh* **Pancake**
BAKING & PASTRY A very thin quick bread or cake made from a batter that is poured into a hot skillet or onto a hot griddle. It can be sweet or savory.

Pan rallado / Migas *pahn rah-YAH-doh* **Bread crumbs**
CONDIMENTS Fresh or dried bread that has been ground to a crumb. The dried variety can be made with stale bread or bread that has been toasted.

Panucho *pah-NOO-choh*
DISH (Mexico) A tortilla that has been fried on only one side. The bottom is crisp and the top (nonfried side) holds a topping such as beans or meat.

Papa *PAH-pah* **Potato**
FRUIT & VEGETABLE *See* **Patata.**

Papadulze *pah-pah-DOOL-seh*
DISH (Mexico) Corn tortillas that are dipped in pumpkin seed sauce, stuffed with chopped hard-cooked egg, and rolled.

Papa morada *PAH-pah moh-RAH-dah* **Purple potato**
FRUIT & VEGETABLE *See* **Patata morada.**

Papa rellena *PAH-pah reh-YEH-nah*
DISH (Peru/Cuba) A large potato fritter. Mashed potato is stuffed with a ground beef mixture and shaped into a ball. It is then coated with flour and deep-fried.

Papas a la huancaína *PAH-pahs ah lah wahn-kah-EE-nah*
DISH (Peru) A dish of boiled and sliced potatoes smothered with a creamy and slightly spicy cheese sauce (huancaina sauce). The potatoes are typically set over a few lettuce leaves and are garnished with olives and chopped eggs.

Papas fritas *PAH-pahs FREE-tahs* **French fries**
DISH Potatoes that are cut into thick or thin strips and then deep-fried. The term refers to the technique of cutting a potato into long, lengthwise strips, which is called frenching.

Papaya *pah-PAH-yah* **Papaya**
FRUIT & VEGETABLES A large, oval-shaped fruit with a smooth, yellow skin that grows to about nine inches in length and two pounds in weight. When ripe, the flesh is densely succulent and sweet with a slight tart flavor. In its center are numerous edible, black seeds that are often discarded.

Papel de aluminio *pah-PEHL deh ah-loo-MEE-nee-oh* **Aluminum foil**
EQUIPMENT Thin sheets of aluminum. They can be found in rolls or individual sheets. The foil is opaque, extremely pliable, and can withstand freezing temperatures and very high heat.

Papel de arroz *pah-PEHL deh ah-RROHS* **Rice paper**
GRAINS & CEREALS Very thin, edible sheets made from white rice flour, tapioca, and water. The dried translucent sheets must be rehydrated in hot water in order to become pliable and workable. Rice paper is used as a wrapper for meat and vegetables and can be fried after it has been rehydrated.

Papel encerado *pah-PEHL ehn-seh-RAH-doh* **Wax paper**
EQUIPMENT A moisture-proof, nonstick paper that has been covered with a thin coating of wax on both sides Microwave safe, it can be used in the oven when lining baking pans so long as the batter fully covers the paper.

Papitas fritas *pah-PEE-tahs FREE-tahs* **Potato chips**
FRUIT & VEGETABLES Thinly sliced, deep-fried potatoes.

Pargo *PAHR-goh* **Snapper**
FISH & SHELLFISH The common name for the *lutjanidae* family of saltwater fish of which there are about 250 species. Found in tropical and subtropical regions of the ocean, they are known for their teeth and snapping mouth which is compared to that of an alligator in quickness.

Pargo / Huachinango *PAHR-goh / wah-chee-NAHN-goh* **Red snapper**
FISH & SHELLFISH A saltwater fish found in warm waters. The most popular fish in the snapper family, it gets its name from the red color of its skin and eyes, which is obtained from the high amounts of carotenoids in its diet. It is a firm, white-flesh fish that flakes when cooked.

Pasa *PAH-sah* **Raisin**
FRUIT & VEGETABLES A dried grape that is dehydrated mechanically or by the sun. Available in a variety of sizes and colors (black, green, purple, and yellow), raisins are intensely sweet with a deep tart flavor. They can be eaten raw or used in both sweet and sour recipes.

Pasa de corinto *PAH-sah deh koh-REEN-toh* **Dried currant**
FRUIT & VEGETABLES A small, dried, seedless Zante grape. Similar to a raisin, it has an intense flavor and is used mostly in baking. It is not in the same family as the fresh black, red, and white currants, which are related to the gooseberry.

Pasapuré *pah-sah-poo-REH* **Potato ricer**
EQUIPMENT A handheld kitchen tool, resembling a large garlic press, used to press soft ingredients through the small holes of a metal plate. This results in food broken down to the size of grains of rice.

Foodmill
EQUIPMENT *See* Molinillo.

Pasta *PAHS-tah* **Pasta**
GRAINS & CEREALS Noodles made from a dough of flour, water, and sometimes egg that is cooked by boiling. They come in hundreds of shapes and sizes and can be dried or fresh. Italian law stipulates that dry pasta can be made only from durum wheat flour. This flour has a slight yellow tinge that gives pasta its characteristic yellow color.

Paste
CONDIMENT A thick puree that is used as a spread or condiment.

Pasta alargada *PAHS-tah ah-lahr-GAH-dah* **Long pasta**
GRAINS & CEREALS A type of pasta that is categorized by its length. Longer than it is wide, it averages about ten inches in length. It can be dried or fresh.

Pasta al huevo / Fideos al huevo *PAHS-tah ahl WEH-voh / fee-DEH-ohs ahl WEH-voh* **Egg noodles**
GRAINS & CEREALS Pasta made from wheat flour, water, and eggs or egg yolks. Egg noodles are flat and can be thick or thin, long or square shaped. They are sometimes found wound up in nests and are available fresh or dried.

Pasta corta *PAHS-tah KOHR-tah* **Short pasta**
GRAINS & CEREALS Pasta that is compact, thicker, and denser that the long variety.

Pasta culinaria *PAHS-tah koo-lee-NAH-ree-ah* **Batter**
BAKING & PASTRY *See* Pasta para rebozar.

Pasta de aceitunas *PAHS-tah deh ah-seh-ee-TOO-nahs* **Black olive paste**
CONDIMENTS Crushed black olives that may be seasoned with lemon, anchovies, and olive oil. Pasta de acetiunas is used as a condiment or spread over toast as a canapé.

Pasta de anchoas *PAHS-tah deh ahn-CHOH-ahs* **Anchovy paste**
CONDIMENTS A paste used as a condiment for its distinctive salty taste. It is made from a combination of mashed anchovies, water, vinegar, and spices. It can be used in recipes or spread on toast as a canapé.

Pasta de annatto *PAHS-tah deh ah-NAH-toh* **Annatto paste**
HERBS & SPICES The pulp surrounding the achiote seed in an annatto tree. Found in paste and powder form, this derivative is used primarily as a coloring agent for items such as cheese, rice, butter.

Pasta de camarones *PAHS-tah deh kah-mah-ROH-nehs* **Shrimp paste**
  CONDIMENTS A pink-colored paste made from ground-up fermented shrimp. Pungent in flavor and odor, it is a condiment used in many Asian recipes.

Pasta de guayaba / Bocadillo *PAHS-tah deh gwah-YAH-bah / boh-kah-DEE-yoh* **Guava paste**
  FRUIT & VEGETABLES Guava fruit pulp that has been cooked with pectin and sugar and flavored with citric acid. It is set and shaped into a firm block that can be sliced and served as a snack or dessert. It is used as a pastry filling or served with cheese.

Pasta de tomate *PAHS-tah deh toh-MAH-teh* **Tomato paste**
  CONDIMENTS Cooked tomatoes that have been strained and reduced to a thick paste. It is found canned or in squeeze tubes.

Pasta en láminas *PAHS-tah ehn LAH-mee-nahs* **Pasta sheets**
  GRAINS & CEREALS Pasta dough that has been flattened into a thin layer.

Pasta fresca *PAHS-tah FREHS-kah* **Fresh pasta**
  GRAINS & CEREALS Pasta made with semolina flour and egg instead of water. It is highly perishable and must be kept refrigerated prior to cooking. It cooks in only a few minutes—a fraction of the time it takes to cook dry pasta.

Pasta para rebozar / Batido / Pasta culinaria *PAHS-tah PAH-rah reh-boh-SAHR / bah-TEE-doh / PAHS-tah koo-lee-NAH-ree-ah* **Batter**
  BAKING & PASTRY An uncooked mixture containing flour and/or eggs. It can be thick (semisolid) or thin (liquid) and is typically cooked in an oven.

Pasta rellena *PAHS-tah reh-YEH-nah* **Filled pasta**
  GRAINS & CEREALS Pasta that has been stuffed with ingredients (a filling).

Pasta seca *PAHS-tah seh-KAH* **Dry pasta**
  GRAINS & CEREALS A paste made primarily from durum semolina flour and water or egg that is shaped and dehydrated by mechanical driers. It comes in varying shapes from long to short, fat to thin, flat to round.

Pasta wonton *PAHS-tah wohn-TOHN* **Wonton wrappers**
  BAKING & PASTRY Small, square sheets of dough made from flour, egg, and water. Also known as wonton skins, they can be made fresh or purchased commercially. Purchased wrappers contain a small amount of cornstarch between the sheets to prevent them from sticking together

Pastel *pahs-TEHL* **Pie / Cake**
  BAKING & PASTRY *See* **Pye** and **Torta**.
  (Puerto Rico) Similar to a tamal, a stuffed cake wrapped in banana leaves. The dough is made from mashed plantains or a starchy root vegetable. It can be filled with beef, chicken, or seafood and is flavored with raisins, capers, olives, and sofrito. After the pastel is formed and wrapped, it is steamed or boiled. Pasteles are commonly eaten during the Christmas holidays.
  (Spain) A savory nine-inch pie filled with meat, fish, or vegetables.

Pastel / Masa *pahs-TEHL / MAH-sah* **Pastry**
BAKING & PASTRY Unleavened dough made from flour, water, and a fat to make pies and tarts. It is also a term used to describe baked goods (cakes, pies, tarts).

Pastelería *pahs-teh-leh-REE-ah* **Baked goods / Bakery / Pastry arts**
BAKING & PASTRY (1) Items produced by the baking process and include breads, cakes, pastries, pies, tarts, quiches, and cookies. (2) An operation that produces and/ or sells baked goods. (3) The art of pastry and dessert making.

Pastelitos *pahs-teh-LEE-tohs*
DISH (Cuba) Pastries made from puff pastry that is stuffed with a sweet or savory filling and glazed with a sweet glaze. Each filled pastelito is formed in its own traditional shape: guava (rectangular), cheese (twist), a combination of guava and cheese (triangular), or beef (round).

Pasteurizar *pahs-teh-oo-ree-SAHR* **Pasteurize**
COOKING METHOD / TECHNIQUE To heat a food item for a short period of time to kill disease-causing pathogens. Pasteurizing is not intended to kill all microorganisms, just most of the ones that are likely to cause disease. It is primarily done to milk but is also used for juices, wine, and beer.

Pastilla de caldo *pahs-TEE-yah deh KAHL-doh* **Bouillon cube**
CONDIMENTS See **Cubito de caldo**.

Patacones *pah-tah-KOH-nehs*
DISH The term used in Venezuela, Colombia, Costa Rica, and a couple other countries to describe fried, unripe plantain. They are similar to tostones except they are sliced thin and fried only once.

Patata / Papa *pah-TAH-tah / PAH-pah* **Potato**
FRUIT & VEGETABLES A starchy tuber, crop vegetable. Hundreds of varieties of potatoes exist. All have thin, edible skin and can range in color from white to yellow to red and even blue. A potato's flesh is creamy white and can be waxy (high moisture/low starch—good for boiling) or starchy (low moisture/high starch—good for baking and mashing).

Patata dulce *PAH-pah DOOL-seh* **Sweet potato**
FRUIT & VEGETABLE See **Boniato**.

Patata morada / Papa morada *pah-TAH-tah moh-RAH-dah / PAH-pah moh-RAH-dah* **Purple potato**
FRUIT & VEGETABLES A small, oval potato with a dark grayish black skin. The flesh is purple colored, very dense, and holds its shape well. A Peruvian heirloom potato from the Andes, it is believed to be one of the first harvested potatoes.

Patata russet *pah-TAH-tah ROO-seht* **Russet potato**
FRUIT & VEGETABLES A large, oblong potato with a rough, brown skin. Its white flesh is high in starch, making it suited for baking, mashing, and frying.

Patatas bravas *pah-TAH-tahs BRAH-bahs*
  DISH (Spain) Fried, cubed potatoes that are smothered in a spicy tomato sauce.

Pato *PAH-toh* **Duck**
  MEAT A bird whose characteristic dark red–colored flesh is much darker than that of chicken. It has a thick layer of fat surrounding its breast that is prized as a cooking fat when rendered. Both domesticated and wild varieties of duck are eaten.

Pato, hígado *PAH-toh, EE-gah-doh* **Duck, liver**
  MEAT An organ meat that is used in making the delicacy foie gras. It is very fatty and rich tasting.

Pato, medio muslo *PAH-toh, MEH-dee-oh MOOS-loh* **Duck, thigh**
  MEAT The dark meat found in the upper leg portion used for making duck confit.

Pato, pechuga *PAH-toh, peh-CHOO-gah* **Duck, breast**
  MEAT The cut of meat found directly in front of the rib cage, it is dark red in color and has a layer of fat under its skin.

Pato real *PAH-toh reh-AHL* **Mallard**
  GAME One of the ancestors of the domesticated duck. Its green head and yellow bill are very recognizable.

Pavo *PAH-boh* **Turkey**
  MEAT A large, domesticated bird with a recognizable wattle that hangs below its chin. Traditionally cooked whole on Thanksgiving, turkey is also popular as a deli meat.

Pavo, carcasa *PAH-boh, kahr-KAH-sah* **Turkey, carcass**
  MEAT The remains of the bird after the meat has been removed.

Pavo, medio muslo *PAH-boh, MEH-dee-oh MOOS-loh* **Turkey, thigh**
  MEAT The upper portion of the bird's leg that constitutes the dark meat.

Pavo, muslo entero *PAH-boh, MOOS-loh ehn-TEH-roh* **Turkey, leg**
  MEAT The entire lower extremity of the bird from the hip to the foot that constitutes the dark meat.

Pavo, pechuga *PAH-boh, peh-CHOO-gah* **Turkey, breast**
  MEAT The pectoral muscle that constitutes the white meat. It is low in fat and can get dry when cooked.

Pectina *pehk-TEE-nah* **Pectin**
  GENERAL A gelling agent and thickener naturally found in the cell wall of plants. Most commonly used to make jelly, jam, and preserves, it is added to fruit mixtures that do not contain enough natural pectin. It is available in liquid and powdered form.

Pejelagarto *peh-heh-lah-GAHR-toh*
  DISH (Mexico) A traditional dish from the state of Veracruz in Mexico. Fish is served in a chunky tomato sauce flavored with onions, chiles, capers, olives, and herbs. A whole fish or fillets can be used.

Pelador *peh-lah-DOHR* **Vegetable peeler**
EQUIPMENT A small kitchen tool used to remove the skin or peel of a fruit or vegetable. It comes in a variety of shapes and sizes but all of them have a small razorlike blade attached to a handle.

Pelar *peh-LAHR* **Peel**
COOKING METHOD / TECHNIQUE To remove the outer skin of a fruit or vegetable.

Skin
COOKING METHOD / TECHNIQUE *See* **Despellejar**.

Pelaya *peh-LAH-yah* **Lemon sole**
FISH & SHELLFISH A species of flounder, a small, white-fleshed fish that is mild in flavor and low in fat. It is also known as English sole.

Pepinillo *peh-pee-NEE-yoh* **Gherkin**
CONDIMENTS A very small cucumber, one to three inches in length, that is pickled and sold in jars or cans. The French call it a cornichon.

Pepino *peh-PEE-noh* **Cucumber**
FRUIT & VEGETABLES A long, green cylindrical fruit with a thin, edible skin. At times the skin is waxed and then peeled and not eaten. The flesh is white and mildly flavored with a juicy and crisp texture. It has small, edible seeds found along the center that are sometimes removed. It is typically eaten raw.

Pepino encurtido *peh-PEE-noh ehn-koor-TEE-doh* **Pickle**
FRUIT & VEGETABLES A cucumber that has been marinated in a brine or vinegar mixture.

Pepino en vinagre al eneldo *peh-PEE-noh ehn bee-NAH-greh ahl eh-NEHL-doh* **Dill pickle**
CONDIMENTS A cucumber that has been pickled in brine flavored with dill seed.

Pepino hothouse *peh-PEE-noh hoht house* **Hothouse cucumber**
FRUIT & VEGETABLES A practically seedless cucumber with a thin, bumpy skin. It is longer than a traditional cucumber (at least one foot long) and is packaged in plastic for protection since its skin is not covered in wax. It is also known as an English cucumber

Pepitas *peh-PEE-tahs* **Pumpkin seeds**
HERBS & SPICES The seeds of the pumpkin that have had their white husks removed. The small, green seeds have a nutty flavor and a crunchy texture. They are available with or without their husks as well as raw or roasted.

Pepitas de chocolate *peh-PEE-tahs deh choh-koh-LAH-teh* **Chocolate chips**
CONDIMENTS Small, round chunks of chocolate.

Pepitas de mantequilla de cacahuete *peh-PEE-tahs deh mahn-teh-KEE-yah deh kah-kah-WEH-teh* **Peanut butter chips**
CONDIMENTS *See* **Pepitas de mantequillas de maní**.

Pepitas de mantequilla de maní *peh-PEE-tahs deh mahn-teh-KEE-yah deh mah-NEE* **Peanut butter chips**

CONDIMENTS Sweetened commercial peanut butter that has been formed into small drops or disks.

Pera *PEH-rah* **Pear**

FRUIT & VEGETABLES The round or bell-shaped fruit that grows on a pear tree. Its thin, edible skin ranges in color from green to yellow to red. Its flesh is cream colored and can be firm or succulent with a slightly sweet flavor. The fruit ripens best after its been picked. There are more than five thousand varieties of pears.

Perca *PEHR-kah* **Perch**

FISH & SHELLFISH A small, freshwater fish that ranges in size from a half a pound to three pounds. Mild-flavored and firm-fleshed, it has a yellow green–colored skin with dark vertical stripes. It is also known as yellow perch or river perch.

Perdiz *pehr-DEES* **Partridge**

GAME A medium-size game bird averaging about one and a half pounds that is a member of the pheasant family.

Perejil *peh-reh-HEEL* **Parsley**

HERBS & SPICES A bright green leaved plant used as an herb. It has a fresh, slightly pungent flavor. Two varieties are used in cooking—curly leaf and flat leaf—which are distinguishable by the shape and texture of their leaves. Available fresh or dried, parsley is used in recipes, as a palate cleanser, and as garnishes.

Perejil chino *peh-reh-HEEL CHEE-noh*

HERBS & SPICES *See* **Cilantro.**

Perifollo *peh-ree-FOH-yoh* **Chervil**

HERBS & SPICES A member of the parsley family. It has tender, green leaves that impart a mild anise flavor. It is an ingredient in fines herbes.

Pernil *pehr-NEEL*

DISH (Puerto Rico) Roasted pork shoulder marinated in citrus juice, vinegar, garlic, dried oregano, and olive oil.

Perretxiko *peh-rreh-TEE-koh*

DISH (Spain) A white wild mushroom that is native to the Basque region of Spain.

Perro caliente *PEH-rroh kah-lee-EHN-teh* **Hot dog**

MEAT An American-style frankfurter. It is a cured sausage made from pork or beef and served in a special oblong soft bun. Typical accompaniments include ketchup, mustard, and pickle relish.

Pesas de hornear *PEH-sahs deh ohr-neh-AHR* **Baking beans**

EQUIPMENT Small, round, often ceramic balls used when blind baking. Baking paper is placed over pastry and then topped with the balls, which allows for even heat distribution and keeps the pastry from rising too much. Dried beans and rice can be substituted for the ceramic balls.

Pescadilla *pehs-kah-DEE-yah* **Whiting**
FISH & SHELLFISH A small silver-skinned fish averaging about three pounds in weight. It has a firm, white flesh that has a mild flavor. Whiting is typically available whole, fresh, salted, and smoked.

Pescado *pehs-KAH-doh* **Fish**
FISH & SHELLFISH An aquatic animal that has fins, a backbone, and gills. Fish range in shapes and sizes and can come from both fresh and salt water. Saltwater fish have larger bones which are easier to remove than those of freshwater fish.

Pescado ahumado *pehs-KAH-doh ah-oo-MAH-doh* **Smoked fish**
FISH & SHELLFISH Fresh fish that has been cured and flavored by smoke. Salmon, trout, and white fish are popular for smoking.

Pescado plano *pehs-KAH-doh PLAH-noh* **Flat fish**
FISH & SHELLFISH A flat and oval-shaped fish whose eyes both lie on the same side of its head. Flat fish are firm, white-fleshed fish that are easy to fillet. Flounder, halibut, sole, and turbot are examples.

Pescado redondo *pehs-KAH-doh reh-DOHN-doh* **Round fish**
FISH & SHELLFISH A round-bodied fish with eyes on both sides of the head. It has a backbone that runs along its upper body and fillets located on either side. Examples are cod, bass, trout, snapper, and salmon.

Peso *PEH-soh* **Scale**
EQUIPMENT A device used to measure the weight of an object.

Pesto *PEHS-toh* **Pesto**
CONDIMENTS An uncooked, Italian sauce made with basil, garlic, pine nuts, Parmesan cheese, and olive oil. Traditionally the ingredients are crushed or pounded in a mortar with a pestle until a sauce forms.

Pez de San Pedro *pehs deh sahn PEH-droh* **John Dory**
FISH & SHELLFISH A deep-sea fish with long spines protruding from its head. Its skin is light yellow green in color with a dark circular spot on its side. Its mild-tasting flesh is versatile and can be cooked in a number of ways.

Pez espada *pehs ehs-PAH-dah* **Swordfish**
FISH & SHELLFISH A large, saltwater fish recognized by its long, swordlike protrusion extending from its nose. Its flesh is dense and meaty yet mild in flavor. Due to its large size (average weight is 350 pounds) its meat is typically sold in steaks and chunks.

Pez loro *pehs LOH-roh* **Parrot fish**
FISH & SHELLFISH A saltwater fish found near reefs in warm waters. It is often a by-catch of snapper. Recognizable by its brilliant blue, yellow, pink, and green–colored

skin, it gets its name from the shape of its mouth and teeth which resemble the beak of a parrot.

Pibes *PEE-behs*
DISH (Mexico) A broad term for a tamal baked in banana leaves.

Pibil *pee-BEEL*
DISH (Mexico) Recado-marinated pork or chicken cooked in an underground pit (pib) that has been layered with banana leaves.

Pibipollo *pee-bee-POH-yoh*
DISH (Mexico) A large tamal (about one foot in length) stuffed with chicken and wrapped in banana leaves.

Picada *pee-KAH-dah*
DISH *See* **Sope.**

Picadillo *pee-kah-DEE-yoh*
DISH (Cuba) A ground beef hash made from beef or a combination of beef and pork and seasoned with onions, garlic, green peppers, tomato sauce, and seasoning. Raisins may or may not be added.
(Mexico) Ground beef flavored with tomato sauce, raisins, and spices. It is often used as a filling for empanadas, tamales, and chiles rellenos.

Picante *pee-KAHN-teh* **Spicy**
DESCRIPTOR Hot; producing a burning sensation in the mouth.

Picar / Desminuzar *pee-KAHR / dehs-mee-noo-SAHR* **Mince**
COOKING METHOD / TECHNIQUE To cut food into very small, irregularly shaped pieces.

Chop
COOKING METHOD / TECHNIQUE *See* **Cortar.**

Picarones *pee-kah-ROH-nehs*
DISH (Peru) Ring-shaped pumpkin fritters served with a sugarcane syrup.

Pichón *pee-CHON* **Pigeon**
GAME *See* **Paloma.**

Picos / Picón *PEE-kohs / pee-KOHN* **Picos blue**
DAIRY Creamy, assertive, and full- flavored cow's milk blue cheese from northern Spain that is wrapped in maple leaves. It is also called Picon.

Pies de cerdo *pee-EHS deh SEHR-doh* **Pig's feet**
MEAT The feet and ankles of a pig that contain high amounts of collagen and will turn soft and gelatinous when cooked for a long time over low heat. Also known as trotters, they are available pickled, smoked, and fresh.

Piel *pee-EHL* **Casing / Skin**
MEAT The thin, tubular membrane from animal (sheep, hogs, cattle) intestines that has been cleaned and dried and is used to encase sausage stuffing.

GENERAL A naturally occurring protective outer covering. For plants, it is known as the peel; for animals, it is a source of fat and flavor.

Piel / Cáscara *pee-EHL / KAHS-kah-rah* **Zest**

FRUIT & VEGETABLES The skin of citrus fruit. Rich in essential oils, it is very fragrant and flavorful. Only the colored part of the skin is the zest—the white interior part is the bitter-tasting pith.

Piel de fruta escarchada *pee-EHL deh FROO-tah ehs-kahr-CHAH-dah* **Candied peel**

BAKING & PASTRY The skin of fresh fruit, typically citrus fruit, cut into strips, boiled in sugar syrup, dusted with granulated sugar, and then dried. It can be eaten as is or used as a garnish.

Pierna *pee-EHR-nah* **Leg**

MEAT A limb that supports an animal's body and is used for locomotion. Animals can have two to four legs.

Piloncillo *pee-lohn-SEE-yoh*

CONDIMENTS (Mexico) Cone-shaped, unrefined, brown sugar that has a deep molasses flavor. It has a hard texture and needs to be cut or chipped at in order to be used.

Pimentón *pee-mehn-TOHN* **Paprika**

HERBS & SPICES A spice made from ground, dried sweet red peppers. The type of pepper used determines the color and flavor of the spice which can range from sweet to pungent to hot. The variety also determines the intensity of its red color.

Bell pepper

FRUIT & VEGETABLE *See* **Pimiento**.

Pimentón ahumado *pee-mehn-TOHN ah-oo-MAH-doh* **Smoked paprika**

HERBS & SPICES A spice made by slowly drying red peppers over an oak-burning fire for several weeks resulting in a sweet and smoky flavor. It comes in three varieties sweet (*dulce*), bittersweet (*agridulce*), and hot (*picante*). Very popular in Spanish cuisine. It is also referred to as pimentón de la vera, which refers to the area in Spain where it is made.

Pimienta *pee-mee-EHN-tah* **Peppercorn**

HERBS & SPICES The very small berry that grows on the pepper plant (a vine) and is used as a spice for its spicy and hot flavor.

Pimienta blanca *pee-mee-EHN-tah BLAHN-kah* **White peppercorn**

HERBS & SPICES The ripe berry of the pepper plant that has had its skin removed and is then dried.

Pimienta de Jamaica *pee-mee-EHN-tah deh hah-MAH-ee-kah* **Allspice**

HERBS & SPICES The berry of the evergreen pimiento tree. The name comes from its flavor, which is a combination of nutmeg, cinnamon, black pepper, and cloves. It is used in both sweet and savory cooking and is also referred to as Jamaica pepper. Allspice can be purchased in whole or ground form.

Pimienta negra *pee-mee-EHN-tah NEH-grah* **Black peppercorn**
HERBS & SPICES A picked and dried unripe berry from the pepper plant. It is the strongest-flavored peppercorn.

Pimienta verde *pee-mee-EHN-tah BEHR-deh* **Green peppercorn**
HERBS & SPICES The soft, unripe berry of the pepper plant. Green peppercorns are preserved in brine or salt.

Pimiento / Ají / Chiltoma *pee-mee-EHN-toh / ah-HEE / cheel-TOH-mah* **Bell pepper / Sweet pepper**
FRUIT & VEGETABLES A fruit and member of the *Capsicum* genus. It has a mildly sweet flavor and crisp, juicy texture. Its color ranges from green to orange to red and it gets its name from its bell shape.

Pimiento choricero seco *pee-mee-EHN-toh choh-ree-SEH-roh SEH-koh*
FRUIT & VEGETABLES (Spain) A dried sweet red pepper. Small and round, it is used to flavor soups and sauces. It is also known as a nora pepper.

Pimiento italiano *pee-mee-EHN-toh ee-tah-lee-AH-noh* **Banana pepper**
FRUIT & VEGETABLES Part of the chile pepper family, a long, yellow pepper, slightly sweet with mild heat, whose shape resembles a that of a banana.

Pimientos morrones *pee-mee-EHN-tohs moh-RROH-nehs* **Roasted red peppers**
FRUIT & VEGETABLES (Spain) Roasted red peppers that are skinned and seeded. They can be made fresh and are also available in jars or cans.

Pimiento rojo / Ají rojo *pee-mee-EHN-toh ROH-hoh / ah-HEE ROH-hoh* **Red bell pepper**
FRUIT & VEGETABLES A bell-shaped pepper with a sweet flavor and crisp juicy flesh. It is a green pepper that has been allowed to ripen on the vine resulting in its red color and sweet flavor.

Pimientos *pee-mee-EHN-tohs* **Roasted red peppers**
FRUIT & VEGETABLES *See* **Pimientos morrones**.

Pimiento verde / Ají verde *pee-mee-EHN-toh BEHR-deh / ah-HEE BEHR-deh* **Green bell pepper**
FRUIT & VEGETABLES A mild and slightly sweet-flavored bell pepper with a crisp and juicy texture. When young, all bell peppers are green and according to their variety will turn yellow, red, or orange if allowed to mature on the vine.

Piña *PEE-nya* **Pineapple**
FRUIT & VEGETABLES The tropical fruit that grows on the pineapple plant and is long and cylindrical in shape with thin, pointed leaves sprouting from its top. Its bumpy, inedible skin must be cut off to expose the yellow- colored flesh, which is juicy and sweet but can be acidic and tart depending on ripeness or variety. The fruit must be

picked when mature, as it will not ripen off the vine, but its acidity can decrease if it is left at room temperature for a couple of days.

Pinchar *peen-CHAHR* **Prick**

COOKING METHOD / TECHNIQUE (1) To create small holes in food. (2) To slightly pierce.

Pincho *PEEN-choh* **Skewer**

EQUIPMENT See **Brocheta**.

DISH (Spain) A small skewered appetizer. It can also refer to food meant to be picked up with a toothpick.

Pincho moruno *PEEN-choh moh-ROO-noh*

DISH (Spain) A skewer of meat, traditionally pork, seasoned with a paste made with cumin, paprika, and olive oil. Pincho moruno literally translates as "Moorish skewer."

Piñón *pee-NYOHN* **Pine nut**

NUTS & OILS The small, edible seed of the pine tree found in a pinecone, which require a labor-intensive process to remove. Ivory-colored, high-fat pine nuts are found inside a thin, dark shell that must be removed before they are eaten.

Pintada *peen-TAH-dah* **Guinea fowl**

GAME A small bird with a dark, strongly flavored meat, ranging from one to four pounds in weight. Care must be given when cooking it as it can dry out easily.

Pinzas *PEEN-sahs* **Lobster claws**

FISH & SHELLFISH The sharp and curved extremities of a lobster.

Pinza *PEEN-sah* **Tweezers**

EQUIPMENT (1) A pincer. (2) A small handheld tool used for grabbing or placing small objects.

Tong

EQUIPMENT See **Tenaza**.

Pionono *pee-oh-NOH-noh*

DISH (Venezuela) A rolled caked filled with caramel, fruit, or cream.

Piononos *pee-oh-NOH-nohs*

DISH (Puerto Rico) Stuffed and rolled sweet plantains. Ripe plantains are sliced lengthwise and fried. A stuffing is then added and they are rolled up.

Piparrada *pee-pah-RRAH-dah*

DISH (Spain) A Basque term that refers to a dish having tomatoes and green peppers as its main ingredient. It also refers to a sauce commonly used to accompany eggs, fish, and meat that is made from a puree of sautéed tomatoes, onions, and red and green peppers.

Pipian *PEE-pee-ahn*

DISH (Mexico) A sauce made from ground pumpkin seeds.

Pisca *PEES-kah* **Pinch**
  MEASUREMENTS An imprecise unit of dry measure. The amount of a substance held between thumb and index finger.

Pisco *PEES-koh*
  BEVERAGE (Peru) A distilled beverage made from grapes that grow in Peru. It is clear in color and slightly viscous.

Pisco sour *PEES-koh SAWH-ehr*
  BEVERAGE (Peru) A mixed cocktail made from a combination of pisco, lemon juice, egg white, sugar, and bitters.

Pistacho *pees-TAH-choh* **Pistachio nut**
  NUTS & OILS The nut that grows on the pistachio tree. Its hard, tan shell splits naturally when ripe and contains a green-colored nut. Shells are sometimes artificially dyed a red color for aesthetic purposes. Pistachios can be purchased shelled or unshelled.

Pisto manchego *PEES-toh mahn-CHEH-goh*
  DISH (Spain) A vegetable stew made with onions, potatoes, zucchini, green peppers, and tomatoes. Similar to a ratatouille, it originates from the La Mancha region in central Spain.

Pitahaya *pee-tah-AH-yah* **Pitahaya / Pitaya**
  FRUIT & VEGETABLES A member of the cactus family, an oval-shaped fruit that has a prickly, inedible, bright pink skin. The juicy flesh is white and filled with small, edible seeds that add a crunchy texture. Its very mild flavor is used as a palate cleanser. It is also known as dragon fruit.

Plancha *PLAHN-chah* **Griddle**
  EQUIPMENT A flat, often rimless cooking pan. It can be a freestanding pan placed over a burner or be built into a stove-top.

Plátano *PLAH-tah-noh* **Plantain**
  FRUIT & VEGETABLES A very large variety of banana with a firmer texture and higher starch content. It can be prepared when ripe or unripe but must be cooked before being eaten. As the plantain matures the skin changes color from green to black and the texture from firm to soft.

Plátano / Banano / Cambur / Gineo *PLAH-tah-noh / bah-NAH-noh / kahm-BOOR / gee-NEH-oh* **Banana**
  FRUIT & VEGETABLES A long, curved fruit that changes color from green to yellow to brown as it ripens. Its flesh is a pale beige color and softens as the fruit matures. The fruit grows in clusters and ripens best off the plant.

Plátano enano *PLAH-tah-noh eh-NAH-noh* **Ladyfinger banana**
  FRUIT & VEGETABLES A small, stubby banana that has a thin skin and sweet flavor.

Plátano maduro *PLAH-tah-noh mah-DOO-roh*
DISH (Cuba) Fried sweet plantains.

Plato *PLAH-toh* **Plate**
EQUIPMENT A flat vessel on which food is served. It can be slightly concaved with a rim. A plate comes in various shapes and sizes but is traditionally round. It is also known as dishware.

Plato hondo / Bol *PLAH-toh OHN-doh / bohl* **Bowl**
EQUIPMENT An deep, open-top vessel used to serve food. It can be small for individual use or large to serve a group.

Plato principal / Plato fuerte *PLAH-toh preen-see-PAHL / PLAH-toh foo-EHR-teh* **Entrée**
GENERAL The main course of a meal.

Poco hecho *POH-koh EH-choh* **Medium rare**
COOKING METHOD / TECHNIQUE The doneness of meat described by its internal temperature, color, and juiciness. The meat should be warm and red in the center and its temperature should reach 130°F-140°F.

Polenta *poh-LEHN-tah* **Polenta**
GRAINS & CEREALS A dish made from boiled cornmeal.

Pollo *POH-yoh* **Chicken**
MEAT A domesticated fowl. Its meat is a type of poultry and its flavor is mild and somewhat neutral. A chicken can weigh between two and ten pounds. Almost the entire bird and its eggs are eaten.

Pollo, ala *POH-yoh, AH-lah* **Chicken, wing**
MEAT Considered white meat, it is sold individually or attached to the breast.

Pollo, carcasa *POH-yoh, kahr-KAH-sah* **Chicken, carcass**
MEAT The entire body of the chicken after it has been slaughtered.

Pollo, cuartos *POH-yoh, KWAHR-toh* **Chicken, quarters**
MEAT A quarter of a whole chicken, made up of the leg or breast meat. Leg quarters contain one thigh and drumstick, and the breast quarter contains one breast and wing.

Pollo, filete de pechuga *POH-yoh, fee-LEH-teh deh peh-CHOO-gah* **Chicken, breast fillet**
MEAT The white meat portion found in front of the ribs, it is the most popular chicken part.

Pollo, hígado *POH-yoh, EE-gah-doh* **Chicken, liver**
MEAT Organ meat. It is mild tasting, as far as liver goes. Sold whole due to their small size.

Pollo, medio *POH-yoh, MEH-dee-oh* **Chicken, half**
MEAT Half of a whole chicken made up of one breast, wing, thigh, and drumstick.

Pollo, medio muslo *POH-yoh, MEH-DEE-oh MOOS-loh* **Chicken, thigh**
MEAT The portion of the chicken's leg above the knee joint. It contains all dark meat.

Pollo, muslito *POH-yoh, moos-LEE-toh* **Chicken, drumstick**
MEAT The bottom portion of the leg below the knee joint. Contains all dark meat.

Pollo, muslo *POH-yoh, MOOS-loh* **Chicken, leg**
MEAT All dark meat chicken made up of two parts: the thigh and drumstick.

Pollo, pecho entero *POH-yoh, PEH-choh ehn-TEH-roh* **Chicken, double breast**
MEAT The entire breast portion of one chicken, made up of two individual breast fillets that are still attached to each other.

Pollo, tiras *POH-yoh ehn TEE-rahs* **Chicken, strips**
MEAT Chicken meat that has been cut into thin strips. The strips can be made from both white and dark meat, but are usually made from the breast meat.

Pollo troceado *POH-yoh troh-seh-AH-doh* **Chicken, diced**
MEAT Chicken meat that has been cubed.

Polvorear / Espolvorear *pohl-boh-reh-AHR / ehs-pohl-boh-reh-AHR* **Dust**
COOKING METHOD / TECHNIQUE To lightly coat food with a powdered substance.

Polvorones *pohl-boh-ROH-nehs* **Mexican wedding cake / Cookies**
BAKING & PASTRY Shortbreadlike cookies that are made with flour, ground nuts, and butter. They are shaped into a ball and rolled in powdered sugar. They are served often at weddings, christenings, and special occasions.
(Spain) Small powdered sugar cookies. They are often served with coffee, tea, or a glass of liqueur.

Ponche *POHN-cheh* **Punch**
BEVERAGE A fruit juice–based beverage made from a mixture of ingredients. It can be alcoholic or soft and is usually made in large quantities and served in a punch bowl. Chunks or slices of fresh fruit are often added as garnish.
(Mexico) A fruit-filled punch that is spiked with cane alcohol.

Poner en hielo *poh-NEHR ehn ee-EH-loh* **Ice**
COOKING METHOD / TECHNIQUE To decrease the temperature of a food by placing it over ice or in an ice bath.

Porción *pohr-see-OHN* **Slice**
COOKING METHOD / TECHNIQUE *See* Rebanada.

Pororo *poh-ROH-roh* **Bean**
FRUIT & VEGETABLES *See* Judía.

Porrusalda *poh-rroo-SAHL-dah*
DISH (Spain) A very light brothy soup made with leeks, potatoes, and sometimes pumpkin. The vegetables are lightly boiled in water and then flavored with olive oil and salt.

Postre *POHS-treh* **Dessert**
BAKING & PASTRY Typically the last course of a meal made up of predominantly sweet food such as cakes, cookies, fruit, and chocolate.

Posuelo *poh-soo-EH-loh* **Ramekin**
EQUIPMENT A small, ovenproof baking dish measuring about four inches in diameter and made of glazed ceramic. It is used for serving individual portions.

Potaje *poh-TAH-heh*
DISH (Cuba) Hearty bean stew.

Pote gallego *POH-teh gah-YEH-goh*
DISH (Spain) The cocido made in Galicia. It contains salted pork hocks instead of bacon and does not contain meatballs.

Pozole *poh-SOH-leh*
DISH (Mexico) A hearty stew made with hominy and often with pork. A number of accompaniments (onion, radish, cabbage, pork cracklings) are served with it and vary from region to region. In some areas the broth is also seasoned with chiles and herbs.

Preparar *preh-pah-RAHR* **Prepare**
COOKING METHOD / TECHNIQUE (1) To cook. (2) To put together.

Preservar *preh-sehr-BAHR* **Preserve**
COOKING METHOD / TECHNIQUE To conserve food so that it can be kept for an extended period of time. Techniques include canning, smoking, salting, pickling, and dehydrating.

Primer plato *pree-MEHR PLAH-toh* **First course**
GENERAL See Entrada.

Proteína *proh-teh-EE-nah* **Protein**
GENERAL Large molecules made up of amino acids that are essential to living cells. Protein provides energy to the body and is responsible for repairing cells. It is found predominantly in animal products but is also provided by plant sources.

Puchero / Cocido valenciano *poo-CHEH-roh / koh-SEE-doh BAH-lehn-see-AH-noh*
DISH (Spain) A hearty veal stew made with ham, bacon, chicken, blood sausage, and meatballs. Chickpeas, onions, and potatoes are also added. The stew is eaten in parts with the broth served first with either rice or thin noodles.

Pudín / Budín *poo-DEEN / boo-DEEN* **Pudding**
BAKING & PASTRY A sweet or savory egg and milk–based custard. It can be baked, steamed, or boiled.
(Spain) Meat or fish pâté. It is typically eaten cold with a side of mayonnaise.

Pudín de pan *poo-DEEN deh pahn*
DISH (Cuba) Bread pudding.

Puerco *poo-EHR-koh* **Pork**
MEAT See Cerdo.

Puerco asado *poo-EHR-koh ah-SAH-doh*
DISH Roast pork.

Puerro *poo-EH-rroh* **Leek**
FRUIT & VEGETABLES A member of the onion and garlic family, but much milder in flavor, that resembles a giant scallion. The white flesh, closest to the roots, has a more pronounced onion flavor than the thick, dark green leaves that shoot up from it. The entire leek is edible but the tops of the greens need trimming as they are tough and offer little flavor. Leeks are used in the same way onions are used.

Pulpa *POOL-pah* **Pulp**
FRUIT & VEGETABLES The soft, flesh of a fruit contained within a thin membrane. It contains the juice of the fruit.

Pulpo *POOL-poh* **Octopus**
FISH & SHELLFISH A member of the mollusk family with eight flexible legs or tentacles and no internal skeleton. It grows to an average extended length of two feet and weight of three pounds. If not cooked properly, the meat becomes tough and rubbery. The younger the animal, the more tender the meat.

Pulque *POOL-keh*
BEVERAGE (Mexico) A pre-Colombian drink made from the fermented sap of the maguey plant. Low in alcohol, it is milky white in color. A splash of hot sauce (picante), a squeeze of lime, and salt are often added.

Pulverizar *pool-beh-ree-SAHR* **Pulverize**
COOKING METHOD / TECHNIQUE To make into a powder by crushing, grinding, or pounding.

Punto de inflamación *POON-toh deh een-flah-mah-see-OHN* **Smoke point**
GENERAL The temperature at which a heated fat begins to deteriorate. Once the temperature is reached, the fat will begin to emit smoke. This results in the fat eventually imparting an unpleasant taste and odor. The higher a fat's smoke point, the better suited it is for frying.

Puré *poo-REH* **Purée**
COOKING METHOD / TECHNIQUE n. Solid food that has been ground to a smooth consistency.

(hacer) Puré *ah-SEHR poo-REH*
COOKING METHOD / TECHNIQUE v. To grind food with a blender, food processor, or food mill until it achieves a smooth consistency.

Pye / Pastel / Empanada *PAH-ee / pahs-TEHL / ehm-pah-NAH-dah* **Pie**
BAKING & PASTRY A dish made with a crust and filling. It can be sweet or savory and can have a single or double crust. Crusts can be made from pie dough, puff pastry, phyllo, and cookie crumbs among other things.

Q

Quarto / Cuarto de galón *KWAHR-toh / KWAHR-toh deh gah-LOHN* **Quart**
> MEASUREMENTS A unit of measure of volume equivalent to 32 fluid ounces, 4 cups, or 2 pints.

Quemadura de congelador *keh-mah-DOO-rah deh kohn-heh-lah-DOHR*
Freezer burn
> GENERAL The loss of moisture from food that has been frozen. It results from improperly wrapped food that has been stored in the freezer. It irreversibly changes the texture, appearance, and flavor of food.

Quemar *keh-MAHR* **Burn**
> COOKING METHOD / TECHNIQUE To overcook to the point that the item is dehydrated and has begun to be converted to ash.

> **Sear**
> COOKING METHOD / TECHNIQUE *See* **Sellar**.

Quesadilla *keh-sah-DEE-yah*
> DISH (Mexico) A lightly fried corn tortilla that is filled with melted cheese and can also include a shredded meat or vegetable. The tortilla can be folded in half to hold the filling or two corn tortillas can sandwich it.

Quesillo *keh-SEE-yoh*
> DAIRY (Mexico) String cheese.

Queso *KEH-soh* **Cheese**
> DAIRY A dairy product made from the milk of cows, goats, sheep, and buffalo. The milk protein casein is coagulated through the addition of rennet, an enzyme. The resulting solids are separated from the liquid, pressed, and then aged.

Queso añejo / Queso cotija *KEH-soh ah-NYE-hoh / KEH-soh koh-TEE-hah*
> DAIRY (Mexico) A dry, salty cheese from Cotija in Michoacan.

Queso asadero *KEH-soh ah-sah-DEH-roh* **Oaxaca cheese**
> DAIRY A semisoft, white, cow's milk Mexican cheese. Similar in texture and melting properties to those of mozzarella, it is available in braids, balls, or wheels. Named after the Mexican state of Oaxaca where the cheese was originally made, it has a flavor similar to that of Monterey Jack and is often used for quesadillas or for broiling since it melts so well.

Queso azul *KEH-soh ah-SOOL* **Blue cheese**
> DAIRY A type of cheese that has been injected with a special mold that causes the cheese to develop blue and green veins. The mold also contributes to the cheese's characteristic flavor.

Queso blanco *KEH-soh BLAHN-koh* **Farmer cheese**
DAIRY A fresh cheese made by pressing out most of the moisture from cottage cheese. It is formed into a solid, rectangular or round shape which can be sliced or crumbled. Made from cow, sheep, or goat's milk, it has a slightly sour flavor.

Queso cabrales *KEH-soh kah-BRAH-lehs* **Cabrales**
DAIRY An assertive Spanish blue cheese from the region of Asturias in northern Spain. It is typically made from cow's milk but can also be blended with sheep's or goat's milk. It was traditionally wrapped in sycamore maple leaves but is now covered in a dark aluminum wrapper with a protected stamp signaling its authenticity.

Queso cotija *KEH-soh koh-TEE-hah*
DAIRY *See* **Queso Añejo.**

Queso Chihuahua *KEH-soh chee-WAH-wah* **Chihuahua cheese**
DAIRY A Mexican cheese made from cow's milk that melts well, becoming soft and stringy. Found in braids or balls, the white cheese is similar in flavor to Monterey Jack cheese. It is named after the Mexican state in which it is made.

Queso crema *KEH-soh KREH-mah* **Cream cheese**
DAIRY A soft, white, unripe, spreadable cheese made from cow's milk. Found in tubs and bars, it has a slight tangy flavor.

Queso de Oaxaca *KEH-soh deh wah-HAH-kah*
DAIRY *See* **Queso asadero.**

Queso fresco *KEH-soh FREHS-koh*
DAIRY (Mexico) A fresh, cow's milk cheese that is similar in texture to farmer cheese. Slightly salty, it is usually packed in liquid-filled containers to help keep it moist. It is a crumbly cheese that does not melt well.

Queso fundido *KEH-soh foon-DEE-doh*
DISH (Mexico) Melted cheese. The white queso asadero is typically used and the cheese is melted in the same shallow earthenware dish it is served in.

Queso suizo *KEH-soh soo-EE-soh* **Swiss cheese**
DAIRY Technically a Swiss-made cheese. Emmentaler is one of the most well known Swiss cheeses. American Swiss cheese is any nutty-flavored cheese with holes in it.

Queso telita *KEH-soh teh-LEE-tah*
DAIRY (Venezuela) An artisanal farmers cheese. Mild in flavor, it is sold packed in liquid.

Queso tetilla *KEH-soh teh-TEE-yah* **Tetilla**
DAIRY A cow's milk cheese from Galicia in northwest Spain. It is one of the few cheeses of that region with a certificate of origin. It gets its name from its resemblance to the top of a nipple (*tetilla*). It is a semisoft cheese with a thin but inedible rind and is sweet and creamy tasting.

Queso Zamora *KEH-soh sah-MOH-rah* **Zamora**

DAIRY A hard, sheep's milk cheese made in the province of Zamora in northeast Spain. Protected by a Denominación de Origen, it is aged for six months during which it is rubbed with olive oil and often turned. Its rind is dark brown with the traditional zigzag pattern that is common with manchego. It is a full-flavored cheese with a sharp, buttery, and nutty taste.

Quimosina *kee-moh-SEE-nah* **Renin**

GENERAL An enzyme used to curdle milk and make cheese. Obtained from the stomach of a young calf, it can be purchased in powdered or tablet form.

Quingombó *keen-gohm-BOH* **Okra**

FRUIT & VEGETABLES *See* Okra.

Quinoa / Quinua *KEE-noh-ah / KEE-noo-ah* **Quinoa**

GRAINS & CEREALS Although treated like a grain, the seed of a leafy green vegetable. Very high in protein, it is considered a complete protein since it contains all nine essential amino acids. Light brown in color when dried, it becomes translucent when cooked with a fluffy texture and nutty flavor. It was a staple in the ancient Inca diet.

Quitar el corazón / Descorazonar *kee-TAHR ehl koh-rah-SOHN / dehs-koh-rah-soh-NAHR* **Core**

COOKING METHOD / TECHNIQUE To remove the center portion of a fruit or vegetable.

Quitar las espinas *kee-TAHR lahs ehs-PEE-nahs* **Pit**

COOKING METHOD / TECHNIQUE To remove the seed or stone of a fruit by cutting it out or pushing it out.

R

Rábano *RAH-bah-noh* **Radish**

FRUIT & VEGETABLES A root vegetable ranging in shape from round to elongated and in size from small (one-inch diameter) to large (one and a half feet in length). Its color can be white, red, purple, or black. Its flavor is peppery and its texture is crisp. It is most commonly served raw.

Rábano daikón *RAH-bah-noh dah-ee-KOHN* **Daikon**

FRUIT & VEGETABLES A large radish with a sweet flavor. Its skin is beige and its flesh is white, crisp, and juicy.

Rábano picante *RAH-bah-noh pee-KAHN-teh* **Horseradish**

HERBS & SPICES A plant grown mainly for its large white root. Pungent and spicy in flavor, it is used as a seasoning or condiment—never on its own. When used fresh, it is typically grated. It is also available bottled, preserved in brine.

Rabo de buey *RAH-boh deh boo-WEH* **Oxtail**

MEAT Meat from the tail of cattle, although it used to come from oxen. Rabo de buey is bony and filled with lots of connective tissue that must be cooked by a slow and moist method (stewing or braising) in order for it to become tender, but it is very flavorful.

Rabo encendido *RAH-boh ehn-sehn-DEE-doh*
DISH (Cuba / Puerto Rico) Oxtail stew.

Radicchio *rah-DEE-kee-oh* **Radicchio**
FRUIT & VEGETABLES A red leaf chicory with white veins throughout its leaves. Used often in salads, it has a bitter flavor that mellows when cooked.

Rajas *RAH-hahs*
DISH (Mexico) Thin strips of roasted poblano peppers.

Rallador *rah-yah-DOHR* **Grater**
EQUIPMENT A kitchen tool used to grate or shred food into thin strips or crumbs. It consists of a metal plate that is perforated with holes on which a food is slid back and forth. The size of the hole determines the size of the grate. The typical configuration of the handheld version is a tall, four- to six-sided box where each side can grate food to different thicknesses and sizes. Most are manual but there are also electric versions.

Rallador / Acanalador *rah-yah-DOHR / ah-kah-nah-lah-DOHR* **Zester**
EQUIPMENT A handheld kitchen tool used to remove the zest from citrus fruit. It is made of a small, flat piece of metal perforated with small holes all along its top edge. The holes are placed against the skin of the fruit and the tool is pulled down with mild pressure. This results in small strips of citrus zest being peeled from the fruit.

Rama *RAH-mah* **Stem**
HERBS & SPICES The part of the plant that connects the roots and the leaves.

Rambután / Achotillo *rahm-boo-TAHN / ah-choh-TEE-yoh* **Rambutan**
FRUIT & VEGETABLES A small, egg-shaped fruit with recognizeable long and thin bristles protruding from its skin. Green when unripe, its skin turns a bright red when the fruit matures. The flesh is a translucent cream color that surrounds a single seed. Its flavor is slightly sweet and tart.

Ramen *RAH-mehn* **Ramen**
GRAINS & CEREALS A Japanese noodle dish served in a broth with pieces of meat and vegetables. Also, an instant Asian-style noodle dish sold in plastic packages.

Rape *RAH-peh* **Monkfish**
FISH & SHELLFISH A flat fish found in northern Atlantic waters. Dark brown–skinned and very ugly-looking, it buries itself in the ocean floor and lures prey with a thin filament that is connected to its head. Its flesh is sweet, firm, and dense (not flaky) resembling lobster meat. The edible flesh is found in its tail.

Rasqueta *rahs-KEH-tah* **Scraper**
EQUIPMENT A piece of curved plastic or rubber. It is used to cleanly scrape off batter or dough from a bowl or work area.

Raya *RAH-yah* **Skate**
FISH & SHELLFISH A kite-shaped flat fish with winglike fins. Mild and sweet tasting, the thin fins are the edible portion of a skate. They are often soaked in acidulated water before being cooked to get rid of a naturally occurring ammonia odor. A skate is also known as ray.

Reacción de Maillard *re-ahk-see-OHN deh MAH-ee-yahrd* **Maillard reaction**
COOKING METHOD / TECHNIQUE A browning reaction that takes place between an amino acid and a sugar. In addition to producing a brown color, it also results in the development of complex meaty flavors and aromas.

Rebanada / Rodaja / Trozo / Porción *reh-bah-NAH-dah / roh-DAH-hah / TROH-soh / pohr-see-OHN* **Slice**
COOKING METHOD / TECHNIQUE (1) A flat cut. A slice can be thick or thin. (2) A slit.

Rebanador de torta *reh-bah-nah-DOHR deh TOHR-tah* **Cake slicer**
EQUIPMENT A long, thin, bull-nosed serrated knife used to slice cakes.

Rebozado / Capeado *reh-boh-SAH-doh / kah-peh-AH-doh* **Crusted**
COOKING METHOD / TECHNIQUE Having a hardened covering. Common covering ingredients are bread crumbs, cheese, peppercorns, and herbs and spices.

Rebozar / Cubrir *reh-boh-SAHR / koo-BREER* **Dredge**
COOKING METHOD / TECHNIQUE To lightly coat a food with a dry ingredient, most commonly flour or bread crumbs.

Recado *reh-KAH-doh*
CONDIMENTS (Mexico) A marinating paste that is basic to Yucatán cooking. The thick flavorful paste is smothered on meats and seafood.

Recao *reh-KAH-oh* **Culantro**
HERBS & SPICES Long, narrow, green leaves with an intense and pungent cilantro flavor.

Recetario / Libro de cocina *reh-seh-TAH-ree-oh / LEE-broh deh koh-SEE-nah* **Cookbook**
GENERAL A book of recipes.

Recortar *reh-kohr-TAHR* **Trim**
COOKING METHOD / TECHNIQUE To cut away unwanted parts.

Reducción *reh-dook-see-OHN* **Reduction**
COOKING METHOD / TECHNIQUE The concentrated solution that results after a liquid is reduced.

Reducir *reh-doo-SEER* **Reduce**
COOKING METHOD / TECHNIQUE To concentrate the flavor and increase the viscosity of a liquid by boiling or simmering it until the water content is decreased through evaporation.

Refajo *reh-FAH-hoh*
  BEVERAGE (Colombia) A beverage made by mixing the Colombian product Kola (nonalcoholic Champagne-flavored soda) with beer or rum.

Refrescar *reh-frehs-KAHR* **Cool / Refresh**
  COOKING METHOD / TECHNIQUE (1) To lower the temperature. (2) To restore coolness or freshness. (3) To place a food item under cold water to cool down or to stop the cooking process.

Refresco *reh-FREHS-koh* **Soft drink**
  BEVERAGE A broad term for a nonalcoholic beverage.

Refrigerador *reh-free-geh-rah-DOHR* **Refrigerator**
  EQUIPMENT *See* **Nevera**.

Regador *reh-gah-DOHR* **Baster**
  EQUIPMENT A tool used for basting. Typically it is a long, hollow cylinder with an opening on one end and a rubber bulb on the other that sucks liquid in when squeezed and pours it out when the pressure on the bulb is let go.

Regaliz *reh-gah-LEES* **Licorice**
  HERBS & SPICES The dark brown root of the licorice plant from which an anise or tarragonlike flavor can be extracted. It is used to flavor candies, soft drinks, and medicines.

Regar con grasa *reh-GAHR kohn GRAH-sah* **Baste**
  COOKING METHOD / TECHNIQUE To brush, squeeze, or spoon fat or liquid over meat while it is cooking.

Rehidratar *reh-ee-drah-TAHR* **Rehydrate**
  COOKING METHOD / TECHNIQUE (1) To restore water loss. (2) To add moisture to a dried item.

Rejilla *reh-HEE-yah* **Cooling rack / Roasting rack**
  EQUIPMENT (1) A flat, metal grate used to cool baked goods. It has short legs that raise the grate above the tabletop allowing for air circulation. (2) Fitted inside a roasting pan, a framework of bars that keeps ingredients off the surface of the pan.

Rellenar *reh-yeh-NAHR* **Stuff**
  COOKING METHOD / TECHNIQUE To cram or fill into a cavity or opening.

Remojar / Poner en remojo *reh-moh-HAHR / poh-NEHR ehn reh-MOH-hoh*
Soak
  COOKING METHOD / TECHNIQUE *See* **Empapar**.

Remolacha *reh-moh-LAH-chah* **Beet**
  FRUIT & VEGETABLES A round root vegetable whose color ranges from white to blood beet red. The root is a storage house for carbohydrates. It is prized as much for its edible, nutritious leaves as it is for its sweet flesh.

Remover *reh-moh-BEHR* **Toss / Stir**
COOKING METHOD / TECHNIQUE To turn or shake food lightly.

Repollo *reh-POH-yoh* **White cabbage**
FRUIT & VEGETABLES The white-colored variety of this tight-headed, leafy green vegetable.

Reposar *reh-poh-SAHR* **Rest**
COOKING METHOD / TECHNIQUE (1) To relax. (2) To set aside and not move.

Requesón *reh-keh-SOHN* **Cottage cheese**
DAIRY A mild-flavored, fresh cheese made from pasteurized cow's milk that has been curdled by the addition of an acid and sometimes an enzyme. The cheese stays moist as not all of the whey gets drained. The texture of the cheese is lumpy with curds ranging in size from small to large.

Reserva *reh-SEHR-bah* **Reserve**
DISH (Spain)The term given to a wine of a higher quality, or wine that has been held back and aged before being sold, or both. In some countries, this is regulated but in others it is not.

Reservar *reh-sehr-BAHR* **Reserve**
COOKING METHOD / TECHNIQUE To keep and save for future use.

Restaurante *rehs-tah-oo-RAHN-teh* **Restaurant**
GENERAL A public establishment that prepares and serves food.

Revolver *reh-bohl-BEHR* **Scramble / Stir**
COOKING METHOD / TECHNIQUE (1) To beat, mix, or stir vigorously. (2) To move around.

Riñón *ree-NYOHN* **Kidney**
MEAT A glandular organ taken from cattle, swine, or lambs. Beef kidney is most recognizable as it is multi-lobed. Kidney is best from younger animals as it is more tender and mild flavored.

Rocoto *roh-KOH-toh*
FRUIT & VEGETABLES (Peru) A medium-size, round, red chile pepper that has grown in South America for thousands of years. Its flesh is similar in thickness to that of a bell pepper, but it is very spicy. It is also known as locoto.

Rocoto relleno *roh-KOH-toh reh-YEH-noh*
DISH (Peru)A dish made of rocoto peppers stuffed with a beef mixture that has been flavored with onions, olives, and spices.

Rodaballo *roh-dah-BAH-yoh* **Turbot**
FISH & SHELLFISH A firm, lean, flat fish with a mild-tasting white flesh. Found in cold northern European waters, it is often compared to Dover sole.

Rodaja *roh-DAH-hah* **Slice**
COOKING METHOD / TECHNIQUE *See* **Rebanada**.

Rodaja de pescado *roh-DAH-hah deh pehs-KAH-doh* **Fish steak**
FISH & SHELLFISH *See* **Rueda de pescado**.

Rodillo *roh-DEE-yoh* **Rolling pin**
EQUIPMENT A handheld cylindrically shaped kitchen tool that looks like a thick rod. Traditionally it is made of wood but also comes in silicone, marble, and plastic among other materials. Its main function is to flatten and stretch out dough, but it is also used to crush, pound, and shape ingredients.

Rollo *ROH-yoh* **Roll**
EQUIPMENT A cylindrically shaped object.

Romero *roh-MEH-roh* **Rosemary**
HERBS & SPICES A woody herb with pine needle–shaped leaves that are very fragrant. It has a strong flavor and aroma that are described as lemony and woodsy.

Romesco *roh-MEHS-koh*
DISH (Spain) A pimiento-based sauce that is thickened with bread and almonds and flavored with garlic, white wine, and aguardiente. It is typically served with seafood.

Ron *rohn* **Rum**
BEVERAGE
A distilled beverage made from the fermentation of sugarcane by-products and then aged. There are four basic varieties: light / white, gold / amber, anejo, and dark.

Roncal *rohn-KAHL* **Roncal**
DAIRY Spanish sheep's milk cheese. It is made in one of the seven villages in the Valle de Roncal in the north of Spain. It is a firm cheese with a nutty and piquant flavor.

Ropa vieja *ROH-pah bee-EH-hah*
DISH (Cuba) Shredded flank steak that is stewed in a slightly sweet-tasting tomato sauce. Ropa vieja literally translates to "old clothes," as the dish is said to resemble shreds of old cloth.

Roqueta *roh-KEH-tah* **Arugula**
FRUIT & VEGETABLES *See* **Rúcula**.

Roscón *rohs-KOHN*
BAKING & PASTRY (Colombia) An egg bread that is shaped like a bagel. It is often stuffed with arequipe or guava paste and sprinkled with sugar. Similar to a doughnut, it is eaten for breakfast or as a snack.

Rozar *roh-SAHR* **Rub**
COOKING METHOD / TECHNIQUE To massage or work a paste, marinade, or condiment onto an item.

Rúcula / Roqueta *ROO-koo-lah / roh-KEH-tah* **Arugula**
FRUIT & VEGETABLES A bitter salad green with a pepper flavor. It can be found in both young and mature stages. The younger the leaf, the more mild tasting.

Rueda de pescado / Rodaja de pescado *roo-EH-dah deh pehs-KAH-doh / roh-DAH-hah deh pehs-KAH-doh* **Fish steak**
FISH & SHELLFISH On average, a one-inch-thick, crosswise cut from a large fish that has been eviscerated.

Ruibarbo *roo-ee-BAHR-boh* **Rhubarb**
FRUIT & VEGETABLES A plant with a reddish pink–colored stem and dark green leaves. Although technically a vegetable, it is treated like a fruit. The celerylike stems are the only edible part of the plant. Very tart in flavor, it is always cooked before being eaten and is always mixed with a considerable amount of sugar.

Rutabaga / Nabo sueco *roo-tah-BAH-gah / NAH-boh soo-EH-koh* **Rutabaga**
FRUIT & VEGETABLES A root vegetable that is a cross between the cabbage and turnip. Shaped like a wide and stubby turnip, it has a thin, beige skin and creamed-colored flesh. Similarly to a carrot, it can be eaten raw or cooked. It is also known as Swede.

S

Sabor *sah-BOHR* **Flavor**
GENERAL A sensory experience gotten from the combination of taste, aroma, and touch.

Sacacorcho *sah-kah-KOHR-choh* **Corkscrew**
EQUIPMENT A tool used to remove the cork from bottles.

Sacarina *sah-kah-REE-nah* **Saccharin**
CONDIMENTS An artificial sweetener. Noncaloric but three hundred times as sweet as sugar, it has a bitter aftertaste and is unstable when heated.

Sal *sahl* **Salt**
HERBS & SPICES A dietary mineral made up of sodium chloride. Used as a seasoning to enhance the flavor of food, it is one of the basic tastes. Extracted from salt mines or the sea, it is a solid crystal that can take on a tinge of color (pink, white, gray) as a result of its impurities. It is an important preservative.

Salado *sah-LAH-doh* **Salty**
DESCRIPTOR Tasting of salt.

Salchicha *sahl-CHEE-chah* **Sausage**
MEAT Ground meat mixed with fat, spices, and seasoning and typically stuffed inside a casing. It can be left fresh, or cured, smoked, or dried to develop its flavor and extend its shelf life.

Salchicha blanca *sahl-CHEE-chah BLAHN-kah*
MEAT (Spain) A fresh breakfast-style pork sausage that does not contain paprika.

Salitre *sah-LEE-treh* **Potassium nitrate**
CONDIMENTS A chemical compound used as a food preservative. Also known as salt-peter. It is most commonly used in making sausages and other cured meats.

Sal marina *sahl mah-REE-nah* **Sea salt**
CONDIMENTS Salt obtained by the evaporation of seawater. In addition to the sodium chloride, it has a variety of minerals that give it a unique taste.

Sal mineral *sahl mee-neh-RAHL* **Rock salt**
CONDIMENTS Unrefined salt sold in large chunks. The impurities left in the salt can cause it to take on pale hues of gray, blue, or pink.

Salmón *sahl-MOHN* **Salmon**
FISH & SHELLFISH An anadromous fish (meaning it lives in salt water but returns to fresh water where it was born to spawn). It has a black, silvery skin and an orange pink–colored flesh. It can be purchased fresh, canned, and smoked.

Salmón ahumado *sahl-MOHN ah-oo-MAH-doh* **Smoked salmon**
FISH & SHELLFISH Fresh salmon that has been cured and flavored by smoke.

Salmonella *sahl-moh-NEH-lah* **Salmonella**
GENERAL A bacterial infection that can be transmitted to the human body through foods such as eggs, poultry, or meat. Other foods can pass along the bacteria via cross contamination.

Salmonete *sahl-moh-NEH-teh* **Red mullet**
FISH & SHELLFISH A very small saltwater fish primarily found in the Mediterranean sea. It has reddish-colored skin and firm, lean flesh that is great for grilling or frying. Despite its name it is a member of the goatfish family, not the mullet family.

Salmuera / Agua salada *sahl-moo-EH-rah / AH-gwah sah-LAH-dah* **Brine**
COOKING METHOD / TECHNIQUE A highly concentrated solution of salt and water. Sugar is sometimes added. It is used to preserve, flavor, and increase the juiciness of meats.

Salsa *SAHL-sah* **Sauce**
CONDIMENTS A flavored liquid used to accompany a food. It can be very thin or very thick, sweet or savory, smooth or chunky.

Salsa agridulce *SAHL-sah ah-gree-DOOL-seh* **Sweet-and-sour sauce**
CONDIMENTS A sauce with a flavor balance between sweet and savory. It is usually made by mixing sugar or honey with vinegar or soy sauce to create a sauce, dressing, or marinade.

Salsa barbacoa *SAHL-sah bahr-bah-KOH-ah* **Barbecue sauce**
CONDIMENTS A sauce used to baste barbecued meat and poultry. It typically contains tomatoes, vinegar, sugar, mustard, and spices.

Salsa de ciruela *SAHL-sah deh see-roo-EH-lah* **Plum sauce**
CONDIMENTS A thick, translucent, golden yellow condiment with a sweet and sour flavor. Also known as duck sauce, it is made from plums and apricots that are mixed with sugar, vinegar, and other seasonings.

Salsa condimentada *SAHL-sah kohn-dee-mehn-TAH-dah* **Relish**

CONDIMENTS A sweet or savory condiment made from chopped fruit or vegetables that have been slowly cooked with added seasonings until it thickens.

Salsa de crema *SAHL-sah deh KREH-mah* **Cream sauce**

CONDIMENTS A sauce made by adding milk or cream to a flour and butter paste (a roux). The thickness of the sauce is dependent on the ratio of flour to liquid. It is also known as béchamel sauce.

Salsa de manzana *SAHL-sah deh mahn-SAH-nah* **Applesauce**

CONDIMENTS A cooked puree of apples. Sugar and spices can be added for flavor.

Salsa de ostras *SAHL-sah deh OHS-trahs* **Oyster sauce**

CONDIMENTS A thick, dark brown condiment made from oysters, soy sauce, brine, and sugar. It is a savory sauce used in many Asian recipes or as a straight dipping sauce.

Salsa de pescado *SAHL-sah deh pehs-KAH-doh* **Fish sauce**

CONDIMENTS A dark brown sauce made from fermented fish. A staple in Southeast Asian cooking, it has a pungent aroma and salty flavor. It is used in cooking and as a condiment in dipping sauces.

Salsa de riñonada *SAHL-sah deh ree-nyoh-NAH-dah* **Suet**

CONDIMENTS The fat found surrounding the kidneys in cattle, lambs, swine, and other animals. It must be rendered before being used and must be refrigerated. It has a very low melting and smoke point.

Salsa de soya *SAHL-sah deh SOH-yah* **Soy sauce**

CONDIMENTS A dark brown condiment made from fermented soybeans, water, salt, and wheat or barley. It is salty and pungent in flavor.

Salsa de tomate *SAHL-sah deh toh-MAH-teh* **Tomato sauce**

CONDIMENTS A smooth or chunky sauce made from cooked tomatoes. It can be plain or seasoned, thick or thin, and made fresh or purchased in a can.

Salsa inglesa *SAHL-sah een-GLEH-sah* **Worcestershire sauce**

CONDIMENTS A dark brown, fermented liquid condiment made from vinegar, anchovies, molasses, tamarind, onion, garlic, sugar, salt, and spices. Originally made in Worcestershire, England, it has a deep savory flavor that is used in cooked recipes and dressings.

Salsa tartara *SAHL-sah TAHR-tah-rah* **Tartar sauce**

CONDIMENTS A chunky, mayonnaise-based sauce made with capers, pickles, onion, lemon juice, and seasonings. It is typically served with seafood.

Salsa teriyaky *SAHL-sah teh-ree-YAH-kee* **Teriyaki sauce**

CONDIMENTS A Japanese marinade consisting of soy sauce, sake, ginger, sugar, and seasonings that are boiled and reduced until it thickens to the desired viscosity. The marinade clings to meat or vegetables and because of the sugar, caramelizes the food as it cooks.

Salsa verde *SAHL-sah BEHR-deh*

CONDIMENTS (Mexico) A green-colored, tomatillo-based sauce that typically includes jalapeño pepper and cilantro. Salsa verde literally translates as "green sauce." (Spain) A sauce made by pureeing parsley with garlic, broth, and wine.

Salsify *SAHL-see-fee* **Salsify**

FRUIT & VEGETABLES The root vegetables of the salsify plant. Very long and slender, it has a rough, thin skin that is peeled before cooking. The skin's color is dependent on the variety and can be pale yellow, gray, or black. Salsify has a faint briny flavor and is sometimes referred to as oyster plant.

Salteado *sahl-teh-AH-doh* **Sauté**

COOKING METHOD / TECHNIQUE *See* **Saltear**.

Saltear (a fuego vivo) / Salteado *sahl-teh-AHR (ah-foo-EH-goh BEE-boh) / sahl-teh-AH-doh* **Sauté**

COOKING METHOD / TECHNIQUE To cook food quickly with little fat in a sauté or frying pan. The food is constantly moved around.

Stir-fry

COOKING METHOD / TECHNIQUE To quickly fry food in a small amount of fat in a large pan (typically a wok) while constantly stirring. Stir-frying is often used in Asian cuisine.

Salvado *sahl-VAH-doh* **Bran**

GRAINS & CEREALS The outer layer of cereal grains (wheat, oats, and rice) that is typically removed during the milling process. It is high in fiber and vitamins and minerals. It is used in breakfast cereals and as an ingredient in baked goods.

Salvado de arroz *sahl-VAH-doh deh ah-RROHS* **Rice bran**

GRAINS & CEREALS The outer layer of the rice grain that is high in soluble fiber.

Salvado de avena *sahl-VAH-doh deh ah-BEH-nah* **Oat bran**

GRAINS & CEREALS The outer edible layer of the oat kernel that contains a high amount of soluble fiber.

Salvado de trigo *sahl-VAH-doh deh TREE-goh* **Wheat bran**

GRAINS & CEREALS The rough outer coating of the wheat kernel that contains a high amount of fiber.

Salvia *SAHL-vee-ah* **Sage**

HERBS & SPICES Light bluish green leaves with a fuzzy texture that are used as an herb. Its flavor is described as earthy, minty, and peppery and it is often paired with roasted meats.

Sancocho de patitas *sahn-KOH-choh deh pah-TEE-tahs*

DISH (Puerto Rico) A hearty stew made from pork trotters (feet), starchy root vegetables, and garbanzos.

Sancochado *sahn-koh-CHAH-doh*

DISH (Peru) A beef and root vegetable stew that is abundant in sweet potato and yuca.

Sancochar *sahn-koh-CHAHR* **Parboil**

COOKING METHOD / TECHNIQUE To partially cook an ingredient by boiling it briefly. The ingredient will finish cooking at a later time, most likely with a different technique. Parboiling is used as a time-saving technique to ensure that ingredients with different cooking times will be ready at the same time.

Sancocho *sahn-KOH-choh*

DISH (Colombia) A meat and starchy vegetables stew.

Sancocho de gallina *sahn-KOH-choh deh gah-YEE-nah*

DISH (Colombia) A stew made with chicken and starchy vegetables.

Sandía *sahn-DEE-ah* **Watermelon**

FRUIT & VEGETABLES Typically a large, elongated fruit that averages about fifteen pounds. Its skin is green with white striations and its flesh is red and filled with black seeds. Very juicy, sweet, and refreshing, it has a high water content. There is a seedless variety.

Sándwich / Bocadillo *SAHN-weech / boh-kah-DEE-yoh* **Sandwich**

GENERAL A dish made up of a filling held between two pieces of bread.

Sándwich de miga *SAHN-weech deh MEE-gah*

DISH (Argentina) Thin sandwiches made with crustless, buttered white sandwich bread. Typical fillings are cheese and ham and cheese.

Sangría *sahn-GREE-ah* **Sangria**

BEVERAGE A wine-based punch popular in Spain and Portugal. Its vivid red color inspired its name (Spanish for "bloody"). Made with red wine, soda water, a liqueur such as brandy, and chopped fruit, it is served over ice. White sangria is a variation made with white wine.

Sangrita *sahn-GREE-tah* **Sangrita**

BEVERAGE Popular in Mexico, a tomato-based drink often served to accompany a tequila shot. It is made by blending tomato and orange juice and adding lime juice and hot chiles or Tabasco sauce.

Sapote *sah-POH-teh* **Sapote**

FRUIT & VEGETABLES The general term for a very soft and ripe fruit. There are three unrelated fruit with sapote as part of their name—mamey sapote, black sapote, and white sapote.

Sapote blanco *sah-POH-teh BLAHN-koh* **White sapote**

FRUIT & VEGETABLES A round fruit with a thin, green skin that turns yellow when mature. Its cream-colored flesh is very soft and sweet with the appearance of a tart vanilla pudding. It is not related to mamey or black sapote.

Sapote negro *sah-POH-teh NEH-groh* **Black sapote**
  FRUIT & VEGETABLES A round fruit that looks like a rotting green tomato. The flesh turns a soft dark brown when ripe with an appearance similar to that of chocolate pudding. Its flavor is somewhat bland.

Sardinas *sahr-DEE-nahs* **Sardines**
  FISH & SHELLFISH A term that broadly describes small, soft-boned, saltwater fish such as herring and pilchard. Iridescent and silver-skinned, the fish swim in large schools. These fatty fish are best grilled or broiled and are often found canned.

Sargo *SAHR-goh* **Sea bream**
  FISH & SHELLFISH A small, saltwater fish that lives near the coast and has an average weight of four pounds. Feeding off crustaceans and mollusks results in its very flavorful meat. It has a round-shaped body and silver-colored skin.

Sartén *sahr-TEHN* **Frying pan / Sauté pan**
  EQUIPMENT A shallow, round cooking vessel with low, sloped sides used to cook food with a hot fat. It has a long handle attached to one side and ranges from eight to twelve inches in width. Its shallowness is important as it allows the vapors from the pan to evaporate quickly and prevents the food from steaming. It is also called a skillet.

Sartén antiadherente *sahr-TEHN ahn-tee-ahd-eh-REHN-teh*
Nonstick frying pan
  EQUIPMENT A frying or sauté pan coated with Teflon or another material that does not allow food to adhere to it.

Sartén de hierro *sahr-TEHN deh ee-EH-rroh* **Cast-iron skillet**
  EQUIPMENT A long-handled frying pan made from ironware. Ironware is prized for its heat-absorbing and -retaining qualities. A frying pan typically is round with sloping sides. It has a no-stick finish when seasoned.

Sashimi *sah-SHEE-mee* **Sashimi**
  FISH & SHELLFISH A Japanese preparation of sliced fresh raw fish. It is served accompanied by pickled radish and ginger and a soy dipping sauce.

Sauco *sah-OO-koh* **Elderberry**
  HERBS & SPICES The fruit of the elder tree. Its dark purplish black berry is very tart, and while it can be eaten raw, it is best when cooked. It is most often used for making preserves or wine.

Sazón *sah-SOHN* **Seasoning**
  CONDIMENTS The salt or spice added to a food to enhance its flavor.

Sazonar / Condimentar *sah-soh-NAHR / kohn-dee-mehn-TAHR* **Season**
  COOKING METHOD / TECHNIQUE To enhance the flavor of food by adding a salt or spice.

Scotch *skohch* **Scotch**

BEVERAGE A barley-based whiskey that is made in Scotland and conforms to strict Scottish standards.

Sebo *SEH-boh* **Tallow**

MEAT Rendered beef fat. It is solid at room temperature.

Seco *SEH-koh* **Dry**

DESCRIPTOR (1) Without moisture. (2) Said of a wine that is not sweet.

Secar al aire *seh-KAHR ahl AH-ee-reh* **Air dry**

COOKING METHOD / TECHNIQUE To dehydrate through exposure to air.

Segmentar *sehg-mehn-TAHR* **Segment**

COOKING METHOD / TECHNIQUE To divide or cut into (segments) pieces.

Segmento *sehg-MEHN-toh* **Segment**

FRUIT & VEGETABLE The membrane-enclosed sections found inside a citrus fruit.

Sellar *seh-YAHR* **Seal**

COOKING METHOD / TECHNIQUE (1) To make tight. (2) To prevent something from entering or escaping by securely closing its opening.

Sear

COOKING METHOD / TECHNIQUE A cooking technique wherein meat is browned quickly over high heat and with a small amount of fat. This provides the meat with a golden brown color and crust, and a deep flavor.

Semilla *seh-MEE-yah* **Seed**

HERBS & SPICES A small, embryonic plant enclosed in a hard covering. A seed is referred to as a kernel.

Semilla de adormidera *seh-MEE-yahs deh ah-dohr-mee-DEH-rah* **Poppy seed**

HERBS & SPICES The very small, dark blue gray seed that come from the poppy flower. Crunchy and nutty in flavor, poppy seeds are used in sweet and savory recipes and are popular toppings on breads. They are available in whole or ground form.

Semilla de ajonjolí *seh-MEE-yah deh ah-hohn-hoh-LEE* **Sesame seed**

HERBS & SPICES See **Semilla de sésamo**.

Semilla de apio *seh-MEE-yah deh AH-pee-oh* **Celery seed**

HERBS & SPICES The seed of a celery plant. It is has a strong celery flavor and is available whole or ground.

Semilla de eneldo *seh-MEE-yah deh eh-NEHL-doh* **Dill seed**

HERBS & SPICES The seed of the dill plant with a flavor and appearance similar to that of the caraway seed. Brown, flat, and oval-shaped, it has a stronger flavor than the leaves of the dill plant, which are used as an herb.

Semilla de girasol *seh-MEE-yah deh hee-rah-SOHL* **Sunflower seed**
HERBS & SPICES The seed of the sunflower plant whose hull is black with white stripes. The small, beige-colored sunflower seeds can be dried or roasted and are sold plain or salted. They are available hulled or in the shell.

Semilla de hinojo *seh-MEE-yah deh ee-NOH-hoh* **Fennel seed**
HERBS & SPICES The oval, brownish green seed from the fennel plant. It is similar in flavor and appearance to an anise seed except it is larger. Available whole or ground, fennel seeds can be used in sweet or savory recipes.

Semilla de mostaza *seh-MEE-yahs deh mohs-TAH-sah* **Mustard seed**
HERBS & SPICES The seed of the mustard plant. A small, round seed, its color is deter- mined by the type of plant it comes from. Most common are the yellow or brown mustard seeds but mustard seeds can also be black or white.

Semilla de sésamo / Semilla de ajonjolí *seh-MEE-yah deh SEH-sah-moh / seh-MEE-yah deh ah-hohn-hoh-LEE* **Sesame seed**
HERBS & SPICES The oil-rich seed of the sesame plant. Small, black or cream-colored sesame seeds are used whole in dishes and impart a nutty flavor. Often baked onto breads, bagels, and rolls, they can also be ground into a paste called tahini.

Sémola *SEH-moh-lah* **Semolina**
GRAINS & CEREALS Wheat that is coarsely ground. Seminola can be specifically a coarsely ground hard durum wheat used to make pasta, or a coarsely ground soft wheat used to make breakfast cereal.

Sepia *SEH-pee-ah* **Cuttlefish**
FISH & SHELLFISH A relative of the squid and octopus that resembles a squid and also has ink sacs. Often tenderized before cooking due to its tough and chewy meat.

Sesos *SEH-sohs* **Brain**
MEAT Beef, lamb, or pork organ meat. It is often referred to as a type of offal.

Seta / Champiñón / Hongo *SEH-tah / cham-pee-ny-OHN / OHN-goh* **Mushroom**
FRUIT & VEGETABLES An edible fungus. It can be cultivated or forged in the wild. Its flavor ranges from mild to nutty and earthy, and its color ranges from white to black. There are thousands of varieties with different sizes, colors, and shapes. They are available fresh or dried.

Seta orellanes *SEH-tah oh-reh-YAH-nehs* **Oyster mushroom**
FRUIT & VEGETABLES An edible wild mushroom that is now also cultivated. Its name comes from its fanlike shape that resembles an oyster. Creamy white in color, it has a flavor that mellows when cooked.

Seta portobello *SEH-tah pohr-toh-BEH-loh* **Portobello mushroom**
FRUIT & VEGETABLE A large, brown cultivated mushroom that is recognizable by its wide, flat cap and fully exposed gills. A fully mature cremini, which is a variety of the common white mushroom, it has deep flavor and meaty texture is due to its age and reduced moisture content.

Seta salvaje *SEH-tah sahl-BAH-heh* **Wild mushrooms**

FRUIT & VEGETABLES A mushroom that has been harvested from the wild (not cultivated). Wild mushrooms are available fresh or dried.

Seta shiitake *SEH-tah shee-TAH-kee* **Shiitake mushroom**

FRUIT & VEGETABLES A cultivated Asian mushroom with a wide, dark brown cap and inedible stem. Meaty and a bit chewy in texture, it has a rich flavor. Shiitakes are available fresh and dried.

Shangurro / Changurro / Txangurro *shahn-GOO-rroh / chahn-GOO-rroh / chahn-GOO-rroh*

DISH (Spain) A dish from the Basque region that utilizes the giant crabs (centollos) of the area. The crabmeat is removed from the shell, cooked, and mixed with a spicy sauce before being returned to the shell. It is then topped with bread crumbs and butter and broiled.

Sidra *SEE-drah* **Cider**

BEVERAGE A fermented fruit juice typically made from apples. The alcohol content ranges from 3 to 9 percent. Most ciders are sparkling but they can be found still and there are nonalcoholic varieties.

(Spain) A typical drink of Asturias in the north of Spain. It is a hard and very dry cider. There is a sparkling version that is somewhat similar to Champagne.

Silla *SEE-yah* **Saddle**

MEAT The connected two loins found on either side of the backbone. Resembling a saddle placed on top of an animal, it is often a cut of lamb, veal, or venison.

Siluro *see-LOO-roh* **Catfish**

FISH & SHELLFISH A freshwater fish that has prominent barbels extending from its mouth area resembling whiskers. Its skin is thick and slippery with no scales and should be removed before cooking.

Sin pepitas / Sin semillas *seen peh-PEE-tahs / seen seh-MEE-yahs* **Seedless**

DESCRIPTOR Without seeds.

Sin semillas *seen seh-MEE-yahs* **Seedless**

DESCRIPTOR See **Sin pepitas**.

Sirope *see-ROH-peh* **Syrup**

CONDIMENTS See **Jarabe**.

Sobresada *soh-breh-SAH-dah*

DISH (Spain) A soft chorizo spread that gets its origin from the island of Mallorca. Made by pureeing chorizo and fat from cured ham with seasonings in a food processor, it is used as a sandwich filling or spread on toast.

Socarrat *soh-kah-RRAHT*

DISH (Spain) The crust of rice that forms on the bottom of a paella pan.

Sofrito *soh-FREE-toh*

DISH (Cuba) A sauté of finely chopped onion, green bell pepper, and garlic in olive oil. It is used as the base for many dishes.

(Puerto Rico) A sautéed mixture of cachucha peppers, cubanelle peppers, onion, garlic, plum tomato, cilantro, and recao.

Soja / Soya *SOH-hah / SOH-yah* **Soybean**

FRUIT & VEGETABLES A legume whose pod is inedible. It contains all essential amino acids making it a great source of protein. Eaten fresh, the green soybean has a nutty and buttery taste and meaty texture. Immature soybeans are steamed and served as edamame. Soybeans are a source for many foods including soy sauce, soy milk, tofu, and soybean oil.

Soldaditos de Pavia *sohl-dah-DEE-tohs deh PAH-bee-ah*

DISH (Spain) Log-shaped fresh cod fritters.

Solomillo *soh-loh-MEE-yoh* **Sirloin / Tenderloin**

MEAT (1) A cut of beef located between the short loin and round. Typically cut into steaks, it is a flavorful cut with a firm texture. (2) An elongated muscle found between the rib and the sirloin. Because it is one of the least active muscles, it is very tender. When cut into steaks, it is referred to as filet mignon.

Sopa *SOH-pah* **Soup**

GENERAL A liquid food made by cooking meat and/or vegetables in a water-based solution. Soup can be smooth or chunky, thick or thin.

Sopa aguada *SOH-pah ah-GWAH-dah*

DISH (Mexico) A brothy soup.

Sopa azteca *SOH-pah ahs-TEH-kah*

DISH (Mexico) Another name for tortilla soup.

Sopa de tortilla *SOH-pah deh tohr-TEE-yah*

DISH (Mexico) An iconic Mexican soup made from a chicken-broth base that is flavored with toasted dried chiles. The soup is then garnished with a number of ingredients that may include cheese, avocado, crema, shredded chicken, chicharrones, and fried tortilla strips.

Sopa seca *SOH-pah SEH-kah*

DISH (Mexico) Served before the main dish, a rice dish that is often made with a tomato puree and vegetables. Sopa seca literally translates as "dry soup."

Sope *SOH-peh*

DISH (Mexico) A small, round, disk-shaped corn masa (about two inches in diameter) that is baked or fried and topped with beans, meat, chorizo, and/or cheese. Depending on the region, it can be called picada, garnacha, chalupa, memela, gordita, or migadas.

Sorbete *sohr-BEH-teh* **Sorbet**

BAKING & PASTRY A frozen dessert made with a water-based mixture flavored with a sweetened fruit puree, chocolate, or wine. It does not contain dairy.

Sorrentinos *soh-rrehn-TEE-nohs*

DISH (Argentina) A large, round ravioli stuffed with cheese and basil and served with tomato sauce.

Soya *SOH-yah* **Soy**

FRUIT & VEGETABLES *See* **Soja**.

Subir *soo-BEER* **Rise**

COOKING METHOD / TECHNIQUE (1) To lift. (2) To reach a higher position.

Sudar *soo-DAHR* **Sweat**

COOKING METHOD / TECHNIQUE A cooking technique that softens vegetables without browning them. Vegetables are covered and cooked over low heat in a small amount of fat.

Suero *soo-EH-ròh* **Whey**

DAIRY The liquid portion of milk that separates from the solids (curds) when cheese is made or when milk sours.

(Colombia) Similar to sour cream, the whey from fermented milk.

Sulfito *sool-FEE-toh* **Sulfites**

GENERAL The salt of sulfurous acid used as a preservative in food and beverages. It is said to cause allergic reactions in some people. It is added to wine to stop fermentation and prevent oxidation. Wines that contain sulfites must be labeled.

Suquet *soo-KEHT*

DISH (Spain) A Catalan fish stew thickened with almond puree.

Suspiro limeño *soos-PEE-roh lee-MEH-noh*

DISH (Peru) A two-layer dessert wherein the bottom layer is caramel (*manjar blanco*) and the top layer is meringue that is dusted with cinnamon.

T

Tabla de picar *TAH-blah deh pee-KAHR* **Cutting board**

EQUIPMENT A flat surface made of wood, plastic, or glass upon which to cut. It can be rectangular or round.

Taco *TAH-koh*

DISH (Mexico) A snack food eaten throughout Mexico at all hours of the day. It is broadly defined as a soft corn tortilla wrapped around a filling. There is no limit to what can be stuffed in tacos.

Tacos al carbón *TAH-kohs ahl kahr-BOHN*

DISH (Mexico) Tacos stuffed with charcoal grilled ingredients, which can include meats and vegetables.

Tacu tacu *TAH-koo TAH-koo*
DISH (Peru) A black bean and rice pancake. It is made by mixing mashed black beans and rice, shaping them into a pancake, and frying it in a bit of oil. It is served as an accompaniment.

Tahini *tah-EE-nee* **Tahini**
CONDIMENTS A thick paste made from ground sesame seeds.

Tajadas *tah-HAH-dahs*
DISH (Venezuela) Fried sweet plantains.

Tamal *tah-MAHL*
DISH (Mexico) A prepared masa (cornmeal dough) that is typically stuffed with meat, cheese, or chiles and wrapped in corn husks or banana leaves. Tamales are steamed and unwrapped before being eaten and are often accompanied by crema.

Tamal de dulce *tah-MAHL deh DOOL-seh*
DISH (Mexico) A sweet tamal made with sugar and sweet ingredients instead of savory ones. It is eaten as a snack or for dessert.

Tamal en cazuela *tah-MAHL ehn kah-soo-EH-lah*
DISH Literally translates to tamal in a pot. Pork and dried beef (*tasajo*) are stewed in a pot to which a special ground corn is added and allowed to simmer and thicken. (Cuba) A hearty stew with the consistency of porridge.
(Mexico) A dish made in a large pot on the stovetop or in the oven. It consists of two layers of masa sandwiched between a meat, vegetable, and/or bean stuffing. The pot needs to be tightly covered while cooking.

Tamal en hoja *tah-MAHL ehn OH-hah*
DISH (Cuba) A dish made from a special corn that is ground and made into a dough and flavored with the classic sofrito (onion, garlic, green pepper) and roast pork that is finely chopped. All the ingredients are well blended and steamed in corn husks (tamal in a leaf).

Tamarillo / Tomate de árbol *tah-mah-REE-yoh / to-MAH-teh deh AHR-bohl*
Tamarillo / Tree tomato
FRUIT & VEGETABLES An egg-shaped fruit, about two inches in length, that can be red, purple, or yellow in color. Its soft flesh is filled with edible seeds similar to a tomato's. Its flavor is tangy and sweet. It is almost always cooked as its skin tends to be bitter when raw.

Tamarindo *tah-mah-REEN-doh* **Tamarind**
HERBS & SPICES The brown pod that grows on the tamarind tree and contains small seeds and a tart pulp that becomes more sour when it is dried. The pulp is used as a flavoring condiment for savory recipes.

Tamiz *tah-MEES* **Sieve**
EQUIPMENT *See* **Criba**.

Tamizar / Cerner *tah-mee-SAHR / sehr-NEHR* **Sift**
COOKING METHOD / TECHNIQUE To separate dry ingredients by passing them through a strainer or mesh. Sifting is used to incorporate air and help lighten ingredients.

Tanino *tah-NEE-noh* **Tannin**
DESCRIPTOR An astringent substance that is found in seeds, stems, peels, and bark. It is an expected characteristic in wine and tea.

Tapar *tah-PAHR* **Top**
COOKING METHOD / TECHNIQUE (1) To cover. (2) To provide a topping or layer.

Tapas *TAH-pahs*
DISH (Spain) Bite-size appetizers eaten before dinner, often accompanied by a glass of wine.

Tapioca, perlas de *tah-pee-OH-kah , PEHR-lahs* **Tapioca pearls**
GRAINS & CEREALS Starch extracted from the cassava (yuca) root. Used as a thickening agent, it comes in various forms with the two most common being flour (used like cornstarch) and pearls (which must be soaked before being used).

Taquería *tah-keh-REE-ah*
GENERAL (Mexico) A taco stand.

Taro *TAH-roh* **Taro root**
FRUIT & VEGETABLES The starchy root of the taro plant. Rough, brown, and hairy skin surrounds a cream-colored flesh that is neutral flavored, similar to a starchy potato, and must be cooked before being eaten. Taro has large, green, ornamental leaves (called callaloo in the Caribbean) that can be eaten if cooked.

Tarta *TAHR-tah* **Tart**
BAKING & PASTRY A sweet or savory pastry with a straight-edged, shallow crust. It does not have a top crust. Fillings can be added before or after the crust is baked.

Tarta de queso *TAHR-tah deh KEH-soh* **Cheesecake**
BAKING & PASTRY A cheese-based tart made with a fresh cheese, typically cream cheese (New York style) or ricotta (Italian style). It can have a crust or be crustless and its texture can range from dense to light and airy.

Tarwi *TAHR-wee*
FRUIT & VEGETABLES (Peru) A legume native to the Andean region of South America that is very high in protein. The white bean is used in soups, stews, and salads.

Tasajo / Cecina *tah-SAH-hoh / seh-SEE-nah* **Beef jerky**
MEAT Preserved beef that has been stripped of fat, cut into strips, marinated, cured, and dried.

Tasca *TAHS-kah*
GENERAL (Spain) A bar where tapas and drinks are served.

Taza *TAH-sah* **Cup**

MEASUREMENTS A unit of measure for either wet or dry ingredients. It measures 8 fluid ounces for wet ingredients but varies in weight for dry ingredients.

Tazas de medir / Jarras de medir *TAH-sahs deh meh-DEER / HAH-rrahs deh meh-DEER* **Measuring cups**

EQUIPMENT A kitchen tool used to measure food in liquid or dry form. For dry measurements measuring cups come in sets that consist of 1/4-, 1/3-, 1/2-, and 1-cup sizes. Liquid measurements are taken with a cup that has markings every 1/4- and 1/3-cup intervals.

Té *teh* **Tea**

BEVERAGE A beverage made by rehydrating and steeping the dried leaves or buds of the tea plant in water. The various processing methods for the leaves determine the individual characteristics of each tea. Tea can be served hot or cold.

Té de uña de gato *teh deh OO-nyah deh GAH-toh*

BEVERAGE (Peru) An infused tea beverage made from an Amazonian plant called cat's claw. It is said to have curative properties.

Té negro *teh NEH-groh* **Black Tea**

BEVERAGE A tea made with leaves that are fermented and oxidized before they are dried. This results in tea that has a very strong flavor and dark amber color.

Tejas *TEH-hahs*

DISH (Peru) A confection filled with caramel (manjar blanco) and covered with a sugar coating similar to fondant.

Tejido conjuntivo *teh-HEE-doh kohn-hoon-TEE-boh* **Connective tissue**

MEAT The tough, fibrous tissue that surrounds muscle fibers. Collagen and elastin are forms of this tissue that must either be removed (elastin) or slowly cooked in moist heat to allow it to break down and gelatinize (collagen).

Tejido de bambú / Alfombrilla de bambú *teh-HEE-doh deh bahm-BOO / ahl-fohm-BREE-yah deh bahm-BOO* **Bamboo mat**

EQUIPMENT A flexible mat made of thin bamboo sticks tied together with string. Bamboo mats are primarily used for rolling sushi.

Telojete *teh-loh-HEH-teh* **Pestle**

EQUIPMENT One piece of a two-part kitchen tool called a mortar and pestle. It is a thick, blunt stick used to crush and mash ingredients.

Tembleque *tehm-BLEH-keh*

DISH (Puerto Rico) Coconut flan or pudding.

Temperatura *tehm-peh-rah-TOO-rah* **Temperature**

MEASUREMENTS The degree of hotness or coldness. Measured with the Celsius or Fahrenheit scale.

Temperatura ambiente *tehm-peh-rah-TOO-rah ahm-bee-EHN-teh* **Room temperature**

MEASUREMENTS Ambient temperature. A comfortable dwelling temperature, for scientific purposes it is calculated at 70°F.

Templar *tehm-PLAHR* **Temper**

COOKING METHOD / TECHNIQUE (1) To slowly increase the temperature of an ingredient (as with eggs and milk). (2) A technique used to stabilize chocolate by melting and cooling it. This results in a glossier and more workable (pliable) chocolate. It is necessary when chocolate will be used for decorating or candy making since without tempering chocolate will produce gray streaks on its surface after sitting for some time.

Tenaza / Pinza *teh-NAH-sah / PEEN-sah* **Tong**

EQUIPMENT A tweeezerlike, handheld kitchen tool used for picking up objects. It is often used when grilling.

Tendón *tehn-DOHN* **Tendon**

MEAT An inelastic but flexible band that connects the muscle to the bone.

Tenedor *teh-neh-DOHR* **Fork**

EQUIPMENT A handheld utensil used for eating or serving food. It is made of a handle that has two to five tines protruding from it. Used mostly in the West for eating, a fork stabs or lifts food that then gets lifted to the mouth or taken to the plate.

Tentempié / Botana *tehn-TEHM-pee-eh / boh-TAH-nah* **Snack**

GENERAL A canapé or hors d'oeuvre, a small bite offered before a meal.

Tequeño *teh-KEH-nyoh*

DISH (Venezeula) White cheese wrapped in bread dough and deep-fried. It is one of the most popular snack foods of Venezuela.

Tequesquite *teh-kehs-KEE-teh*

GENERAL (Mexico) Limestone used in the preparation of nixtamal for making masa.

Tequila *teh-KEE-lah* **Tequila**

BEVERAGE A distilled spirit made from the sap of the agave plant. This plant grows particularly well in and around the small town of Tequila (located in the state of Jalisco). Therefore, just like Champagne and Cognac, in order to be classified tequila, tequila must be made in the state of Jalisco. All others are called mescal. Although Mexican law states that tequila must be at least 51 percent agave, the best tequila is 100 percent.

Termometro *tehr-MOH-meh-troh* **Thermometer**

EQUIPMENT An instrument that measures temperature.

Ternera *tehr-NEH-rah* **Veal**

MEAT The meat from a calf one to three months old. Due to its young age, controlled milk-fed diet, and limited movement, its meat is very tender and pale in color.

SPANISH-ENGLISH **T**

Ternera, chuleta *tehr-NEH-rah, choo-LEH-tah* **Veal, chop**
  MEAT An individual cut of veal from the loin area that includes a rib.

Ternera, escalopa *tehr-NEH-rah, ehs-kah-LOH-pah* **Veal, escalope**
  MEAT A boneless veal fillet that has been pounded thin.

Terrina *teh-RREE-nah* **Terrine**
  EQUIPMENT A long, rectangular, glazed ceramic or terra-cotta dish with tall, straight sides and a tight-fitting lid. It is used to shape and chill pâtés.
  MEAT A mixture of ground meat or fish and fat that has been shaped in a terrine, cooked, and then chilled. It Is also known as pâté.

Terrones de azúcar *teh-RROH-nehs deh ah-SOO-kahr* **Sugar cubes**
  CONDIMENTS Sugar crystals that have been mixed with simple syrup and formed into cubes.

Tetera *teh-TEH-rah* **Teapot**
  EQUIPMENT A vessel used for brewing tea. Typically a teapot has a handle, a spout, and often a strainer to hold or catch loose tea leaves.

Tibio *TEE-bee-oh* **Luke warm**
  DESCRIPTOR Tepid. Moderately warm. Neither hot nor cold.

Tiburón *tee-boo-ROHN* **Shark**
  FISH & SHELLFISH A very large saltwater fish with dense, lowfat meat. The meat must be soaked in acidulated water before being cooked to remove its natural ammonia odor. It is sold in steaks or chunks.

Tijeras de cocina *tee-HEH-rahs deh koh-SEE-nah* **Kitchen shears**
  EQUIPMENT Scissors used for cutting food and other kitchen tasks.

Tinga poblana *TEEN-gah pohb-LAH-nah*
  DISH (Mexico) A tomato-based pork stew that is flavored with chipotles and often contains potatoes.

Tinta de calamar *TEEN-tah deh kah-lah-MAHR* **Squid ink**
  FISH & SHELLFISH The dark purple black ink found inside a sac in the squid. It is used for coloring and flavoring.

Tira *TEE-rah* **Shred**
  COOKING METHOD / TECHNIQUE A thin, narrow strip.

Tirabeque *tee-rah-BEH-keh* **Snow pea**
  FRUIT & VEGETABLES A flat, green-colored, thin, fresh bean with an edible pod. It is picked when immature and contains very small peas.

Tiradito *tee-rah-DEE-toh*
  DISH (Peru) Small slices of raw fish similar in size to Japanese sashimi that are marinated with lime juice, ginger, and a spicy chile.

Tocino *toh-SEE-noh* **Bacon**
MEAT *See* Beicon.

Tocino del cielo *toh-SEE-noh dehl see-EH-loh*
DISH (Spain) A very rich custard made without milk and baked in a caramelized pan. The custard is made with egg yolks, sugar, and water.

Tomate *toh-MAH-teh* **Tomato**
FRUIT & VEGETABLES The fruit that grows on the tomato vine. Typically round, but also elongated or pear-shaped, a tomato has an edible thin skin and its flesh is filled with small, edible seeds in its center. When immature, all tomatoes are green and tart and turn sweeter with their color changing to pink and orange then red. There are about seventy-five hundred varieties, each with its own color, shape, and flavor.

Tomate amarillo *toh-MAH-teh ah-mah-REE-yoh* **Yellow tomato**
FRUIT & VEGETABLES A variety of tomato that is not widely available. Usually grown from heirloom seeds, it has a thin, yellow skin and a very sweet flesh.

Tomate cherry *toh-MAH-teh CHEH-rree* **Cherry tomato**
FRUIT & VEGETABLES A small tomato, either red or yellow, about one inch wide. It sweetness is due to its low acidity.

Tomate de árbol *to-MAH-teh deh AHR-bohl* **Tamarillo**
FRUIT & VEGETABLES *See* Tamarillo.

Tomate en rama *toh-MAH-teh ehn RAH-mah* **Vine-ripened tomato**
FRUIT & VEGETABLES A tomato that is left to ripen on the vine.

Tomate hidropónico *toh-MAH-teh ee-droh-POH-nee-koh* **Hydroponic tomato**
FRUIT & VEGETABLES A greenhouse tomato grown in a liquid solution instead of soil. Environmental factors such as light and temperature are controlled, as is exposure to pests and weeds. It allows for tomatoes to be grown when soil and outside temperature are unsuitable.

Tomate pera *toh-MAH-teh PEH-rah* **Plum tomato**
FRUIT & VEGETABLES An egg-shaped tomato with significantly less seeds and pulp than round tomatoes. Its higher proportion of flesh makes it suitable for making sauce. It is also known as a Roma tomato.

Tomate secado al sol *toh-MAH-teh seh-KAH-doh ahl sohl* **Sun-dried tomato**
FRUIT & VEGETABLES A tomato that has been dehydrated by the sun. It has a concentrated, sweet flavor, a wrinkled skin and a chewy texture. Sun-dried tomatoes are available packed in oil or dried and kept in a plastic bag.

Tomate seco *toh-MAH-teh SEH-koh* **Dried tomato**
FRUIT & VEGETABLES A tomato that has been dehydrated by a dehydrator or an oven. It has a concentrated, sweet flavor a wrinkled skin and a chewy texture. Dried tomatoes are available packed in oil or dried and kept in a plastic bag.

Tomatillo toh-mah-TEE-yoh **Tomatillo**
FRUIT & VEGETABLES A small, round, green fruit that is surrounded by a thin, paper-like husk, which is inedible and must be removed. A member of the gooseberry family, the thin-skinned fruit is filled with small, edible seeds in its center. Tart and tangy in flavor, its flesh is firm and can be eaten raw or cooked. It is very popular in Mexican cuisine.

Tomillo toh-MEE-yoh **Thyme**
HERBS & SPICES Member of the mint family, an herb with a woody stem and very small, oval leaves. It has a pungent woody and lemony flavor. It is sold in bunches when fresh but also available dried, and is a member of the traditional bouquet garni.

Toronja toh-ROHN-hah **Grapefruit**
FRUIT & VEGETABLES A large citrus fruit that is more tart than sweet and is somewhat bitter. Its fragrant yellow skin must be peeled and its white pith removed. The interior flesh is made up of juicy segments that can range in color from yellow to a deep reddish pink. Its juice is a popular morning beverage.

Torreja toh-RREH-hah **French toast**
BAKING & PASTRY A dish made from slices of bread that have been dipped in an egg-and-milk mixture and panfried on both sides until golden brown. It is typically topped with maple syrup, fresh fruit, and/or whipped cream.

Torrijas toh-RREE-hahs
DISH (Spain) Bread dipped in a milk-and-egg mixture and panfried. Similar to bread pudding, torrijas are eaten as dessert.

Torta / Pastel TOHR-tah / pahs-TEHL **Cake**
BAKING & PASTRY A baked good made with flour, sugar, and eggs as well as some sort of leavener. It is typically baked in a pan or mold in the oven.

Tortilla tohr-TEE-yah **Omelete**
DISH (Spain) A dish made with beaten eggs cooked in a buttered sauté pan until the eggs set and is then folded in half onto itself. A filling of sautéed vegetables or cheese can be placed inside the folded egg.

Tortilla
BAKING & PASTRY (Mexico) A thin, unleavened, griddle cake made from fresh *masa* (corn dough). It is a staple in Mexican cuisine.

Tortilla a la gallega tohr-TEE-yah ah lah gah-YEH-gah
DISH (Spain) A variation of the tortilla espanola commonly found in Galicia. It contains potatoes, onions, chorizo, and pimientos.

Tortilla española tohr-TEE-yah ehs-pah-NYOH-lah
DISH (Spain) A large potato and onion omelet shaped like a round cake. Cooked entirely on the stovetop, the thinly sliced potatoes and onion are gently cooked in olive oil until limp. The egg is then added to the pan and gently allowed to set until

carefully turned over. The omelet is usually about an inch thick. A slice can be eaten for any meal or a small piece taken as a tapa.

Tortita *tohr-TEE-tah* **Biscuit**
GRAINS & CEREALS *See* **Galleta**.

Tostada *tohs-TAH-dah* **Toast**
COOKING METHOD / TECHNIQUE To brown an ingredient using dry heat.
DISH (Mexico) A fried, crispy tortilla topped with any variety of ingredients, such as shredded chicken, mashed beans, shredded lettuce, crumbled cheese, and a chili sauce. The tortilla can be small and bite-size or larger, about six inches wide.

Tostadora *tohs-tah-DOH-rah* **Toaster**
EQUIPMENT A small electric kitchen appliance that toasts breads. It is typically constructed as a rectangular box with two to four slits on its top where the slices of bread are inserted.

Tostones / Chatinos *tohs-TOH-nehs / chah-TEE-nohs*
DISH (Cuba) Unripe (green) plantains that are sliced, shallow fried, smashed, and fried again. They are salted and served with a wedge of lime.

Totopos *toh-TOH-pohs*
DISH (Mexico) Fried tortilla chips.

Tres leches *trehs LEH-chehs*
DISH A very popular dessert made from a yellow cake that is soaked in a mixture of three milks—whole, evaporated, and condensed. It is typically topped with meringue. It is said to have originated in Nicaragua.

Trigo *TREE-goh* **Wheat**
GRAINS & CEREALS Cultivated grass grown around the world that is used to make flour for a large number of culinary uses. The wheat kernel contains gluten-forming amino acids which provide elasticity and produce very desirable results when baking. The grain is also fermented and used to make beer and distilled alcohol.

Trigo integral *TREE-goh een-teh-GRAHL* **Whole wheat**
GRAINS & CEREALS A wheat kernel that has been minimally processed and contains all three edible parts: the bran, endosperm, and germ.

Trinchar *treen-CHAHR* **Carve**
COOKING METHOD / TECHNIQUE To cut portions of cooked meat using a carving knife.

Tripa / Menudo *TREE-pah / meh-NOO-doh* **Tripe**
MEAT A type of offal, most commonly beef stomach lining but also lamb and pork. It is pale-colored and has a netted honeycomblike-patterned texture. Tripa requires a long cooking time. It is available fresh, pickled, and caned.

Triturar / Hacer tiras *tree-too-RAHR / ah-SEHR TEE-rahs* **Shred**
COOKING METHOD / TECHNIQUE To tear into thin, narrow strips.

SPANISH-ENGLISH **T**

Trituradora *tree-too-rah-DOH-rah* **Food processor**
EQUIPMENT A small, electric kitchen appliance that chops, grinds, slices, and purees food. It consists of a work bowl fitted with an S-shaped blade and a lid that must be securely fastened in place before it can be turned on. The food can be added directly to the bowl or put through the feed tube found on the lid. Food processors come in various sizes.

Grinder
EQUIPMENT *See* Molinillo.

Trocear *troh-seh-AHR* **Chop / Dice**
COOKING METHOD / TECHNIQUE *See* Cortar; Cortar en dados.

Trompeta de la muerte *trohm-PEH-tah deh lah moo-EHR-teh* **Horn of plenty mushroom**
FRUIT & VEGETABLES A trumpet-shaped wild mushroom with a wrinkled-edged cap. Dark grayish black in color with a deep earthy and nutty flavor, it is available fresh and dried.

Trozo *TROH-soh* **Slice**
COOKING METHOD / TECHNIQUE *See* Rebanada.

Trucha *TROO-chah* **Trout**
FISH & SHELLFISH A freshwater fish that belongs to the salmon family. It has silvery skin and small bones and its flesh is firm with a medium fat content.

Trucha ahumada *TROO-chah ah-oo-MAH-dah* **Smoked trout**
FISH & SHELLFISH Fresh trout that has been cured and flavored by smoke.

Trucha arco iris *TROO-chah AHR-koh EE-rees* **Rainbow trout**
FISH & SHELLFISH The most popular of the trout variety, a fish that is easily identified by a broad rainbow-looking band that runs along its side. Its flesh has a mild flavor. It makes spawning trips between fresh and salt water and is both farmed and caught wild.

Trufa *TROO-fah* **Truffle**
FRUIT & VEGETABLES An edible fungus that grows three to twelve inches underground and near trees. Hunted out by pigs and dogs, it is considered a delicacy. There are two main types: black and white. The white is earthy and garlicky. The black is less pungent with earthy aromas. Truffles are served shaved atop hot food.

Tuna *TOO-nah* **Prickly Pear**
FRUIT & VEGETABLES *See* Higo chumbo.

Tupinambo *too-pee-NAHM-boh* **Jerusalem artichoke / Sunchoke**
FRUIT & VEGETABLES *See* Aguaturma.

Turrón *too-RROHN*

DISH (Spain) Similar to nougat, a candy made from almonds and honey. It comes in a crunchy form (alicante) or a soft version (jijona). It is popular during the Christmas season.

Txangurro *chahn-GOO-rroh*

DISH *See* **Shangurro**.

U

Unir *oo-NEER* **Bind**

COOKING METHOD / TECHNIQUE *See* **Ligar**.

Utensilios *oo-tehn-SEE-lee-ohs* **Utensils**

EQUIPMENT Small tools or instruments used to handle food. Basic tableware utensils include a knife (*cuchillo*), fork (*tenedor*), and spoon (*cuchara*).

Uvas *OOH-bahs* **Grapes**

FRUIT & VEGETABLES Edible berries that grow in clusters on vines or shrubs. They can have small seeds in their center or be seedless, and the color of their thin, edible skin ranges from light green to dark purplish black. There are more than a thousand varieties, and depending on their flavor profile, they can be used for wine making, eating, drying, or making into preserves.

Uvas espinas *OO-bah ehs-PEE-nah* **Gooseberry**

FRUIT & VEGETABLES Large berries with a tart-flavored flesh that grow on bushes. Their soft, furry skin comes in a variety of colors ranging from green to white to yellow to red.

V

Vaca frita *BAH-kah FREE-tah*

DISH (Cuba) Flank steak that is boiled, shredded, and marinated with lime, garlic, and lime juice. It is then panfried until crispy.

Vaciador de melón *bah-see-ah-DOHR deh meh-LOHN* **Melon baller**

EQUIPMENT *See* **Cortador de melón**.

Vacuno *bah-KOO-noh* **Beef**

MEAT *See* **Carne de res**.

Vainilla *bah-ee-NEE-yah* **Vanilla**

HERBS & SPICES A long, thin, brown pod that is the fruit of an orchid plant. Vanilla pods are handpicked when green, then boiled and dried, turning their characteristic brown color. The pods are usually split in half lengthwise and their seeds scraped off and used in recipes. Due to the labor-intensive process, vanilla is the second most expensive spice next to saffron. There are three varieties: Bourbon-Madagascar (the most common), Tahitian, and Mexican.

Vainita *bah-ee-NEE-tah* **Green bean**
FRUIT & VEGETABLES *See* Judía verde.

Vapor *bah-POHR* **Steam**
GENERAL Water vapor.

(Cocinar al) vapor *(Koh-see-NAHR ahl) bah-POHR* **Steam**
COOKING METHOD / TECHNIQUE To cook with the heat produced by converting water to steam.

Vaporera / Olla para cocinar al vapor *bah-poh-REH-rah / OH-yah PAH-rah koh-see-NAHR ahl bah-POHR* **Steamer**
EQUIPMENT A device or cooking vessel used to create steam and cook food in it.

Vegetal / Hortaliza *beh-geh-TAHL / ohr-tah-LEE-sah*
FRUIT & VEGETABLES The edible root, tuber, stem, leaf, or seed of a plant.

Vegetariano(a) *beh-geh-tah-ree-AH-noh (nah)* **Vegetarian**
GENERAL A person who does not eat animal products.

Viandas *bee-AHN-dahs*
FRUIT & VEGETABLES (Cuba) Tropical tubers and root vegetables. The most common are yuca, malanga, boniato, and name.

Vieira *bee-EH-rah* **Scallop**
FISH & SHELLFISH A marine bivalve mollusk. Most are free living and swim by opening and closing their very ornate fan-shaped shells. The abductor muscle responsible for the shell's movement is what is eaten. There are two varieties: the smaller and sweeter bay scallop and the larger sea scallop. The shells are often used as serving dishes.

Vinagre *bee-NAH-greh* **Vinegar**
CONDIMENTS An acidic condiment made by converting fermented liquids (wine, beer, and cider) into weak solutions of acetic acid through oxidation. Acetic acid is what gives vinegar its tart taste.

Vinagre al vino *bee-NAH-greh ahl BEE-noh* **Wine vinegar**
CONDIMENTS Vinegar made from red or white wine. It can be aged in wooden casks, which results in a deeper flavor. It tends to be less acidic than cider or distilled vinegar.

Vinagre balsamico *bee-NAH-greh bahl-SAH-mee-koh* **Balsamic vinegar**
CONDIMENTS Vinegar made from the fermented juice of the Italian Trebbiano grape and aged in wooden barrels for a number of years. This aging process produces a dark-colored, sweet-flavored vinegar.

Vinagre de arroz *bee-NAH-greh deh ah-RROHS* **Rice vinegar**
CONDIMENTS Vinegar made from fermented rice or rice wine. It is popular in Japanese, Chinese, and Korean cuisine.

Vinagre de frambuesa *bee-NAH-greh deh frahm-boo-EH-sah*
Raspberry vinegar

CONDIMENTS Vinegar that has been infused with the flavor of raspberries or has been made with fermented raspberry juice.

Vinagre de jerez *bee-NAH-greh deh geh-REHS* **Sherry vinegar**

CONDIMENTS Wine vinegar made from sherry and aged in oak barrels. It is amber colored with a deep complex flavor.

Vinagre de sidra *bee-NAH-greh deh SEE-drah* **Cider vinegar**

CONDIMENTS Vinegar made from cider.

Vinagre de vino tinto *bee-NAH-greh deh BEE-noh TEEN-toh* **Red wine vinegar**

CONDIMENTS Vinegar made from red wine. Some producers age the vinegar in small, wooden casks to deepen and develop its flavor. It is slightly less acidic than distilled white vinegar.

Vinagreta *bee-nah-GREH-tah* **Vinaigrette**

CONDIMENTS A mixture of vinegar and oil that has been seasoned. Often flavored with herbs, spices, and condiments like mustard and honey, it is used as a dressing on salads, vegetables, and cold meats and fish.

Vino *BEE-noh* **Wine**

BEVERAGE An alcoholic beverage made from the fermented juice of grapes. It can be categorized as still (nonsparkling), sparkling (effervescent), or fortified (reinforced with a spirit).

Vino de Borgona *BEE-noh deh bohr-GOH-nah* **Burgundy wine**

BEVERAGE Wine made from grapes grown in eastern France. The most common grapes from the region are the Pinot Noir and Chardonnay.

Vino de Burdeo *BEE-noh deh boor-DEH-oh* **Bordeaux wine**

BEVERAGE Wine made from grapes grown in southwest France. In Britain, this wine is referred to as claret.

Vino de jerez *BEE-noh deh geh-REHS* **Sherry**

BEVERAGE Wine made from white grapes that have been fortified with brandy after fermentation. Protected by a designation of origin, all sherries must be produced in an area known as the sherry triangle located in the south of Spain. Sherry is produced in a variety of styles, most notably dry and light (fino), colored and medium dry (amontillado), and dark and sweet (oloroso).

Vino para cocinar *BEE-noh PAH-rah koh-see-NAHR* **Cooking wine**

CONDIMENTS An inferior wine that has been fortified with salt. Solely used for cooking, it cannot be drunk straight.

Vino porto *BEE-noh POHR-toh* **Port**

BEVERAGE *See* **Oporto**.

SPANISH-ENGLISH V

Vino seco *BEE-noh SEH-koh*
> CONDIMENTS A cooking wine. It is a dry white wine that has been fortified with salt, usually 1.5 percent by volume.

Viruta *bee-ROO-tah* **Shaving**
> COOKING METHOD / TECHNIQUE A very thin, flat slice.

Vitamina *bee-tah-MEE-nah* **Vitamin**
> GENERAL An organic substance required by the body in very small amounts for normal growth and activity. It cannot be synthesized entirely by the body and must be consumed through the diet or through supplements. There are a total of 13 vitamins categorized as either water or fat soluble.

Vodka *BOHD-kah* **Vodka**
> BEVERAGE A distilled beverage. A clear liquid obtained from multiple distillations of a fermented grain (rye, wheat, corn) or root vegetable (potato, beet). The distilled liquid is then filtered through charcoal to remove remaining impurities. The clear spirit is often flavored with fruit or spices.

Voltear *bohl-teh-AHR* **Flip**
> COOKING METHOD / TECHNIQUE (1) To turn over. (2) To throw as to reverse the position.

Turn over
> COOKING METHOD / TECHNIQUE (1) To fold over. (2) To move the position of something 180 degrees.

W

Wasabi *wah-SAH-bee* **Wasabi**
> HERBS & SPICES A Japanese horseradish root. It is used as a spice for its pungent, mustardlike heat that is known to irritate the nasal passages. The long, white root is rarely available fresh (which is grated when used). Most often it is found in paste or powdered form that has been treated with green food coloring.

Wok *wohk* **Wok**
> EQUIPMENT A special round-bottom cooking vessel (pot) used in Asian cuisine. A special ring may be necessary to put over a burner to keep it in place. Made of steel, it is used for many stovetop cooking methods, but is most popular for stir-frying.

X

Xantina *sahn-TEE-nah* **Xanthan gum**
> GENERAL A starch produced by the fermentation of sucrose used as a thickener. It also keeps solutions in emulsions and prevents them from separating.

Y

Yema de huevo *YEH-mah deh WEH-voh* **Egg yolk**

DAIRY The yellow middle of an egg that makes up one-third of the egg's weight. It is spherical in shape and is found within the egg white. Contains protein, fat, phospholipids, most notably lecithin, whose main function is in acting as an emulsifier bringing two immesible liquids together. The depth of its yellow color is determined by the animal's diet.

Yemas de Santa Teresa *YEH-mah deh SAHN-tah teh-REH-sah*

DISH (Spain) Candied egg yolks made by cooking sweetened egg yolks and reshaping them into small circles. They are named after the most famous nun (Saint Teresa) of the convent they were originally made in. Their name literally translates as "Saint Teresa's egg yolks."

Yerba buena *YEHR-bah boo-EH-nah* **Peppermint**

HERBS & SPICES A species of mint that is pungent and peppery flavored with a high menthol content. Its small leaves are dark green and hearty. It is the herb used in making mojitos and Caipirinha.

Yogur *yoh-GOOR* **Yogurt**

DAIRY A thick dairy product made from milk that has been curdled with a friendly bacteria. Slightly tart in flavor, many are flavored with fruit and other flavors. Sugar and gelatin are almost always added to improve the flavor and texture.

Yuca *YOO-kah* **Cassava**

FRUIT & VEGETABLES An elongated root vegetable with a very tough and inedible, brown skin and milky white flesh. It is high in starch and has a neutral flavor. Used to make tapioca, it is also known as cazabe or manioc.

Yuca chupe *YOO-kah CHOO-peh*

DISH (Peru) A soup made from cassava root (yuca).

Yuca con mojo *YOO-kah kohn MOH-hoh*

DISH (Cuba) Boiled yuca served with mojo dressing.

Yuca frita *YOO-kah FREE-tah*

DISH Fried yuca. Peeled yuca is boiled, cut into strips, and then deep-fried.

Z

Zanahoria *sah-nah-OH-ree-ah* **Carrot**

FRUIT & VEGETABLES A root vegetable with curly green tops that grow above ground. The root is sweet and the tops are not eaten. It has a thin skin that is usually peeled. It is long, thin, and typically orange but there are also white, purple, yellow, and red heirloom crops.

Zarzuela de marisco *sahr-soo-EH-lah deh mah-REES-koh*

DISH (Spain) A large shellfish medley cooked in a spicy sauce flavored with tomatoes, brandy, and wine.

Za'tar *SAH-tahr* **Za'atar**

CONDIMENTS An herb and spice mixture used as a condiment. Popular in Middle Eastern cuisine, it is made from toasted sesame seeds mixed with dried oregano, thyme, marjoram, and salt. They are mixed with olive oil and made into a paste that is eaten with bread or spread on meats and vegetables.

Zumaque *soo-MAH-keh* **Sumac**

HERBS & SPICES A red berry that grows in clusters on small shrubs that are dried and ground to a powder and used as a spice. Often used in Middle Eastern cuisine, it imparts a red color and tart citrus flavor to meats and vegetables.

Zurrukutuna *soo-rroo-koo-TOO-nah*

DISH (Spain) A dish made from salted cod that is simmered in a garlic and tomato sauce flavored with choricero peppers. It is typically served with large crusty croutons and a poached egg on top.

QUICK REFERENCE

CUISINE BY COUNTRY

Cocina africana *koh-SEE-nah ah-free-KAH-nah* **African cuisine**

Cocina asiática *koh-SEE-nah ah-see-AH-tee-kah* **Asian cuisine**

Cocina australiana *koh-SEE-nah ows-trah-lee-AH-nah* **Australian cuisine**

Cocina austriaca *koh-SEE-nah ow-stree-AH-kah* **Austrian cuisine**

Cocina británica *koh-SEE-nah bree-TAH-nee-kah* **British cuisine**

Cocina china *koh-SEE-nah CHEE-nah* **Chinese cuisine**

Cocina coreana *koh-SEE-nah koh-ree-AH-nah* **Korean cuisine**

Cocina española *koh-SEE-nah ehs-pah-NYO-lah* **Spanish cuisine**

Cocina francesa *koh-SEE-nah frahn-SEH-sah* **French cuisine**

Cocina griega *koh-SEE-nah gree-EH-gah* **Greek cuisine**

Cocina india *koh-SEE-nah EEN-dee-ah* **Indian cuisine**

Cocina indonesia *koh-SEE-nah een-doh-NEH-see-ah* **Indonesian cuisine**

Cocina italiana *koh-SEE-nah ee-tah-lee-AH-nah* **Italian cuisine**

Cocina japonesa *koh-SEE-nah hah-poh-NEH-sah* **Japanese cuisine**

Cocina marroquí *koh-SEE-nah mah-rroh-KEE* **Moroccan cuisine**

Cocina mejicana/mexicana *koh-SEE-nah meh-hee-KAH-nah* **Mexican cuisine**

Cocina portugesa *koh-SEE-nah pohr-too-GEH-sah* **Portugese cuisine**

Cocina rusa *koh-SEE-nah ROO-sah* **Russian cuisine**

Cocina suiza *koh-SEE-nah SWEE-sah* **Swiss cuisine**

Cocina tailandesa *koh-SEE-nah tah-ee-lahn-DEH-sah* **Thai cuisine**

Cocina vietnamita *koh-SEE-nah bee-eht-nah-MEE-tah* **Vietnamese cuisine**

CUTS OF MEAT / CORTES DE CARNE

Beef	Carne de Res/Vacuno
Beef patty	Carne molida en forma
Chuck	Espadilla
Fillet steak	Filete Corte de solomillo
Flank	Falda Vacio Tapabarriga
Porterhouse	Bife ancho con costilla Lomo vetado con costilla Churrasco redondo
Rib eye	Filete de lomo alto Bife ancho Lomo vetado
Rump steak	Bistec de cadera Colita de cuadril Punta de picana Empuje
Short plate	Tapa de asado Plateada Planchuela
Short ribs	Asado de tira Costilla cargada
Sirloin	Solomillo Bife angosto Lomo liso Bife chico
Skirt steak	Entraña Arrachera
T-Bone	Chuleta con solomillo Bife angosto con lomo Entrecot

Top round	Tapa plana Tapa de cuadril Punta de ganso Cadera
Whole tenderloin	Solomillo entero Lomo

Veal — Ternera

Veal	Ternera
Chop	Chuleta de ternera
Escalope	Escalopa de ternera

Lamb — Cordero

Lamb	Cordero
Chop	Chuleta de cordero
Crown	Corona de cordero
French trimmed	Costillas de cordero
Leg	Pierna de cordero
Rack	Costillar de cordero
Shoulder	Paletilla de cordero
Shoulder steak	Corte de paletilla de cordero

Pork — Cerdo/Carne Puerco

Pork	Cerdo/Carne Puerco
Boneless leg	Pierna deshuesada de cerdo
Chop	Chuleta de cerdo
Cutlet	Filete de cerdo
Escalopa	Escalope de cerdo
Leg	Pierna de cerdo
Loin	Lomo de cerdo
Shoulder	Paletilla de cerdo Pernil
Spareribs	Costillas de cerdo
Tenderloin	Solomillo de cerdo

Chicken	Pollo
Breast fillet	Filete de pechuga de pollo
Carcass	Carcasa de pollo
Double breast	Pecho entero de pollo
Drumstick	Muslito de pollo
Half	Medio pollo
Leg	Muslo de pollo
Liver	Hígado de pollo
Quarters	Cuarto de pollo
Thigh	Medio muslo de pollo
Wing	Ala de pollo

Turkey	Pavo
Breast	Pechuga de pavo
Carcass	Carcasa de pavo
Leg	Muslo entero de pavo
Thigh	Medio muslo de pavo

Duck	Pato
Breast	Pechuga de pato
Liver	Hígado de pato
Thigh	Medio muslo de pato

CORTES DE CARNE / CUTS OF MEAT

Carne de Res/Vacuno	Beef
Arrachera	Skirt steak
Asado de tira	Short ribs
Bife ancho	Rib eye
Bife ancho con costilla	Porterhouse
Bife angosto	Sirloin
Bife angosto con lomo	T-Bone
Bife chico	Sirloin
Bistec de cadera	Rump steak
Cadera	Top round
Carne molida en forma	Beef patty
Chuleta con solomillo	T-Bone
Churrasco redondo	Porterhouse
Colita de cuadril	Rump steak
Corte de solomillo	Fillet steak
Costilla cargada	Short ribs
Empuje	Rump steak
Entraña	Skirt steak
Entrecot	T-Bone
Espadilla	Chuck
Falda	Flank
Filete	Fillet steak
Filete de lomo alto	Rib eye
Lomo	Whole tenderloin

Lomo liso	Sirloin
Lomo vetado	Rib eye
Lomo vetado con costilla	Porterhouse
Planchuela	Short plate
Plateada	Short plate
Punta de ganso	Top round
Punta de picana	Rump steak
Solomillo	Sirloin
Solomillo entero	Whole tenderloin
Tapa de asado	Short plate
Tapa de cuadril	Top round
Tapa plana	Top round
Tapabarriga	Flank
Vacio	Flank

Ternera	Veal
Chuleta de ternera	Chop
Escalopa de ternera	Escalope

Cordero	Lamb
Chuleta de cordero	Chop
Corona de cordero	Crown
Corte de paletilla de cordero	Shoulder steak
Costillas de cordero	French trimmed
Costillar de cordero	Rack
Paletilla de cordero	Shoulder
Pierna de cordero	Leg

Cerdo/Carne Puerco	Pork
Chuleta de cerdo	Chop
Costillas de cerdo	Spareribs
Escalope de cerdo	Escalopa
Filete de cerdo	Cutlet
Lomo de cerdo	Loin
Paletilla de cerdo Pernil	Shoulder
Pierna de cerdo	Leg
Pierna deshuesada de cerdo	Boneless leg
Solomillo de cerdo	Tenderloin

Pollo	Chicken
Ala de pollo	Wing
Carcasa de pollo	Carcass
Cuarto de pollo	Quarters
Filete de pechuga de pollo	Breast fillet
Hígado de pollo	Liver
Medio pollo	Half
Medio muslo de pollo	Thigh
Muslito de pollo	Drumstick
Muslo de pollo	Leg
Pecho entero de pollo	Double breast

Pavo	Turkey
Carcasa de pavo	Carcass
Medio muslo de pavo	Thigh
Muslo entero de pavo	Leg
Pechuga de pavo	Breast

Pato   **Duck**

Hígado de pato	Liver
Medio muslo de pato	Thigh
Pechuga de pato	Breast